I0603802

Alan Wald has been the most important teacher of every generation of historians of US cultural radicalism hatched since the 1970s—this despite the various names on our university diplomas and the alphabet soup of acronyms marking our numerous political commitments. *Lineages of the Literary Left* demonstrates why the common debt to Wald has been an excellent thing. Its twenty essays tackle a heady range of subjects—from Harlem boxing pulp to Japanese proletarianism, from mass dance to world systems theory—but all reflect Wald's characteristic blend of humane detail and expansive historical imagination. Wald's concluding autobiographical reflection, meanwhile, is itself worth the price of admission.

–William J. Maxwell
Professor of English and African American Studies, Washington University in St. Louis

As the doyen of radical literary studies, Alan Wald demonstrated that Marxisms (plural) and other Left thought were as dominant an influence in twentieth-century US culture as Transcendentalism had been in the nineteenth century. This festschrift of some 20 essays on the works of poets, novelists, and the lives of many of them adds to his legacy while following what the editors term his "ecumenical approach." A valuable contribution to the radical and critical tradition in American letters and life.

–Jules Chametzky
Professor Emeritus of English, University of Massachusetts Amherst

Wald has long been our sure-footed guide through the thickets of Left literary and intellectual history. No one knows the convoluted political landscape of the 1930s (or its many legacies) as well as he does. By so comprehensively extending the lines of inquiry he set in motion, this volume is a fitting tribute to his tireless work.

–Andrew Ross
Professor of Social and Cultural Analysis, New York University

Lineages of the Literary Left: Essays in Honor of Alan M. Wald

Lineages of the Literary Left: Essays in Honor of Alan M. Wald

Edited by Howard Brick, Robbie Lieberman, and Paula Rabinowitz

Michigan Publishing

Copyright © 2015 by Howard Brick, Robbie Lieberman, and Paula Rabinowitz
Some rights reserved

This work is licensed under the Creative Commons Attribution-NonCommercial-NoDerivs 3.0 United States License. To view a copy of this license, visit http://creativecommons.org/licenses/by-nc-nd/3.0/us/ or send a letter to Creative Commons, 171 Second Street, Suite 300, San Francisco, California, 94105, USA.

Published in the United States of America by
Michigan Publishing
Manufactured in the United States of America

ISBN 978-1-60785-345-9 (paper)

An imprint of Michigan Publishing, Maize Books serves the publishing needs of the University of Michigan community by making high-quality scholarship widely available in print and online. It represents a new model for authors seeking to share their work within and beyond the academy, offering streamlined selection, production, and distribution processes. Maize Books is intended as a complement to more formal modes of publication in a wide range of disciplinary areas.

http://www.maizebooks.org

This book was produced using PressBooks.com, and PDF rendering was done by PrinceXML.

In memory of Marvin Felheim
(October 9, 1914–July 16, 1979)

Inspiring teacher

Contents

Foreword

Mary Helen Washington

I definitely want to be counted along with many others as part of Alan Wald's literary lineage. I am indebted to Alan for so many things that it is hard to know where to begin. But I will start with his review of my manuscript for my recent book *The Other Blacklist: The African American Literary and Cultural Left of the 1950s.* In response to that manuscript, Alan sent about six pages of corrections, suggestions, revisions, hesitations, and criticisms, along with the most glowing recommendation for my work. To me, that epitomizes perfectly the pull no punches, supportive colleague Alan has always been. I felt buoyed by the support but challenged to do my work and get it right. Over the past ten years, Alan has answered every e-mail query I have sent to him, always with the kind of precise detail that shows the depth, range, and commitment of his scholarship. Who except Alan can name the exact Left status (left-leaning, fellow traveler, procommunist, committed Communist, eccentric communist, etc.) of hundreds of writers and intellectuals, tell you exactly how reliable your sources are, or would know that one of the campers at the left-wing Camp Wo-Chi-Ca was Colin Powell's sister!

Alan's work on the literary and cultural Left is a monumental achievement, but no less monumental is his lifetime work of encouraging, directing, and supporting his colleagues and friends.

Acknowledgments

First and foremost, we want to acknowledge how much fun it has been to coedit this volume together. Our time as graduate students in the American Culture program at the University of Michigan overlapped in the 1970s and 1980s, but this project has given us another opportunity to get to know each other in entirely new ways. We thank the University of Michigan's Department of English Language and Literature and its chair, Professor Michael Schoenfeldt, for generous support of the March 2013 symposium on which this book is based and acknowledge a further contribution toward the publishing subvention granted by the University of Michigan Office of Research. The University of Michigan's Department of History also contributed funding and facilitated a term's leave for Howard Brick to allow him to work on this volume. We are grateful as well to the University of Minnesota, which, through its Imagine Fund Grant, provided Paula Rabinowitz funding for travel and research. We appreciate the great work of Anthony Cece, who designed the book cover, and Aaron Bekemeyer at Michigan and Sarah Carlson and Mark Engelmann at Minnesota, who provided research assistance at various stages of the project.

More than twenty-five University of Michigan departments, institutes, and programs funded the symposium "Lineages of the Literary Left." Our thanks go to those units and to those who participated in the symposium. We appreciate the work of the contributors to this volume, all of whom have added immensely to important and ongoing scholarly conversations about the Literary Left. Of course, our deepest debt is to the honoree of this volume, our adviser, comrade, and friend Alan Wald.

The poem "Love Do Not Ask," from *Poems by Faiz* by Faiz Ahmed Faiz and translated by Victor Kiernan, is reproduced with permission of

Oxford University Press India © Oxford University Press. Unauthorized copying is strictly prohibited.

"Filling Station" from *The Complete Poems: 1927–1979* by Elizabeth Bishop is reprinted by permission of Farrar, Straus and Giroux, LLC. Copyright © 1979, 1983 by Alice Helen Methfessel.

"The Solution," originally published in German in 1964 as "Die Losung," translated by Derek Bowman, Copyright © 1964, 1976 by Bertolt-Brecht-Erben/Suhrkamp Verlag, and "The Caledonian Market," originally published in German in 1964 as "Der Kaledonische Markt," translated by John Willet, Copyright © 1964, 1976 by Bertolt-Brecht-Erben/Suhrkamp Verlag, from *Bertolt Brecht Poems 1913–1956* by Bertolt Brecht, edited by John Willet and Ralph Manheim. Used by permission of Liveright Publishing Corporation.Langston Hughes's poems used by permission of Random House.

Grateful thanks to Mary Cantwell Nelson for permission to quote from the unpublished manuscripts of Robert Cantwell and to Judith Benet Richardson for permission to quote from the poems of Genevieve Taggard. John Callahan allowed permission to quote from Ralph Ellison's papers, and the General Commission on Archives and History (United Methodist Church) gave permission to quote from the Dorothy McConnell papers.

Introduction: Literary Lineages

Howard Brick, Robbie Lieberman, and Paula Rabinowitz

This volume collects recent scholarship on intellectual, literary, and cultural movements and figures associated with left-wing politics beginning in the early twentieth century and continuing into our own time, largely in the United States but elsewhere in the world as well. These essays honor the contribution of Alan M. Wald's pathbreaking research, which for almost half a century has demonstrated that attention to the complex lived experiences of writers on the Left provides a new context for viewing major achievements as well as instructive minor ones in US fiction, poetry, drama, and criticism. His many books and articles, which are listed in the accompanying bibliography, have illuminated the creative lives of figures such as James T. Farrell, Willard Motley, Muriel Rukeyser, Philip Rahv, Richard Wright, Ann Petry, Kenneth Fearing, and Arthur Miller. Wald has delved into a consideration of Sidney Hook and pragmatism, developed a theory of Popular Front culture, and dissected the complexities of the anti-Stalinist Left. His investigations have opened the archives of Irving Howe, Sol Funaroff, Alfred Hayes, Paule Marshall, Sherry Mangan, Samuel Sillen, Rebecca Pitts, and other unduly neglected writers such as Jo Sinclair, Carlos Bulosan, John O. Killens, and Joy Davidman, among the many more across the Left who people Wald's magisterial studies in modern American culture. Collectively, the thinkers and actors intimately linked with social struggle who are analyzed in these diverse essays can be understood to form intertwined lineages of the Literary Left. Moreover, the critics and historians comprising this tribute attest to the varied lineages threading together myriad scholarly traditions as well. Throughout we stress the concluding "s," indicating the plural and multiple tendencies, fields, and methods expanding the Literary Left.

Linage, precursor spelling of *lineage* according to the University of Michigan's *Middle English Dictionary,* has a contradictory cast, collating an escalating series of descendants, at once expansive and particular:

> (1) Ancestry, descent, family stock, lineage; (2) A line of descendants; posterity, offspring, progeny; also, an individual descendant; (3) A specific family; also, members of one family, relatives, kinsmen; (*b*) family relationship, consanguinity; (*c*) an alliance by marriage; (4) A tribe, nation, or people; an ethnic group; (*b*) one of the tribes of the Israelites; (5) A region inhabited by one of the tribes of Israel; a tribal territory or encampment. The race of man, the human race, mankind. . . .

According to the *Oxford English Dictionary,* the first recorded use of lineage, spelled "linage," predates Chaucer (from circa 1330) and has continued in usage to the present day. As is clear from the ascending list, its varied meanings create a complex system of linkages among and between people. Beyond the family ancestry and lines of descent and kinship implied are larger connections that ally tribes, nations, ethnicities, and people—the entirety of humanity. And more than that, this matrix includes the territory inhabited by them—that is, we of the world. So, in one configuration of the term, we are all together now, but if we look more closely, because one definition particularizes a tribe of Israel and the land it inhabited, one begins to see why *Lineages of the Literary Left* makes sense as a title. It is not because we are the descendants of this particular tribe—unnamed—and thus perhaps mythical and singular. Rather, our concerns as activist scholars seek to incorporate everyone—the human race—through diverse ideas and practices aimed at inclusion and social justice; yet invariably, as happens with small and fragmented sects identifying spatially and temporally, these lineages threaten to collapse in on themselves even as they continuously proliferate and disagree. Lineages disperse.

Surely the lineages of the Literary Left traced in this volume incorporate aspects for all the myriad definitions of linage found in the *Middle English Dictionary*—of descent, and thus of forebears, of sects and their fractious posterity, of alliances and schisms, of times and places and beyond these of human history itself. The contributors to this volume are linked through an intellectual project to recast the literary and cultural histories of the twentieth century through attention to biography, theoretical readings of obscure and canonical works of fiction or poetry, anti-imperialism and antiracism, and theorizing the varied collective cultural and political projects associated with something like a revolutionary leftist agenda—within the Communist Party or among its critics on the Left. Moreover, we are connected as colleagues, friends, or students through the legacy of Alan Wald's work as scholar and teacher over the course of a half century: we are among those constituting various lineages of the Literary Left.

A modern American current of imaginative literature fashioned with radical (left-wing) political intent or associated with social protest can be recognized, at its start, in the work of such writers as Edward Bellamy, Charlotte Perkins Gilman, W. E. B. Du Bois, Jack London, and Upton Sinclair. Something more in the nature of a movement linking the political Left and radical artistic work emerged in the 1910s with the appearance of the magazine *The Masses* (1911–17) and continued through the 1920s and 1930s with its successor, the *New Masses* (1926–48), and with other radical journals, such as the *Partisan Review* (1934–2003). Associated with the Socialist Party and the Communist Party as well as their varied political offshoots, left-wing literary movements seemed to subside during the first decade of the Cold War, yet leftist literary lineages persisted and assumed new forms in the second half of the twentieth century, including the magazine *Masses & Mainstream* (1948–63), successor to the *New Masses,* as well as less obviously leftist publications, including pulp fiction, children's literature, and work in other popular media.

The earliest studies of these lineages appeared in the late 1950s, culminating in the first thorough account, Walter Rideout's *The Radical Novel in the United States, 1900–1950* (1956), followed by *Writers on the Left: Episodes in American Literary Communism* (1961) by Daniel Aaron, the Harvard University emeritus English professor whose work inspired Wald's and helped shape that of many others. Part of the postwar scholarly assessment of American Communism after the movement had declined (due both to internal flaws and official repression), *Writers on the Left* appeared just as a rejuvenated New Left was emerging in the United States.

While Wald's work and most of the essays collected here focus on elements of the Literary Left in the United States, comparable movements have appeared throughout diverse traditions of modern world literature: in France, from Victor Hugo and Émile Zola to the surrealists, existential Marxists, and poststructuralist critics; in Britain, from William Morris to W. H. Auden, Stephen Spender, George Orwell, Doris Lessing, and beyond; in China, from Lu Xun, the May Fourth movement, and the League of Left-Wing Writers; in Japan, in the work of Takiji Kobayashi, Yuriko Miyamoto, and the Proletarian Arts Foundation to the postwar writer Kenzaburō Ōe; and in Latin America, represented by Pablo Neruda, Carlos Fuentes, Gabriel Garcia Marquez, and many others. By including essays on Japanese, European, and Middle Eastern writers and activists, we hope this volume will spark comparable reassessments of the international dimensions of these literary practices, spawning even more lineages in the process. Furthermore, by dissecting the political biographies of activists and scholars whose work falls beyond the ambit of literature, we foreground how the Literary Left informed and learned from broader leftist movements within academia and various communities.

There are many different ways to group the twenty essays comprising *Lineages of the Literary Left*. We have grouped them thematically—poems, lives, novels, histories—but the interconnections among them crisscross these categories. Roughly, they all consider twentieth-century literary and cultural productions, including poems, novels, pageantry, dance, painting, sculpture, performance, and journalism, created in and for varied milieu from New York's Union Square to Moscow's Red Square associated with radical social movements. In addition, some essays reassess the scope and assumptions behind America's literary history and its periodization and focus attention on the long process, begun in the 1960s, of rethinking the boundaries of intellectual history and cultural studies. These efforts dramatically altered the scholarly definition of canonical literary works deserving historical and textual attention and redrew the boundaries of national culture. Some essays address methodological issues raised when biographies and archives are probed for traces of forgotten histories (emphasizing the salience of this mode of writing the literary biography of ghosts developed in Wald's work). As such, they often acknowledge the complicated status of activist writers and scholars in the United States and other parts of the world and thus point to new directions in social and cultural criticism that politically engaged intellectuals may pursue in the coming years. Many of the essays also consider theoretical debates about history, social movements, and political praxis, especially as they are expressed through text, gesture, or image. To do so, they delve into popular cultural forms (parades and pageants, manga and pulp) in the United States, the Soviet Union, and Asia to reconsider seemingly nonpolitical forms, such as the lyric or a woodcut. Many essays examine the affinities and tensions across classes, nations, races, and genders among left-wing intellectuals' lives and within their cultural and scholarly expressions. Often these raise the vexed question of Stalinism within various leftists' lives, activities, and organizations and as such offer further recoveries of lost biographies, traditions, and works. Various essays probe the complex political investments of scholars and activists in strategies to confront war and promote peace, challenge imperialism and analyze decolonization, or model revolutionary acts. Each of these occasionally disputatious approaches can be said to have grown directly from the scholarship of Alan M. Wald.

As the most important scholar of the twentieth-century American cultural Left in the world, Wald has made immeasurable contributions to rethinking American literary history and Marxist critical practices. As this volume attests, his work is the touchstone, the point of departure, for what is virtually a boom in studies of the Literary Left of the 1930s—and now of the entire twentieth century. Standing at the crossroads of literary criticism and historiography, Wald's scholarship develops from his unique approach to biography, often gleaned from deep archival research and wide-ranging interviews. This method is significant not only for literary critics and theorists; he has also taught many of us how to be historians of the American Left. Wald's recently completed three-volume history of Communist Party affiliations among disparate groups of writers—*Exiles from a Future Time, Trinity of Passion,* and *American Night* (University of North Carolina Press)—joins his earlier volumes on the anti-Stalinist Left to provide a major rethinking of the relationships among politics, modernism, periodization, popular culture, and social movements. The three-volume study continues his superb crafting of biographical critique or critical biography: the deep respect he pays to the details of private lives and lived experiences as a lens for gleaning a sense and sensation of literary expression. Wald's is a method aimed at unpacking literary form within and through literary history. In short, his work does more than outline diverse alternative tracks within history; the generative aspect of his work, on view in these essays, posits how lineages of the Literary Left probe the myriad vicissitudes of twentieth-century American literature.

Wald has written on almost every left-wing writer in the United States and done so in a range of styles and venues. He is a careful, erudite, and subtle scholar, versed in critical theoretical nuances and dedicated to the most painstaking archival, ethnographic, and oral historical research, but he is also concerned with broadening the audience for his work to include general readers and, most important, political activists by speaking and publishing widely. For instance, as editor of the University of Illinois Press series "The Radical Novel Reconsidered," Wald brought back into print works long ignored, helping us understand the complex countertradition of radical cultural practices suppressed during the virulent Red Scare of the 1950s. In addition, he regularly reviews new scholarship within the broad field of literary radicalism for a number of journals and as such brings these studies to wider attention within the public sphere as well as academia. As Wald's scope has expanded, he has developed a new model for periodizing the twentieth century, one that accounts for the peculiar and varied forms of what he calls "Communist literary modernism" operating across classes and within their fractured ethnic, racial, sexual, and gendered communities.

Wald's scholarly work can be divided into two parts: the earlier emphasis of his career retrieved and reexamined the American anti-Stalinist Literary Left, culminating in his definitive study *The New York Intellectuals.* His method focused on excavation, digging up the names, life stories, and works of literary radicals critical of the Communist Party USA (CPUSA). The three books from this period are compendiums of this cohort of writers, but they also develop a style of reading that views a literary work as a complex, even theoretical, gloss on political affiliations and biographical details. Wald's method of searching lives and movements has influenced many of the contributors to this volume—T. V. Reed, Chris Vials, Dayo F. Gore, Julia Mickenberg, Robbie Lieberman, and Bill Mullen—even when those being considered (Robert Cantwell, Dorothy McConnell, Beulah Richardson, Pauline Koner, Charlotta Bass, and W. E. B. Du Bois, respectively) were far from the Trotskyist Left. Attention to genre—for instance, poetry and poetics, as in the essays by Harvey Teres on Elizabeth Bishop, Sarah Ehlers on Genevieve Taggard, Rachel Rubin on Langston Hughes and Don West, and Tariq Ali on the poetry of defeat and resistance—has been essential to Wald's methodology since the appearance of his double biography of poets Sherry Mangan and John Wheelwright, *The Revolutionary Imagination.* That book adapted ideas developed in Fredric Jameson's *Marxism and Form* and *The Political Unconscious* by connecting genre, form, and history to relatively unknown modernists, whose anti-Stalinist politics, Wald argued, were keys to their formal innovations.

While retaining the biographical thoroughness of his early work, in his more recent studies Wald has dissected complex narrative structures—focused primarily through the lenses of racial and ethnic identities and Utopian desires for collectivity and alternative sexualities—to demonstrate how literary movements come into being and express themselves symbolically. Incorporating and recasting a series of standard literary and political tropes in order to find a voice within an oppressive structure (be it Cold War America, racism, heterosexism, imperialism, or political ostracism), these authors often then found themselves and their ideas transformed through both internal psychological dynamics and external political forces. *Exiles from a Future Time* is the first volume of Wald's impressive trilogy on the post-1930s Communist cultural scene. It begins with a playful yet powerful discussion of "strange Communists" to explore a weird history based in the idiosyncratic stories of individual writers but suggesting a larger field, unnoticed by scholars of either the CPUSA or twentieth-century American literature. The second volume, *Trinity of Passion,* provides a significant new approach to the critical understanding of the place of the Spanish Civil War in deepening antifascist sentiments among black, Jewish, and gay writers during and after World War II. The final volume, *American Night,* completes the saga by addressing the impact of the Cold War on various writers and brings Wald's multifaceted story of Communist literary modernism's legacies into the 1960s.

The trilogy on communist-oriented writers has led Wald to expand his object of study to include popular fiction, B movies, children's books, and cover art for pulp fiction as he followed the varied trajectories of their lives. It turns out that anticommunist paranoids who saw mid-twentieth-century American popular culture as saturated by left-wing ideology were right, and it is because of Wald's research that we know how thoroughly ingenious were those on the margins of mainstream American apparatuses of culture—working through publishing houses, book clubs, reading groups—in fashioning an oppositional stance within an industrial setting. Often at one and the same time, these "strange communists" bent in accommodation to political repression but also pried open various media, forms, and genres for personal expression in surprising and counterintuitive ways. One can see the influence of Wald's capaciousness, his open approach to the full range of an author's works, in Joseph G. Ramsey's reading of Ed Lacy/Len Zinberg's boxing pulp or in E. J. San Juan, Jr.'s consideration of Benjamin Appel's political bildungsroman about the Philippines. The impact of Wald's challenge to arbitrary cultural divisions—for example, insisting that one needs to read pulp fiction together with political theory in order to fully grasp the writing career of many left-wing authors—is apparent in Konstantina M. Karageorgos's and Nathaniel Mills's revisionist approaches to canonical authors Richard Wright and Ralph Ellison, respectively, whose writings were deeply imbued with both philosophy and popular culture. Wald's sense that the impact of proletarian literature extends beyond its limited period of the Great Depression can be seen in Heather Bowen-Struyk's ethnographic exploration of the contemporary youth culture appeal in Japan of a 1929 proletarian novel, *The Crab Cannery Ship.*

Ultimately, Wald's three recent books stand with his earlier works as visionary and revisionary histories of midcentury American literature. Rendering a sense of how movements shape thought through collective biography and political history, and are in turn shaped by the variety of individuals' experiences and sensibilities, has been a hallmark of Wald's archival and ethnographic scholarship. As the essays in this volume demonstrate, Wald's ecumenical approach, which draws on the sensibilities of the New Left to frame his readings of the Old Left and beyond—detailed in his own contribution to this volume, where he turns his method on himself—has changed the narrative that literary historians construct about modernism and postmodernism and thus expanded current American Studies thinking about culture, nationalism, citizenship, and race. Opening movements to scrutiny—and doing so through attention to individuals—influenced the composition of the collective-biographical focus of Michael Löwy's genealogy and typology of Jewish radicals; the attention Howard Brick gives to the rise of the distinct "world systems" approaches of Eric Wolf and Immanuel Wallerstein; Cary Nelson's reconsideration of poststructuralism, Marxist scholarship, and Joseph Stalin's legacy; and the challenges to traditional and racist historiography of slavery that James Smethurst discerns in the work of African American writers and artists.

In all, *Lineages of the Literary Left* incorporates a wide range of studies by scholars concerned with the modern literary and cultural Left in the United States and throughout the world. Bringing together distinguished and emerging scholars of the cultural Left from around the country and abroad—some of whom were students *with* Wald, some students *of* Wald, and others students of his students—the volume maps approaches to modern literary language and image, reconsiders the methods that have been refined and invented in that work, and charts new directions in left-wing cultural studies. This volume makes clear that the Literary Left is an expansive category: its lineages extend beyond the written word to include actors and dancers, painters and sculptors, philosophers and street performers, and scholars and activists. And its history is neither limited by national borders nor traditional periodization.

Inspired by the political activism of the 1960s, Alan Wald's work has continued to graph the lineages first recorded by Rideout and Aaron and has traced new threads within its territories and tribes. Charting a capacious field, Wald has inspired the editors and contributors to this volume and scores of others around the world to follow suit. He is a consummate teacher, at once generous and rigorous. Many of us also speak of Wald's enthusiasm, erudition, and attention to detail in critiquing our work in stories that are similar to the one recounted by Mary Helen Washington in the foreword. Wald's energy and seriousness are infectious. Like him, we often ignored advice to play it safe and instead followed our passions, political and aesthetic, by ferreting out the hidden stories and histories of a fascinating cohort of cultural workers committed to doing more than interpreting the world.

[PART I]

Poems

[1]

The Mirror of the World: Poetry, Defeat, and Resistance

Tariq Ali

When I was invited to contribute to this collection, I thought I would discuss poetry as a mirror of the world. The real subject I want to address—though I fear it might appear too pessimistic—is the experience of defeat, which is relevant to us all. I *will* discuss poetry but within the rubric of defeat: what it has meant in the past, the distant past as well as the more immediate past, and what it means in different shapes and forms for the present. Poetry itself has been with us in some shape or form since humanity learned to express itself. Poetry, initially, could be simple sounds or very ancient or primitive music. It is a form of expression that comes into the modern world, and then it becomes something completely different. Yet there has always been in it, too, an element of resistance.

The Ancient Mirror

The first fragments of poetry were discovered in ancient Mesopotamia, in the Indus Valley, or in ancient China. Some of these fragments of poetry are interesting because they talk about the struggle to live. It is a resistance, if you like, against nature; it expressed the effort to survive.

The first two great works that have remained with us are, in a way, very modern. Look at the two great poets of the ancient Greek world: Homer and Hesiod. Homer writes about war, about the traumas and troubles of war, and what happens when soldiers stay away from their families for a long time as well as about the effect that all this has on how wars are fought in all its gory detail: this is a world that can be understood in terms of modern experience as well. Hesiod is, for us, a very different Greek poet. We know much more about him: we know where he came from and who his father was, and we know about the society in which he lived. If you take Hesiod's great work *Works and Days,* it again has a modern feel to it, although written in very ancient times.

Hesiod's ancient Greek society possessed great wealth. Its dazzling urban culture was very well known, but the wealth came from the countryside: wealth—from wine, oil, and corn—that was controlled by private landed proprietors. In the countryside lived peasants, game, and migrant laborers there for seasonal work. When there were no more jobs available, the laborers moved on. Hesiod describes all of this in different ways in *Works and Days,* making it a very contemporary piece of work. And his father was a migrant worker. Hesiod described him, effectively, as someone in flight, and he was fleeing, you can be sure, not from wealth and good things but from loathsome poverty, the loathsome poverty that Zeus visits upon men. Hesiod says, "Work is no disgrace; it is idleness which is a disgrace."[1] This is relevant today—and not just in contemporary Greece, which is a place of great hardship. If you talk to young people today in many parts of the world—in the United States as well as in Europe and Asia—they will tell you that too. They will tell you that when you do not work, when you have nothing to do—and even when you're dependent to survive or to live a basic existence on ever more scarce state subsidies—it is very shaming.

We have in these two great ancient Greek poets an image of the world that does not go away, however much it changes. Many, many similar poems (though perhaps not of that scale) come from other cultures as well. In China, poems tended to be incredibly vicious satires against the rulers of the day—biting, scabrous, satirical, and angry. In India, you have the great work the *Vedas,* the religious work of ancient Hindu culture. There you find a hint of Homer: descriptions of wars, the gory details, the gods and goddesses. In fact, some of the names of the gods were not too dissimilar, whether Egyptian, Greek, or Indian, for we have learned about the links between post-Aryan India and ancient Greek culture. This shows us that at the very beginnings of the modern world, a European element fused with something very different from it, and the result was to create what is now known loosely as Western civilization. There was then, in some sense, a common old world.

The Age of Revolution

But let us move on to the periods of revolution and, first, the European revolutions. The English revolution of the seventeenth century divided the country through a long civil war, which led to the execution of King Charles I, the first king to be executed in Europe. People forget that there was an open and transparent discussion about this act. Should we kill the king or not? It is one of the most fascinating discussions in English history. There were contingent reasons: "He lies. We try and make deals with him, but he goes behind our back. He organizes against us. What to do? If he's going to organize a counterrevolution, then the only alternative is to try him and kill him." There was a trial, and after it they killed the king, creating the new republic, the Commonwealth, with Oliver Cromwell at its head.

Cromwell appointed a secretary of state, a very brilliant young scholar John Thurloe, who built the network of English spies, the original British intelligence service. When Thurloe called his weekly Monday morning meeting to discuss the state of Europe and the strategy of the English revolutionary republic toward the rest of Europe, sitting across the table from him were three of the greatest poets of the time: John Milton, John Dryden, and Andrew Marvell. What were they discussing? Not poetry, I can tell you that. The discussions were about what was happening in Europe: the political debates of the time, who their enemies were, how their enemies were acting, and what to do. Milton played an absolutely decisive role in some of these discussions, and after the defeat of the revolution by the Restoration, he produced what is regarded as a masterpiece of English literature, *Paradise Lost.* That poem is a record of defeat. That is the way we can best understand it, as a work by someone as centrally involved in the struggle of revolution and its defeat as Milton was: you can imagine the pain he felt. And so, in a way that surprised people *Paradise Lost* portrayed Satan, the rebel angel, very sympathetically. Milton has him say "Better to reign in Hell, than serve in Heav'n."[2]

The culture that was produced by defeat saw literary and poetic masterpieces, but it also saw another thing we witness today. When there is a big defeat, a lot of people, especially from within the intelligentsia and radical circles as well, shift allegiances. This is not new. Christopher Hill, the late and great English Marxist historian, wrote much on this phenomenon—the fact that some of the most ultra-Left critics of Cromwell ended up supporting the Restoration. Yet the impact of that revolution remained, and it was discussed, as we know, all over Europe. "The English have killed their king. Why? How?" When the French Revolution occurred, once again there was a debate over whether to guillotine Louis and Marie Antoinette; those debating the issue decided to go ahead. Interestingly enough, in one of the most intelligent comments to be written by a European monarch, Marie Antoinette's brother, the Austrian emperor, sent her a letter two years prior that recognized what was happening. I summarize: "I'm getting reports of what is going on in France; it's absolutely atrocious. The role you're playing is beyond belief. Why are you behaving so stupidly? Don't you understand what's going on around you? If you carry on like this, it will end badly."

The French revolutionary process ignited subsequent European revolutions, and the next wave of poets—the progenitors, if you like, of radical commitment, the poetry of commitment—were inspired by the French Revolution. We might start with William Wordsworth, but he became disillusioned very quickly. His disillusionment began in 1793 when the revolution took a more radical course. Then he denounced it and said, "This is not what I wanted." But you know the course of events in France did not depend on what Wordsworth wanted or not. He retreated to a pastoral conservatism, and Percy Shelley wrote these lines, to him, in public:

> In honored poverty thy voice did weave
> Songs consecrate to truth and liberty;
> Deserting these, thou leavest me to grieve
> Thus having been, that thou shouldst cease to be.[3]

I say that about a lot of people today. Nonetheless, in the decades after the French Revolution we see an amazing outpouring of poetry from the great romantic poets Shelley, John Keats, and Lord Byron.

Shelley was without doubt the most radical. In his book on Johann Goethe, Georg Lukács, the Hungarian Marxist critic, describes Shelley as a revolutionary genius at least in a poetic visionary context; he cites Shelley's *Prometheus Unbound* as a work that "celebrate[d] the liberation of Prometheus" as a sign of "the real struggle for liberation of humanity."[4] Before *Prometheus Unbound,* Shelley had written one of the great radical poems in English, *The Mask of Anarchy,* following the massacre of Peterloo. He was on holiday in Lake Livorno in Italy, and news came that English soldiers had gone into Manchester and massacred poor people demonstrating for social and political rights. Written on the spur of the moment, Shelley had to negotiate endlessly for anyone to publish the poem. Two stanzas were initially censored, but even the poem as first published was very radical:

As I lay asleep in Italy,
There came a voice from over the sea,
And with great power it forth led me,
To walk in the visions of poesy.[5]

Then he introduces Liverpool's cabinet to his audience. First the foreign secretary, Lord Castlereagh:

I met Murder on the way—
He had a mask like Castlereagh—
Very smooth he looked, yet grim;
Seven bloodhounds followed him:

All were fat; and well they might
Be in admirable plight,
For one by one, and two by two,
He tossed them human hearts to chew
Which from his white cloak he drew.[6]

Then Shelley introduced the chancellor of the exchequer, Lord Eldon:

Next came Fraud, and he had on,
Like Lord E____, an ermined gown;
His big tears, for he wept well,
Turned to mill-stones as they fell.[7]

And so on. It is a long poem, and then he ends with an invocation—a call for an uprising, which created absolute mayhem. The conservatives went crazy. Shelley wrote in "Men of England":

Sow seed—but let no tyrant reap;
Find wealth—let no imposter heap:
Weave robes—let not the idle wear;
Forge arms—in your defense to bear.[8]

In other words, if you are attacked, defend yourself with weapons. I don't know where the notion comes from that this was Mahatma Gandhi's favorite poem, because the poem is definitely not a pacifist one.

In the one that Lukács liked best, *Prometheus Unbound,* Shelley ends too with an appeal to the people of England:

Rise like lions after slumber.
In unvanquishable number—
Shake your chains to earth like dew
Which in sleep had fallen on you—[9]

So, if you remain inactive and passive, you chain yourselves. This tradition lasted—it is in William Blake, too—but it grew out of the French Revolution, out of its defeat, that is, though it was a defeat they did not want to accept. These poems said that there are new possibilities. Don't be pessimistic because the French Revolution has been defeated, that Wellington had defeated Napoleon at Waterloo in 1815—these poems were written in 1819—for we go on! That was the message of the poems.

Communism

Then we come to communism and the Russian Revolution. When certain scholars get obsessed simply with the question of numbers, the number of casualties, I worry that this obsession can lead to simplistic conclusions. One of those conclusions is that between fascism and communism, Adolf Hitler and Joseph Stalin, there is no difference. Yet there is a huge difference, which can be summarized in the following fashion: without the Red Army, fascism would have overtaken Europe. The two key battles of World War II were the Battle of Stalingrad and the Battle of Kursk. They broke the backbone of fascism. That's one point, and not a small thing. Second, the origins of the two philosophies or ideologies are completely different. One was an ultranationalism backed by big capital. Fascism was the last resort of capital, and capital backed it. The profit margins of the big capitalist industries during the Third Reich shot up. Krupp, Thyssen, and all these rogues that are still around took profits of 300–400 percent, based on slave labor. This is not the same thing as communism.

Yes, Stalin was a monster. Atrocities were committed, but you didn't need a world war to defeat the Soviet Union. It imploded. Why did it implode? Because the desire for reform came from within the country: first in 1956 and then later after 1985 under Mikhail Gorbachev. That Gorbachev mishandled the reforms and was naive beyond belief regarding the intentions of the West is another question, but the desire for reform came from within, and the people were desperate for changes. None of the Soviet bloc countries had to be physically conquered to bring those regimes to an end: yet indeed, that was the only way fascism could be destroyed.

Judeocide was fascism's worst crime but not its only crime. Add the number of Slavs killed and the number of Russians who died in World War II. But as I said, compiling numbers is not the point. It is simplistic and decontextualized. For that matter, you could add the United States to the list of perpetrators and great numbers of people killed: just a million in Iraq not so long ago under the occupation; a million dead, and five million orphans left behind. By just citing numbers, we see that the deaths are horrific. But what does it mean? If you say that therefore the United States is the same as Benito Mussolini's Italy, that America is a fascist state—which some angry people do say—we know that the equation is nonsensical.

It is foolish, when we now have the distance of history, to talk about these things in this way. How can one compare the poets produced by communism to most of the rubbish produced by fascists? It is not true that fascism did not produce any masterpieces. Unfortunately, one cannot deny that they did. We have Louis-Ferdinand Céline, the French novelist; I do not like him, but he was a genius. As Leon Trotsky wrote about Céline in 1933, "He walked into great literature as other men walk into their own homes."[10] Jean-Paul Sartre feared that the bastard would outlive us all. You have to recognize this, but by and large the artistic standing of fascists simply was not like his.

One poet who came to his peak following a defeat—that is, the victory of fascism in Germany—was Bertolt Brecht. Some of his finest poetry was written in the aftermath. We must say of all these Communist poets—Brecht in Germany, Pablo Neruda in Chile, Nâzim Hikmet in Turkey, Faiz Ahmed Faiz in Pakistan, Louis Aragon in France—and of the great surrealist poets, André Breton and others, who were not officially Communists but part of the culture of the Left in that time, that they were rock-solid internationalists. Their links to communism made them think about the world as a whole. Their attraction to communism de-provincialized them for life. They couldn't just write about themselves or their own countries. They thought about the world. In our household in Pakistan—a Communist household—we would get all the left-wing magazines from Britain as a matter of course. We also had magazines from the United States: *The Nation,* the *New Masses,* and *Masses and Mainstream.* Many of the figures in Alan Wald's books are familiar to me from what I used to read in the 1950s and 1960s as a teenager at home. That happened because of being in a Communist family, if you like, outside the Soviet Union.

Weirdly, even Stalin (son of a so-and-so that he was) appreciated poetry. There is the famous case of Osip Mandelstam, a great poet who wrote some bad poems in praise of Stalin. (Stalin knew they were not good poems; he was a brutal dictator, but he was not stupid.) Then Mandelstam composed the famous "Stalin Epigram," a poem that he never wrote down. He would recite it to small groups of friends in tiny apartments in Moscow, and it is a most wonderful poem. He referred to Stalin's mustaches as two cockroaches: it was a vicious poem.[11] Naturally, things like this don't stay quiet. The poem spread by word of mouth. Finally someone wrote it down, and it landed on Stalin's desk. Stalin read the poem quite dispassionately, but he wasn't sure whether it was good or not, so he rang Boris Pasternak. It turns out that Pasternak survived the purges in part because in 1915, he had reviewed a collection of Georgian poetry in a Moscow literary newspaper, noting that one of those who showed promise was a young poet named Iosif Dzhugashvili. It was Stalin, of course, who thought "Well, the guy must be genuine, because I was a nobody then," and he never forgot that. So Stalin rang Pasternak up and said, "It's Stalin here." You can imagine the trembling on the other end of the line. "What do you think of Mandelstam? Would you say he's one of our greatest poets?" Now, we don't know how Pasternak replied. Pasternak himself said that he replied, "Yes, he is the greatest," but we don't know. In any case, it was too late because Mandelstam was in a prison, and conditions were bad. He died there. He wasn't executed. He died from the bad conditions of the Gulag.

The Poets' International

The internationalism of the Communist poets was, in any case, remarkable—Brecht's especially so, because he had read everything. In particular, he was attracted to the imperialist poetry of Rudyard Kipling, not because he agreed with Kipling but because he loved the rhythms of Kipling's verse, which are fantastic. Kipling was the only poet who managed to capture the rhythms of speech of working-class white soldiers in imperialist lands. A poem that Kipling wrote about the British soldiers in India serving Queen Victoria gives us the Cockney rhythms of these working-class white soldiers:

> 'Ave you 'eard o' the Widow at Windsor [That's Victoria.]
> With a hairy gold crown on 'er 'ead?
> She 'as ships on the foam—she 'as millions at 'ome,
> An' she pays us poor beggars in red.
> (Ow, poor beggars in red!)
>
> Then 'ere's to the Widow at Windsor.
> An' 'ere's to the stores an' the guns,
> The men an' the 'orses what makes up the forces
> 'O Missis Victorier's sons.
> (Poor beggars! Victorier's sons!)[12]

Brecht was fascinated by this poem, and he wrote a wonderful response—an unfinished poem written at the market on Caledonian Road in London titled "The Caledonian Market." In it, he offers no sympathy for those serving in an imperialist army:

> Oh, East is East and West is West,
> The hireling minstrel cried.
> But I observed with interest
> Bridges across that great divide.

And huge guns trundling east I've seen
And cheerful troops keeping them clean.
Meanwhile from east to west backrolled
Tea soaked in blood, war wounded gold.
And the Widow at Windsor, all dressed in black,
Grins, takes the money, stuffs it in her pocket
And gives the wounded a pat on the back,
And sends them down to the Caledonian Market.
Their walk may have lost its spring,
But they try to hobble around the stalls
And buy a second hand wooden leg instead
To match their equally wooden head.[13]

Brecht had no sympathy for those who were serving in an imperialist army. And the same Brecht, Communist Brecht, when he saw an uprising in Berlin against the East German regime in 1953 after the death of Stalin and saw workers gunned down, what did he do? The slander is that he supported it, but he never supported it. He wrote a quatrain in the Asian style in the shape of a letter to the Politburo called "The Solution":

After the uprising of the 17th June
The Secretary of the Writers Union
Had leaflets distributed in the Stalinallee
Stating that the people
Had forfeited the confidence of the government
And could win it back only
By redoubled efforts. Would it not be easier
In that case for the government
To dissolve the people
And elect another?[14]

What could be more vicious satire than that? He had called out leaders, suggesting they "dissolve the people."[15] What more could he have offered as a "solution" than that? His revolutionary sensibility survived defeat.

Let us switch from Europe to the Arab world in 1967, haunted as it was by the experience of the defeat in war that year. The great Syrian Arab poet Nizar Qabbani wrote a poem titled *Marginal Notes in the Book of the Setback.* It is a huge poem. Here is but one key section, wherein, like Shelley in the nineteenth century, Qabbani invokes something other than setbacks:

Arab children,
Corn ears of the future,
You will break our chains,
Kill the opium in our heads,
Kill the illusions.

Arab children,
Don't read about our suffocated generation,
We are a hopeless case.
As worthless as a watermelon rind.
Don't read about us,
Don't ape us,
Don't accept us,
Don't accept our ideas.
We are a nation of crooks and jugglers.
Arab children,
Spring rain,
Corn ears of the future,
You are the generation
That will overcome defeat.[16]

I was thinking about this poem when the Arab Spring began in Tunisia and Tahrir Square. How happy it would have made Qabbani to see the beginnings of a process that has not yet come to an end. This tradition in our poetry and the poetry in the Indo-Pakistan subcontinent remains strong to this day, even though we no longer have huge gatherings. Young people watch recitations of these old poems on the Internet and on YouTube nonstop.

In Pakistan, the great Communist poet Faiz Ahmed Faiz wrote some beautiful poetry. He was a great love poet, a lyric poet. Eventually he wrote this great poem to his mistress, who was badgering him and harassing him, saying, "You've become a bore; you've become political. / You don't see me." In reply, he wrote a poem called "Love, Do Not Ask." The poem says:

Love, do not ask me for that old love again,
Once I thought life, because you lived, a prize—
Time's pain nothing, you alone were pain;
Your beauty kept earth's springtime from decay. . . .
It was not true, all this, but only wishing;
Our world knows other torments than love,
And other happiness than a fond embrace.
Dark curse of countless ages, savagery
Inwoven with silk and satin and gold lace,
Men's bodies sold in street and marketplace,
Bodies that caked grime fouls and thick blood smears,
Flesh issuing from the cauldrons of disease
With festered sores dripping corruption;
These sights haunt me too and will not be shut out;
Not be shut out, though your looks ravish still.

This world knows other torments than of love,
And other happiness than a fond embrace;
Love, do not ask for my old love again.[17]

The poem goes on. It had a huge impact, because these poems, written by very intellectual poets, reached the masses when they were sung by great divas. The same occurred in the Arab world: Qabbani's poetry and that of others was sung by Um Kalthoum, Egypt's great singer and actress, and when Um Kalthoum sang it, it was heard by the nation. Whether they were banned or not, truck drivers played CDs as they drove their trucks from one country to the other, listening to this poetry.

When the partition of India happened, Faiz wrote a wonderful poem saying that this is not the road we wanted. He described this independence as a "pock-marked dawn": "A day that will not come out because night has still gripped it. This is not what we were promised." Then he ends: "Carry on our struggle. It's not over yet." And before he died, he wrote the poem "Aaj Ke Naam," or "In Today's Name," for the people of the country and for the poor. Unlike today, such poems were sung by people and were addressed to people; such poetry was a mass phenomenon. We had poetry readings with ten, fifteen, twenty thousand people. My earliest memories are of these gatherings, with improvised poetry competitions held between the different poets who spoke before us.

Consider the very great Turkish poet Nâzim Hikmet, who was locked up in a Turkish prison. There were huge campaigns for his release and appeals signed by everyone. He fled to the Soviet Union, but when there was an amnesty in Turkey he returned. They tried to kill him again and conscripted him into the army. The doctor who inspected him said, "They have told me to declare you healthy, but three days in the sun, my friend, given the state of your heart, and you will die. You will drop dead, and they will say, 'he had a heart attack and died.' You'd better get out." He took a small boat and with a fisherman sailed out into the sea where there were lots of Soviet and East European ships. By luck, that day he found a Romanian ship. The ship's men did not know who he was, but the sailors saw people crying for help. Hikmet describes finally being hauled onto that ship and going into the captain's room. The captain says, "Who are you?" Hikmet says, "I'm Nâzim Hikmet, the Turkish Communist poet, and they're going to try and kill me, so I need to get out. Take me wherever you can." The captain laughs and points, and behind him there is a picture of Hikmet, part of the campaign, saying "Free Nâzim Hikmet."[18]

For all who are interested in the state of the world and its ecology, consider Hikmet's interesting poem "On Living":

> Living is no laughing matter;
> you must live with great seriousness
> like a squirrel for example—

I mean without looking for something beyond and above living,
I mean living must be your whole occupation.

Living is no laughing matter;
You must take living seriously,
So much so and to such a degree

that, for example, your hands tied behind your back, your back to the wall, or else in a laboratory

in your white coat and safety glasses,
you can die for people—
even for people whose faces you've never seen,
even though you know living
is the most real, the most beautiful thing.[19]

And Hikmet ended with a materialist invocation.

This earth will grow cold,
a star among stars
and one of the smallest,
a gilded mote on blue velvet—
I mean *this,* our great earth.
This earth will grow cold one day,
not like a block of ice
or a dead cloud even
but like an empty walnut it will roll along
in pitch black space . . .
You must grieve for this right now
—you have to feel this sorrow now—
for the world must be loved this much
if you're going to say "I lived" . . .[20]

This was written in February 1948, at the height of the Cold War.

Beyond Defeat

I regret not discussing my favorite Israeli poet, Aharon Shabtai, who writes in Hebrew and writes to his people poems of startling intensity, warning them, "Don't say you don't know. You do know what's going on and one day what will you say when you are sitting in a court of law, and they say to you, why did you do this? You cannot say we did not know." Poets like this in the world make us see the power of poetry. It remains universal, whether Shelley or Qabbani. This power will not go away, regardless of other things that have happened. Sometimes while looking at Alan Wald's work or my own or that of others, I get a feeling that what we are talking about is Atlantis. We're trying to find the best examples of what Atlantis was like—a submerged continent, gone. That's only part of the story, though, because even in mythology they don't say that everyone who lived on Atlantis died with the continent. Some survived. Some went elsewhere. Some moved to other continents and lived to fight another day. There are two emotions in our lives today. One is despair, and sometimes we all feel it, but it is an emotion that induces passivity. Then there is hope. Not overly optimistic hope, but hope even in bad times. Even in times of defeat. Hope is an active emotion and always has been. It is an emotion I have always favored, even when one feels incredibly depressed, when the atrocities go on and on.

What we have to do when the atrocities take over and shake the world is to fight back with our fists, our pens, our books, whatever we can. I am not one of those who believe that it is all over. In some parts of the world, other people realize this. The movements that arose in South America have made of that continent the most independent lands today. One of the many acts of Hugo Chavez that I admire occurred on the four hundredth anniversary of the publication of *Don Quixote*. The Ministry of Culture in Caracas ordered that a million copies be printed. Each household that had become newly literate, due to the education programs Chavez promoted, would be given a free copy of *Don Quixote*. When Chavez was mocked—"Who will read it?" they said—he replied, "I don't care who reads it—perhaps their children or their grandchildren. They should have it in the house." That is a message for us too: We write as members of a generation that is now departing. Many of our friends have gone, but we write not for ourselves and not for the past generations but for the future. It is like Qabbani's poetry. When I write, I think not about my friends who will or will not read the book but of the young people who might—and of what they might make of it. In this continuity that we try to achieve—a continuity for human emancipation and self-liberation—there is something that carries on. Socialism failed once, and its enemies want to vilify it forever. Capitalism has failed at least seventy times since it was invented, and it goes on and on. I say that one failure is not enough to write us off completely.

Notes

1. Hesiod, *Work and Days*, Perseus Digital Library, http://www.perseus.tufts.edu/hopper/text?doc=urn:cts:greekLit:tlg0020.tlg002.perseus-engl:274.
2. John Milton, *Paradise Lost*, Book 1, line 242.

3. Percy Bysshe Shelley, "To Wordsworth," Sonnet Central, http://www.sonnets.org/shelley.htm#400.
4. Georg Lukács, "Hölderlin's *Hyperion*" (1934), in Georg Lukács, *Goethe and His Age,* translated by Robert Anchor (London: Merlin, 1968), 153.
5. Percy Bysshe Shelley, "The Mask of Anarchy: Written on the Occasion of the Massacre at Manchester," University of Pennsylvania, http://knarf.english.upenn.edu/PShelley/anarchy.html.
6. Ibid.
7. Ibid.
8. Percy Bysshe Shelley, "A Song: 'Men of England," Poetry Foundation, http://www.poetryfoundation.org/poem/183987.
9. Percy Bysshe Shelley, "Prometheus Unbounded," Poetry Foundation, http://www.poetryfoundation.org/poem/174403.
10. Leon Trotsky, "Céline [and Poincaré]: Novelist [and Politician]," Anti-Caste, http://www.anti-caste.org/trotsky-celine-and-poincare-novelist-and-politician.html.
11. Osip Mandelstam, "The Stalin Epigram," Poets.org, http://www.poets.org/viewmedia.php/prmMID/16806.
12. Rudyard Kipling, "The Widow at Windsor," DayPoems, http://www.daypoems.net/poems/1797.html.
13. Bertolt Brecht, "The Caledonian Market," in *Poems, 1913–1965,* edited by John Willet and Ralph Manheim (New York and London: Methuen, 1979), 233.
14. Bertolt Brecht, "The Solution," in *Poems, 1913-1965*, 440.
15. Ibid.
16. Tariq Ali, *The Clash of Fundamentalisms: Crusades, Jihads, and Modernity* (London and New York: Verso, 2002), 117–21.
17. Faiz Ahmed Faiz, "Love, Do Not Ask," translated by Victor G. Kiernan, in *Poems by Faiz* (London: Allen and Unwin, 1971), 65.
18. For more details, see "Nâzim Hikmet Biography," Famous Poets and Poems, http://famouspoetsandpoems.com/poets/nazim_hikmet/biography.
19. Nâzim Hikmet, "On Living," Famous Poets and Poems, http://famouspoetsandpoems.com/poets/nazim_hikmet/poems/13749. For a slightly different translation, see Nâzim Hikmet, *Beyond the Walls: Selected Poems,* translated by Ruth Christie, Richard McKane, and Talât Sait Halman (London: Anvil Press Poetry, 2002), 165.
20. Nâzim Hikmet, "On Living."

[2]

What's Left of Lyric: Genevieve Taggard and the Redefinition of Song

Sarah Ehlers

In her 1934 *New Masses* essay "Romanticism and Communism," Genevieve Taggard argued that the "proper function of poetry" might only be comprehended "after the false principle of the individual, a little universe sealed away from all the rest of life, has been ridiculed to death." According to Taggard, truly revolutionary poetry had not yet been written. But she began to discern its outlines by looking to the past—to "the genial, sober, salty, level-headed, profound type of the older literatures" where there were "no gods and giants, but men, grown to full capacity."[1] In "Romanticism and Communism" as well as in the prose "Note Books" included throughout her 1936 volume *Calling Western Union,* Taggard suggested that "the poetry about to be born"—by rigorously eschewing the "individualism," "self-interest," and belief in the "godlike perfection" of man that she associated with romanticism—would find its most lasting form by harnessing both the arts of the past (those that predate the nineteenth-century "bourgeois revolution") and the advances of the present. *Calling Western Union* was in many ways a case in point: the book's title drew on the early–twentieth-century emergence of telecommunications to imagine radical political poems as "emergency messages sent via Western Union," and yet its poems were formed as, and informed by, traditional folkloric genres such as the chant, the ballad, and the song.[2]

It is hardly surprising then that in a radio broadcast likely aired from New York City in the late 1930s, Taggard fused the "poetry of the future" to the modern technology of the radio by way of a traditional form.[3] Near the end of the broadcast, she read aloud her "Definition of Song," a poem originally published in a May 1936 issue of the *New Masses* and then collected in *Calling Western Union.* Despite the poem's obvious association with traditional song, she told her listeners why the poem "belongs to our modern world":

> This is a poem against individualism in the arts, against the outworn idea of the lonely genius, the prima donna, the hero of literature; a poem that talks about the art of doing things together. And so this is poetry inspired by the city, and by modern ways of doing things. *Participation for all.* After I read this poem you will see why I think the person who listens is important to the poet. A good poet tries to say what his listener needs to hear.[4]

The technology of the radio magnified a fantasy that informed not just the construction of Taggard's 1930s poetry but also the formation of radical Depression-era poetics more broadly: that a poem might communicate directly with readers and, as a result, intervene immediately in social life. Reverberating through the airwaves, a poem could reach the "ears of millions," and a poet such as Taggard could (not unlike labor union leaders of the time) use the radio to promote political solidarity.[5]

Taggard's notion of poetic transmission was only augmented by radio—not necessarily produced by it. As Taggard herself suggested, the new "medium" of the radio "returns to us, marvelously amplified, the old art of the ballad makers and the troubadours."[6] This statement begs the question, however, of how a return to the arts of the past can produce the future of poetry. In what follows, I argue that the poems and prose pieces collected in *Calling Western Union* chart the formal means by which Taggard attempted to imagine and construct the "poetry of the future." During the 1930s, Taggard was caught at a difficult crossroads as she tried to conceptualize a poetry that could not yet exist. The notion that wireless radio transmission could disperse her singular speaking voice into "a million vibrating lines" is but one iteration of her poetic impulse to eradicate the "futile," "false," and "manufactured" opposition between the "Individual" and "Society" that characterized the art of "the liberal and the Romanticist."[7] Taggard's interest in radio reveals a significant aspect of how she engaged questions of political representation in her Depression-era poetry. For Taggard, romantic poetics and their modernist inheritance were premised on models of political identity that opposed the individual to society and, as a result, could not possibly represent the forms of community that might be produced from new economic and political alignments. In *Calling Western Union,* Taggard pursued this critique through experimentation with the lyric mode: she worked to reconfigure the romantic lyric subject by contemplating new possibilities for collective expression. Her poems ultimately return us to the lyric's etymological connection with the Greek lyre, its classical association with singing in front of an audience, as she attempted to do away with the modern notion that a lyric "I" speaks only to itself in solitude.

Taggard was a prolific poet and critic, but her importance as a radical woman writer and public intellectual has remained relatively obscure. She published her first volume of poems, *For Eager Lovers,* in 1922, and her work regularly appeared in such widely circulating publications as *Poetry: A Magazine of Verse* and the *New Masses.* In addition to cofounding *The Measure: A Journal of Poetry* in 1921, she coedited the *Masses/Liberator* anthology *May Days* in 1925 and published a critical biography of Emily Dickinson in 1930. By the time *Calling Western Union* was published in 1936, Taggard was not only an increasingly recognized scholar (*The Life and Mind of Emily Dickinson* went into its second printing in 1934) and leftist critic (she worked as a contributing editor for the *New Masses*) but was also an important poetic voice on the Communist Left. Taggard's early poems, admired by critics as diverse as Harriet Monroe and Mike Gold, demonstrate her experiments with traditional verse genres as well as the development of her "Marxist sensibility."[8] *Calling Western Union,* which includes iconic Depression-era poems such as "Mill Town" and "Up-State Depression Summer" alongside earlier poems such as "Everyday Alchemy" and "Revolution," indicates "a revision of her radical self to meet the demands of the increasingly radicalized environment of the 1930s."[9] While conservative critics would "convict" Taggard of the "vice" of "sentimentality," her poems were heartily embraced by Depression-era audiences who recognized them as compelling representations of everyday experiences "in the light of a new set of social and revolutionary values."[10]

Often working against those contemporary scholars who have echoed historical criticisms of Taggard's poetry, scholars such as Nancy Berke, Cary Nelson, Charlotte Nekola, Paula Rabinowitz, and Alan Wald have argued convincingly for the literary-historical importance of Taggard's imaginative work.[11] But more than excavating the work of Taggard, I recover the ways in which radical leftist poets rethought the conventions of the poetic lyric, a mode typically associated with pure self-expression. Taggard is a central figure for illuminating alternative historical conceptions of lyric that emerge against the notion, prevalent in modern literary criticism, that the lyric is self-enclosed. A study of Taggard's radical poetics allows us, in Walter Kalaidjian's terms, to "see how our own contemporary allegiance to possessive individualism is not so much a 'natural' as it is a historically contingent credo."[12]

In this sense, the phrase "Left of Lyric" has a double meaning. First, it references a political spectrum. I want to think about how 1930s writers associated with the Communist Left attempted to move a conventional lyric, reliant on bourgeois notions of expression, politically Left. Second, I evoke the phrase "Left of Lyric" in terms of the perceived wreckage of poetry circa 1929. During the 1930s, radical writers were as anxious as they were hopeful about poetry's capacity to address the failures of capitalism and shifting international formations. Poetic language, for many such writers, was not the language of social renewal but a "dead language." What could Depression-era writers possibly make of the lyric when there seemed to be nothing left of it?

From a historical standpoint, Taggard's work speaks to a prevailing suspicion on the Left that romantic and modernist versions of the poetic lyric and the lyric subject ran counter to radical utopian visions of revolutionary community and, in many ways, to poetic attempts to document scenes of working-class, antiracist, and anti-imperialist struggle. In her 1937 poem "This Body Politic," for instance, Ruth Lechlitner figures the "I" as a "slave" to fascist dictatorship, and she chides the "lyric" poet for singing the "stone-age myth" and the "dream of dinosaurs" while the "ego" of the exploiter "flowers."[13] And critic Michael Davidson uses Muriel Rukeyser's well-known line "Not Sappho, Sacco" to schematically describe an aesthetic shift "from an austere lyricism, for whom Sappho was the model, to forms...that blur generic terms."[14] As her arguments in "Romanticism and Communism" suggest, Taggard saw the traditional romantic lyric as the refuse of a crumbling capitalist system and a defunct bourgeois literary order. Her poems in *Calling Western Union* thus approach a conceptual gap as she attempts to cast off traditional lyric practice in order to declare the death of bourgeois individualism. What emerges, I argue, is not simply a turn away from the lyric; in fact, Taggard considered herself a poet who could never "stop experimenting with lyric effects."[15] In *Calling Western Union,* Taggard reconstructs forms of lyric expression and lyric address and, in so doing, rethinks the lyric's long association with song. This reconceptualization of lyric—this experimentation with "lyric effects"—opens new possibilities for collectivity within the space of the poem itself.

My arguments about how Taggard heaved the lyric leftward are informed by recent work in the field of historical poetics, particularly the assertion that we should conceive of lyric not as a transhistorical genre but rather as a mobile concept that has meant different things at different times and, in the case of Taggard, for different political reading communities.[16] A close study of Taggard's radical poetics allows us to excavate a set of historical and political conditions for the production of the modern lyric that previously have been obscured. In the wake of the 2008 economic collapse, poets and critics have renewed their attention to the social functions of lyric, questioning the relationship between lyric subjectivity and neoliberal notions of political recognition.[17] It is my contention that "old" anticapitalist left-wing poets such as Taggard provide discourses for understanding, in historical and theoretical terms, the ideological contours of the lyric subject as well as the links between experiments with lyric and the imagination of radical forms of collectivity.

Taggard's body of radical poetry, in its concerted efforts to explore the problems and failures of individualism, provides a particularly apt means to explore how Depression-era political poets approached—or reproached—the lyric. Scrupulously reading how radical poets such as Taggard put pressure on the lyric from within opens up new possibilities for historical and theoretical reevaluations of lyric specifically and of the development of artistic modernity across the twentieth century more broadly. While a host of recent monographs has explored the ways in which modern American poets articulated the effects of global capitalism, these projects for the most part have set Old Left poetry aside.[18] For instance, Joel Nickels asserts that Wald's conception of the "revolutionary imagination" is "much closer" to the "ambitions" and "attitudes" of canonical modernist poetry than scholars have realized.[19] But then Nickels doesn't read any Old Left poetry, choosing instead works where no obvious political message or orientation manifests. Nonetheless, Nickels indicates how important the recovery of revolutionary imaginative work is for broad reevaluations of the landscape of early twentieth-century poetry.

At the Death of Poetry

During the 1930s, radical writers commonly decried early twentieth-century poetic culture for being too steeped in esoteric forms and bourgeois models of individualism. Many politically committed poets thus imagined poetry as dead, a rhetorical device that allowed them to separate a presumably inert modern poetry from an emerging radical artistic culture that would reestablish poetry's connection to the social world. In their view, the art of poetry would be revitalized—indeed, reborn—through new forms that communicated directly to mass audiences as well as imagined revolutionary models of subjectivity and community. In "Romanticism and Communism," Taggard uses images of death and rebirth to sketch the future of revolutionary poetry. Near the start of the essay she asks, "Should the poetry about to be born belong to the Romantic Family?" Her answer, of course, is decidedly *no.* The "Romantic Family," she avers, is surely a "bourgeois" one, and the future communist poetry must reject the romantic inheritance that she traces from Rousseau to Shelley, Whitman, and T. S. Eliot.[20] In "Note Book II" from *Calling Western Union,* Taggard suggests that "Rousseau's doctrine, boiled down and taken over by a host of artists[,] insisted that man must recreate his divine self by retreating from the maze of social forms." This approach is "backward," stultifying the "forward advance" of the working-class masses.[21] According to Taggard, to believe that the romantic thinker or artist "expresses our revolutionary meaning today is nonsense."[22]

Whether or not Taggard's account of the romantic tradition is oversimplified (or even built on misreading), it provides a convenient foil for her vision of poetry's future. In *Calling Western Union,* Taggard conceives the passageway to a new aesthetic through an imagination of a poet's death. In "Note Book I," the first short prose passage in *Calling Western Union,* and in "Funeral in May," the poem immediately following, the death of a poet becomes a symbol for the figurative death of a condition for poetry as well as the social order that had sustained it. "Note Book I" continues the arguments that Taggard began in "Romanticism and Communism," identifying one of the main assumptions hindering the development of revolutionary poetry: "the romantic notion that the individual is capable of godlike perfection." She continues, "This is poison food, and those who eat it die a lingering and pallid death. But before he dies the poet repeats the doctrine that poisoned him. He feeds his audience on the gigantic fiction of a *Free Personality.*"[23] In "Funeral in May," Taggard again employs the figure of a poet's death in order to reconceive poetic expression. Here, death signals not only the eradication of an old order but also the potential for new representational possibilities.

"Funeral in May" begins at the deathbed of a worn-out poet. This poet imagines himself as Christlike—a self-declared "mouthpiece of the divine" whose "voice starts from the throat in gold song / in the breathing peace of the lord." But try as he might, God has eluded him. Alas, the poet has been "forsaken by metaphor" and damned to the worst of fates: "to be literal literal." In his dying gasp he begs: "Lovely metaphor, redeem me from sin / and deliver us from meaning." "Then he died," the poem succinctly declares, "snap like any business man / worry overstrain / burst a blood vessel."[24]

The imagined death of a poet in "Funeral in May" is but one of many examples of how radical Depression-era poets mobilized the trope of poetry's death in order to figure how poetry might be revitalized to serve new political functions. At the close of *Exile's Return,* for instance, Malcolm Cowley posits that decadent modernist poet Harry Crosby's 1929 suicide became an emblem for the defunct notion that art "was purposeless, useless, wholly individual and forever opposed to the stupid world."[25] The figure of the dead poet might be seen to serve multiple functions in Taggard's poem. Perhaps he is a model of an authoritarian modernist figure (a representative of what Taggard referred to in another poem as the "Sick Generation") whose death signifies a break with particular coteries and aesthetics she associates with 1920s high modernism. Or he might be seen as representative of a dying romantic tradition in which, according to Taggard, "individual grandeur" trumped the "common good."[26]

What is potentially more compelling, however, is how the figuration of the poet's death in "Funeral in May" marks a shift in conceptions of the lyric. In "Funeral in May," the figure of the solitary poet is buried and then literally written over when the "voice of the infidel" enters and instructs the poem's other "infidels" to inter the poet and mark his grave. They use the dead poet's mirror as a headstone, scrawling his epitaph in the space where his image would have appeared:

Set here for his grave-stone
His perfect companion the mirror. Put it here out of doors,
In its blank write his epitaph out. *Newsreel our day.*
Let windy leaves toss in its flash.
When we gather fresh laurel
Blow blasts on the factory whistle. Ring loud early bells.
Dance in the meadows
young and old
stalwart and swarthy.[27]

Using the mirror for a gravestone is, at first, a bit of a joke. Calling the mirror the poet's "perfect companion," the poem pokes fun at his narcissism and solipsism. But this gesture takes a more serious turn when the "voice of the infidel" gives the command to write out "*Newsreel our day*" in the mirror blank. The act of filling in the blank space where the dead poet's image would have appeared effectively replaces the individual poet with the very historical realities he tried to avoid and transcend. The insertion of the possessive pronoun "our" is significant here as well, marking the shift from a poetics based in a singular "I" to one that embraces a plural "we." Even while a singular voice (the "voice of the infidel") orchestrates the scene, a collective "we" gathers "fresh laurels" and dances to the sounds of the factory's "whistle" and "early bells."

This gesture is consonant with Taggard's critiques of the romantic tradition and her invocation of what she variously called "group life" and "common good." The vision of such a form of collectivity can be seen in the last section of "Funeral in May," when "the voice of the infidel" again issues the command "Turn funeral to fete." The new poetry being formed at Taggard's "fete" will not be rooted in individual egos or achievements but rather in collective action. This poetry will be grounded in present-day social and cultural life, and it will incorporate the sounds of the field and the factory. This vision culminates in the poem's last section, when the "voice of the infidel" calls out:

> Turn funeral to fete.
>   Here we inter folly
> Gluttonous villainy stupidity the vanity of man.
> Again and again we must dance on the grave of this death
> Beating down with determined feet what is already dead;
> Weeds growing here will wear to rags where we step.
> Dance
>   it is May
>   of all Mays the gayest with promise.
> You who are skilled with the songs lead the way with your singing.[28]

These last lines of "Funeral in May" suggest how the imagined death of a poet, and thus a paradigm for a particular poetics, provides a productive space for crafting a radical poetics. This is especially apparent in the line "Here we inter folly," which is rife with double meanings. The poem reiterates the literal act of interring (of placing in a grave) the dead poet and thus the follies of an irrelevant poetic culture. But "inter" also suggests a state of transition, of being in between the death of one paradigm and the birth of another. "Folly" here might not just refer to the senseless practices represented by the dead poet (the "Gluttonous villainy stupidity the vanity of man"). A second definition of "folly" is evoked whereby "folly" refers to an ornate structure serving no practical purpose. This meaning of "folly" emphasizes how in burying the old poet, the notion that poetry does not have a practical political function is also buried. It is especially significant, then, that the funeral-turned-fete takes place in May, considering the month's association with the May Day parades that celebrated working-class solidarity.

Most significantly, the poem ends with a command that allows us to understand a key formal innovation of Taggard's radical poetics: "You who are skilled with the songs lead the way with / your singing."[29] In this line, Taggard's poem begins to chart a shift from an individuated lyric "I," one modeled on bourgeois forms of subjectivity and addressing only itself, to an emerging address to a collective "you" in the process of formation. This might be read as a gesture toward what Taggard calls in "Romanticism and Communism" a poetry that "sees the individual in relationship to something bigger than himself and knows that all meanings lie in the relationship of artist to audience, of one word to another."[30]

What seems most at stake in Taggard's poem is how the "you" is invoked—and why and where. At the moment of the "poor poet's" death, the "voice of the infidel" enters and issues the command to "Bury the poet deep in his words." This infidel speaks to the others in the poem (those carrying out the commands), but this "voice" also calls out to, and therefore implicates, the reader. While it might seem counterintuitive to read a poem such as "Funeral in May" in relation to lyric, the poem works out a critique of lyric through the death of the bourgeois poet and the address to a plural "you" that emerges in his wake, suggesting the reemergence of lyric on radical grounds rather than its complete eradication. If in romantic and modern lyrics the poet expresses his thoughts only to himself (even when the poem purports to address another), then Taggard boldly reasserts the presence of another—of "you"—in order to disturb such claims to pure self-expression. Virginia Jackson explains that the logic of address that dominates post-romantic theories of lyric reading "converts the isolated 'I' into the universal 'we' by bypassing the mediation of any particular 'you.'"[31] Taggard hints at a similar logic early in "Funeral in May" when she describes the dying poet's amplified voice as a "splendid echo," and she reformulates this logic when she ends the poem by urging the addressee to replace the poem's speaker and "lead the way with your singing."

Taggard's poem thus suggests the emergence of a new form of address in which the lyric utterance is intended for public circulation—much in the same way a radio broadcast could "reach the ears of millions."[32] In this way, "Funeral in May" challenges models of lyric address that make "the overhearing of a persona our principal means of understanding a poem."[33] Jackson explains that within this framework for reading, saying "I" stands in for saying "you." Here, "the poet's solitude stands in for the solitude of the individual reader—a self-address so absolute that every self can identify it as its own."[34] Certainly, Taggard never intended her own lyrics to be read this way. On the back flap of her 1938 *Collected Poems,* she stresses a different form of identification between poet and reader. Taggard explains that she "tried to use the 'I' in a poem only as a means of transferring feeling to identification with anyone who takes the poem, momentarily, for his own. 'I' is then adjusted to the voice of the reader."[35] What Taggard begins to accomplish in "Funeral in May" is in the spirit of how she described her lyric poems in 1938, but there are some fundamental differences. Rather than merely interrupting lyric's solipsism by positing an "adjusted," or slightly altered, identification between poet and reader (or speaker and listener), in "Funeral in May" Taggard foregrounds a second-person "you" that in effect is a political community in the process of formation. In Taggard's logic, the "you" is not merely a fictive placeholder—an imagined audience that in the end is the poet's own voice echoing back to her. Rather, the "you" is a modification of the speaking "I": it is called on to replace the "I" with a collective singing that eschews the "individualistic absolutism" that Taggard associates with the romantic tradition.

The Redefinition of Song

In "Funeral in May" Taggard might, through the death of a poet, place us at a death of the romantic lyric as such—or, at least, at a historical gap where the meaning of lyric was reconfigured. In other words, she attempted a revision of lyric that looks something like its death. In her experiments with structures of lyric address, Taggard also foregrounded the importance of singing and song, both within her own lyric practice and as part of the history of lyric itself. As Wald notes, from the beginnings of the Communist movement in 1919, "the form of poetry favored by US Left activists and political leaders was very much in the tradition of workers' songs, ballads, and folk culture."[36] Throughout the 1930s and 1940s and in *Calling Western Union* especially, Taggard invoked "song" as a means to imagine poetry's potential to represent the voices of a revolutionary collective. She, like many other radical poets, seemed to idealize verse genres such as the ballad and song that are associated with oral transmission. Such genres were imagined as immediately accessible: capable of stirring the emotions of a wide audience and intervening directly in social life. Song, in this sense, becomes an example of what Cary Nelson describes as poetry becoming "an occasion for a working-class oral community—not, as literary studies has often held it to be, the sign of an isolated and self-contained subjectivity but a discourse opening a space for sharing experiences and developing collective agency."[37] In *Calling Western Union,* poems such as "At Last the Women Are Moving," "Feeding the Children," and "Mass Song," for instance, use metrical regularity, chant-like repetition, and refrain in ways that reference the poems' immediate use for political action and their potential circulation among those ready "to walk city miles with many."[38]

Taggard's invocation of song also teaches us something about lyric and its history. The "voice of the infidel" in "Funeral in May" challenges (indeed, replaces) a bourgeois romantic version of the lyric speaker by referencing the lyric's classical associations with song and with choral performances of song and dance. In Taggard's history of lyric singing, then, both Sappho *and* Sacco are relevant touchstones. The lyric is connected to the lyre of ancient Greek poets such as Sappho—a reference to the earliest form of lyric as a song performed for a specific audience. Taggard was an established teacher and scholar, and her drafts and notebooks are punctuated with related notes on Greek poets and philosophers; she often drew on classical forms in her poems ("At Last the Women Are Moving," for instance, is written in hexameter).

Taggard seems to practice this mode of lyric singing in the draft of an unpublished poem titled "In the Plural":

> It was sung into me
> It was sung out of me
> And into me
> And out of me
> What became part of me
> And did I make
> A single song[39]

There is a tension between the poem's proposed title—"In the Plural"—and the singular "I" receiving and singing a song. The poem fragment implies that the "I" of a poem is not a self-expressive speaker but instead is a conduit for the message or song referred to by the pronoun "it." The singing "I" receives song in a way that mirrors the acts of reading that Taggard describes in another poem from *Calling Western Union,* "Life of the Mind 1934." In that poem, Taggard frames the experience of the work through a parenthetical aside: ("*The words in the books are not true / If they never act in you.*") This suggested reading practice—which emphasizes experience, intuition, and action over philosophizing—is similar to assimilating "song" as "part of" oneself.[40] While the pronoun "it" emerges as a reference to a disembodied song, it is nonetheless transformed through embodied acts of singing ("It was sung into me" and "became part of me") and listening (words "acting in you").

Taggard uses song to challenge predominant models of lyric reading. As "Life of the Mind 1934" suggests, this also requires her to assume her role as teacher. Alison Van Nyhuis has argued that throughout *Calling Western Union* Taggard uses various framing devices that "remind readers that Taggard conducts the collection's revolutionary movements."[41] One of the ways Taggard accomplishes the work of framing the poem is by turning individual pieces into pedagogical acts. "Definition of Song" suggests this strategy right away, with a title foregrounding that the purpose of the poem is to "define" song for its audience. The poem then begins with affirmation and lament:

Singing is best, it gives right joy to speech
Six years I squandered, studying to teach,
Expounding language. Singing it is better,
Teaching the joy of song, not teaching the letter.[42]

Here, the "joy" of song is opposed to time squandered "studying to teach" and "expounding language." The syntactical construction of the second line suggests both that the "I" of the poem "squandered" her time and that the "I" itself should assume a less authoritative position. The "I" is placed in the middle of the line, not at the beginning of the line, and is modified by "squandered" as if to intimate that the pronoun itself is wasted. This is further elaborated in the second section, which argues that "of all forms of song surely the least / Is solo." It is here that in defining (or redefining) song, Taggard explores the possibility of collective expression:

Singing is the work of many voices.
Only so when choral mass rejoices.
Is the lock sprung on human isolation
And all the many welded into one.[43]

In a letter to Granville Hicks, Taggard identified "Funeral in May" and "Definition of Song," along with her poems "Image," "Remembering Vaughan," and "Lark," as her "legacy to the Left."[44] Taken together, these poems dramatize the importance of Taggard's metaphoric killing off of a forlorn poet cloaked in symbol and metaphor and suggest her new attention to representing the collective voice of the "infidels" who dance and sing "on the grave" of bourgeois poetic traditions. In "Lark," which closes *Calling Western Union,* it is again "singing" that will call forth "the day-rise, the day-rise, the great day-rise" of revolution, and it is only the "Singer, Singer fair, so fair" who can envision what is to come. The last lines of "Lark" suggest that for Taggard, the effects of lyric (or "lyric effects," to recall her phrasing) are not always immediate. On one level, of course, Taggard redefines poetic expression in order to create solidarity in the present. But on another level, what she most seeks is something like a reverberation: an imagination of future historical and political conditions that could change the parameters for the production of lyric.

Recently, scholars of US poetry have begun to explore how contemporary activist poets proffer critiques of the liberal subject by, in the words of one critic, imagining "forms of collective being subsisting at the margins of the marketplace."[45] Such studies aptly demonstrate how contemporary political poets reinvent traditional modes of solitary self-expression in order to formulate a dissenting voice that privileges the communal over the individual. But poetry scholars have yet to fully consider the longer history of which those innovations are a part. As I demonstrate through the example of Taggard, salvaging "what's left" of Depression-era radical poetry—excavating those narratives that have been "left out"—might help us to conceive new frameworks and genealogies for understanding activist, anticapitalist poetry and its efforts to speak from a space of collective dissent. She was sure that Communism would produce revolutionary art, but she also indicated that the conditions for the production of such art would not exist in her lifetime. Taggard teaches the contemporary critic that if we are to summon the future of poetry, we must look to its past—or, to paraphrase Taggard, harness the energy of past hopes in our search for forms that will last.

Notes

1. Genevieve Taggard, "Romanticism and Communism," *New Masses* (September 25, 1934), 20.
2. Nancy Berke, *Women Poets on the Left: Lola Ridge, Genevieve Taggard, Margaret Walker* (Gainesville: University Press of Florida, 2001), 89.
3. Genevieve Taggard, "The Poetry of the Future," n.d., Genevieve Taggard Papers, Archives and Manuscripts Collection, New York Public Library, 1. While the transcript for Taggard's radio broadcast is undated in her archive, its frequent references to New York City indicate that it was recorded there; in the transcript she references her "new book," *Collected Poems, 1918–1938,* likely placing the broadcast in the late 1930s or early 1940s.
4. Taggard, "The Poetry of the Future," 18–21.
5. For the role of radio in efforts to promote working-class solidarity, see Lizabeth Cohen, *Making a New Deal: Industrial Workers in Chicago, 1919–1939,* 2nd ed. (Cambridge: Cambridge University Press, 2008), 134–43, 341–57.
6. Ibid., 22. Taggard's notion that radio "returns us" to the oral arts of balladeers recalls Susan Stewart's notion of a "distressed genre" or "new antique." Susan Stewart, *Crimes of Writing: Problems in the Containment of Representation* (Oxford: Oxford University Press, 1991).
7. Taggard, "The Poetry of the Future," 6; Taggard, "Romanticism and Communism," 20.
8. Alan Wald, *Exiles from a Future Time* (Chapel Hill: University of North Carolina Press, 2002), 280.

9. Berke, *Women Poets on the Left,* 88.

10. Walter Kalaidjian, *The Edge of Modernism: American Poetry and the Traumatic Past* (Baltimore: Johns Hopkins University Press, 2006), 135. Kalaidjian cites Cleanth Brooks's criticisms of the contributors (including Taggard) to *Proletarian Literature in the United States.* Rebecca Pitts, "Tough, Reasonable, Witty," *New Masses,* October 27, 1936, 22.

11. See, for example, Berke, *Women Poets on the Left;* Cary Nelson, *Repression and Recovery: Modern American Poetry and the Politics of Cultural Memory, 1910–1945* (Madison: University of Wisconsin Press, 1989); Cary Nelson, *Revolutionary Memory: Recovering the Poetry of the American Left* (New York: Routledge, 2001); Charlotte Nekola and Paula Rabinowitz, eds., *Writing Red: An Anthology of American Women Writers, 1930–1940* (New York: Feminist Press, 1987); Paula Rabinowitz, *Labor and Desire: Women's Revolutionary Fiction in Depression America* (Chapel Hill: University of North Carolina Press, 1991); and Alan Wald, *Exiles from a Future Time* (Chapel Hill: University of North Carolina Press, 2002).

12. Kalaidjian, *The Edge of Modernism,* 138.

13. Ruth Lechlitner, *Tomorrow's Phoenix* (New York: Alcestis Press, 1937), 18.

14. Michael Davidson, *Ghostlier Demarcations: Modern Poetry and the Material World* (Berkeley: University of California Press, 1997), 138–39.

15. Genevieve Taggard, *Long View* (New York: Harper Brothers, 1942), 110.

16. This is perhaps best exemplified by Virginia Jackson and Yopie Prins's thesis that what we call "lyric" is an abstraction produced by modern literary criticism. Virginia Jackson and Yopie Prins, "General Introduction," in *The Lyric Theory Reader: A Critical Anthology,* edited by Virginia Jackson and Yopie Prins, 108 (Baltimore: Johns Hopkins University Press, 2013), 1–8. See also, Virginia Jackson, *Dickinson's Misery: A Theory of Lyric Reading* (Princeton, NJ: Princeton University Press, 2005).

17. Christopher Nealon, *The Matter of Capital: Poetry and Crisis in the American Century* (Cambridge, MA: Harvard University Press, 2011), 140. For the relationship between lyric and forms of liberal-democratic subjectivity, see Margaret Ronda, "'Not Much Left': Wageless Life in Millennial Poetry," Post45, October 9, 2011, http://post45.research.yale.edu/2011/10/not-much-left-wageless-life-in-millenial-poetry/, and Jennifer Ashton, "Labor and the Lyric: The Politics of Self-Expression in Contemporary American Poetry," *American Literary History* 25, no. 1 (January 2013): 217–30.

18. See Michael Davidson, *On the Outskirts of Form: Practicing Cultural Poetics* (Middletown, CT: Wesleyan University Press, 2012); Oren Izenberg, *Being Numerous: Poetry and the Ground of Social Life* (Princeton, NJ: Princeton University Press, 2012); Joel Nickels, *Poetry of the Possible: Spontaneity, Modernism, and the Multitude* (Minneapolis: University of Minnesota Press, 2012); and Nealon, *The Matter of Capital.*

19. Nickels, *Poetry of the Possible,* 21.

20. Taggard, "Romanticism and Communism," 18.

21. Genevieve Taggard, *Calling Western Union* (New York: Harper Brothers, 1936), 47.

22. Taggard, "Romanticism and Communism," 19.

23. Taggard, *Calling Western Union,* 31.

24. Ibid., 34–36.

25. Malcolm Cowley, *Exile's Return: A Literary Odyssey of the 1920s* (New York: Penguin, 1994), 287–88.
26. Taggard, *Calling Western Union,* 31.
27. Ibid., 36.
28. Ibid., 37.
29. Ibid.
30. Ibid., 18–19.
31. Jackson, *Dickinson's Misery,* 129.
32. On the solitary nature of lyric publics, see Michael Warner, "Publics and Counterpublics," in *Publics and Counterpublics,* 65–124 (New York: Zone Books, 2002).
33. Jackson, *Dickinson's Misery,* 129.
34. Ibid., 128.
35. Genevieve Taggard, *Collected Poems, 1918–1938* (New York: Harper Brothers, 1938), n.p.
36. Wald, *Exiles from a Future Time,* 18.
37. Nelson, *Revolutionary Memory,* 197.
38. Taggard, *Calling Western Union,* 6. The transformations in Taggard's poetry from "lyric" to "song" mirror developments in leftist music and song culture, and her ideas about collective expression were influenced by her collaborations with left-leaning composers. For instance, her revolutionary poem "Lark" was set as a choral work by Aaron Copland. When Taggard's Sarah Lawrence colleague William Schuman began composing more accessible arrangements for "unskilled" singers, he ostensibly began with a draft of one of Taggard's poems. Such experiences prompted her to aver in *Long View* that "Song is collective. (Poetry should be)" (104). For Taggard's collaborations with Copland and Schuman, see Howard Pollack, *Aaron Copland: The Life and Work of an Uncommon Man* (Urbana: University of Illinois Press, 2000), 327–28, and Steve Swayne, *Orpheus in Manhattan: William Schuman and the Shaping of America's Musical Life* (New York: Oxford University Press, 2011), 123–32. For a history of leftist song culture, see Robbie Lieberman, *"My Song Is My Weapon": People's Songs, American Communism, and the Politics of Culture, 1930–50* (Urbana: University of Illinois, 1995).
39. Genevieve Taggard, Draft of "In the Plural," n.d., Genevieve Taggard Papers, Archives and Manuscripts Collection, New York Public Library.
40. Taggard, *Calling Western Union,* 56 (italics in original).
41. Alison Van Nyhuis, "Revolution and Modern American Poetry: Genevieve Taggard's *Calling Western Union,*" *Revista Canaria de Estudios Ingleses* 62 (2011): 32.
42. Taggard, *Calling Western Union,* 7.
43. Ibid., 7.
44. Quoted in Wald, *Exiles from a Future Time,* 233.
45. Ronda, "'Not Much Left.'"

[3]

The Darker Brother and the Cracker Boy: Langston Hughes, Don West, and Poetry as Social Conversation

Rachel Rubin

I am the darker brother.
They send me to eat in the kitchen
When company comes,
But I laugh,
And eat well,
And grow strong.
-Langston Hughes

"Rise up, you Cracker boy. Sing your ballads,
Dream your future."
-Don West

In 1947, Langston Hughes and Don West, a radical white poet and organizer from Devil's Hollow, Georgia, arranged to make guest appearances in each other's college writing classes at Atlanta University and Oglethorpe University, respectively. Hughes and West, who were born just four years apart and published their first books five years apart, had known each other for several years and were both huge-selling poets by this time, despite the way the publishing deck was stacked against them as an African American and a poor white Southerner and as political radicals: both achieved this status by operating largely outside of the mainstream publishing world. For instance, Hughes's book *A New Song* was published by the International Workers' Order (IWO); Louise Patterson, a leader in the IWO, used to read Hughes's poems at talks and hawk the books. West's books, similarly, were sold through union meetings and other gatherings of sharecroppers, miners, and farmers in what Jeff Biggers calls a "populist poetry crusade."[1]

The idea for the exchange of classroom visits by Hughes and West initiated from the mutual respect and interest the two felt for each other, sometimes manifested in the physical envelope of front and back matter: West thanks Hughes in the acknowledgments to his 1946 collection *Clods of Southern Earth* for "teaching me through the beauty of his own work," and Hughes in turn called West's work "the poems of our heartbeats" in 1951, a comment that was used on the back cover of West's 1973 collection *O Mountaineers!*[2] But Hughes's and West's presence in each other's writing classrooms was also a literalization of an important part of their relationship: in their fond if not close acquaintanceship, the two poets were able to school each other in particular and consequential ways. The structure of the twin classroom visits, then, raises and enacts a fascinating question: what did these two poets teach each other—particularly as they worked through a shared radical politics toward what we might then call a radical poetics? And how does treating poetics as a *conversation* challenge more static visions of poetry as words on the page emerging from singular vision? As in the epigraphs above, this essay will attempt both to move toward and signal a conversational analytical approach by presenting all quotations of Hughes's and West's poems side by side instead of in tandem (adapting a practice both familiar and generative in art history classrooms).

Linking Hughes and West in an analytical enterprise serves as a kind of scholarly twofer: Hughes's broad inclusion into the American canon is able to direct our attention back to West, whose work had been out of print for nearly twenty years until the 2004 publication of Biggers and Brosi's reader *No Lonesome Road* (with much of it remaining out of print today). But this dimension of Hughes's legacy also directs us back to the more radical and formally challenging aspects of Hughes's work that actually get less attention now than *before* his widespread anthologizing (and before his own self-sanitizing following his appearance before the House Un-American Activities Committee in 1953, reflected in what he chose to include in his *Selected Poetry* in 1967). Many of Hughes's most explicitly leftist poems, mostly from the 1930s, remained out of print or uncollected until after his death, with the 1973 appearance of *Good Morning, Revolution* (edited by Faith Berry) and the 1994 appearance of *Collected Poems.* In particular, the relationship between Hughes and West highlights the interracialism that was such an important part of their poetic projects, especially interracialism born of class solidarity. Further, while promotion of class solidarity characterized much literature of the American Left, the "conversation" between Hughes and West is instructive in the way that it reveals a process by which the two poets helped each other grapple with what that solidarity would mean in terms of both politics and poetics.

Although in the twenty-first century even most US high school students are familiar with Hughes—who after all received a literal stamp of approval from the US Postal Service in 2002—West, even with some sustained recent attention (from Jeff Biggers, Chris Green, and James Lorence), largely remains a victim of the historical amnesia regarding the Literary Left that still has not been fully addressed. West's fourth volume of poetry, *Clods of Southern Earth* (1946), sold over twelve thousand copies by subscription before even coming from the press, and it sold nearly one hundred thousand copies during its run. This was reported in the *Atlanta Constitution* as a record for a first book of poetry—which is remarkable even though *Clods* was not, in fact, West's first book of poetry—but West, succinctly tagged a "mountain socialist" by his colleague and Highlander School cofounder Myles Horton, remains mostly unknown.[3]

"Walt Whitman in Overalls"[4]

West was born into a Gilmer County, Georgia, farming family at a moment when, as James Lorence puts it, "Appalachia was already immersed in an irreversible transition that strained the bonds of family and community that had sustained mountain people for more than a century."[5] West's father, a subsistence farmer and father of eight, moved the family to Cobb County so he could take up cotton sharecropping while West was in his teens. By the age of fifteen, West had attended school for a total of five terms and had begun traveling seven miles by mule to Oakland Junior High School. Then an uncle got him a place at the Berry School, a school for children living in poverty in the Georgia mountains, where he worked his way through school until he left or was expelled in 1926 after clashes with school authorities over a variety of issues, including the administration's paternalism, an uncritical screening of *Birth of a Nation,* and the dismissal of a popular staff member.

After completing three years of high school in this way, West was accepted to Lincoln Memorial University in Harrogate, Tennessee. He supported himself and his sister through college by gathering laundry, sweeping floors, and washing dishes, still finding time to be a campus leader and to carry baskets of food to the poor (purportedly, however, he often had to borrow the money to buy it). From Lincoln Memorial he went to Vanderbilt University, where his classmates included prize-winning writer Jesse Stuart (who wrote the introduction to West's first book of poetry, *Crab-Grass*) and poet James Still, both of whom had also graduated from Lincoln Memorial. The three Appalachian writers, who were friends, came to be known as "the barefoot boys" at genteel Vanderbilt; although they followed quite different career paths, each found subject and inspiration in his rural background. In a 1978 interview, Still said that West was the "poet of the disinherited," while Stuart "wrote most of the books."[6] West completed a degree at Vanderbilt's School of Religion and began preaching in slums and in little mountain churches; according to Stuart, who refers to West in his autobiography as "Ron East," West was removed from several churches for his social justice vision:

> "What brought you here?"
> "I'm getting my D.D. this year, preaching and working in the slums."
> "Same old Ron East!"
> "In flesh and blood but not in spirit. I've been kicked out of three churches since I preached in the mountains. I've seen so much human suffering, Stuart, that I've grown bitter. I've been trying to save human beings on earth instead of preaching to them of a reward in heaven."[7]

This abrupt severing of relationships with churches would continue for decades, culminating in a dismissal for refusing to sign an anticommunist oath in 1956. By that time, West had been beaten unconscious, run out of town, and robbed of his home, library, and personal papers in a series of fires set by the Ku Klux Klan.[8]

In the mid-1930s, West began to publish poetry in several of the same Left-sponsored venues that Hughes did. Both poets published in the Communist *New Masses* and *Daily Worker* and in the *Harlem Liberator.* Both poets felt the need in later collections (such as Hughes's 1959 *Selected Poems* and West's 1951 *The Road Is Rocky*) to obscure or omit their poems' initial publishing venues. And both had work included in the important 1935 anthology *Proletarian Literature in the United States;* in addition to the thematic parallels established by the principles of the anthology, there are interesting structural parallels, with both Hughes's and West's contributions using rhythmic folk song as model—for Hughes's "Ballad for Lenin" and for West's "Southern Lullaby":

> I am Chico, the Negro,
> Cutting cane in the sun.
> I lived for you, Comrade Lenin.
> Now my work is done.[9]

> Eat, little baby, eat well,
> A Bolshevik you'll be,
> And hate this bosses' hell-
> Sucking it in from me . . .[10]

The anthology encouraged this use of folk ballad as poetic material, including a small gathering of "Folk Songs" slotted into the "Poetry" section with both credited and uncredited lyrics.[11]

West embarked on a lifetime of political activism and organizing, devoting himself to a range of issues in labor, civil rights, and education. He was involved in the 1929 Gastonia textile workers' strike, and he frequently organized among miners. As Hughes did, West played a leading role in the defense of Angelo Herndon when Herndon's case went to the Supreme Court in 1935 and 1937. A somewhat breathless summary, written in 1948 and supposedly drawn from the pages of the *Daily Worker*, is included in West's Federal Bureau of Investigation (FBI) file:

> [S]ubject wrote poem "Listen, I am a Communist" in 1934; fled Atlanta, Georgia in 1934 when sought on charges of inciting to insurrection; spoke at Boston, Mass. 1934 under auspices International Labor Defense demanding release of Ernst Thaelmann [*sic*]; jailed 1935 Pineville, Kentucky, for activities in connection with miner's strike; subject on national committee of C.P. in 1936 drive for election of BROWDER and FORD when subject was in Louisville, Kentucky; also listed as state organizer of Workers Alliance of Kentucky and member of National Unemployed Committee for Browder and Ford in 1936; subject was present at reception of MAUDE WHITE, only negro [*sic*] member Central Committee of C.P. At New York City 6-21-37; subject listed as Georgia born organizer of the C.P. of Kentucky at the time. Confidential informant advises subject became a Communist and was a member in 1945 and 1948. . . . Subject presently residing on farm, Route 4, Douglasville, Georgia.[12]

West was fired from Oglethorpe and several other positions under a cloud of relentless red-baiting, but until his death in 1992, he continued to write poetry, farm, and organize in Appalachia. He viewed these activities as necessarily intertwined, although he acknowledged that sometimes his other work took away from the time and energy he could spend writing poetry. By the time of West's death, the FBI had compiled twelve hundred pages of files on him for various organizing activities under a number of different aliases.

Dear Don

West first initiated direct contact with Hughes in 1943, writing him a letter from Lula, Georgia, in which he declared, "I admire you and your writing as much as I do anyone I know of."[13] The next day West wrote again to ask for permission to read one of Hughes's poems during one of his "regular broadcasts" on the radio station WGGA in Gainesville, Georgia.[14] By this time, West had long been studying Hughes's literary and nonliterary works and had dedicated a poem to him: "Brown Brother." In this poem, West refers to the other poet's accomplishment as his ability to "sing the songs your people think," invoking both his and Hughes's use of song in their contributions to *Proletarian Literature in the United States.*[15] As this direct contact between the two poets continued, West began to adopt certain poetic strategies and priorities that had characterized Hughes's own work.

One visible effect of Hughes on West is through what can be called the construction of a radical patriotism. Hughes had a career that straddled World War II (as did West), which for many African American writers and artists was extremely complicated in terms of their sense of Americanness. The segregated military worked to reinscribe the ideology of racism, even as serving in it called upon black men and women not only to be American heroes but also to allow themselves to be claimed as such. In fact, resisting the racism of the military required that African Americans had to insist upon their own patriotism and Americanism in the face of exclusion by the very institutions that bolstered and informed that patriotism. It is uniquely paradoxical—and as the war ended, of course, the paradox evolved into the now-familiar trope of the returning ethnic war hero who fought for American democratic ideals abroad and against Hitler's racial policies, then returned to second-class citizenship at home. (Examples of this trope can be found in the cartoons of African American Communist Ollie Harrington, for instance, or in Peter LaFarge's song "Ballad of Ira Hayes," along with Toni Morrison's novel *Sula* and Leslie Marmon Silko's novel *Ceremony.*)

In addition to the paradoxes of World War II consensus politics for the poet of color, Hughes's desire to structure a radical patriotism was also profoundly shaped by his closeness to the organized Left and the movement for international Communism. This closeness continued, with varying degrees of openness, well beyond the so-called Red decade and was manifested (though not pigeonholed) by the places where Hughes published, the content of his writings, the friendships he maintained with leftist literary figures, the talks he attended or gave, and so on. To make himself part of a communist Left within the framework of struggle against white supremacy in the United States, and within an artistic dedication to promoting black American forms as valid art, meant that Hughes had to answer head-on the question of who has the right to claim and use patriotic symbols and themes. Of course, this question became sinister for both Hughes and West, who were accused not only of being lovers of Stalin but—most important—of being un-American when called before the House Un-American Activities Committee. Invoking his days as a preacher, West would draw parallels between Catholic McCarthyites and Judas, calling them both "children of the devil."[16]

Taking up this challenge to claim and define Americanism was an important contribution of Hughes, despite his defanging that has followed both the McCarthyite attacks on him and his schoolroom appropriation. Some of his better-known poems work this ground, particularly "I, Too, Sing America," the poem from which I have taken half of the title for this essay, which invokes the Whitmanesque inclusiveness of America and envisions, confidently, a transformed system in the American future, and "Let America be America Again" (1938), which was first collected in *A New Song*, published by the International Workers Order. This artistic goal of Hughes' is also visible in his less-anthologized poems, including ones that Hughes (under the coercion of red-baiting) suppressed himself or even repudiated during the 1950s, such as "One more 'S' in the USA" and "Good Morning, Revolution," which opens with the speaker describing "Revolution" as his "pal" and goes on to insist that

> You know, the boss where I used to work,
> The guy that gimme the air to cut down expenses . . .
> Said you was a trouble maker, a alien-enemy . . .[17]

Clearly, one of the boss's silliest mistakes here is calling the revolution "alien" when it is plainly native—and friendly, depending upon one's economic class. The narrative voice of the poem, by contrast, comes across as so carefully "American," with its "say, listen," its "pal around," and its "gimme the air," that "American" is almost defamiliarized—which has the effect of opening up its definition. It is also worth noting that in this poem, the gender and even racial identity of the speaker are indeterminate—although the spelling and colloquial language, as well as the talk about "the boss," make it clear that the speaker is a worker.[18]

Hughes populates much of his poetry, and his prose as well, with characters who insist, through words, actions, voice, and carefully seeded identifying markers, upon their own exemplary Americanness. He then yokes this Americanness together with a class-conscious political vision that is inseparable from the idea of "the people's poet" that has come to be so tightly associated with him—for better or for worse, depending on who is doing the associating. An example is "Air Raid over Harlem." In this poem, the narrative voice is Harlem, personified. This consciousness-possessing "Harlem" imagines a movie that would send a "red" and endearingly American message to "Mr. Hearst": that message is "Jim Crow can kiss my ass," for "THE BLACK AND WHITE WORKERS ARE FREE."[19] The intent here is to wrest the idea of Americanism from a definition that promotes and maintains the status quo, both in society and in art—here represented by the movies.

While others adopted the politics and poetics of "radical patriotism"—one example is Kenneth Patchen—it formed a visible current between Hughes and West. West found this strategy particularly congenial to his own enterprise; he pursued a revisionist history of the United States across decades of his writing. West insistently traced the progressive values of working Americans, black and white, back to the first settlers of Georgia. Therein, according to West, lies the true history of the United States, a tale that has yet adequately to be told: "Someday I intend to do it, to tell about these people with rough hands, big feet, and hard bodies; about the real men and women of the South."[20] These "plain folk" represent real patriots, in West's mind, as opposed to those who lay claim to the name while propping up economies of hate and exploitation. Hughes singled out West's efforts to redefine "patriotism" by writing in 1951 that West's poems are "as American as Rte. 66."[21] Thus, both Hughes and West can be seen to overlay the notion of patriotism with class consciousness, making a working-class revolution a peculiarly American promise, even as each one, early in his career, acknowledged the Soviet example.

West also shared with Hughes a vision of the poet's role as one who directs this native American class consciousness, calls it to action as would a union organizer organizing a collective job action or a preacher calling for professions of faith through acts of charity (both jobs that West held at different times). By the 1930s, metaphors of awakening and arising on the part of the downtrodden were well established—from adoption of the opening line of "The Internationale" ("Arise, ye pris'ners of starvation") to Joe Hill's "Workers of the World, Awake" to Clifford Odets's *Awake and Sing!* Hughes too worked within this idiom but laid out a role for the poet as the "awakener," repeatedly injecting a call to "Listen!" into his poems: "Mr. Roosevelt, listen!"; "Listen, hungry ones!"; "Listen to yo' prophets, / Little Jesus!"; "Say, Listen, Revolution,"; "Listen, Christ,"; "Revolt! Arise!"; and so forth.[22] West's poems appear to answer, and join, this challenge of Hughes's:

Call to Creation

Listen!
All you beauty-makers
Give up beauty for a moment.
Look at harshness, look at pain,
Look at life again.[23]

Listen, I'm an Agitator

Listen . . . ! I'm an agitator—
    They call me "Red,"
The color of Blood,
    And—"Bolshevik!"[24]

West's poem appeared first in the *Daily Worker* in a more direct iteration that declared "I am a Communist / A Red / A Bolshevik!"[25]

As the one who speaks for "the black millions," or as "poet in overalls,"

Hughes and West both enacted the identity formation of the politicized poor through formal choices that consciously elevate nonliterary artists—quilt makers, balladeers, fiddle players, revival workers in West's case; blues singers, cabaret dancers, jazz musicians in Hughes's case; as their most important "literary" ancestors.[26] (In one or two of West's poems, he also invoked jazz musicians, clearly as a kind of tribute to Hughes, because these poems are so touchingly Hughesian.) Both Hughes and West populated many of their poems with nonliterary artists: Hughes's "sleek black boys in a cabaret," for instance, and West's "ballad singer."[27]

As James Smethurst points out, the slogan of the Communist-organized League of Struggle for Negro Rights, of which Hughes was the president, was "Promote Negro Culture in Its Original Form with Proletarian Content."[28] This notion of "infusing . . . old forms with new consciousness" provided a way for the poet to examine and acknowledge a particular subculture or folk form while remaining dedicated to the broader worker identity.[29]

For Hughes and West, in addition to gestures they made in their poetry toward "folk" forms, imbuing "old forms with new consciousness" meant the poeticizing of everyday life—and also the simultaneous, corresponding, politicizing of everyday life. A succinct example is the ending of Hughes's laconic "Elevator Boy" and the instructive (and efficient) double meaning of West's "Georgia Scene":

I been runnin' this
Elevator too long.
Guess I'll quit now.[30]

Cropper
    down the cotton row
Landlord
    in the saddle
Rowboat
    by the river bank
Paddle, boy, paddle![31]

Like Hughes, West seeks to give an ideologically suggestive picture of the familiar.

One way Hughes and West created the politicized ordinary is by staging multiple voices in their work so that the poetry itself is a kind of collective; as Edwin Rolfe wrote in *To My Contemporaries*, to achieve radical poetics "the mind must first renounce the fiction of the self."[32] In other words, this is poetry of alliance, as opposed to poetry of individualism or introspection. (Of course, both Hughes and West wrote that kind, too.) Hughes created a sense of class-based unity by voicing multiple members of the working class calling for it. He attempted to make his poetry plural. And this poetic plurality goes hand in hand with achievements that his characters might make in the world of politics—if they make their own efforts plural. For instance, Hughes's "Sister Johnson Marches" (1938) and West's "Last Wish" (1946) both begin in the singular but move, over three stanzas, from "I" to "we." Hughes's titular character declares "Here I am with my head held high!" while the narrative voice in West's poem relates that her lover was "kilt by factory wheels, / Workin' in Atco Mill."[33] By the end of the poem, though, Hughes gives us "people / Marching in a mass," and West's speaker describes wanting "to see my people jine / To tear thur misery down . . ."[34]

Hughes's influence on West is particularly strong here. West puts this elevation of plurality literally at the front of his *Clods of Southern Earth,* which he opens with a note titled "Appreciation": "Whether this book is good or bad, a lot of folks had a hand in it—a Georgia sharecropper, a Carolina mill hand, twenty-four dead coal miners in Kentucky, and a lot more. I don't know all their names, but they helped."[35] West's poetry likewise speaks in the voices of many different people—marked off, among other things, by the various vernacular Englishes they speak. Further, as "Sister Johnson Marches" and "Last Wish" demonstrate, Hughes and West are both examples of the rare male poet who writes sometimes in the voice of a woman speaker. Their dearest hope is that someday people will join their voices together for workers' rights as Hughes and West have joined them together in the chorus that is their poetry.

Dear Langston

As much as he admired Hughes—indeed, likely because of it—there were important lessons that West wanted to give back to Hughes, because it is on this question of class-based unity that West sought to move Hughes farther along. West admired and imitated Hughes's materialist and economic approach but saw Hughes circulating what West knew to be a deliberately created myth about American racism: that the real racists are the poor. Instead, the class position of African Americans and poor white Southerners should make them natural allies, if only poets could help undo the false teaching that the ruling class has used to obscure this fact. In an anxious fan's letter, West wrote to Hughes in 1943:

> I admire you and your writing as much as I do anyone I know of. But I think I shall always say that its [*sic*] wrong for any educated Negro to single out the "cracker," "poor white trash" and any other group of working white folks, as the chief enemy of the Negro people.[36]

West was reacting to Hughes's use of the word "cracker," citing one of his columns in the *Chicago Defender,* although Hughes also used the epithet in poems such as "Ballad of Sam Solomon" (published in the *Afro-American* in 1941). West's poem "Voice of the Cracker" is enriched when read as a response to Hughes, creating a poetic conversation to accompany their epistolary one:

Sam Solomon called on
Every colored man
To qualify and register
And take a stand.

The crackers said, Sam,
If you carry this through
Ain't no telling what
For the pattern was set
From the big houses
We'll do to you.[37]

And you've heard
That I'm the lyncher
Of Negroes,
The man with hood and night shirt!

But I tell you
You've heard falsely!
By those who now point
The unfriendly finger at me...[38]

West insisted that the same forces that benefit from racism against African Americans have encouraged a lasting myth—that poor white Southerners, or "crackers," are naturally racists—as a strategy to drive a wedge between groups of working people who should be allies. The word "redneck," for instance, almost a stand-in for racist, used to signify someone who worked under the hot sun and got burned. (And as far back as the early decades of the twentieth century, in the context of coal mining "redneck" signified "union man," whether white or black, in reference to the red bandana that constituted the strikers' "uniform.") West wanted Hughes to acknowledge that white supremacy and "redneck" bashing serve to bolster each other rather than standing in opposition—or even in reaction—to each other. In other words, the lesson that West hoped to impart had specificity beyond the optimistic elevation of class-based interracial unity put forth by a number of his contemporaries. He had a more particular—and less common—point to make: *don't fall for the notion that the real racists are working-class whites. That is a trick.* Instead, the real racists are the wealthy who have profited from racism, who have built empires from it, both during and after slavery. While acknowledging that racism has taken root in poor white Southerners, that they have "often been in mobs and such like," West insisted that this is because they "have had their minds filled with poison" by those who profit from mutual distrust or worse between black and white workers.[39] Indeed, there are ways in which West's body of work prefigures certain theoretical frameworks of *whiteness studies,* because his poetics depends on the ways in which labor and economics have created the two mutually defining categories of "white" and "black." West concluded his letter by saying,

> I still feel that it is the working white man and not the smooth, slick, boss who is the best potential ally of the Negro people in their struggle for equality in the South. And, to put it the other way around, I think also that the Negro people are the best ally of the white workers of the South in their struggle for better conditions, more democracy, etc.[40]

West pursued this notion in his poetry:

> Redneck, Cracker
> Goober picker
> Eat poke sallet
> Drink pot liquor.
>
> Wool hat, hooger,
> You're my brothers
> All of us had
> Poor white mothers.
>
> Linthead, white trash,
> Red dirt eaters
> Lonesome water
> Makes repeaters . . .
>
> We are the ones
> The rich folks claim
> That lynch the Blacks
> And bring us shame.[41]

Unfortunately, the trick is still quite functional; popular political rhetoric shows that ideologically based criticism of wealthy right-wing politicians is often accomplished by calling them poor—as in the way Sarah Palin's wealthy family was often called "rednecks" or "snowbillies" and the way *Rolling Stone* investigative journalist Matt Taibbi compared bailed-out bankers to "a family of hillbillies . . . sleeping nine to a bed."[42]

Historical evidence supports West's contention of the closeness between stereotyping of Appalachians and black Americans. James Klotter has shown, for instance, that the stereotypes used to disparage white Appalachians are frequently reapplied versions of the stereotypes used to disparage African Americans. He points out that accounts by the earliest literary writers, historians, folklorists, and sociologists found Appalachians to be wily, superstitious, and lazy, open to visitors but at the same time likely to engage in violence. "Instead of 'Sambo' and 'Nat' came 'Abner' and 'Joab,'" writes Klotter. (Klotter even quotes one writer's account of Kentucky mountaineers that dwelled upon how much the group loved to eat watermelons!)[43]

Reviews of West—even some of those in leftist media—condemned him on the very terms in which he sought to move Hughes along. Mainstream reviews bristled over West's instructive tone, in some cases coming across as angry over his "gettin' above his raising." A reviewer in the *New Masses,* meanwhile, strikingly proves West's point by citing his inability to get past his own "hillbilly" baggage—first objecting to West's use of nonstandard forms of English and then adding condescendingly that he supposes it's still nice to hear progressivism coming from an area where "we thought blood and rope to be eternal phenomena."[44]

Long after his correspondence with Hughes, West continued to underscore the financial benefit to the bosses of perpetuating this divide. In an introduction to a 1982 reader, *In a Land of Plenty,* he writes:

> That old Southern family stuff that you've heard so much about, always meaning the aristocratic, slave-owning tradition, is worn about as thin as the blood of those families today. Our people, the real Southern mass majority of whites, are the ones the Negroes were taught to call "pore white trash." And we, in turn, were taught the hateful word "N——." Nice little trick, isn't it? Hitler used it, too. And it is still being used today, by the whites from the big houses, who engineer lynchings and make it seem that the responsibility is the white workers.[45]

West was not unaware of what the cost of this had been in the South for black Americans. In another letter, he wrote to Hughes:

> God knows any Southern white man should apologize to any man of another color before questioning any statements he may make about the Southern whites, regardless of how bad.
>
> I know it, too.[46]

West makes the same admission in the poem he dedicated to Hughes, "Brown Brother," acknowledging the category "whiteness" in a way that denaturalizes it:

> We are proud and boast the whiteness
> In the pigment of our skin
> Never think to measure rightness
> By a soul that burns within.[47]

But West still insists. And he connects his insistence to the radical revision of American history that he—like Hughes—wants to perform. Focusing on the epithet Hughes has used, West writes:

> What I am trying to do is to make the word "cracker" mean what it originally meant in Georgia. For a long time Georgia prohibited slavery, you know. Because these early ex-jail bird settlers were set against any form of slavery

> and oppression. They were the original crackers. They had some damned good ideas and principles, too.[48]

West appeared to be optimistic about the everyday workability of black-white alliance in class struggle: he penned a poem titled "Unity Is an Ax," a title that, for those from the country, is at once declamatory and homey. In addition to this call to political unity, West seemed to believe that *poetic* unity is also an ax, as demonstrated concretely by his refusal in 1982, late in his career, to copyright a volume of his poetry, *In a Land of Plenty.* Instead, he added the instruction that anyone who needs it should use it:

> Purposely this book is not copyrighted. Poetry and other creative efforts should be levers, weapons to be used in the people's struggle for understanding, human rights, and decency. "Art for Art's sake" is a misnomer. The poet can never be neutral. In a hungry world the struggle between oppressor and oppressed is unending. There is the inevitable question, "Which side are you on?"
>
> To be content with things as they are . . . is to take sides with the oppressor who also wants to keep the status quo. To challenge the power of oppression is the poet's responsibility. . . .
>
> Thus no copyright, no effort to restrict use. Groups or individuals are welcome to reproduce or use any or all parts of this book.[49]

To concretize the idea of American left-wing poetry as an "intertextual social conversation," Cary Nelson created one long poem by patching together lines and stanzas from the actual poems of more than a dozen left-wing poets from the 1930s and 1940s.[50] Unfortunately, Nelson's ahistorical gimmick actually undercuts itself by leveling out the particularities of give and take, by more or less removing the context that Mikhail Bakhtin points out is continually shaping both art and history. And the gimmick misunderstands the nature of the dialogic by turning it monologic, taking out the challenges, the responses, the pushes—and the changes. The relationship of West and Hughes shows us two poets from rather different places and perspectives working out together and in their writing what it would mean to be a poet for radical social change. To be inclined to do this, to want to participate in this social conversation, neither man needed to receive orders from the Communist Party or its organs to create "positive heroes," romantic factory settings, or glowing portraits of Communists. And furthermore, as they carried out the conversation, they didn't feel the need to agree all the time—or to maintain the same level of commitment to particular organizations. In other words, when we look at the poetry of Langston Hughes and Don West as a collective endeavor, we are not talking about the artists' individualism or interiority being squashed by a centralized authority—another cherished American political myth. We are talking about a cooperative and adaptable effort to move toward a radical poetics for the poet-agitator.

Notes

1. Jeff Biggers, "The Fugitive of Southern Appalachian Literature: Reconsidering the Poetry of Don West," *Journal of Appalachian Studies* 5, no. 2 (Fall 1999): 160.
2. Don West, *Clods of Southern Earth* (New York: Boni and Gaer, 1946), n.p.; West to Langston Hughes, September 30, 1943, Langston Hughes Papers, Beineke Rare Book and Manuscript Library, Yale University, New Haven, Connecticut (hereafter Langston Hughes Papers). My attention to paratextual matter as meaningful "envelope" is inspired by the brilliant and portable framework of John Sekora's "Black Message/White Envelope: Genre, Authenticity, and Authority in the Antebellum Slave Narrative," *Callaloo* 10 (1987): 482–515.
3. Alex Hite, "Poetry Books Are Written by Georgians," *Atlanta Constitution*, August 4, 1946. West nonetheless retains hero status for some, as concretized in the Appalachian Studies Association's Heroes/Heroines of Appalachia commemorative T-shirt series, which featured West in 2001. A shirt in this series has a picture of West and one of his poems in its entirety:

   Up up mountain toilers
   And hear what I tell
   In a land of plenty
   There's hunger and hell.

   We dig and we shovel
   We weave and we sweat
   But when comes the harvest
   It's little we get . . .

   O this is the story
   Of you and the rest
   And if I am lying
   My name's not Don West.

4. Hite's review of *Clods of Southern Earth* in the *Atlanta Constitution* dubbed West thus.
5. James Lorence, *A Hard Journey: The Life of Don West* (Urbana and Chicago: University of Illinois Press, 2007), 2.
6. "James Still: Interviewed by J. W. Williamson," *Interviewing Appalachia: The* Appalachian Journal *Interviews, 1978–1992,* edited by J. W. Williamson and Edwin T. Arnold (Knoxville: University of Tennessee Press, 1994), 64.
7. Jesse Stuart, *To Teach, To Love* (New York: World Publishing, 1970), 161.
8. Alan Wald, *Exiles from a Future Time: The Forging of the Mid-Twentieth-Century Literary Left* (Chapel Hill: University of North Carolina Press, 2002); Don West, *No Lonesome Road: Selected Prose and Poems,* edited by Jeff Biggers and George Brosi (Urbana and Chicago: University of Illinois Press, 2004); Chris Green, *The*

Social Life of Poetry: Appalachia, Race, and Radical Modernism (New York: Palgrave Macmillan, 2007).

9. Langston Hughes, "Ballad for Lenin," in *Proletarian Literature of the United States,* edited by Granville Hicks et al. (New York: International Publishers, 1935), 167.
10. Don West, "Southern Lullaby," in *Proletarian Literature of the United States,* 199.
11. In his chapter on West in *The Social Life of Poetry,* Chris Green performs rhythmic analysis of several of West's poems to demonstrate concretely West's employment of the ballad form.
12. Paul Tierney, report on Donald Lee West, FBI Records Obtained through Freedom of Information Act: FBI File 100-559, October 27, 1948, http://documents.theblackvault.com/documents/fbifiles/West_Donald_L.-Pittsburgh-3_text.pdf.
13. West to Hughes, September 30, 1943, Langston Hughes Papers.
14. West to Hughes, October 1, 1943, Langston Hughes Papers.
15. Don West, "Brown Brother," in *No Lonesome Road: Selected Prose and Poems,* edited by Jeff Biggers and George Brosi (Chicago and Urbana: University of Illinois Press, 2004), 111.
16. Quoted in Douglas Flamming, *Creating the Modern South: Millhands & Managers in Dalton, Georgia, 1884–1984* (Chapel Hill: University of North Carolina Press, 1992), 194.
17. Langston Hughes, "Good Morning, Revolution," in *The Collected Poems of Langston Hughes,* edited by Arnold Rampersad (New York: Knopf, 1994), 162.
18. Ibid.
19. Hughes, "Air Raid over Harlem," in *Collected Poems,* 185–88.
20. Don West, "Foreword," in *O Mountaineers!* (Huntington, WV: Appalachian Press, 1974), 19.
21. Hughes to West, June 24, 1951, Langston Hughes Papers.
22. Hughes, *Collected Poems,* 242, 208, 94, 224, 228, 146.
23. Hughes, "Call to Creation," in *Collected Poems,* 203.
24. West, "Listen, I'm an Agitator," in *Clods,* 24.
25. West, "I Am a Communist," *Daily Worker,* March 13, 1934, 5.
26. Hughes, "A New Song," in *Collected Poems,* 144; West, "Listen, I Am an Agitator," 24.
27. Hughes, "Harlem Night Club," in *Collected Poems,* 90; West, "Ballad Singer," in *Clods,* 133.
28. James Smethurst, *The New Red Negro: The Literary Left and African-American Poetry, 1930–1946* (New York: Oxford University Press, 1999), 79.
29. Ibid.
30. Hughes, "Elevator Boy," in *Collected Poems,* 85.
31. West, "Georgia Scene," in *O Mountaineers,* 91.
32. Edwin Rolfe, *To My Contemporaries* (New York: Dynamo, 1936), 59.
33. Hughes, "Sister Johnson Marches," in *Collected Poems,* 146; West, "Last Wish," in *Clods,* 53.
34. Ibid.

35. West, *Clods,* n.p.

36. West to Hughes, September 30, 1943, Langston Hughes Papers.

37. Hughes, "Ballad of Sam Solomon," *Afro-American,* July 5, 1941.

38. West, "Voice of the Cracker," in *Clods,* 141.

39. West to Hughes, September 30, 1943, Langston Hughes Papers.

40. Ibid.

41. West, *No Lonesome Road,* 160.

42. Matt Taibbi, "Secrets and Lies of the Bailout," *Rolling Stone,* January 4, 2013, http://www.rollingstone.com/politics/news/secret-and-lies-of-the-bailout-20130104.

43. James C. Klotter, "The Black South and White Appalachia," in *Blacks in Appalachia,* edited by William Turner, Edward J. Babbell, and Nell Irwin Painter (Lexington: University Press of Kentucky, 1985), 52.

44. Lorence, *A Hard Journey,* 25.

45. Don West, *In a Land of Plenty: A Don West Reader* (Minneapolis: West End Press, 1982), 17.

46. West to Hughes, October 10, 1943, Langston Hughes Papers.

47. West, "Brown Brother," 111.

48. West to Hughes, October 10, 1943, Langston Hughes Papers.

49. West, *In a Land of Plenty,* n.p.

50. Cary Nelson, *Revolutionary Memory: Recovering the Poetry of the American Left* (New York: Routledge, 2001), 158.

[4]

Somebody Loves Us All

Harvey Teres

Part 1.

Once upon a time the struggles of working people were a subject of real interest in the United States. During the 1930s, the decade of the Great Depression and growing interest in radical politics, a significant number of writers, critics, and intellectuals turned their attention to the politics and experiences of the working class, often but not always impelled by their interest in Marxism and sometimes through their relationship with the Communist Party, its front organizations, or in fewer cases the Trotskyist movement. This led to an unprecedented range of literary efforts to inject fresh depictions of working-class life into American literature—sometimes of heroic, victorious characters and struggles, sometimes of weakened characters and hard defeats.

At times, critics prevailed upon writers to portray at least glimmers of the socialist future to come, and sometimes they would encourage writers to dramatize principles of Marxism so that abstract philosophy might become living reality. For some of the more thoughtful critics and writers of that tumultuous decade, it was, surprisingly, the literary criticism of the archconservative T. S. Eliot that offered a way to think about how writers might successfully integrate a belief system like Marxism into their writing. Eliot's essay "Dante," for instance, published in 1920 as one of thirteen highly influential essays in *The Sacred Wood,* ranked Dante among the world's greatest writers because of his extraordinary ability to "deal with his [Christian] philosophy, not as a theory . . . or as his own comment or reflection, but in terms of something perceived."[1] Few writers, of course, achieved what Eliot was praising—the integration of beliefs with life vividly lived through the senses and correlative thoughts. For this reason above all others, little literature produced within the orbit of political parties and agendas both then and now has become a permanent part of our culture.

Writers' interest in working-class experience during the 1930s did not often dwell on the working class's aesthetic experience; in fact, the interest often led to a suspicion of the category of aesthetics altogether, to an antiaesthetic (if by "aesthetic" we mean cognitive and affective responsiveness to the artful manipulation of form and technique or to nature). Working-class or proletarian literature of the day was often premised on the notion that subtle and sophisticated literary elements reflected the tastes of privileged elites and therefore needed to be stripped away, leaving in their place a less refined but more direct, engaged, and authentic representation of reality. Such literature was meant to conform to a working-class outlook alleged to be shaped by hardship and struggle that left little appetite for artistic subtleties. Writers and critics tried to resolve the remaining aesthetic issues by linking Marxism and political and social exigencies to resistant forms and genres. Although some of these literary figures—such as Jack Conroy and Richard Wright—rose out of poverty, most were of the middle class, as were, significantly, most of their readers. In this regard, the decade was not unlike others insofar as its writers and artists more or less remained a separate stratum despite admirable efforts to engage with working people. In the end, they tended to conflate writing about the working class with knowing the working class.

The 1930s produced literature that typically portrayed working people on the job, on strike, at meetings, debating tactics, suffering injuries or illness, expressing their dissatisfaction, or dreaming of a different life or brighter future. Women writers added new emphases on sexual and marital relations, childbirth and child care, all types of domestic labor, and resisting patriarchal values inside and outside the home (which sometimes included workplace discrimination and harassment), while African American writers emphasized the crucial matter of race relations and added elements from the rich tradition of black culture. Granted, this signaled an unprecedented commitment to aspects of working-class life that hadn't before been such a strong draw for American writers, but as Alan Wald has amply pointed out in his many illuminating studies of the literature of the American Left, much was left out. A rarity in the literature of the times was an interest in working people as aesthetic beings—as individuals, for instance, with a profound need for the production and enjoyment of craft both on the job and off. Whatever compensatory pleasures they were able to enjoy—either self-generated or experienced as consumers of the movies and its attendant celebrity culture, music, sports, fashion, the comics, or other forms of popular culture—these did not figure strongly in the literature devoted to the experiences of working people. The reason is not hard to see: writers and critics intent on exposing the depredations of capitalism in crisis and its oppression of the masses were not disposed to dwell upon the minor notes of pleasure that ordinary people managed to enjoy in order to enhance the quality of their lives. When Zora Neale Hurston chose to dwell on such compensatory pleasures, she was excoriated by more orthodox critics (famously by Richard Wright) for her lack of seriousness and evasion of political realities.

Alan Wald and others have labored mightily to remedy our amnesia toward whatever attributes proletarian literature possessed, but they also acknowledge the limitations of the proletarian literary movement; more important, by focusing less on ideology and more on what Raymond Williams called "structures of feeling," these literary historians have uncovered a considerably more diverse literature and culture generated by progressive and often Popular Front politics from the 1930s into the McCarthy period. In terms of formal experimentation and subtlety, psychological rigor, and thematic range, this body of work surpassed the literature of the proletarian literary movement, and it has been exceedingly well served by Wald and other committed and enthusiastic literary historians.[2]

One of the few figures who saw that writers and critics, even those committed to working-class politics, were not looking closely enough at the aesthetic experiences of ordinary people was the radical democrat John Dewey. His 1934 classic *Art as Experience* is testimony to this fact. As Robert Westbrook pointed out in his admirable *John Dewey and American Democracy* (1991), Dewey had not written much about art in any of his previous works, but the exigencies of his own thinking, the socioeconomic crises of the times, and the close relationship he had developed with the maverick art collector Albert Barnes all caused him to place art and aesthetics at the center of his thinking.[3] *Art as Experience* was and remains one of the most compelling arguments ever made on behalf of transgressing the boundaries between art and everyday experience through underscoring their continuities. For Dewey, the philosophical and critical gaze, long directed at the art object itself, needed to refocus on aesthetics as it informs a wide spectrum of human experience. Indeed, Dewey defined "the work of art" not as the art object but rather as "what the product does with and in experience."[4] Typically, "art is remitted to a separate realm, where it is cut off from that association with the materials and aims of every other form of human effort, undergoing, and achievement."[5] To restore the importance and direct relevance of art, theory had to "restore continuity between the refined and intensified forms of experience that are works of art and the everyday events, doings, and sufferings that are universally recognized to constitute experience."[6] Dewey argued that if this perspective were correctly pursued, a "detour" would be necessary from the idealization of the art object seen as a discrete entity apart from its continuity with the rest of life and the qualities it shares with common experience. He described the preferred path as follows:

> In order to *understand* the esthetic in its ultimate and approved forms one must begin with it in the raw; in the events and scenes that hold the attentive eye and ear of man, arousing his interest and affording him enjoyment as he looks and listens: the sights that hold the crowd—the fire-engine rushing by; the machines excavating enormous holes in the earth; the human fly climbing the steeple-side; the men perched high in air on girders, throwing and catching red-hot bolts. The sources of art in human experience will be learned by him who sees how the tense grace of the ball-player infects the onlooking crowd; who notes the delight of the housewife in tending her plants, and the intent interest of her goodman in tending the patch of green in front of the house; the zest of the spectator in poking the wood burning on the hearth and in watching the darting flames and crumbling coals. These people, if questioned as to the reason for their actions, would doubtless return reasonable answers. The man who poked the sticks of burning wood would say he did it to make the fire burn better; but he is none the less fascinated by the colorful drama of change enacted before his eyes and imaginatively partakes in it. He does not remain a cold spectator.[7]

Like many other radicals of the time, Dewey was convinced that the richest aesthetic experiences of ordinary Americans were thwarted by what he termed "oligarchical control from the outside of the processes and products of work."[8] This, rather than machines themselves or industrialization per se, was "the chief force in preventing the worker from having that intimate interest in what he does and makes that is the essential prerequisite of esthetic satisfaction. . . . As long as art is the beauty parlor of civilization, neither art nor civilization is secure."[9] Though Dewey's language was more guarded than that of many of his fellow radicals during the 1930s, his recommended socialistic solution was unmistakable: "No permanent solution is possible save in a radical social alteration, which effects [*sic*] the degree and kind of participation the worker has in the production and social disposition of the wares he produces."[10]

Yet Dewey was not an advocate of proletarian literature. Although he appreciated this literature's attention to new experiences and materials, which he acknowledged could have the effect of encouraging previously marginalized people to express themselves because of barriers broken, the restriction of literature to the themes of the factory worker or the agendas of political movements "does not give fair play and outlet to [the artist's] vital interest. It forces his perceptions into channels previously worn into ruts and clips the wings of his imagination."[11] Implicitly for Dewey, any political movement worth its salt or any serious critical inquiry made by experts must begin by acknowledging the centrality of aesthetic experience that is as daily as dinner and detached from direct political awareness or engagement.

Suppose we were to take Dewey's recommendation to begin with aesthetics "in the raw"—that is, in the intensified moments of interest and pleasure experienced by ordinary people in their workaday worlds. What sort of literary or critical endeavors might provide the kind of insight and imagination that Dewey had in mind? I suggest we might begin by directing more of our attention to the "work" of art—that is, to how individual texts do things "with and in" the experiences of the reader and readers in the aggregate. We might also spend more time evaluating literature that depicts the manifold experiences of ordinary people, whether or not these texts conform to preferred political movements or goals. Finally, as a way of updating our interest in working-class experience and addressing the challenges of the early twenty-first century, we might develop public humanities research projects that take us off campus and into surrounding communities in order to learn more about the aesthetic experiences of our fellow citizens.

Part 2.

A well-heeled woman stops at a gas station and is taken aback by the ghastly grease and oil that seem to be everywhere. But soon she notices that it is family-operated and that despite the grime, someone has actually tried to beautify the place. She becomes curious and takes increasingly careful note of a few decorative objects that offer the family a respite from the grim ugliness—a small table, a doily, a houseplant. A bit wryly, but not without appreciation and even a tincture of awe, she exclaims, "Somebody loves us all."

Elizabeth Bishop's 1955 poem "Filling Station" provides a rare glimpse into an important part of our world that nonetheless remains largely invisible: the aesthetic experiences within the everyday lives of working people. As we'll see, it's a quirky poem whose privileged speaker's tone is often elusive, but it's also a poem that illustrates the ways in which class and gender shape attitudes toward working people, including the importance of beauty in their lives. As such, I regard it as a touchstone for vital experiences we rarely discuss and little understand. Who, after all, is interested in the aesthetic experiences of working people besides working people themselves? Certainly cosmetic and fashion companies and advertisers for beer and cars are. The corporate world, with its army of employees whose task it is to cash in on the latest styles that they themselves strive to shape or predict, is heavily invested in pleasing the senses of ordinary people and thereby influencing consumption-driven taste. The entertainment industry too—Hollywood movies, pop and country music, television—makes serious efforts to appeal aesthetically to the masses, again where consumer choices are at stake.

Can we add academics to the list of those concerned with the aesthetic experiences of working people? Perhaps, but truth be told, few have shown much interest. A scholar such as Alan Wald, who has devoted a career to understanding the culture and literature produced by Marxism in the United States, has had much to say about writers and literature devoted to representing the interests and experiences of working-class Americans. Indeed, when in the preface to Wald's most aesthetically responsive book, *The Revolutionary Imagination: The Poetry and Politics of John Wheelwright and Sherry Mangan,* he commits himself to exploring "the implications of [the anti-Stalinist Left's] political tradition for literary creation itself," he means to direct his attention to elements of literary form and technique that make for literature's special effects upon readers.[12] When he combines alertness to these matters with his exploration of the radical politics and movements that influenced these poets and their readers, he offers us a vantage point from which we can observe the relationship between art and the people. This is a valuable step toward engagement with the actual experiences of the very subjects whose political fate concerns us. It's a step that places us as middle-class academics on the edge of a vast, largely unfamiliar terrain whose inhabitants many of us rarely listen to and barely know.

More effectively than nearly any poem I know, Bishop's "Filling Station" dramatizes a chasm of this kind. Here is the poem in full:

Oh, but it is dirty!
—this little filling station,
Oil-soaked, oil permeated
To a disturbing, over-all

Black translucency.
Be careful with that match!

Father wears a dirty,
Oil-soaked monkey suit
That cuts him under the arms,
And several quick and saucy
And greasy sons assist him
(it's a family filling station),
All quite thoroughly dirty.

Do they live in the station?
It has a cement porch
Behind the pumps, and on it
A set of crushed and grease-
Impregnated wickerwork;
On the wicker sofa
A dirty dog, quite comfy.

Some comic books provide
The only note of color—
Of certain color. They lie
Upon a big dim doily
Draping a taboret
(part of the set), beside
A big hirsute begonia.

Why the extraneous plant?
Why the taboret?
Why, oh why, the doily?
(Embroidered in daisy stitch
With marguerites, I think,
And heavy with gray crochet.)

Somebody embroidered the doily,
Somebody waters the plant,
Or oils it, maybe. Somebody
Arranges the rows of cans
So that they softly say:
ESSO—so—so—so
To high-strung automobiles.
Somebody loves us all.[13]

The poem begins with an exclamation—"Oh, but it is dirty!"—that implies a good deal about the speaker. The five words at first suggest a forceful, opinionated, and finicky speaker who reacts in horror to the slovenly state of the filling station. She is imperious—a snob, an elitist—but to what extent? Is this horror or mock horror? The exclamation point suggests that she is genuinely appalled, but is there not also a bit of self-deprecatory irony in her exclamation, as though she comes to her judgment reluctantly, knowing that it might be construed as arrogant (thus the "but" in "but it is dirty," as if she is arguing with herself)? The filling station is part of a world she likely encounters infrequently and is unfamiliar with. Is she fully confident in her own superiority as she mocks the filling station and the family within, or might she be aware that she is a bit squeamish? The lines that immediately follow suggest the former, though her perspective later changes. Returning to the first line, we discover that it stands alone visually but not grammatically because the subject of the sentence, the filling station, emerges only in the second line, where its presence is doubly diminished by its being named with a diminutive: it's a "*little* filling station" (my emphasis). The speaker then describes the station using a bit of playful hyperbole, calling it "oil soaked, oil permeated / to a disturbing, over-all / black translucency." Once again the speaker's fastidiousness is apparent, but by claiming to be disturbed and not just disgusted, she lightly suggests that more is at stake than simply being repelled by the scene. Her further claim that the entire station appears to be covered with oil—to the point that it has congealed over time to a shine—must be an exaggeration, as is the snarky warning of the following line, "Be careful with that match!"

The joke reminds me of the joke made by Jody Starks at Janie's expense during their public argument—one of several climactic scenes in Zora Neale Hurston's *Their Eyes Were Watching God.* Jodie rebukes Janie for the poor job she has done cutting a plug of tobacco for a customer and yells, "Don't stand dere rollin' yo' pop eyes at me wid yo' rump hangin' nearly to yo' knees." The narrator steps in and informs us that "[a] big laugh started off in the store but people got to thinking and stopped. It was funny if you looked at it right quick, but it got pitiful if you thought about it for awhile. It was like somebody snatched off part of a woman's clothes while she wasn't looking and the streets were crowded."[14] My guess is that many readers respond in like manner to the speaker's joke in "Filling Station." Though I don't believe, as one critic has maintained, that the poem as a whole dwindles as one sees it more clearly, certainly the joke does.[15]

The condescension continues in the second stanza: "Father wears a dirty, / oil-soaked monkey suit / that cuts him under the arms." The speaker rejects the expected "The father," favoring the feigned intimacy of "Father" in an effort to ventriloquize the more homely appellation she imagines the family uses; thus, she mildly mocks the locution. "Monkey suit," with its uncomplimentary analogy, refers to the father's overalls, which are apparently a size too small, suggesting a shortage of funds to purchase a pair that fits. That "monkey suit" is also a term for a tuxedo intensifies the irony. He is accompanied by "several quick and saucy

/ and greasy sons." Here "several" substitutes for the precise count we might expect from someone more interested in the family than is the speaker, who has apparently overheard some off-color and off-putting interactions between the father and his sons. The speaker closes the stanza with yet another reminder of just how dirty the filling station is, as if this is necessary given that no fewer than eight of the previous twelve lines describe the ubiquitous filth.

The third stanza begins with the appalled, rather amazed speaker asking, "Do they live in the station?" In an effort to answer her own question, she observes that "behind the pumps" is a "cement porch" and on it a sofa upon which lies "a dirty dog, quite comfy." The sofa is part of a set of wickerwork that is "crushed and grease- / impregnated"—unsightly to her but sufficient at least to satisfy the dog. Though the speaker remains fixated on the shabbiness of the place, she has discovered that this is someone's home and that the family's pet seems content. Perhaps more important, though, is that her gaze steadily penetrates toward the interior of the station. This concentration—from the pumps to the porch to the wicker sofa to the dog—seems to work against the speaker's blithe dismissal of the place in her earlier joke about the match. Despite her many reservations, she is being drawn in.

This concentration deepens in the next stanza as the speaker's gaze lingers over additional objects on the porch. She notices comic books that at first she claims supplies some color to the place and then quickly corrects herself by the partial retraction of "certain color." Apparently the comics are smudged with grease and oil like everything else. She then bores in on several other objects. The comic books "lie / upon a big dim doily / draping a taboret / (part of the set) beside / a big hirsute begonia." A taboret is a low stool or stand. It is a word that many readers will not know. "Doily," which is especially apposite because it allows Bishop to place a "D" in front of the word "oily," will be familiar to more readers but also to more women than men. The same for "begonia." It is beginning to dawn on the speaker that she is describing feminized objects inside the larger masculine space of the filling station. (At this point the earlier phrase, "grease- / *impregnated* wickerwork" [my emphasis], begins to take on greater significance.) Yet the emphatic alliteration of these lines with their obtrusive, reverberating "d" and "b" sounds ("a big *d*im *d*oily / *d*raping"; "*b*eside / a *b*ig hirsute *b*egonia") continues the speaker's derision as she burlesques the props on the porch.

But that derision diminishes in the next stanza when the speaker's curiosity takes over, and she pauses to ask a series of blunt, dramatic questions with their pounding dactyls and trochees: "Why the extraneous plant? / Why the taboret? / Why, oh why, the doily?" Though irony persists in that last line, her inquiry has acquired an urgency and even a level of sincerity that represents a new note. Her genuine interest is underscored by the important parenthetical that immediately follows, a key afterthought in which she makes a determined effort to discern the precise stitches used in the doily: "(Embroidered in daisy stitch / with marguerites, I think, / and heavy with gray crochet.)" The heretofore detached and superior speaker is now consumed by details that only fellow practitioners or admirers of the crafts of embroidery and crocheting will notice and appreciate. (The change in tone is evident in the settled sound of the rhymed "gray crochet.") This group includes the speaker and, as the speaker is in the process of discovering, the invisible woman in the station. The two of them comprise a kind of female confederacy that transcends class difference, for not many men will ever notice a doily, not to mention daisy stitches or marguerites. Even fewer will know that a daisy stitch resembles the petals of a flower or that a marguerite is a spiked cluster that resembles a star. The engaged speaker has at least momentarily passed through a stubborn social barrier. She is focused enough now on the porch to observe small details, and what had been merely looking turns into seeing for the first time—seeing the craftsmanship of a poor woman intent on beautifying a bleak workplace that is also her home. The speaker is becoming more aware of the entire family's conditions of existence, which are revealed to be more than grease and oil.

In the final stanza the speaker turns her thoughts to the invisible caretaker: "Somebody embroidered the doily. / Somebody waters the plant, / or oils it maybe." Here, finally, is momentary recognition, if not exactly respect—but lest the speaker succumb to sentimentality, she follows this recognition with another condescending joke. Yet the joke in turn is quickly supplanted by the speaker's description of another of the invisible woman's efforts: "Somebody / arranges the rows of cans / so that they softly say: / ESSO—so—so—so / to high-strung automobiles." As Bishop herself pointed out in the very last letter she wrote before her death, "so, so, so" is an utterance used to soothe "high-strung" horses, so here we see the handiwork of a woman creatively transposing a locution from a preindustrial or premechanical context to a modern one, in effect trying to soothe or tame the careening cars that pass her by.[16] (In fact, in contrast to the harsher sounds of previous stanzas, the entire final stanza is saturated in soothing "s" sounds.) The woman's gesture has intriguing implications for a world changing from a quieter, more agrarian way of life to a more kinetic, industrialized one.

That this filling station is located in Brazil matters (Bishop at first proposed titling the poem "Station #2, Rio to Bahia"), despite Bishop's own view that she hadn't thought of the poem "as being an especially Brazilian poem."[17] It turns out that this mid-twentieth-century ESSO station is an example of the American corporate presence in Brazil, ESSO having been the international trade name for John D. Rockefeller's Standard Oil Corporation as a phonetic version of the company's initials. (ExxonMobil, currently the world's largest publicly traded international oil and gas company, is the descendant of it.) The station is also an early example of a shift of global capitalism toward developing the service and consumer industries. Given this context, we recall that the speaker of this poem is in fact a consumer, and the family is her service provider. It is an economic interaction between two classes of people (and perhaps across racial lines, although race does not overtly figure in the poem) that differs from interactions contingent upon developments at the point of production in the typical representations of class difference or class conflict in the decades before Bishop's poem. In this, it resembles Wilson's gas station in the valley of ashes in F. Scott Fitzgerald's *The Great Gatsby* or the roadside dramas of the Joad family in John Steinbeck's *The Grapes of Wrath* more than it does the factory epics of the proletarian literary movement. As we shall see, Bishop's treatment of class difference differs markedly from the apocalyptic, often Manichaean representations of class conflict that have not typically been found in literature since the 1930s. But that does not make her poem any less illuminating when it comes to the dynamics of class interaction.

The final line of the poem is the wonderfully evocative but ultimately ambiguous "Somebody loves us all." Most readers probably assume that the speaker is referring to the woman, a kind of angel of the house. Other readers will interpret the last line as a nod to the heavens. There is also disagreement about the tone of this final line. Is it heartfelt, or does it express incredulity? Does it represent a revelation, or is it merely a bemused acknowledgment, perhaps with a shrug of the shoulders, of something the speaker considers inexplicably bizarre? Put another way, is the speaker's response more like Rainer Maria Rilke's before the sublime Torso of Apollo, resolving to change his life, or is it more like Samuel Johnson's reaction, as told by James Boswell, upon hearing a Quaker woman preach: "Sir, a woman's preaching is like a dog's walking on his hind legs. It is not done well; but you are surprised to find it done at all"?

I would like to think, as I imagine many readers would, that the speaker undergoes something of an epiphany at the end of the poem as she discovers that she shares a certain kinship with the woman of the house—"Somebody loves *us* all" (my emphasis)—thereby transcending ideologies of class premised on her social and aesthetic superiority over the woman. Such an interpretation would not necessarily rule out a religious perspective, in which the speaker experiences wonder as she realizes that "somebody" is actually a benevolent God who has miraculously placed within the woman and within "us all" an aesthetic instinct—a capacity to create beauty and to be uplifted by it. Whether we view "somebody" as the woman or as God, the common thread here is that at the end of the poem the speaker declares a degree of empathy and even solidarity with the woman and her family in spite of the social barriers that had previously kept them apart.

That said, it is not unreasonable to view the end of the poem quite differently. This is a speaker, after all, who at several points has partially nullified her curiosity with condescending jokes. Although the arc of the poem suggests that she is slowly being drawn into the family's world, she seems compelled to stop or even reverse her progress through her priggish humor. It is therefore possible to regard her final assertion that "Somebody loves us all" as a kind of retreat from the effort to understand what she has observed rather than an empathetic response. It is not hard to imagine that upon uttering this glib rationalization, she promptly gets in her car and drives off.

But if we to turn from the speaker's experience to our own as readers, we see that fixing upon one interpretation or the other is not of paramount importance. Regardless of what our final assessment of the speaker is, her creation by Bishop has the effect of generating the reader's empathy for the family. We may admire the speaker because she is revealed as someone who has shown solicitude toward the mother and thus the family, or we may disapprove of her snootiness. (I am discounting a response in which we revel in the speaker's arrogance, because I do not think it would be consistent with what we know about Bishop's life and her other poems, which, like "A Miracle for Breakfast," "Jerónimo's House" and other "house" poems, avoid condescension.) The important thing is that in both cases Bishop has enjoined us to watch the speaker watching the family; in watching, our perspective is at least as deep as the speaker's insofar as we also peer into rarely observed lives and see an effort to insert beauty into their hardscrabble world, but it is in fact wider because the speaker is also within our purview—Bishop provides us a means, if we choose, to understand her words within a larger ensemble of social relations. Although Elizabeth Bishop is no longer an unfairly neglected writer—on the contrary, she is now firmly ensconced as a major canonical poet of the twentieth century—and although she has never been a poet known for her political commitments, it might behoove progressive academics to value her and poets like her more highly, not least for the emphasis they place on direct observation and alert attention to aspects of everyday life that are often considered trivial or apolitical. In fact, these trivialities are the stuff of meaning and the source of deep commonality that could provide a basis for new approaches to solidarity.

Bishop attempts to see the invisible poor around her and invites her readers to see as well, and she reminds us of the humanizing need for beauty that is found everywhere. Poems such as "Filling Station" are especially pertinent today when awareness of the quality of life of the working poor is pitifully inadequate, especially given the many dire social problems that threaten our nation and remain unaddressed: the shrinking real income of most Americans, the growing inequality between rich and poor, the decline in social mobility because of diminished opportunity, the continuing high unemployment rate, and the absence of any national strategy for solving these problems. Under these circumstances, efforts to interact with marginalized constituencies in sustained and reciprocal relations through publicly engaged scholarship—to see and hear and understand our fellow citizens—are crucial to the progressive impulses within literary studies and are vital to the public at large. Let us do as Dewey suggested and Bishop did in "Filling Station": seek out aesthetic experience "in the raw." Let us redraw the boundaries of our profession in order to seek out our working-class fellow citizens and build dialogue and relationships around neglected matters of vital importance: whether and where they encounter beauty and what that encounter feels like, the function these encounters play in their lives, the influence of arts education, the role of artistic skill and evaluation of quality, the relation between aesthetic and spiritual or religious experience, and the moral and political effects of their encounters. These have been perennial concerns of aestheticians and critics alike, and there is reason to believe that there are insights to be gained by raising these issues directly with working people. I would also hazard that along with academics, activists and organizers would benefit by an approach to political engagement that gives aesthetics the attention it deserves.

As literary scholars and citizens, our commitments to aesthetic experience, literary and artistic excellence, and social and economic justice are not mutually exclusive; they are deeply intertwined. We can supplement the kind of archival, revisionist scholarship that arises out of an abiding commitment to working people and movements for social change—exemplified by the outstanding contributions of scholars such as Alan Wald and his many students—and take the bold step of reaching out to the working people who surround us, listening to them and learning from them, and using the results of these interactions to build a more robust profession and a more vital democracy.

Acknowledgements

I would like to express my gratitude to friends and colleagues who read or heard a draft of this essay and offered many valuable suggestions: Paul Elitzik, Ken Frieden, Roger Hallas, Brooks Haxton, Sanford Sternlicht, and David Yaffe.

Notes

1. T. S. Eliot, "Dante," in *The Sacred Wood* (1920; reprint, London: Methuen, 1980), 170–71.
2. See, for example, Michael Denning, *The Cultural Front: The Laboring of American Culture in the Twentieth Century* (London: Verso, 1996); Barbara Foley, *Radical Representation: Politics and Form in U.S. Proletarian Fiction, 1929–1941* (Durham, NC: Duke University Press, 1993); Cary Nelson, *Repression and Recovery: Modern American Poetry and the Politics of Cultural Memory, 1910–1945* (Madison: University of Wisconsin Press, 1989); Robert Shulman, *The Power of Political Art: The 1930s Literary Left Reconsidered* (Chapel Hill: University of North Carolina Press, 2000); Alan Wald, *Exiles from a Future Time: The Forging of the Mid-Twentieth-Century Literary Left* (Chapel Hill: University of North Carolina Press, 2002); Alan Wald, *Trinity of Passion: The Literary Left and the Antifascist Crusade* (Chapel Hill: University of North Carolina Press, 2007); Alan Wald, *American Night: The Literary Left in the Era of the Cold War* (Chapel Hill: University of North Carolina Press, 2012). For an alternative perspective that takes in the full range of literary and cultural achievement of the 1930s, see Morris Dickstein, *Dancing in the Dark: A Cultural History of the Great Depression* (New York: Norton, 2009).
3. By all accounts, Barnes was a cantankerous figure who was careful to restrict admission to his galleries, which were chock full of impressionist and postimpressionist masterpieces. What was so unusual about this was that he tended to restrict the rich and the powerful while granting admission to ordinary people. This was consistent with his other commitments—to racial equality, the New Negro movement, and African American art. Barnes's galleries, now known as the Barnes Foundation, recently moved into its new home in downtown Philadelphia.
4. John Dewey, *Art as Experience* (1934; reprint, New York: Perigee Books, 1980), 3.
5. Ibid., 3.
6. Ibid., 3.
7. Ibid., 4–5.
8. Ibid., 343.
9. Ibid., 343–44.
10. Ibid., 343.
11. Ibid., 190.

12. Alan Wald, *The Revolutionary Imagination: The Poetry and Politics of John Wheelwright and Sherry Mangan* (Chapel Hill, University of North Carolina Press, 1983), xiv.
13. Elizabeth Bishop, *The Complete Poems, 1927–1979* (New York: Farrar, Straus and Giroux, 1983), 127–28.
14. Zora Neale Hurston, *Their Eyes Were Watching God* (1937; reprint, New York: Perennial Library, 1990), 74.
15. See David Bromwich, "Elizabeth Bishop's Dream-Houses," in *Skeptical Music: Essays on Modern Poetry,* 116–31 (Chicago: University of Chicago Press, 2001).
16. Elizabeth Bishop, Letter to John Frederick Nims, October 6, 1979, in *One Art: Letters,* edited by Robert Giroux, 638–39. (New York: Farrar, Straus and Giroux, 1994).
17. Joelle Bielle, ed., *Elizabeth Bishop and the* New Yorker: *The Complete Correspondence* (New York: Farrar, Straus and Giroux, 2011), 158.

[PART II]

Lives

[5]

A Black Woman Speaks: Beah Richards's Life of Protest and Poetry

Dayo F. Gore

Toward the end of 1951, artist-activist Beulah Richardson penned a powerful and lengthy performance poem titled "Genocide." Scripted in three parts, the poem's "1st Voice" is that of a "Negro woman," accompanied by a "chorus of ten voices; children from ages 3 to 21." In the piece the Negro woman declares:

> 1st Voice: And my pain is unended. For this government's policy toward me is ever changing but unchanged. . . . Look at me! I am the living, indisputable fact of "American Democracy." I am the constitution unamended; I am the citizen undefended.
> Chorus: Humiliated, insulted, betrayed and outraged.
> 1st Voice: . . . I'll not speak spite . . . but life. And to speak of life I must tell of death. Now you must see that I am flesh and blood.
> Chorus: And more than that.
> 1st Voice: You must see that I am black and because of that a strange democracy has been practiced upon me.
> Chorus: Say it plain.
> 1st Voice: It kills me. By government policy I am slain.
> Chorus: Maimed, slaughtered, lynched, framed.
> 1st Voice: It kills me. This American Democracy . . . . . . it kills me![1]

The poem was written and performed to support the publication of *We*

Charge Genocide: The Historic Petition to the United Nations for Relief from a Crime of the United States Government against the Negro People, issued by the Communist Party–affiliated Civil Rights Congress (CRC) under the leadership of its director, lawyer and Communist Party USA (CPUSA) member William Patterson.[2]

The piece makes visible the devaluing of black life within a brutally racist justice system and what these activists often called "legal lynching." It also evocatively illustrates the centrality of necropolitics, what Achille Mbembe theorizes as the subjugation of life to the power of death, in structuring African American citizenship.[3] Richardson's poem connects these forces of state power to longer histories of oppression and resistance that are foundational to the nation, and she performed the piece at numerous events publicizing *We Charge Genocide.* Indeed, during the early 1950s Richardson, who worked on numerous CRC campaigns and served as a writer for Paul Robeson's *Freedom* newspaper, garnered much of her early success and publicity as a poet performing and writing in support of such left-leaning activities.

Richardson's early years as a political artist and activist, however, are rarely acknowledged in discussions of her stellar career as an actor on stage, in film, and on TV. She is better remembered by her stage name Beah Richards and her 1967 Oscar-nominated role as Sidney Poitier's mother in *Guess Who's Coming to Dinner,* in her Tony Award–nominated performance in James Baldwin's *The Amen Corner* (1965), or even her role in the 1990s as Dr. Benton's mother on the long-running television series *ER.* Although these dramatic turns solidified Richardson as a serious film and stage talent and highlight her longevity as a successful actor, they do not tell the full story. For a more complete understanding of Richardson's artistic path one must also pay attention to the political commitments that led her to make a career out of playing older black women in a range of politically charged films and stage performances.

Richardson's artistic development, creative alliances, and political affiliations were strongly informed by her long-standing investments in the cultural practices and political analyses developed while she was part of a New York–based black leftist network. This included a dynamic group of black women radicals who coalesced as a collective in the 1940s and 1950s. Among this group of women were writers such as Lorraine Hansberry and Alice Childress and veteran activists such as Louise Thompson Patterson, Maude White, and Thelma Dale. While some of the women were stalwart members of the CPUSA, their activism defies neat categorizations and convenient ideological labels, as these women pushed back against narrow leftist political lines and passionately asserted black women as powerful voices of resistance who could speak to multiple and interconnected forms of oppression.[4]

In the introduction to his essay collection *Writing from the Left: New Essays on Radical Culture and Politics* (1994), Alan Wald highlights this community of black leftists as a key example of a sustained "Communist cultural tradition" as they "pre-figured" Black Arts practices and "intersected with the new Black Arts movement" of the 1960s.[5] However, as new studies on black radicalism and the long black freedom struggle illustrate, the politics and cultural work carried out by the black women in this collective not only prefigured the Black Arts Movement and Black Power politics but also feminist politics and cultural work of the 1960s and 1970s.[6]

In tracing Richardson's artistic development within the black Left, this chapter extends to black women writers on the Left Wald's incisive use of biography to chart a radical literary tradition and builds on many of his insights regarding connections between the Old and New Left cultural work to illuminate the ways black women radicals from the 1940s and early 1950s remained engaged as artists and activists in the black freedom struggle and feminist politics well into the 1970s. Finally, in exploring the black Left context of Richardson's political development and emergence as an artist and activist, this chapter urges greater attention to and a more nuanced reading of Richardson's later cultural work for the ways it sustains these radical politics and serves as an example of the legacies of an earlier black Popular Front politics.[7]

"A Black Woman Speaks . . ."

More than fifteen years before her Oscar-nominated role, Richardson, a thirty-one-year-old poet and activist, took the stage at the Women's Workshop of the American People's Congress for Peace in Chicago. The workshop, organized by American Women for Peace (AWP) and the Women's International Democratic Federation (WIDF), represented a range of progressive interracial women's peace organizations.[8] With more than five hundred women in attendance, Richardson read from her poem, "A Black Woman Speaks . . . of White Womanhood, of White Supremacy, of Peace." Speaking "in searching honesty," she warns the mostly white audience that "white supremacy is your enemy and mine," that "the only difference is degree," and asks, "What will you do? Will you fight with me?" In concluding, Richardson urges her audience to join black women in the "wholehearted fight" for "peace in a world where there is equality."[9] Conference participants gave Richardson a standing ovation and awarded her a conference prize, and the AWP published the poem as a pamphlet.[10]

The reading marked Richardson's ascent within a national leftist milieu in which she would come into her own as an artist, an activist, and a theorist. Her radical voice would take shape as she moved from her hometown of Vicksburg, Mississippi, to New Orleans and southern California before settling in New York City in the 1950s. Richardson's desire to leave behind what she considered a stifling life in Vicksburg motivated her travels.

In the 1940s, Richardson attended Dillard University in New Orleans, where she found a much-needed escape and introduction to city life. After graduating with a BA in 1948, she moved to California, settling first in San Diego and then Los Angeles. Richardson connected with progressive activists in both cities, but it was while in Los Angeles that she became familiar with a Communist Party–affiliated West Coast black Left and joined the Los Angeles chapter of American Women for Peace.[11] A March 1951 *Daily People's World* article announced actress Beulah Richardson as the entertainer at a series of programs organized by the "newly formed" Los Angeles Harbor Committee for Protection of the Foreign Born, which supported activists facing anticommunist attacks.[12]

It was perhaps these California connections that led to Richardson's opportune meeting with William Patterson and Louise Thompson Patterson, both key figures in the CPUSA-affiliated black Left and frequent travelers to the West Coast.[13] In a July 1951 letter to William Patterson, Richardson highlighted the significance of their initial exchanges: "Upon first meeting you . . . I faced and accepted the full responsibility of the Negro writer. . . . [M]y first loyalty is to the cause of freedom. Your approval of my latest work makes me feel that I am, in some measure, meeting that responsibility." She also requested that he "say to Louise [Thompson Patterson] that the promise made to her and to Ms. McGee to do a poem on womanhood, is now kept and that I feel it to be my best work to date."[14] This suggests that it was not simply discussions with William Patterson but also conversations with Louise Patterson and Rosalie McGee—the wife of Willie McGee, a black veteran sentenced to death for the rape of a white woman—that had inspired and provided direction for Richardson's writing of *A Black Woman Speaks.*

Richardson's self-described "best work to date" placed her in conversation with a number of black women radicals who articulated an intersectional analysis of race and gender and pushed their white women comrades to recognize white supremacy as a women's issue and acknowledge their own racial and economic privilege. In February 1947, Thelma Dale clearly articulated these politics at the International Council meeting of the WIDF. Seeking to win support for her perspective "that there can be no real equality for all women until Negro women are also give[n] equality," Dale outlined black women's experiences with "the double oppression of both racial and sex discrimination."[15] Less than five years, later Richardson would expand on these concerns, histories, and relational inequalities in her celebrated eleven-page poem.

Richardson's piece details the ways white supremacy works to construct a racialized notion of womanhood and maintain a destructive hierarchy among women. This construction deemed white women superior and normative and thus coded all discussions of women's activism and women's issues. Richardson explains: "I would that I could speak of white womanhood / as it will and should be / when it stands tall in full equality. / But then, womanhood will be womanhood / void of color and of class, / and all necessity for my speaking thus will be past. / Gladly past."[16] Illuminating the centrality of race and class in dominant constructions of the images of US women, Richardson also imagines a possible future in which economic inequalities and socially constructed hierarchies of difference would no longer exist. For Richardson, "full equality . . . void of color and of class" was not a longing for idealized sisterhood or the erasure of difference but instead was a clear reminder of the ways failing to interrogate calls for women's equality ultimately recenters white womanhood. In this way, her vision moved beyond a humanistic ideal of universal inclusion that was inevitably conceptualized through a normative white subject, foreshadowing instead interventions that would be more fully articulated decades later by black feminist activists such as the Combahee River Collective, cofounder of the Black Women's Liberation Committee and SNCC activist Frances Beal, and scholars theorizing the interrelated and intersectional constructions of gender.[17]

Richardson's work articulates how race and class gendered women differently. Explicating a history of interdependence and oppression that bound black and white women together, she writes "and what wrongs you murders me / and eventually marks your grave / so we share a mutual death at the hand of tyranny."[18] For Richardson, this relationality developed within a long history of US white supremacy and gender oppression rooted in the institution of slavery. As black women toiled under the chattel slavery of a white heteropatriarchy, white women bowed to this same white heteropatriarchy by accepting a constructed ideal of (white) womanhood.[19] Richardson critically reads racialized sexuality as a key source of tension between black and white women activists, yet she also invokes a more standard gendered view of racial violence as she asserts that it was the lynching of black men in defense of white womanhood that gave her voice, asserting, "It is right that I a woman black, should speak of white womanhood. / My fathers, My brothers My husbands, My sons die for it."[20]

"Some Sense of Oneness": Joining a Network of Black Women Radicals

Soon after Richardson's July reading, William Patterson wrote to her praising the poem for its "depth and poignancy, great political wisdom and truth" and urging her to embrace her role as a "leader." He also invited Richardson to New York for a few weeks during his birthday celebration in late August. The invitation included an offer to cover her expenses and set up meetings "with a number of groups," including women active in "legal lynching" campaigns and those "close to Paul and the paper *Freedom.*"[21]

In September 1951, Yvonne Gregory wrote an article for *Freedom* praising Richardson as a voice of "all Negro women in anger and tenderness" and recounting her arrival in New York, including an enthusiastically received reading of her poem and a celebratory welcome party held for her at *Freedom*'s offices.[22] Once in New York, Richardson put into action one of the strongest themes in *A Black Women Speaks* as she immediately became active in the struggle to challenge a racist justice system and end "legal lynching." She joined in organizing a September event framed as the Sojourn for Truth and Justice. The protest sought to bring black women from across the country to Washington, D.C., to meet with the Justice Department and demand a "redress of grievances."[23] Richardson served on the initiating committee that included *California Eagle* newspaper editor Charlotta Bass, writer Alice Childress, Rosalie McGee, Shirley Graham Du Bois, and Louise Thompson Patterson.[24] The organizers made the focal point of the event black women who had experienced firsthand the brutality of Jim Crow justice such as Josephine Grayson, wife of one of the recently executed Martinsville Seven. The protest also centered on the wives of black leaders facing anticommunist investigations.[25]

The D.C. gathering also spotlighted black women radicals' efforts to link women's organizing and civil rights activism. Richardson took a leading role in creating these connections, as she advocated for the sojourn as an exclusively black women's protest.[26] Her clear voice in this organizing effort reflects her emergence as a strategic leader in this network as well as the support she must have found among fellow activists for sustaining a space within the movement for black women's civil rights organizing and cultural work.

The success of the protest sparked the formation of the civil rights organization Sojourners for Truth and Justice (STJ). The STJ defined itself as "an independent non-affiliated Negro women's organization," even as it built a core of support around black women who had a history of working in Communist Party–affiliated groups.[27] The STJ also claimed to speak and work for the "fifteen million Negro citizens," a domain that in both mainstream and radical organizations had long been dominated by black men.[28]

Richardson appears to have been away during the founding meetings of the STJ, but by the end of the year she had published several articles on her travels south in *Freedom,* completed her "Genocide" poem in support of the CRC's *We Charge Genocide* petition, and was being scheduled for a national tour to help the "promot[ion] and sale" of the publication. "Already you have been away too long and we need you and miss you," declared Angie Dickerson of the CRC as she negotiated requests for Richardson's speaking tour.[29] With such encouragement, Richardson would become a fully active member in the New York black leftist communities, relocating to the city to write for *Freedom,* work on campaigns such as the Trenton Six and *We Charge Genocide* through the CRC, and serve as a member of the STJ.

"By Government Policy I Am Slain": Working and Writing for Freedom

By the 1950s, under the leadership of William L. Patterson, the CRC became a major advocate for black people caught in the US criminal justice system.[30] Often mobilizing around cases that the National Association for the Advancement of Colored People (NAACP) proved unable or unwilling to take up, the CRC led the charge in articulating a radical civil rights politics that connected the mistreatment of African Americans within the US legal system to the daily economic and social injustices that black people encountered as a result of the US government's investments in the structures of white supremacy.[31] The organization relied on the work of national staff members and activists such as Halois Moorhead and Maude White Katz as well as numerous black women volunteers including Richardson, Yvonne Gregory, Bessie Mitchell (the sister of one of the Trenton Six), and renowned elder stateswoman Mary Church Terrell to carry out this work.

When Beulah Richardson joined the CRC in late 1951, the organization was recovering from a series of devastating campaign losses, as the

Martinsville Seven had been executed in February and Mississippi had executed Willie McGee in May. The CRC seemed to respond to these setbacks with an intensified focus and a more radical stand against legal lynching and the US government. This can be seen in part in the publication in November 1951 of *We Charge Genocide: The Historic Petition to the United Nations for Relief from a Crime of the United States Government against the Negro People.* Compiled and written by William Patterson and a group of CRC activists, the publication detailed a long history of racial discrimination, economic exploitation, and violence against African Americans in the United States, taking the groundbreaking step of framing such concerns as a human rights issue deserving international intervention. A prominent portion of the petition outlined the numerous cases of legal lynching that occurred in the United States, including the recent Rosa Lee Ingram case and the Martinsville Seven and Willie McGee cases. William Patterson announced the petition in Paris and traveled throughout Europe denouncing the limits of US democracy. As noted above, Richardson also played a central role in publicizing the work and performed her poem "Genocide" at the book's US launch. *We Charge Genocide* proved particularly successful at exposing white supremacy as the US government's Achilles' heel within international Cold War debates over human rights and democracy.[32]

Richardson's piece with its "Mood: Urgent and Angry" not only powerfully dramatized the publication's charges but also captured the renewed urgency and defiance felt by many CRC activists after the tragic deaths of the Martinsville Seven and Willie McGee. The poem begins by recounting the long history of injustice faced by African Americans, "1st Voice: Mine, the hands that picked cotton. . . . Two hundred years of my unpaid labor made the country the nation it is now. . . . Since then through deceit, gradualism, hypocrisy, another hundred years of semi-slavery. . . . This government's policy toward me is ever changing and unchanged." Throughout Part I, Richardson enumerates the ways an antiblack discourse frames the genocidal project. "So it is the government's policy to make of me the enemy. White is right and black is evil. All that's evil must be shunned and slain."[33] Richardson points in large part to this discourse and the structures of Jim Crow as the source of black deaths, both social and literal. She writes:

> Chorus: Jim crow is the rule.
> 1st Voice: On the busses, planes and trains. . . . . [*sic*]
> Chorus: Jimcrow.
> 1st Voice: It maims; how it offends dignity. Along the street. . . . . . [*sic*]
> Chorus: Jimcrow.
> 1st Voice: On the Job. . . . . . [*sic*]

> Chorus: Jim Crow
> 1st Voice: Where I live, where I play, / in the courts of every state.
> Chorus: Say it plain.
> 1st Voice: Death! And when I die, Jimcrow marks the spot where my / outraged corpse must lie.[34]

In this section, Richardson articulates a powerful link between the practices of Jim Crow segregation, which by the mid-1950s would be increasingly framed psychologically in public discourse, and the brutal violence and inequities that African Americans experienced in their daily lives.[35] For Richardson, Jim Crow operated not simply as a social barrier but also as a purveyor of white supremacy and black death directly connected to the government-sanctioned practice of "legal lynching." Invoking the recent state executions of black defendants, Richardson writes in the voice of the chorus:

> But Willie McGee died, he was electrocuted and the women themselves harassed and persecuted. . . . . [*sic*] White supremacists not so easily defied, nor their doctrine easily denied. Fifty were not enough. There must be more, ever more voices crying "Tell me, has white supremacy ended your poverty, your pain your misery?"[36]

Richardson then returns to the 1st Voice, a Negro woman, to highlight the interracial and economic workings of white supremacy that link legal lynching and labor exploitation, proclaiming:

> And with all the killing, what's to be gained? / Money for the rulers—injustice and death for the people black and white. American workers have a common enemy. . . . The widows who stand at the mine pits mourning their dead buried deep by the greed of the coal industry and the widows of the seven men of Martinsville lift their angry cry; "Whose is the responsibility?"[37]

Thus, Richardson brings to light the multiple ways that white supremacy justifies black death and the economic exploitation of both black and white workers. However, while committed to connecting the assertions in *We Charge Genocide* to other economic and political struggles, Richardson continued to present antiblack discourses as marking a very specific and deadly history as she sought a response "to my dead . . . bidding me speak . . . . , [*sic*] bidding me find a way to tell of how and why they were pushed into death alive."[38]

"The Revolt of Rosa Ingram": Black Women Radicals and the Rosa Lee Ingram Case

After 1951, Richardson continued to deploy her artistic talents in support of the organizing work of both the CRC and the STJ even as both organizations faced a growing onslaught of government harassment. The almost decade-long campaign to free Rosa Lee Ingram emerged as perhaps one of the most important struggles against legal lynching that Richardson worked on. The case involved Ingram, a recently widowed sharecropper, and two of her teenage sons who were all convicted and sentenced to death (later reduced to life imprisonment) for the November 1947 murder of John Ethron Stratford. Stratford had died after a dispute with Ingram turned violent and her sons came to her aid. Presenting a black women as the symbolic figure in a criminal case and validating a black defendant's use of deadly force in defending her own life, the Ingram campaign provided radical black women an important source of inspiration and a powerful vehicle for articulating black women's lived experience. Both the STJ and the CRC's Women's Committee for Equal Justice (WCEJ) worked to situate the Ingram case within a longer history of black women's experiences of violent sexual assault at the hands of white men.[39]

Richardson's poetry again served as the signature cultural articulation of these organizing politics. In 1953, she penned the "The Revolt of Rosa Ingram," a lengthy unpublished piece that was performed and circulated broadly through WCEJ chapters. In this poem, Richardson poignantly captures the intersecting histories of a racist criminal justice system and the sexual violence faced by black women in the United States. As a dramatization of the incident from Mrs. Ingram's perspective, "The Revolt of Rosa Lee Ingram" highlights Stratford's murder as an act of resistance to sexual assault. Following the vein of "Genocide," "The Revolt of Rosa Lee Ingram" also indicts a Jim Crow legal system that condones racial violence and "legal lynching" yet denies a black woman the right of self-defense:

> Tis the lawless laws of this land / that killed this man . . .
> It's the policeman's billy. / The policeman's gun.
> It's lynchers running loose / and nothing ever done.
> It's jails packed full of innocent folks
> with the real criminals judging in the courts.[40]

Reflective of a feminist politics that would not gain mainstream acceptance for decades, the final pages of the poem defend Mrs. Ingram's right to her own body, asserting, "these are the laws that killed this man / no wonder he could'nt [*sic*] understand / my body belongs to me. / But be calm my sons / men and women will come. / Must come / to defend a woman's right to her own body."[41] Although men and women did come to support the Ingram campaign, the Ingrams would remain in prison until their parole in 1959.

"Experience Weighs Heavily on My Attitude": From Beulah Richardson to Beah Richards

The imprisonment of the Ingrams outlasted all of the Communist Party–affiliated organizations that campaigned for their release, including the short-lived STJ and the more established CRC. But the dynamic group of black women radicals who had taken leadership in these spaces proved to have greater political longevity. Beulah Richardson, whose poetry and performances helped give artistic expression to the theoretical and political visions articulated in a range of black Left-led organizing efforts, was sustained through Cold War anticommunism by relying on the network of black leftist cultural workers with whom she explored new strategies for connecting her activism and creative craft.

Taking the stage name Beah Richards, she found more or less steady employment throughout the late 1950s and 1960s. She starred in Alice Childress's 1955 off-Broadway production *Trouble in Mind,* served as an understudy to Claudia McNeil in the celebrated 1959 production of Lorraine Hansberry's *A Raisin in the Sun,* and toured with the show's national company. Richards also moved into film with a role in the 1959 *Take a Giant Step,* starring Ruby Dee, and an uncredited role as the family maid in the 1962 film *The Miracle Worker.* By 1967, Richardson had established herself nationally as a film and television actor and garnered several central roles in a number of interracial and implicitly political productions. These include roles as a local abortion provider fearful of imprisonment in *In the Heat of the Night;* as the black mother Rose Scott in *Hurry Sundown,* starring Jane Fonda and Michael Caine; and, in her signature role—although only seven years his senior—as Sidney Poitier's empathetic and supportive mother alongside Roy Glenn, Spencer Tracy, and Katharine Hepburn in *Guess Who's Coming to Dinner?*[42]

Yet even with her rising star and access to more mainstream venues for her creative talents, Richardson remained connected to black leftist organizations and the close-knit network of black women radicals. Having come together and honed their politics in the 1940s and 1950s, the women demonstrated little hesitation in engaging contemporary political questions. With the founding of *Freedomways* in 1961, Richardson joined a number of these veteran black women radicals in support of the publication. A slightly revised version of Richardson's 1951 poem "A Black Woman Speaks" accompanied a 1961 article by Maude White Katz titled "Negro Women and the Law."[43]

Figure 5.1. Beah Richards as Mama Caleba in the film *In the Heat of the Night* (directed by Norman Jewison, 1967).

Richardson also penned several articles for a 1964 special issue on the "southern battlefronts."[44] She traveled south to report on the ongoing political activism in Alabama and in her home state of Mississippi. Richardson's three-part series recounts her experiences in Greenwood and Birmingham in 1963 during a period of major grassroots mobilizations led by SNCC and the NAACP. Echoing a global political outlook shaped by her work on the *We Charge Genocide* publication, Richardson defines the struggle as a revolutionary "fight for human rights, not Negro rights or equal rights.[45] She also continued to support black defendants unjustly jailed. In 1971, Richardson joined with former comrades such as Louise Thompson Patterson, Ossie Davis, and Marvel Cooke as a named supporter of the National United Committee to Free Angela Davis and the Angela Davis Legal Defense Fund. They helped to mobilize support for Davis's freedom and provided crucial organizational leadership during the two-year campaign.[46]

Indeed, Richardson's lifelong work among the black Left continued to fuel her well into the 1970s. Writing to Louise Thompson Patterson in late 1976, Richardson clearly still found the communities of support to be powerful guideposts for her work, proclaiming that "I feel as if magically I've gone backwards." Richardson's comments referred most directly to the surprising revival of her poem, "A Black Woman Speaks," as a stage performance. Undoubtedly, this air of familiarity also spoke to the strength of black feminist organizing. Nevertheless, for Richardson, the moment felt incomplete. She remarked that the contemporary period of revival lacked "the same joyousness we had when first we organized the Sojourners . . . some sense of oneness that of course we know is there" even as she conceded that "experience weighs heavily on attitude."[47]

Such a statement might at first glance appear quite counterintuitive.

But on closer analysis, Richardson's nostalgia speaks to the importance of the political bonds and solidarity that initially held this group of black women radicals together and proved to be a sustaining force in their personal lives and activism. Richardson's comments testify to the continued strength and political engagement of this important network of veteran black women radicals but also reveal how much she relied on the lessons and relationships developed during these earlier years, long after the organizational work ceased.

Indeed, for Richardson, the "sense of oneness" and "loyalty...to the cause of freedom" that defined her art and activism during the 1950s appears to have sustained a fundamental part of her political analysis and cultural work. Such political investments are suggested in her portrayal of Mama Caleba/Mrs. Bellamy, the local store owner who performs backroom abortions in the film *In The Heat of the Night.* Richardson depicts this seemly minor character (clearly meant to signal the exotic world of southern black rural life) as a multilayered flirtatious, defiant, and vulnerable black woman who pointedly gives voice to the racial tensions at the heart of Sidney Poitier's character as she inquires of him, "Why you want to help the police like that? They're stealin' your soul. They chew you up and spit you out."[48] Perhaps Richardson also drew on the feelings of "joyousness" and a "sense of oneness" that she found so inspiring while working with the Sojourners to enliven her performance in the 1998 film *Beloved.* Richardson evocatively conveys an image of "joyousness" and invokes "some sense of oneness" in the electric scene in which she, as the character Baby Suggs, calls the children, women, and men of the black freed community into the ring to laugh, dance, and "weep, just weep for the living, for the dead."[49]

Figure 5.2. Beah Richards as Baby Suggs in the film *Beloved* (directed by Jonathon Demme, 1998).

Notes

1. Beulah Richardson, "Genocide," 1–2, unpublished mimeograph copy, microfilm reel 26, frames 58–70, Civil Rights Congress Papers, Schomburg Center for Research in Black Culture, New York Public Library (hereafter CRC Papers).
2. Civil Rights Congress, *We Charge Genocide: The Historic Petition to the United Nations for Relief from a Crime of the United States Government against the Negro People* (New York: Civil Rights Congress, 1951)
3. Achille Mbembe, "Necropolitics," translated by Libby Meintjes, *Public Culture* 15, no. 1 (2003): 21–22. For a discussion of "legal lynching," see Rebecca Hill, "Introduction," in *Men, Mobs, and Law: Anti-Lynching and Labor Defense in U.S. Radical History,* 1–26 (Durham, NC: Duke University Press, 2008).
4. I explore their activism in more detail in Dayo F. Gore, *Radicalism at the Crossroads: African American Women Activists in the Cold War* (New York: New York University Press, 2011). See also Mary Helen Washington, "Alice Childress, Lorraine Hansberry, and Claudia Jones: Black Women Write the Popular Front," in *Left of the Color Line: Race Radicalism and Twentieth Century Literature of the United States,* edited by Bill Mullen and James Smethurst, 183–204 (Chapel Hill: University of North Carolina Press, 2003).
5. Alan Wald, *Writing from the Left: New Essays on Radical Culture and Politics* (London and New York: Verso, 1994), 4.
6. For examples of this new work that examine the writings and activism of black women on the Left, see Gore, *Radicalism at the Crossroads;* Cheryl Higashida, *Black Feminist Internationalism: Women Writers of the Black Left* (Urbana: University of Illinois Press, 2011); Erick McDuffie, *Sojourning for Truth and Justice: Black Women, American Communism, and the Making of Black Left Feminism* (Durham, NC: Duke University Press, 2011); Mary Helen Washington, *The Other Blacklist: The African American Literary and Cultural Left of the 1950s* (New York: Columbia University Press, 2014).
7. Ian Rockborough-Smith, "'Filling the Gap': Intergenerational Black Radicalism and Popular Front Ideals of *Freedomways* Magazine's Early Years (1961–1965)," *Afro Americans in New York Life and History* (January 2007): 7–36; Nikhil Pal Singh, *Black Is a Country: Race and the Unfinished Struggle for Democracy* (Cambridge, MA: Harvard University Press, 2005).
8. Jacqueline Castledine, *Cold War Progressives: Women's Interracial Organizing for Peace and Freedom* (Urbana: University of Illinois Press, 2012), and Harriet Hyman Alonso, *Peace as a Women's Issue: A History of the U.S. Movement for World Peace and Women's Rights* (Syracuse, NY: Syracuse University Press, 1993).
9. Beulah Richardson, *A Black Woman Speaks of White Womanhood, White Supremacy and Peace* (New York: American Women for Peace, 1951): 1, microfilm, Sc Micro F-11727, Schomburg Center for Research in Black Culture, New York Public Library.
10. Ibid., "Foreword"; Yvonne Gregory, "Poet Demands Equality for Negro Womanhood," *Freedom,* September 1951, 7.
11. *Beah: A Black Woman Speaks* (directed by LisaGay Hamilton, 2003); Mel Gussow, "Beah Richards, 80, Actress in Stalwart Role," *New York Times,* September 16, 2000, 13A.
12. "Harbor Rallies to Expose Witch Hunt," *Daily People's World,* March 27, 1951, 12.

13. As mentioned above, William Patterson was a leading member of the CPUSA and director of the CRC, and Louise Thompson Patterson came of age as part of the Harlem Renaissance milieu and was an active member in the Party since the 1930s.

14. Beulah Richardson to William Patterson, July 1951, microfilm reel 5, frame 337, CRC Papers, part 2.

15. Thelma Dale, "The Status of Negro Women," February 3, 1947, 6, microfilm, part II, reel 34, National Negro Congress Papers, Harvard University; Richardson, "Foreword," *A Black Woman Speaks.*

16. Richardson, *A Black Woman Speaks,* 1.

17. Combahee River Collective Statement, "A Black Feminist Statement," in *Words of Fire: An Anthology of African-American Feminist Thought,* edited by Beverly Guy-Sheftall, 232–40 (New York: New Press, 1995); Frances Beal, "Double Jeopardy: To Be Black and Female," in *Words of Fire,* 146–56; "Mapping the Margins: Intersectionality, Identity Politics, and Violence against Women of Color," *Stanford Law Review* 43 (July 1991): 1241–99.

18. Richardson, *A Black Woman Speaks,* 3. See also Elsa Barkley Brown, "What Has Happened Here': The Politics of Difference in Women's History and Feminist Politics," *Feminist Studies* 18 (Summer 1992): 302–7.

19. Richardson, *A Black Woman Speaks,* 6.

20. Ibid., 3, 10.

21. William L. Patterson to Beulah E. Richardson, August 1, 1951, microfilm, reel 5, frame 336, CRC Papers, part 2.

22. Gregory, "Poet Demands Equality," 7.

23. "A Call to Negro Women," 1951, pp. 1–3, box 13, folder 3, Louise Thompson Patterson Collection, Woodruff Library Special Collections, Emory University, Atlanta (hereafter Louise Thompson Patterson Collection); Lorraine Hansberry, "Women Voice Demands in Capital Sojourn," *Freedom,* October 1951, 6.

24. "A Call to Negro Women," 1.

25. Hansberry, "Women Voice Demands in Capital Sojourn."

26. Charlotta Bass to Beulah Richardson, 19 September 1951, box 12, folder 19, Louise Thompson Patterson Collection. It appears from the letter that Richardson and Bass had a disagreement over the event as being exclusively for black women.

27. "A Call to Negro Women," 2–3.

28. Ibid.; "Draft Constitution and By-Laws of the Sojourners for Truth and Justice," p. 1, box 12, folder 17, Louise Thompson Patterson Collection.

29. Angie Dickerson to Miss Beulah Richardson, December 10, 1951, microfilm reel 5, frame 335, CRC papers, part 2; Beulah Richardson, "Victims' Kin Rebuke Tobias, Want Justice," *Freedom* (December 1951): 1.

30. The CRC emerged from the consolidation of several organizations, including the International Labor Defense and the National Federation for Constitutional Liberties.

31. Gerald Horne, *Communist Front? The Civil Rights Congress, 1946–1956* (Madison, NJ: Fairleigh Dickinson University Press, 1988).

32. Gerald Horne, *Black Revolutionary: William Patterson and the Globalization of the African American Freedom Struggle* (Urbana: University of Illinois Press, 2013).

33. Richardson, "Genocide," 1.

34. Ibid., 3.

35. For a discussion of this turn in a range of writings and studies, including Gunnar Myrdal's work and James Baldwin's writings, see Penny Von Eschen, *Race against Empire: Black Americans and Anticolonialism, 1937–1957* (Ithaca, NY: Cornell University Press, 1997), 153–66.

36. Richardson, "Genocide," 5.

37. Ibid., 5–6.

38. Ibid., 6.

39. Charlotta Bass, "Sojourners for Truth and Justice Bulletin" (draft), 2, box 12, folder 18, Louise Thompson Patterson Collection and WCEJ, "The Case of Mrs. Ingram," reel 8, frame 152, CRC Papers.

40. Beulah Richardson, "The Revolt of Rosa Lee Ingram," n.d., 9, microfilm reel 15, frames 322–32, CRC papers, part 2. A reference to Ingram being in prison for "nearly seven years" suggests that the poem was written in 1953 or 1954.

41. Ibid., 10.

42. Ira Peck, "No Time for Bitterness," *New York Times,* May 2, 1965, C5; Mel Gussow, "Beah Richards, 80, Actress in Stalwart Roles," *New York Times,* September 16, 2000, A13.

43. Maude White Katz, "Negro Women and the Law," *Freedomways* (Summer 1962): 278–86.

44. *Freedomways* (Winter 1964).

45. "Beulah Richardson, "Two Southern Cities," *Freedomways* (Winter 1964): 60.

46. "Angela Davis," *Freedomways* (Summer 1971): 197; "Blacks Urged to Aid Miss Davis in Trial," *New York Times,* October 20, 1970, 27; Joy James, "Introduction," in *Angela Y. Davis Reader,* edited by Joy James, 1–25 (New York: Blackwell, 1998).

47. Beulah Richardson to Louise Thompson Patterson ("Beulah to Lou"), March 6, 1976, box 11, folder 7, Louise Thompson Patterson Collection.

48. *In the Heat of the Night,* directed by Norman Jewison (1967 Los Angeles, Mirisch Corporation).

49. *Beloved,* directed by Jonathan Demme (1988, Burbank, Touchstone Pictures and Harpo Films).

[6]

The Missing Peace: Charlotta Bass and the Vision of the Black Left in the Early Cold War Years

Robbie Lieberman

On February 19, 1960, the *Pittsburgh Courier* published a review of Charlotta Bass's semiautobiographical book *Forty Years: Memoirs from the Pages of a Newspaper.* Under Bass's editorship, the *California Eagle,* one of the oldest black newspapers in the US West, had become an important voice for challenging inequality and discrimination. On the heels of her forty years with the *Eagle,* Bass became the first African American female to run for vice president. Nominated by Paul Robeson, she was on the 1952 Progressive Party ticket, a third party already diminished by a crushing defeat in 1948 after its standard-bearer Henry Wallace, an outspoken opponent of the Cold War, had momentarily raised the hopes of the Communist Left. In its review of Bass's memoir, the *Courier* described her as "the indomitable as well as intrepid former editor of the California Eagle," noting the paper as "a reflection of the vigorous thought and actions of a woman who dared to meet every challenge. She believed in America and the American Constitution. She believed in the Declaration of Independence. She believed in God."[1] While recognizing Bass's lifelong commitment to democracy and minority rights, the *Courier* had little to say about her interest in peace. Much of the journalistic and scholarly work on the black Left during the early Cold War years suffers from the same omission. Scholars attend to black internationalism or the use of nonviolence in the civil rights movement but rarely discuss peace issues, including concerns about nuclear weapons, military spending, and war, nor do they probe the relationship of these issues to antiracism, feminism, and anticolonialism.[2] Scholarship on Bass focuses on her as a community activist and newspaper editor in Los Angeles and portrays her alternately as a "race woman," a protofeminist, or a "radical precursor of the black power movement."[3] Only Gerald Gill, in a chapter on her 1952 vice presidential campaign, seriously addresses her interest in peace and the links she drew between US foreign policy and the status of African Americans.[4]

Figure 6.1. *Portrait of Charlotta Bass*, Providence (?), ca. 1901–10. Postcard with a photograph of a young Charlotta Bass. The photograph may have been taken in Providence, where Bass (then Charlotta Spears) lived with an older brother and worked at the *Providence Watchman*, an African American newspaper. Credit: Charlotta Bass Collection, Southern California Library (Los Angeles).

Charlotta Bass's views after World War II underscored her broad, global perspective, particularly her outspoken and lasting support for peace and freedom. Her story helps fill a gap in peace movement history, which often leaves out African Americans (with the exception of well-known pacifists such as Bayard Rustin), and in African American history, which often leaves out peace activism. My focus here is on the interplay between the personal and political: the experiences that contributed to Bass's interest in peace, the way in which she articulated her concerns, and the impact of her outspoken peace advocacy on her life. Her story is one of several that helps to break down the divide between the African American freedom movement and the peace movement, usually portrayed as unrelated struggles in the popular mind and in much scholarly literature, especially in the historical writing on the black Left.

Accounts of Bass's life put her date and place of birth sometime between 1874 and 1890 either in Rhode Island, Ohio, or South Carolina. As a child, Charlotta Spears was deeply affected by reading Edward Bellamy's utopian novel *Looking Backward.* Her family thought that socialism was un-Christian and would only get her into trouble, but her mother did take her to the first organizational meeting of the National Association for the Advancement of Colored People (NAACP) in their Rhode Island town, and that became another defining moment in her life. Spears moved to Los Angeles at the age of eighteen, becoming editor and publisher of the *California Eagle* in 1912, a position she held for nearly forty years until she was forced to sell the paper during the Red Scare. In the years prior to World War II, she helped win a series of victories for equal rights, including fighting the first cases against restrictive covenants and successfully ending discrimination in employment at the Southern California Telephone Company, the Los Angeles General Hospital, and the Los Angeles Transit Company. She was known for her ability to build effective coalitions and she worked with and played leadership roles in many organizations. Her writing and activities focused on the local scene, but she was hardly indifferent to foreign affairs. In the 1930s, she spoke out against fascism and promoted independence in Africa. The weekly radio program she created in the late 1930s shared local, national, and international news from the black press.[5]Along with many other African Americans, Bass strongly supported World War II, believing that it would lead to democracy and equal rights at home and abroad. She was not naive and knew that such rights would not come without a struggle. Her nephew Ellis Spears learned this during his military training in Mississippi, which he called "the worst State in the Union for the Negro race." He wrote to Bass that his experience there was "terrible" and that "if you could only see some of the things that happened here you would wonder what we are fighting for."[6] Bass opposed A. Philip Randolph and the March on Washington movement—among her reasons was his "bipolar view of race relations" (that is, black and white), which did not square with her multicultural experience in Los Angeles. In practice, however, she participated in the "double V" campaign, supporting the war effort while continuing to fight discrimination and segregation at home.[7] Again like many others, she was bitterly disappointed by the lack of progress after the war. As she saw it, instead of seeing a victory for equality, African American veterans were welcomed home from war by lynch mobs, as occurred in Georgia and Mississippi. Fueling these attacks at home were US Cold War priorities, and she assailed the way that US policy makers gave anticommunism priority over anticolonialism and antiracism. From that time on—whether running for office, writing her regular column, or speaking out against the Red Scare—Bass articulated explicit links between peace and freedom despite the political and personal costs.

In its 1960 review, the *Courier* concluded that "insofar as it reflects the perplexity of many Negroes with fighting hearts," Bass's book was "a provocative study of how you may start out right and end up in a maze." The "maze" was presumably her association with Communists and Progressives. These associations confounded her efforts to promote social justice and peace in the era of the Cold War and the Red Scare, made the *Courier* reluctant to engage her peace advocacy, and narrowed the scholarship about Bass.[8]

The views of peace proponents associated with the Communist Left in the early Cold War years were predicated on defending the Soviet Union. While the Soviet Union claimed to stand for peace, its internal policies highlighted the hypocrisies of that claim, just as ongoing racial inequality in the United States belied US claims of standing for freedom. There was a grain of truth in each of these cases, as E. P. Thompson pointed out, but the relevant point here is that leaders in the Communist-affiliated peace ranks, such as Paul Robeson, knew and kept quiet about the horrors of the Soviet Union.[9] This made their peace advocacy problematic. Yet it is important to note that Robeson and W.E.B. Du Bois and those who shared their outlook—among them noteworthy black women such as Lorraine Hansberry, Shirley Graham Du Bois, Eslanda Robeson, and Charlotta Bass—had a view of peace that went beyond a defense of Soviet policies. It rested more broadly on (1) the idea of a shared humanity, which people could learn about through an exchange of cultures; (2) a disgust with US Cold War policies (i.e., support for European colonialism, the development of nuclear weapons, and the threat of war), policies they held responsible for creating greater economic and racial inequality; and (3) in many cases (such as Hansberry's) an abhorrence of war and violence. For many, their sense of the potential in human beings to treat each other with decency and dignity also stemmed from their own experiences, especially from travel abroad including visits to the Soviet Union. Robeson's experience was emblematic; as he stated before the House Un-American Activities Committee, "In Russia I felt for the first time like a full human being. No color prejudice like in Mississippi, no color prejudice like in Washington. It was the first time I felt like a human being."[10] In Bass's case, the global travel came later, though her reactions were quite similar. Nonetheless, such multicultural experience and exchange was central to her activism in Los Angeles and her strong belief in a shared humanity was part of her Christian outlook on the world.

To be sure, not everyone who abhorred war, promoted an exchange of cultures, and criticized US Cold War policies was willing to work with Communists. But as the *Courier* explained about Bass, she was among those who "chose to work, without too much question, with any and all groups" who shared her concerns. Titled "A Conundrum: Whither?" the article ended with a more sympathetic question: "Where should Negroes like Mrs. Bass have run when the 'Commies' came on the scene?" From the perspective of the black Left, the choices were limited; one could join the cold warriors in trying to exploit the US government's rhetorical commitment to democracy and freedom around the world in order to make gains on the home front (the approach of mainstream civil rights leaders), or one could oppose US Cold War policies and work with those who were willing to critique the hypocrisies of the US commitment to freedom at home and abroad. The latter choice often led to working with communist front organizations that refused to criticize the Soviet Union.

Despite the fact that Bass's words—especially during the 1952 Progressive Party campaign—mirrored those of the Communist Party, there was continuity between her earlier community organizing and her post–World War II national electoral campaigns and increasing commentary on international affairs. A good example was the way she recalled her service in 1943 as the first African American to serve on a grand jury in Los Angeles County. After listening to her fellow jurors make a number of disparaging remarks about Mexican Americans, she responded, "As I look at you, I am . . . afraid that your ignorance and prejudice will be your undoing. Unless you wake up, and together, all of us, you and I—Mexican, Negro, Asian, European, and African—create a world of peace dedicated to the real brotherhood of man, I am afraid we are lost."[11] Her view of equality and freedom had always been universal, even when her focus and activities had been local. All people were children of God, she believed, and they deserved the same rights and opportunities.[12] The Red Scare and her need to defend herself against attacks that she was a Communist brought this continuity to the forefront.

Perhaps more important, there was one deeply personal reason for Bass's more intense focus on peace issues after World War II. Her nephew, John Kinloch, was killed in action after he volunteered to join the first integrated combat regiment in 1945, believing that it represented what the war was about. Kathleen Cairns suggests that Kinloch's death radicalized Bass; Cairns calls it the "final spark" that fueled a "growing cynicism."[13] Kinloch's death was clearly a vital motivating factor for Bass's focus on peace issues from then on, feeding her anger at the treatment of black veterans after World War II and her opposition to the war in Korea. But bitterness about national priorities—seeing "the flower of our youth" sent to Korea while there were few resources devoted to ending segregation—was not merely an expression of cynicism.[14] In her political activity and in her column, she rejected "the tacit agreement that blacks would keep their noses out of foreign relations in exchange for a slow but steady expansion of civil rights."[15] Differentiating her views from that approach—arguably a far more cynical one than her own—she sharply criticized US foreign policy, linking the struggle for democratic and human rights abroad to the struggle for equality at home. Like her compatriots Du Bois and Robeson, Bass saw peace and freedom as inextricably linked while focusing on her own government as the greatest obstacle to the achievement of these ideals.

Kinloch had come to California as a teenager in the late 1930s and Bass became his guardian so he could attend UCLA as a California resident. He worked on the *Eagle,* soon becoming its managing editor, as Bass groomed him to take over the paper. After he was drafted, Kinloch wrote to her from Europe about the enormous impact she had on his life.

> [W]ith all the sincerity at my command . . . I want to thank you for six wonderful years of learning. I want to thank you for the opportunity you gave me to find out what the world is about, and for teaching me that there are people for whom honesty is a creed that is lived up to.
>
> You remember that when I came to you, I was on the road to becoming one of those smart New York 'young cynics' with faith in nothing [but] items with dollar signs. I want to thank you for the convictions which I grew to hold after having worked at the EAGLE. I know what a pain in the rear I have been . . . that you have had Job's patience in three directions.[16]

Kinloch described what was the "turning point" for him, a "heroic" speech he heard Bass give, and concluded, "I swore that night that I would try to live with as clear and conscious faithfulness to the people's cause as you have."[17]

The comment on being "a pain in the rear" refers in part to Kinloch's fascination with the movies, which led him to disappear for hours on end, even when there was work to be done. By all accounts he was a gifted writer; he had published poems in the *New Masses* and the *Saturday Review,* and he had visions of becoming a Hollywood screenwriter.[18] He was already becoming a leader in his own right, organizing a junior council of the NAACP and performing on a nightly radio show while serving as writer and editor on the *Eagle.* There is evidence that suggests Kinloch was drafted for political reasons—in order to destroy the paper, Bass believed, since he played such a vital role in its operations.[19]

Kinloch was ambivalent about the war and the possibility of being drafted, as evidenced in his poetry, yet he shared the hopes of the black Left that it would open up opportunities to create a more genuine democracy at home.[20] His letters from Europe expressed his high hopes for the future; the war, he believed, would usher in a new world. In fact, he claimed that this new world was already becoming visible in Europe. He wrote to his mother in November 1944 of

> a whole world lunging forward on the high road to freedom. . . . The holy places of evil in this world are getting the stuffing kicked out of them—by the big feet of us common everyday Joes. There are holy places of evil back home that will know our footsteps, too. . . . The dead will not have died in vain, for their children will live in freedom. Our children, too, the shining black faces, will live the tomorrow that their parents could only dream. They will because none of us shall fail to continue the struggle even when this fighting here is done.[21]

At the same time he refused to glorify war, "even a good one, a necessary and just one like this."[22]

Less than a month later, he wrote "Aunt Charlotte" to tell her about "the biggest, best shock of the war," namely that "Negroes will be accepted as volunteers for combat replacements in white infantry units at the front! NO SEGREGATION!"[23] He told her he had volunteered and, surely aware of the risk he was taking, asked her not to tell his mother. But mostly he expressed excitement about how this would move the struggle forward. Kinloch's letters repeatedly asked "Aunt Charlotte" to try to get him status as a war correspondent so he could tell the stories of the "Negro troops" from close up. Such stories would highlight the views of black GIs who were "determined that democracy will have to come alive" for them "when the shooting's over." He relayed the story of one soldier who had told him how he felt about his job as a rigger: "It was damned near poetry the way he explained it." Kinloch's quoting of this GI's story ended with these words: "I don't care what anybody tells me, I know that job is important. When I get home I'll know I have every right to living like an American should."[24] It is not clear whether Bass ever responded, but whether she did or not she must have felt some guilt about not attending to his request to get him official status as a war correspondent. He sent a letter dated February 5, 1945, saying he had a kind of "eerie feeling" from writing and not hearing back (it had been nearly three months since he had heard from her), and again he pressed her to work on his request. Kinloch may have even had a premonition that he was not going to come back alive; in one of his last letters to his mother he made a plea for her to heal the breach between her and "Aunt Charlotte" and be proud of all the important work her sister was doing.[25]

When Kinloch was killed in combat nine weeks after joining the infantry (in which African Americans could only serve as privates), young activists in Los Angeles formed the John Kinloch Club in his honor, and a few years later they opened the Bass-Kinloch Cultural Center. Bass's renewed determination to change the world, focusing on the links between peace and freedom, may be seen as yet another way of honoring Kinloch's memory. She continued to express a firm belief in the US Constitution while criticizing the ongoing lack of equality for racial minorities at home—including high-profile cases of mistreatment of black veterans—but she now devoted more effort to decrying US foreign policy.

Bass had formally been a Republican, despite occasional detours, throughout her adult life. She served as the western regional director for Wendell Wilkie's presidential campaign in 1940 but publicly broke with the Republican Party after World War II. She had clearly been moving closer to the Communist Party's position on a number of issues since the early 1940s and in 1948, she supported the Progressive Party campaign, serving as cochair of Women for Wallace. She consistently criticized US Cold War policies in the pages of the *Eagle,* even as it became clear that this would invite attack. Surely her shifting commitment, particularly her devotion to peace issues, had something to do with the loss of her nephew. For one thing, it would have been hard to view his death as a necessary sacrifice, given the lack of changes in race relations at home after the war. As mentioned above, she was already convinced that he had been drafted to silence the *Eagle*'s voice. She had been very close to Kinloch, and it is not hard to imagine her anguish about his death leading her to a stronger interest in peace, an issue that already fit her Christian beliefs and was now underscored by the people she most admired, such as Robeson.

When Bass ran for Congress in 1950 on the Independent Progressive Party ticket—the same year Du Bois ran for Senate in New York on the American Labor Party ticket on a platform of peace and civil rights—her peace platform included opposing "preventative war," admitting China to the United Nations, outlawing atomic and hydrogen bombs, and supporting independence for colonial peoples.[26] In the early 1950s, she also chaired Sojourners for Truth and Justice, a black women's organization that linked peace and freedom, protesting the war in Korea and the lack of democracy that was evident in the cases of the Martinsville Seven, Willie McGee, and Rosa Lee Ingram.[27] Bass had many other links to the Communist Left, even as she continued her association with the NAACP and her church, and she was still known in Los Angeles as an organizer who excelled at building successful coalitions around particular causes.[28]

Figure 6.2. Charlotta Bass receives a bouquet of flowers at a congressional campaign rally in 1950. To her right is Reuben Borough, Progressive Party candidate for California treasurer; on the left is the folksinger Ernie Lieberman. Credit: Charlotta Bass Collection, Southern California Library (Los Angeles).

Even so, Bass sounded more and more like Paul Robeson and W. E. B. Du Bois, who both faced attack for their words, activities, and associations, especially those having to do with peace. In his controversial speech at the 1949 Paris Peace Congress, Robeson argued that African Americans would not go to war on behalf of a government that denied them democratic rights at home: "We do not want to die in vain any more on foreign battlefields for Wall Street and the greedy supporters of domestic fascism. If we must die, let it be in Mississippi or Georgia! Let it be wherever we are lynched and deprived of our rights as human beings!"[29] In the wake of the attacks on Robeson that followed, Bass brought him to Los Angeles to sing on the occasion of the *California Eagle*'s seventieth anniversary, and the paper characterized him as "the great Negro leader of ALL the people."[30] Her regular column in the *Eagle* pointed to the hypocrisy of politicians who seemed more concerned about democracy in Europe or Asia than at home. Speaking about the "senseless slaughter" in Korea, for example, she invoked John Kinloch's death, one of several times she juxtaposed the sacrifices that African Americans made abroad to their precarious position at home. In a speech about Harriet Moore, who was killed along with her husband Harry T. Moore (Florida's NAACP leader) after the Ku Klux Klan planted a bomb in their home, Bass pointed out that Mrs. Moore's brother was flown home from Korea in uniform to attend her funeral.[31]

Figure 6.3. John Kinloch in front of the *California Eagle* offices circa 1941. Credit: Charlotta Bass Collection, Southern California Library (Los Angeles).

From the late 1940s on, Bass strongly and publicly objected to proponents of peace being dismissed as communists. In 1948, she demanded that the *Daily News* retract its "libelous" statement that she was a member of the Communist Party while continuing to use the pages of the *Eagle* to legitimize the struggle for peace.[32] Her May 11, 1950, column foreshadowed Du Bois's indictment by the Justice Department as head of the Peace Information Center, a position from which he gathered signatures on the Stockholm Peace Petition that called on the nations of the world to outlaw atomic weapons. Bass wrote that anyone who spoke out

> against the destruction of civilization by the construction of death bombs is considered an enemy of the government and is subjected to a loyalty test and public abuse. Any organization or newspaper that sees no cause for provoking a war with Russia is giving comfort and support to the Communist Party in its effort to overthrow our government, is what the Hearst and other Wall Street controlled newspapers would have you believe. But, Brother, it ain't true.[33]

Bass explored this theme in other columns over the next several months. In her August 4, 1950, column, she commented on the irony of the New York City police breaking up a peace demonstration: "Sponsors of the meeting had applied for a permit which had been denied on the grounds that to hold a rally for peace would create a disturbance."[34]

At a time when the causes of peace and civil rights were becoming divided, in part as a result of the Red Scare, Bass took the unusual position of supporting the integration of the armed forces *and* opposing war, surely a position that Kinloch would have appreciated. Bass's campaign for vice president on the Progressive Party ticket in 1952 continued to hammer home themes of peace and freedom. In a speech in Brooklyn, she talked about spending priorities:

> We say—take the $65 billion that Republicans and Democrats are voting for death, and use those dollars to build a new life. Those billions could lift the wages of my people and all people, ensure everyone of jobs and old age security, educate and train and give new hope to our young people in decent schools, free our sharecroppers, build new hospitals and new medical centers. Yes, the $8 billion that is being spent to rearm Europe and crush Asia could rehouse all my people living in the slums of Harlem and Bed-Stuy and in every city in the nation.[35]

In California, Bass also emphasized the Progressive Party's peace program: "Peace by negotiation. Peace which will bring an end to the war in Korea. Peace which will bring an end to the war on the Negro people here at home by wiping out jim crow [*sic*] and oppression. Peace which will outlaw the murderous Ku Klux Klan."[36] She went on to mention jobs, a strong Fair Employment Practices Act, outlawing lynching and the poll tax, and establishing old age pensions, all of which added up to "Peace which will truly make this one nation, indivisible with liberty and justice for all."[37]

Responding to the Progressive Party's opposition to US Cold War policies, *Time* magazine issued a vicious denunciation of the party's presidential ticket. Its 1952 article titled "National Affairs: Shocking Pink" referred to the Progressive Party's presidential candidate Vincent Hallinan as the "'peace candidate'"—the quotations meant to indicate that he wasn't really interested in peace at all. It described Bass as "dumpy, domineering . . . [c]hildless . . . bitterly radical," mentioning as well that she had visited Russia.[38] The red-baiting took its toll. She had already been forced to sell the *Eagle.* A few years later, her sorority rescinded her membership. She had to justify her views to her church. (In a "Dear Pastor" letter, she wrote that she was "a loyal American in every sense of the word.")[39] All of these were painful experiences, but they did not change her view of the world or prevent her from continuing her activity. In her farewell column in the *Eagle* on April 26, 1951, Bass concluded, "I am very confident that within my lifetime yet I will see first class citizenship achieved for all my people, true democracy for all Americans, and peace in all the world!"[40] She never stopped working for peace and democratic rights.

Bass continued to organize her community from a global and leftist perspective even in her retirement community in Elsinore, outside of Los Angeles. In the mid-1960s, she proposed the publication of a small monthly magazine, the *Elsinore Voice.* Suggesting that it would be "a family publication to inform the outside world [of] the health benefits of Elsinore," her proposal also suggested that the magazine would be

> Dedicated to world peace and the abolition of war, atomic or otherwise, establishment of a friendly trade relationship with Russia, admission of China to the U.N., support of Freedom Marchers in their effort to abolish all forms of segregation and discrimination[.] . . . decent housing in all sections of the city, free of discrimination[,] . . . adequate pension for the aged.[41]

To sum up the development of her beliefs, we can say that Charlotta Bass was committed to Christianity, American democracy, and racial equality. But equally important, she was opposed to the Korean War, the buildup of nuclear weapons, and colonialism. Her accomplishments included a number of firsts, several of which have been mentioned above. She was also ahead of her time in discussing what it meant to be African American (as opposed to Negro) and in her awareness of the triple oppression of black working women.[42] But her individual achievements are beside the point here.

There were many other black leftists who shared Bass's perspective, who desperately wanted to build a world of racial equality but whose vision did not end there. Ossie Davis and Canada Lee, Carlton Goodlett and Claudia Jones, Lorraine Hansberry, William Worthy, Eugene Gordon, Shirley Graham Du Bois, and Eslanda Robeson all shared the view that Bass expressed at the end of her autobiographical book: "We who fight on the side of the people believe that the great enemies of mankind are poverty and disease, inequality and war."[43] They shared her global perspective, the links between peace and freedom that she spelled out, and her advocacy of both causes. Thus, their stories help to expand our conceptualization of the black Left in the early Cold War years, adding an important dimension to our understanding of these individuals and the movement of which they were a part. Peace was an integral part of their vision for a world free of colonialism, racism, gender inequality, and poverty. Because of their pro-Soviet outlook, their view sounded—and to many people continues to sound—at best naive, at worst duplicitous (and certainly treasonous to Cold War proponents). But I argue that there was an unmistakable sincerity and significance in their pleas for peace, precisely because of their refusal to separate peace from other issues. Their expression of a broad vision of peace was considered un-American and brought surveillance, attack, and repression. But this was not only because of their pro-Soviet outlook; it was also because of the particular way in which they linked the cause of peace with freedom and justice. Mary McLeod Bethune had spoken to these connections earlier, and both Martin Luther King, Jr. and Coretta Scott King made similar arguments at various times.[44] But Bass and her contemporaries spoke out in the early years of the Cold War, when only Communists, it was assumed, promoted peaceful coexistence with the Soviet Union, opposed the Korean War and the buildup of atomic weapons, and agitated against colonialism. They all may not have been strict pacifists (though a number of them were), but they shared a critique of what we would now call structural violence, which had to be addressed in order to move the world closer to conditions that could foster a positive peace.[45]

Why has the black Left's interest in peace received so little attention? Peace historians have addressed the issue of racial inequality on occasion, but they tend to focus on the internal dynamics of peace movements and fail to address African American perspectives on peace in a serious way.[46] For purposes of this collection, it is more compelling to consider why scholars of the black Left—whether their work is historical or literary—pay so little attention to writing and activism around peace issues.

There are two major tendencies. The easier one to explain is the group of scholars who simply want to avoid questions about black activists' ties to the Communist movement. Whether they fear tainting the legacy of their subjects or their own reputations, they don't see the evidence because they have internalized the anticommunism that prevailed during the Red Scare era, or for some other reason, these scholars understate or neglect the black Left's concerns about peace issues.[47] This approach mirrors the Cold War liberal approach to civil rights in its post–World War II phase (and to the early scholarship on the civil rights movement). Fear of anticommunist attacks on the civil rights movement throughout the first quarter century of the Cold War meant not only distancing the movement from the likes of Robeson and Du Bois but also warning young people to stay away from Communists and attacking Martin Luther King, Jr. when he spoke out against the Vietnam War.[48]

But we need another explanation for those who acknowledge Communist ties in many other areas. What are we to make of those who forcefully challenge the old view that Communists exploited the black freedom movement for their own purposes but simply refuse to use the word "peace"? To be fair, Charlotta Bass's impact was most significant in Los Angeles, and there is reason to honor her leadership on a local level. Yet this does not explain viewing her post–World War II writings and activities as a "departure" from her otherwise admirable work rather than as an integral and important extension of her local accomplishments to a more global scope.[49] And again, even those who accept or even celebrate her and others' ties to the Communist Left focus almost exclusively on black liberation struggles or black feminism even as their subjects specifically emphasized peace as a priority. The strong commitment to peace issues is inescapable if you look at Du Bois and Robeson and the many others who took their cues from those two. These activists did not write and speak about "internationalism." The word they used was "peace," and yet one searches in vain for the latter term in most scholarly studies on the black Left.[50]

Perhaps the neglect of peace issues stems from lack of interest among those focused on race-class-gender equality and/or issues of sexuality. Moving beyond Bass, there are suggestive cases to point to in the realm of literature. To take just one instance, the neglect of black authors' interest in peace can be seen in the scholarship on Ann Petry's novel *The Narrows.*

In the brilliant scholarship about *The Narrows,* there is barely a mention of peace. Yet the main character, the setting, and, arguably, even the inevitable conclusion are tied to war and militarism as well as to the race and class issues that have received close attention.[51] In one intriguing example, Farah Jasmine Griffin's insightful chapter on *The Narrows* seeks to restore its leftist politics, beginning with Petry's intentions. Griffin says that Petry's argument for the significance of "sociological fiction," rooted in Western culture and influenced by Marxism, echoes Du Bois's claims in his famous essay "Art as Propaganda." But Petry added one more feature to such propaganda, suggesting that socially conscious writers might be merely people with a conscience, a large portion of whose cultural heritage "stems from the Bible," even if it includes Marxism as well.[52] Petry zeroed in on the Old Testament story of Cain and Abel. As quoted by Griffin:

> In one way or another, the novelist who criticizes some undesirable phase of the status quo is saying that man is his brother's keeper and that unless a social evil (war or racial prejudice or ante-Semitism [*sic*] or political corruption) is destroyed man cannot survive but will become what Cain feared he would become—a wander[er] and a vagabond on the face of the earth.[53]

It is not insignificant that "war" is first on Petry's list of social evils—just as it was not an accident when Lorraine Hansberry made a similar list of social evils in response to an interview question.[54]

Griffin tells us how the main character in *The Narrows,* Link Williams, is a combination of Paul Robeson and W. E. B. Du Bois: a gifted athlete and a handsome young man with the ambition of becoming a historian and writing about slavery. Yet Link goes off to serve in the military and comes back a changed person, with no direction. There is no discussion, in either the novel or the scholarship, about what happened to him during his service in the army, but it clearly has destroyed his ambition.[55] The setting of *The Narrows* is a town controlled by a munitions factory, and the family that owns it is responsible for Link's death; indeed, the one who pulls the trigger is not only the husband of the white woman with whom Link has an affair but also an officer in the US Army.[56] The high expectations of African Americans, including those on the Left, coming out of the World War II–era military and the way those hopes were dashed by continued brutal violence, even against those who supposedly fought for democracy, is again a central theme. But the Cold War context matters a great deal, since it helps explain *why* those expectations were not met. Anticommunism and preparations for war against the Soviet Union, support for European allies in their struggle to hold on to their colonies (lest they turn to communism), growing militarism on the home front—these were tied to the continuation of race and class oppression, as Robeson, Du Bois, Bass, Petry, and many others articulated at the time.

Scholars' reluctance to highlight peace as a major theme in Petry's novel is similar to the neglect of Bass as a peace activist. This perhaps explains why one of the more accurate summations of Bass's life and legacy comes from an essay written by a middle school student who doesn't yet know any better. "Charlota Bass did raise the issues in her relentless pursuit for peace and equality."[57] More broadly speaking, the split between the causes of peace and freedom, for which the Cold War and the Red Scare were mainly responsible, has echoes today in a scholarly divide between the two topics that has barely begun to be breached.

Surely the broad, significant legacy of the black Left from the Cold War era, a legacy that encompasses the linked struggles for peace and freedom, merits more attention than it has thus far received.

Notes

1. "A Conundrum: Whither?," Courier Correspondence, February 19, 1960, box 1 Additions, Charlotta Bass Papers, MSS 002, Southern California Library for Social Studies and Research, Los Angeles, California (hereafter Bass Papers).
2. See, for example, the work of Fanon Che Wilkins, Brent Hayes Edwards, Brenda Gayle Plummer, Robin Kelley, and many others on black internationalism. Exceptions to this include Jacqueline Foertsch, *Reckoning Day: Race, Place, and the Atom Bomb in Postwar America* (Nashville: Vanderbilt University Press, 2013); Jacqueline Castledine, "Quieting the Chorus: Progressive Women's Race and Peace Politics in Postwar New York," in *Anticommunism and the African American Freedom Movement,* edited by Robbie Lieberman and Clarence Lang, 51–79 (New York: Palgrave Macmillan, 2009); and Carole Boyce Davies, *Left of Karl Marx: The Political Life of Black Communist Claudia Jones* (Durham, NC: Duke University Press, 2008). Gerald Horne also addresses peace issues in several of his books, though he does so rather uncritically. Bass and her contemporaries did not use the term "structural violence," but that concept was central to the way they connected various issues to their desire for peace.
3. Regina Freer, "L.A. Race Woman: Charlotta Bass and the Complexities of Black Political Development in Los Angeles," *American Quarterly* 56 (September 2004), 607–32. http://lion.chadwyck.com/display/printView.do?area=abell; "The Press as Pulpit: Charlotta Bass and the *California Eagle,*" in Kathleen Cairns, *Front-Page Women Journalists, 1920–1950,* 73–106 (Lincoln: University of Nebraska Press, 2003); "Charlotta A. Bass: Radical Precursor of the Black Power Movement," in Rodger Streitmatter, *Raising Her Voice: African-American Women Journalists Who Changed History,* 96–106 (Lexington: University Press of Kentucky, 1994).
4. Gerald Gill, "'WIN OR LOSE—WE WIN': The 1952 Vice-Presidential Campaign of Charlotta A. Bass," in *The Afro-American Woman: Struggles and Images,* edited by Sharon Harley and Rosalyn Terborg-Penn, 109–18 (Port Washington, NY: Kennikat, 1978). The other study that addresses Bass's communist connections and her peace interests directly, offering a rare glimpse into the wide range of her interests and affiliations, is Robert Gottlieb et al., *The Next Los Angeles: The Struggle for a Livable City* (Berkeley: University of California Press, 2005).
5. Biographical notes, 1959, author unknown, box 2, Bass Papers; "Biographical Notes on Mrs. Charlotta Bass," The Progressive Party of Ohio, 1952, box 1 Additions, Bass Papers; Cairns, *Front-Page Women Journalists,* 92, 97.
6. Ellis E. Spears's letter is from Camp Van Dorn, Mississippi, May 10, 1943, box 1 Additions, Bass Papers.
7. Freer, "L.A. Race Woman," 9; Cairns, *Front-Page Women Journalists,* 100. Bass did not share Randolph's intense anticommunism, but her opposition in this case also stemmed from discomfort with all-black organizations. See Scott Kurashige, *The Shifting Grounds of Race* (Princeton, NJ: Princeton University Press, 2010), 153.
8. Among those who write admiringly of her efforts to combat discrimination in

employment and housing in Los Angeles up through World War II yet cast her post–World War II peace activism in negative terms or avoid it altogether are Streitmatter, Freer, Cairns (cited above). In *Bound for Freedom*, Douglas Flamming echoes the negative portrayal of Bass put forward by *Time* magazine, writing of her as a "peace candidate" and claiming that after her nephew's death Bass "adopted his leftist views." See *Bound for Freedom: Black Los Angeles in Jim Crow America* (Berkeley: University of California Press, 2005), 366, 370.

9. See Martin Bauml Duberman, *Paul Robeson* (New York: Knopf, 1988), 208–9, 352–54.
10. "Testimony of Paul Robeson before the House Committee on Un-American Activities, June 12, 1956," History Matters, http://historymatters.gmu.edu/d/6440.
11. Bass tells this story in her self-published memoir. See Charlotta Bass, *Forty Years: Memoirs from the Pages of a Newspaper* (Los Angeles: Self-published, 1960), 127.
12. She presented herself as a member in good standing of the Baptist Church and as a Progressive and a loyal American. See, for example, a draft of a dinner speech to be given in Brooklyn, April 18, 1952; see also a September 29, 1952, transcript of a broadcast, box 1 Additions, Bass Papers.
13. Cairns, *Front-Page Women Journalists*, 98, 102.
14. "The Negro in the World Crisis," Typescript, p. 8, box 1 Additions, Bass Papers. Cases of racial injustice in the immediate post–World War II years are discussed in Gerald Horne, *Communist Front? The Civil Rights Congress, 1946–1956* (Rutherford: Fairleigh Dickinson University Press, 1988).
15. The quote is from John Henrik Clarke, who says that Du Bois put it even more aptly, suggesting that black people were offered a "bribe" in which they would be granted more equal status in the United States in exchange for "the slavery of all mankind." See "Black America Fashions Its Foreign Policy," 13, John Henrik Clarke Papers, box 28, Schomburg Center for Research in Black Culture, New York Public Library, Astor, Lenox and Tilden Foundation.
16. John Kinloch to Aunt Charlotte, December 20, 1943, box 1 Additions, Bass Papers.
17. Ibid. The "heroic" speech to which he referred included sharp criticism of A. Philip Randolph.
18. See R. J. Smith, *The Great Black Way: L.A. in the 1940s and the Lost African-American Renaissance* (New York: Public Affairs, 2006), 29–30. Kinloch was optimistic that the movies were about to open up and that he would be able to sell some scripts.
19. She made an appeal on the grounds of Kinloch's vital service to the paper that was clearly unsuccessful. Letter fragment from Charlotta A. Bass, box 1 Additions, Bass Papers. In a letter to his mother explaining why he can't come East, Kinloch reveals the desperate financial situation the paper is in and how badly "Aunt Charlotte" needs him. In a fragment of a letter about his being drafted, he writes, "A preliminary investigation of my case revealed that *political pressure* had been exerted within the Selective Service System and that documented evidence prepared by my lawyer had been withheld from the draft appeal board." John to Mother, August 22, 1941; Dear Mother, July 4, 1943; box 2 Additions, Bass Papers. The US government's suspicion and monitoring of the black press has been well documented. See, for example, Patrick Washburn, *A Question of Sedition: The Federal Government's Investigation of the Black Press during World War II* (New York: Oxford University Press, 1986).
20. See his poem "A POME. FOR FOLKS. WHO WONDER. WHAT. THE HELL,"

quoted in Smith, *The Great Black Way,* 55–57. The poem begins with suspicion about the patriotism being whipped up and memories of the last war and ends with a call to combat Hitler and defend the fight for freedom as "COURAGEOUS, TO LIVE FOR, TO DIE FOR."

21. John Kinloch to Mother, November 16, 1944, box 1 Additions, Bass Papers.
22. "The danger of fascism in America is sharply reduced," he wrote, "when you have millions of soldiers with first-hand knowledge of the lying deception about 'the glory of war.'" John Kinloch to Mother, December 10, 1944, box 1 Additions, Bass Papers.
23. John Kinloch to Aunt Charlotte, January 2, 1945, box 1 Additions, Bass Papers. The letter is dated 1944, but this is clearly a mistake.
24. John Kinloch to Mom, Somewhere in France, September 14, 1944, box 1 Additions, Bass Papers.
25. John Kinloch to Mom, France, January 28, 1945, box 1 Additions, Bass Papers.
26. Flyer headed "For Action on Your Problems . . . Elect Charlotta A. Bass," n.d., box 1 Additions, Bass Papers.
27. See Erik McDuffie, "A 'New Freedom Movement of Negro Women': Sojourning for Truth, Justice, and Human Rights during the Early Cold War," *Radical History Review* 101 (Spring 2008): 81–106. Other clear links to the Communist Left, if we use guilt by association as a measure, included her serving on the national board of the Civil Rights Congress, signing on to the petition that William Patterson presented to the United Nations charging the US government with genocide against African Americans, and having an address book listing many other Communists and fellow travelers.
28. One such cause was that of Wesley Robert Wells, whose story Gerald Horne relates in *Communist Front?,* 323–27.
29. This was the sort of talk that led to the Peekskill Riots in August and September 1949 in which anticommunist attacks on Robeson and those who attended his concert there resulted in more than 150 people being sent to the hospital. On Peekskill and its aftermath, see Robbie Lieberman, *The Strangest Dream: Communism, Anticommunism and the U.S. Peace Movement, 1945–1963* (Syracuse, NY: Syracuse University Press, 2000), 73–80.
30. "Paul Robeson Sings in Los Angeles May 12, Auspices California Eagle," *California Eagle,* April 27, 1950, 1.
31. She mentioned the Moores in several speeches. This particular point was made in a 1952 campaign speech for the Progressive Party found in box 1 Additions, Bass Papers.
32. Charlotta A. Bass, "Notice of Libelous Statements Published and Demand for Retraction," August 31, 1948, box 1 Additions, Bass Papers. It is certainly possible that she was discouraged, like Robeson, from joining the Communist Party because she was of more use to the party if she did not formally become a member, but I have not found evidence to this effect.
33. Charlotta A. Bass, "The Sidewalk," *California Eagle,* May 11, 1950, 3, 5.
34. "Thousands Defy N.Y. Police Ban as They Gather for Peace Rally," *California Eagle,* August 4, 1950, 1.
35. Draft of speech for Brooklyn dinner, April 18, 1952, p. 7, box 1 Additions, Bass Papers.

36. California speech, 1952, p. 6, box 1 Additions, Bass Papers.

37. Ibid.

38. "National Affairs: Shocking Pink," *Time,* March 17, 1952. The language used to describe Bass was also code for calling her a lesbian. Thanks to Paula Rabinowitz for pointing this out.

39. August 14, 1956, letter from Marian Jackson, Iota Phi Lambda Sorority to Charlotta Bass, box 2; letter to "Dear Pastor," May 5, 1953, box 1 Additions, Bass Papers.

40. "The Sidewalk," *California Eagle,* April 26, 1951.

41. Suggestions for magazine, n.d., box 1 Additions, Bass Papers.

42. Bass wrote of the triple oppression of black women in a typescript of a speech in Brooklyn, p. 6. In an open letter to the editor of *Ebony* magazine, March 20, 1953, she critiqued the word "Negro" and suggested that the correct name for black people was "African Americans." Both documents are in box 1 Additions, Bass Papers.

43. Bass, *Forty Years,* 341–42. She applied for a social security card in Illinois, which shows a birth date of February 1890. "United States Social Security Death Index," FamilySearch. https://familysearch.org/pal:/MM9.1.1/JR2G-4TY. Charlotta Bass, April 1969, citing US Social Security Administration, Death Master File, database (Alexandria, Virginia: National Technical Information Service, ongoing).

44. See, for example, Mary McLeod Bethune, "'Closed Doors': Mary McLeod Bethune on Civil Rights," in *Sisters in the Struggle: African American Women in the Civil Rights–Black Power Movement,* edited by Bettye Collier-Thomas and V. P. Franklin (New York: New York University Press, 2001), 19. In a 1985 speech, Coretta Scott King said that "we cannot afford to separate peace from freedom and justice. World Peace cannot be achieved as long as massive poverty, racism, and repression are tolerated. And freedom and justice will remain a distant goal for millions of suffering people as long as the nuclear arms race and militarism are allowed to dominate the world economy." King is quoted in Juliet E. K. Walker, "War, Peace and Structural Violence: Peace Activism and the African-American Historic Experience," Occasional Paper No. 14, July 1992, Indiana Center on Global Change and World Peace, Indiana University, Bloomington.

45. The theory of structural violence was developed by Norwegian peace researcher Johan Galtung, but the idea (if not the term) was used by a number of peace proponents—Communists among them—who differentiated between what Martin Luther King, Jr. later called "positive peace," meaning the presence of justice, from "negative peace," the absence of war. Thus, the black Left in particular offered an important perspective that has not been duly noted.

46. Joyce Blackwell explores these issues to some extent in *No Peace without Freedom: Race and the Women's International League for Peace and Freedom, 1915–1975* (Carbondale: Southern Illinois University Press, 2004). Melinda Plastas, *A Band of Noble Women: Racial Politics in the Women's Peace Movement* (Syracuse, NY: Syracuse University Press, 2011) is more focused on internal dynamics as opposed to ideas. Marian Mollin has done the most to address both peace and freedom in a serious manner; see *Radical Pacifism in Modern America: Egalitarianism and Protest* (Philadelphia: University of Pennsylvania Press, 2011). From the freedom movement side, there is an acknowledgment, but no sustained discussion, of some black intellectuals' interest in peace in Kimberly Philips, *War! What Is It Good*

For? Black Freedom Struggles and the U.S. Military from World War II to the War in Iraq (Chapel Hill: University of North Carolina Press, 2012).

47. Flamming's work is the best example of this tendency as he views the attacks on her somewhat uncritically, but a number of other scholars just omit her peace activism and focus on what they see as her more positive legacy—that is, her earlier work challenging employment and housing discrimination. One of the strangest examples of missing the connections that Bass drew between peace, freedom, and equality comes toward the end of Streitmatter's chapter on her work as a journalist: "She ended one of her last speeches with a threat that could have as easily been delivered by Malcolm X. . . . 'Beware, ye nations of the world! The people are speaking out loudly and more coherently than ever before in their demand for peace and their share of the fruits of their labor.'" When did Malcolm X talk about "the people" and "their demand for peace"? Streitmatter, *Raising Her Voice,* 106.

48. See Robbie Lieberman, "Another Side of the Story': African American Intellectuals Speak Out for Peace and Freedom during the Early Cold War Years," in *Anticommunism and the African American Freedom Movement,* 38–40.

49. In Flamming's final chapter, titled "Departure," he suggests that Bass's "real departure was political." (Her physical departure was her move to Harlem, which was short-lived.) Flamming, *Bound for Freedom,* 365.

50. Again, the handful of scholars willing to seriously engage peace issues and the black Left include Jacqueline Foertsch, Jacqueline Castledine, Carole Boyce Davies, and Gerald Horne.

51. Alan Wald points out all this and more, including the story of the Treadway gun taught in the local public schools, one of which is named "Arsenal" (the Treadways are responsible for Link's murder). Yet his insightful and detailed analysis of the novel, of which there are few, does not lead him to consider that a desire for peace was part of Petry's outlook. See Alan Wald, *American Night: The Literary Left in the Era of the Cold War* (Chapel Hill: University of North Carolina Press, 2012), chap. 6.

52. Petry is quoted in Farah Jasmine Griffin, "Hunting Communists and Negroes in Ann Petry's *The Narrows,*" in Alex Lubin, *Revising the Blueprint: Ann Petry and the Literary Left* (Jackson: University Press of Mississippi, 2007), 141.

53. Ibid.

54. Robbie Lieberman, "'Measure Them Right': Lorraine Hansberry and the Struggle for Peace," *Science & Society* 75, no. 2 (April 2011): 206–35.

55. This is the major theme in Willard Motley's *We Fished All Night,* but he spells out how each of his three characters is destroyed by his military experience. Motley was a pacifist and a conscientious objector in World War II, yet another African American writer who linked peace and freedom.

56. Here we are reminded of John O. Killens's *And Then We Heard the Thunder* or even William Gardner Smith's *Last of the Conquerors,* in each of which it slowly dawns on the main character that the real enemy is not so much the Germans as the white Americans.

57. The essay, titled "Charlotta Bass" by Victoria E. Garten of St. Mary's Catholic School, won first place in the Middle School category of 2007 Black History Month essay winners and appears in Chelsea DeWeese, "Celebrating Black History Month in the West," *Arizona Daily Sun,* February 24, 2007, azdailysun.com/news/local/education/article_628bfe33-84d0-5e34-8c58-1acf3b8a7a8e.html.

[7]

Dancing for Stalin: Pauline Koner's "Russian Days" and the Question of Stalinism

Julia L. Mickenberg

Pauline Koner (1912–2001), an American dancer, choreographer, and student of former Ballet Russes choreographer Michel Fokine, arrived in Moscow on December 16, 1934, to begin a two-month tour of the Soviet Union at the invitation of the Soviet government. Koner, as she often told people, the "first American dancer officially invited to the Soviet Union since Isadora Duncan," had moved to the "new Russia" in 1921 to start a dance school.[1] Koner's stay in Russia, extended from two months to nearly two years, echoed the experience of that pioneering American dancer in significant ways.

Koner's arrival in Bolshevik Russia coincided with the funeral of Sergei Kirov, the popular Leningrad party chief and Joseph Stalin's potential successor. Koner watched the event from her hotel window.[2] As she peered through the glass at the "sad but beautiful spectacle," she remarked to herself that Russia had lost a "great person." Notwithstanding this quiet tribute in her diary, Koner was barely aware of the Kirov murder's significance, nor could she have been.[3]

Thirty years earlier, Isadora Duncan's initial visit to Russia was also framed through the lens of a funeral that portended revolutionary changes. Duncan claimed to have arrived in St. Petersburg in January of 1905 on the night of a funeral cortege for victims of the Bloody Sunday massacre, in which czarist troops attacked thousands of peaceful protestors. Duncan insisted that the sight of the funeral cortege convinced her to commit "[herself] and [her] forces to the service of the people and the down-trodden." Indeed, she remarked, "if I had never seen it, all my life would have been different."[4]

While the Bloody Sunday massacre launched the 1905 revolution (which failed but unleashed the energies that would culminate in 1917), Kirov's assassination would launch a very different kind of revolution. The Kirov assassination became the pretext for Stalin's launch of the Great Terror, in which more than a million people were accused of espionage, sabotage, and other anti-Soviet crimes, sent to prison camps, and murdered.[5] The coincidence of Kirov's murder with Koner's arrival in Moscow eerily foreshadowed the complicated dynamics of the Russian chapter in Koner's career.

Koner was twenty-two when she arrived in Moscow, exactly half as old as Duncan had been when at forty-four she came at the invitation of the Soviet government to live in the "new Russia," but close to Duncan's age at the time of her initial trip to czarist Russia in 1904–5. That visit and tours in 1908 and 1913 had earned Duncan a major following among imperial Russia's artistic avant-garde.[6] However, during the years Duncan actually made her home in Russia (from 1921 to 1924), her vision of liberating new Russia's youths through Duncan-style dance was largely unrealized. Her Moscow school was never adequately supported by the Soviet government, her dance was no longer appreciated (Soviet critics called her overweight, past her prime, and out of touch with the new ethos) and her love life was a disaster. (She married and within two years divorced the prominent Russian poet Sergei Esenin, who drank too much, abused Duncan, and eventually committed suicide).[7]

In contrast, we might say that Koner's Russian days were a great success, professionally and personally. She had more work than she could physically manage at a time when dancers in the United States were struggling under the impact of the Great Depression. Her dances were lauded by Russian critics and audiences. She taught at the Soviet Union's most prominent and prestigious institute of "physical culture," and her plans to establish her own dance group "to complete what Duncan began" appeared close to realization.[8] Finally, Koner discovered "physical love" with a man who respected her work and inspired her creatively.

But looked at in another way, Koner's Soviet sojourn failed to live up to its promise. True, Koner found professional success and love in Russia, but only at a high cost. She fell for a married man who had no intention of leaving his wife. Far more troubling, Koner's success was ultimately predicated on her accommodation to a Stalinist ethos. While in the Soviet Union, her dance and choreography gradually shifted from largely apolitical "ethnic" dances toward more political work as she, like Duncan before her, aimed to produce dances for Russia's "new youth."[9] In the final weeks of Koner's Soviet sojourn, she choreographed and performed a militaristic dance, witnessed by Stalin himself, as part of a seventy thousand–person physical culture parade held in Leningrad.

While Duncan would not live to write about her "Russian days," she did nothing during those days that she would later regret. Koner, in contrast, never fully acknowledged to American audiences what was clearly the culmination of her work in the Soviet Union. She was not well versed in "proletarian dance art" and only became (marginally) involved in the flourishing revolutionary dance movement in the United States after she returned from Russia.[10] It is Koner's simultaneous "not knowing" and active involvement, her literal performance of Stalinism and not just her coincidental arrival at the moment of Kirov's death, that make her a useful vehicle for thinking about the question of Stalinism for Americans who put their confidence in the Soviet project.

Duncan's characterization of dance as a spiritual or religious practice makes it an apt expressive mode for exploring the relationship that many people had to the Soviet Union, one that was grounded more in instinctive faith than in rational logic. "I salute the birth of the future international community of love," Duncan said of postrevolutionary Russia. "A new world, a newly created mankind; the destruction of the old world of class injustice, and the creation of a new world of equal opportunity." She aimed to bring her dance, "a high religious art," to this new mecca, where her "dancer of the future . . . whose body and soul have grown so harmoniously together that the natural language of the soul will have become the movement of the body" could help fulfill "the ideals of the new world."[11]

After 1917, Duncan and Koner were among the legions of American "new women" who closely watched events in the "new Russia" and, increasingly, went to experience the "new life" themselves: from suffragists celebrating women's franchise under the new regime following the revolution to reformers noting the Soviet provisions for maternal and child health to rebels against constricting sexual mores who marveled over the Soviet Union's free abortion and easy divorce.[12] But by the time of Koner's arrival in the mid-1930s, conservatives as well as a fair number of socialists and dissident Marxists associated Stalin's regime with violence and oppression. Even so, for a large part of the Left as well as many liberals, the Soviet Union still resonated with a revolutionary sense of democratic possibility and particularly with new possibilities for women.[13] This attitude persisted despite the fact that unexplained disappearances, including disappearing Americans, were already a regular feature of Soviet life, and violent retribution was an accepted mode of dealing with so-called enemies of the revolution—and had been since 1917.[14]

By the 1930s, optimism about the "new Russia" required greater and greater leaps of faith or willed ignorance. As Milly Bennett, a writer for Soviet Russia's first English-language newspaper, the *Moscow News,* flippantly wrote to a friend in 1932, "the thing you have to do about Russia is what you do about any other 'faith.' You set your heart to know they are right . . . and then, when you see things that shudder your bones, you close your eyes and say . . . 'facts are not important.'"[15]

What are the implications of ignoring "the facts" of Stalin's reign? Or of glorifying the man himself, even if that glorification was only a gesture, not something heartfelt? Alan Wald's scholarship has grappled with the legacy of Stalinism for the American Left and has offered a model for nuanced usage of a term that is often uncritically employed. In the context of US politics, "Stalinist" is often used as a blanket term for followers of the Communist Party USA (CPUSA) and, more specifically, to allude to their dogmatic qualities. Wald's work suggests that the term needs to be understood with greater precision to describe the way in which the CPUSA came to serve as "a bureaucratic instrument of the Thermidorean reaction in the Soviet Union" while recognizing that it was far from being entirely that for many committed activists in its ranks.[16] Wald argues that the CPUSA was both genuinely revolutionary in some respects—for example, in its efforts on behalf of workers and the unemployed and in its commitment to racial equality—but in other respects the Party bred ideological rigidity and undemocratic practices. Even more seriously, unquestioning loyalty to the Soviet Union among a large swath of the American Left led to widespread disavowal of and even justifications for state-sanctioned terror and repression. In this respect, Americans actually *in* Russia make for some of the most complicated case studies in Stalinism, for in this case the term is not simply an abstraction employed by opponents of the Popular Front milieu in the United States.

In the Soviet context, Stalinism meant something very specific, as David Hoffman, a historian of Russia, explains:

> Stalinism can be defined as a set of tenets, policies, and practices instituted

> by the Soviet government during the years in which Stalin was in power, 1928–1953. It was characterized by extreme coercion employed for the purpose of economic and social transformation. Among the particular features of Stalinism were the abolition of private property and free trade; the collectivization of agriculture; a planned, state-run economy and rapid industrialization; the wholesale liquidation of so-called exploiting classes, involving massive deportation and incarcerations; large-scale political terror against alleged enemies, including those within the Communist Party itself; a cult of personality deifying Stalin; and Stalin's virtually unlimited dictatorship over the country.[17]

In the Soviet context, an ethos of paranoia, fear, secrecy, and ideological rigidity defined the terms of daily life, particularly for Soviet citizens, to a large extent.

Even so, significant numbers of Americans of varying political persuasions (many of them not card-carrying members of the Communist Party) sought a kind of redemption in Soviet Russia.[18] "Dupe" seems both inadequate and inaccurate as a label for fellow travelers such as Koner. Echoing Duncan's notion of dance as religious expression, Koner told herself that she wanted to create the "New Soviet Dance," a "great new art" that would communicate "the triumphant joy the victory and hope of the new Russian Soviet life." And indeed, she tried to choreograph and perform dances that would communicate the vital spirit she felt that she witnessed among young people in the Soviet Union, people raised to believe in a socialist future. But by reading her diary, one gets the sense that although she loved working with Russian young people, what she really wanted was to develop as an artist, and she had found in Russia the opportunity for that to happen beyond anything she'd ever experienced. As she wrote in her diary within weeks after her arrival, "Today brought a great event in my life. My dancing and theories are taken seriously."[19]

The militarist performance with which Koner concluded her Russian days represented, above all, a desire to display her skills as a dancer and choreographer before a large audience filled with important people. But she also was deeply energized by her students, particularly the young women. As Roger Markwick notes of the generation who came of age in the 1930s, "this generation combined a sentimental, 'feminine' commitment to marriage, motherhood and Motherland with an inherent belief that they were 'strong women' and equal partners in the heroic Soviet project with men.'"[20] Even as the Stalinist regime emphasized motherhood and family life (outlawing abortion and divorce in 1936), rather than driving women out of the public sphere and into the home, both necessity and enthusiasm kept women in the workplace as well. Young women were widely celebrated in Stalinist culture as full partners in the Soviet projects of industrialization and mobilization for a war that seemed increasingly imminent. Koner, not much older than her students, was likely enthralled by the "cult of the heroine" that showcased the new Soviet woman "as an emancipated representative of progress and modernization."[21]

Why dance as a medium for considering Americans' relationship to Stalinism? Dance is written into the body; it is a language believed to be capable of communicating otherwise inexpressible inner feelings and truths. This notion, drawn from the ideas of French music theorist François Delsarte, who at the turn of the century developed a system of movements that he claimed corresponded to specific emotional states, informed Isadora Duncan's movement and her claims for "the dance's" power.[22] US dance critic John Martin's theory of metakinesis updated Delsarte to suggest dance's uniquely expressive properties: "Because of the inherent contagion of bodily movement, which makes the onlooker feel sympathetically in his own musculature the exertions he sees in somebody else's musculature, the dancer is able to convey through movement the most intangible emotional experience."[23]

Soviet theater director Vsevolod Meyerhold incorporated Delsartian thinking into his system of actor training, called biomechanics, that was based on the idea that "all psychological states are determined by specific physiological processes."[24] Meyerhold was a proponent of physical culture—an umbrella term for an array of physical education in the Soviet Union but one that emphasized the cultural dimensions of movement—and especially favored gymnastics. According to David Hoffman, "Soviet authorities . . . sought to shape the body as well as the mind, and in fact believed that physical exercise was essential to mental health and the transformation of consciousness. . . . Gymnastics emerged as a favored form of physical culture precisely because it taught not only discipline and control but also synchronization through group exercises believed to be capable of integrating and uniting individuals."[25]

Although Delsarte's ideas were influential in the Soviet Union, their impact was felt more directly in theater and film than in dance proper, primarily because of ballet's enduring place in Russian culture. What this meant was that American dancers, though cognizant of their debt to Russia's great traditions in dance (from the *Ballets Russes* to the performances of Anna Pavlova), believed that when it came specifically to modern dance technique, Russians had more to learn than to teach. "Revolutionary dancers" in the United States, like revolutionary writers, actors, artists, and filmmakers, closely watched developments in Russia after the Bolshevik Revolution, but they considered modern dance—a form far more popular in the United States than in the Soviet Union—to be more in tune with the new Soviet society than ballet was. Consequently, American dancers believed that they could make a unique contribution to further revolutionary developments in the arts.

Duncan, whose expressive dance is generally seen as the basis for modern dance, had envisioned dancers whose movements proclaimed the "freedom of woman." And she hoped to see her vision realized in a nation, Soviet Russia, that proclaimed "all humanity"—or at least all workers—as its constituency. However, Duncanism, seen as too ideologically amorphous, had lost its hold in Russia, arguably by the time Duncan settled there, but certainly by the late 1920s. As dance scholar Irina Sirotkina explains, by this time "The new aesthetic ideal was biomechanical exercises for healthy-looking workers and athletes, and not wave-like movements for girls in tunics."[26]

"Physical culture" became in the Soviet Union one of the only arenas for movements that in the United States might be classed as modern dance. Thus, it was not coincidental that Koner could only develop as a choreographer in the Soviet Union (and not simply as a dancer) once she became involved with the Lesgaft Institute of Physical Culture, an association that put her squarely within the Stalinist project of militarizing Soviet youths.[27]

A number of prominent modern dancers involved with the revolutionary dance movement in the United States, among them Edith Segal, Anna Sokolow, Mignon Garland, and Dhimah Meidman (all Jewish), made pilgrimages to Soviet Russia in the 1930s. In that decade, the revolutionary dance movement represented a significant trend within modern dance more broadly. For almost all these women, Isadora's influence was inescapable. Young Jewish women who studied "Duncan dance" at settlement houses in the 1910s became leading lights in the revolutionary dance movement in the 1930s; once in Russia, those who practiced "plastic dance" understood that they were being seen as inheritors of Duncan's lineage.[28]

Koner was of the same generation as Segal, Sokolow, and other leading figures in the revolutionary dance movement that thrived in New York City beginning in the 1930s, but she was only tangentially connected to it. (Koner performed in a number of shows sponsored by groups associated with the Left after her Russian tour, but on the whole she claimed to be more interested in creating art than in creating or performing "socially conscious works.") Though not specifically trained in Duncan-style dance, Koner recognized Duncan as an early influence and, as noted above, consciously imagined herself to be "complet[ing] what Duncan began" in the Soviet Union.[29] Koner was the daughter of secular Russian Jewish immigrants to the United States and grew up in the generally socialist milieu that encompassed a large proportion of immigrant Jews in New York City in the early twentieth century. Her father, a lawyer, developed a medical plan for the Workmen's Circle, a Jewish socialist fraternal organization founded in 1900.[30] In addition to ballet training with the Russian émigré Michel Fokine, Koner studied Spanish dance with Angel Casino, a well-known teacher of what was then a popular style of dance. At age seventeen Koner had toured with Michio Ito, a dancer from Japan who had been influenced by Duncan and the Ballet Russes (both of whom he saw in Europe) and by eurhythmics, a system of rhythmic movement that, like Delsartism, emphasizes kinesthetic awareness. Koner's New York solo concert debut (in 1930) was with another Japanese dancer, Yeichi Nimura, whose training in ballet and Spanish dance complemented his dance adaptations of traditional Japanese elements.[31]

Koner's eclectic training, exotic looks (she had long dark hair, olive skin, and high cheekbones), and tremendous adaptability launched her reputation as an ethnographic or neoethnic dancer, performing dances based on a variety of traditions, including many with a Far Eastern flavor. In 1932 and 1933, she spent nine months studying and dancing in Egypt and Palestine. A long-running interest in the East and in ancient civilizations drew her to Egypt, but she took a special interest in Palestine because of her Jewishness. Tel Aviv in the early 1930s was a "city of pioneers": there, alongside orthodox Jews praying, Koner saw "young settlers from the kibbutzim, energetic, sunburned, work-steeled bodies, and minds honed by the difficulties of survival—a look of life in their eyes and a warmth in their heart. . . . The atmosphere breathed enthusiasm, hope, and progress." Koner "felt vibrantly free, as if [she] had shed an invisible layer of skin, and proud of [her] Jewishness."[32]

Although Koner felt proudly Jewish while in Palestine, she performed "Jewish" dances—among the many styles in her repertoire—less as a Jew performing her own heritage and more as ethnographic interpretation. According to dance scholar Rebecca Rossen, "whether she was performing as an Indian priestess in *Nilamani* (1930), a Javanese temple dancer in *Altar Piece* (1930), or a Hasidic boy in *Chassidic Song and Dance* (1932), Koner separated herself from the ethnic material she used by presenting her work as creative interpretation and not authentic replication." Like Ruth St. Denis (a contemporary of Duncan's), Koner performed such dances in order to demonstrate her own universality, "or her ability to represent a variety of Others."[33]

Figure 7.1. Pauline Koner wearing a flamenco dress performing a Spanish dance, circa 1935–36. Photograph, Pauline Koner Papers, 1905–2000, New York Public Library for the Performing Arts. Credit: Jerome Robbins Dance Division, New York Public Library for the Performing Arts, Astor, Lenox and Tilden Foundations.

For many Jewish Americans with Russian roots, both Palestine and the Soviet Union were popular sites of "magic pilgrimage," both homelands of a sort with utopian promise, both places where "new people" were being created along with new civilizations.[34] While Palestine called as a Jewish homeland, the Soviet Union offered Jews with roots in Russia a chance to reformulate, now in terms of "class and political solidarity," their emotional connection to a land once known for its brutal oppression of Jews.[35] Indeed for Jews, as for African Americans, part of the Soviet Union's attraction was the possibility of having distinctions such as race or ethnicity no longer matter.[36]

Koner would not consciously go to Russia as a Jew, nor was she even particularly committed to the Soviet project (of "changing man" and reorganizing social and economic relations)—at least at first.[37] On a visit to the Soviet Union in 1934 for their twenty-fifth wedding anniversary that year, Koner's parents had presented her press book to the Soviet concert bureau. Possibly because of Koner's training with Fokine, officials were enthusiastic and almost immediately invited Koner to dance in the Soviet Union, offering her a round-trip ticket and a two-month contract with excellent pay. In the midst of the Depression, the offer sounded too good to be true.[38] Moreover, both the ethnic variety encompassed by the Soviet Union and the ostensible universality of Communist internationalism promised to take Koner's work in exciting new directions.

Over her two years in the Soviet Union, Koner had so many engagements she could barely keep up with her own schedule. Within the first few weeks she had performed a special concert for leading artists in Moscow with great success: "Now everyone is talking about me," she wrote in her diary. She met many of the great figures of the Soviet arts—Sergei Eisenstein, Vsevolod Meyerhold, Vsevolod Pudovkin, and others—and all of them took her work seriously, offering pointed commentary and welcoming her into a community of artists. In Leningrad at the Marinsky Ballet School she gave lessons in "oriental style," "Spanish style," "Fokine style," and her own style. "People were thrilled," Koner remarked in her diary as she marveled at her own success. She saw non-Russian minorities dance in their native styles, finding dances such as "the hunter's dance, the duck dance, and the shaman" to be "primitive but interesting." In contrast, she saw Russian attempts at modern dance as "banal" and without "nuance." Still, she had never experienced such "serious active interest in forwarding the dance art," and she felt that she had something unique to offer. "Russia needs a new form in its dancing. It knows what it wants as far as theme is concerned but its form is outdated. It's up to me to get those together and I shall."[39] As her two months were nearing their end, she decided that she wanted to stay in Russia: "I am being convinced slowly but surely that Russia is the place for me," she wrote in her diary. "The place where I can mold my future. It has the inspiration I need the possibilities I need. I am planning to start a group here, to start the new Russian dance. Perhaps my fate has all my life guided me to this point. . . . I am filled with new ideas and hopes."[40]

While she found Soviet *dance* less than inspiring, Koner was deeply affected by other aspects of life in Russia. For instance, she was entranced by her visit to a factory: by the immensity of the machines and the workers' pride, interest, and enthusiasm. And she was deeply moved by the spectacle of a May Day parade, by the "electric currents vibrat[ing] in the air" as Stalin passed and by the rhythmic movements of marchers through the square.[41]

As Koner came into her own professionally, she also discovered a new kind of love with the successful Soviet filmmaker Pudovkin, a married man twenty years her senior; their relationship was physical, intellectual, *and* creative: "He is a person whom I can admire, respect, and learn from," she wrote in her diary. "I do not feel as though I am only body only something to give sensation. I am a person am respected as such and an artist. To talk! To lose oneself in a wild enthusiasm! In the hot surging flame of creation!"[42]

After a year of touring, Koner was invited to teach at the Lesgaft Institute of Physical Culture in Leningrad. This work, though exhausting, was energizing, "stimulating, and creative.... The pupils in Leningrad are young and fresh, a new type of youth, Soviet youth," she wrote in her diary. "Full of enthusiasm, life, and energy, full of a desire to work and strength to accomplish. They are bubbling with ambition. I shall be able to create interesting compositions with them and hope to form a permanent group, a New Soviet Group."[43]

The Lesgaft students inspired Koner to choreograph her first dance in Soviet Russia: "The theme is the triumphant joy the victory and hope of the new Russian Soviet life. My subject is the red flag. I do not dance one who sees carries or feels the flag, no, I dance the flag itself. All its movement and all for which it stands." Noting this new composition, she began to seriously contemplate: "What will the new Soviet dance be?" Her notes here are choppy, confused: "find the definite themes such as the hope the health the youth the happiness of Soviet form...feeling of vigor delight of the new generation their desire to learn to grow to go ever higher and accomplish more. Yes that is the proper line to take." Yet Koner's certitude crumbled as she admitted almost in the same breath that her emotional state is "very bad," that she has realized the "impossibility" of her love for Pudovkin.[44] Her work became a respite from these emotions, but she also found it hard to separate the two, especially given Pudovkin's influence on her work.

After one of the first evenings Koner spent with Pudovkin (before their affair began) and his colleague, the scenarist Natan Zarchi, Koner had written of Pudovkin in her diary: "He is a strange, hysterical, but brilliant person and I may be able to get much inspiration from him."[45] Ten days later, she noted the "tremendous impression" she made on Pudovkin during a concert that evening,[46] and she described the discussion she had later that evening with him, Zarchi, and her interpreter Valia:

> We have discovered an interesting form of dance using contemporary dynamic music—legato move pause legato
> dynamic pause
> dynamic shorter—legato
> legato—legato
> pause
> dynamic dynamic
> final crescendo.
> We also discussed thematic material and how to attack thematic material. I am inspired and thrilled with new impetus to work. I am beginning to ori-

> ent myself to this mode and have a strong notion that I shall spend a much longer period in Russia than I originally planned perhaps I shall even make my headquarters here.[47]

Two days later, Koner spent much of the day reading Dalcroze's book *Eurythmics Art and Education,* noting to herself, "I find that I have instinctively been doing what Dalcroze advocates," and adding, "I am being convinced slowly but surely that Russia is the place for me."[48]

Emile Jacques-Dalcroze and François Delsarte were tremendously important to Soviet filmmakers, including Pudovkin, who, like other film and theater directors, drew upon Dalcroze's system of rhythmic gymnastics to understand ways in which sound and gestures could most effectively communicate human emotions.[49] Pudovkin likely recommended the book to Koner in order that she might think more systematically about the relationship between music, movement, and emotion (i.e., "thematic material"). Indeed, Pudovkin, who emerged as one of the leading filmmakers of the Stalin era (he was awarded the Stalin Prize in 1951) and whom scholars have since accused of "devot[ing] his great talent wholly to the service of the Party," proved instrumental in convincing Koner that her work should forward the goals of the revolution (i.e., should "view the new victory as your victory").[50]

A Leningrad newspaper describes Koner teaching "machine dances" (a variety of the dances pioneered by the Soviet composer Nikolai Foregger in which bodies mimic the movement of machines), but extant photographs point to the fact that Koner also embraced a more organic vision for the "new Soviet dance." Images from what appears to be a rehearsal on the Leningrad beach show young people in bathing suits moving in unison or posed in evocative *tableaux vivants.* Their collective gestures suggest freedom, joy, possibility, and dynamism, echoing the style cultivated by German *ausdruckstanz* (expressive dance) and also echoing Pudovkin's shots of expansive spaces with grasses swaying in the wind. Formations incorporate a primitively fashioned bow and arrow, sheets, and a crown of flowers worn by Koner. Dancers reach toward the sky, their arms gesturally repeating the leafy branches that several students grasp. Koner also dances solo, improvising for her students or perhaps for the photographer: she stretches, reaches, lunges, twists, kicks, bends, leaps, and even spirals in midair. Here we see something like an accommodation between Duncan-style "plastic dance" and the new Soviet physical culture.

The culmination of Koner's work in the Soviet Union was choreographing a "mass dance" as part of a seventy thousand–person Physical Culture parade that took place in Leningrad in July 1936, with Stalin himself in the audience. Physical Culture parades were a typical feature of Soviet mass meetings and celebrations, visible manifestations of youthful fitness and discipline.[51] This was Koner's first attempt at "group choreography." She recognized that it could mean "the beginning of an important phase in my career." But more important, she told herself, "it means interesting work for myself."[52] This was to be her "Dance of the New Youth."

Figure 7.2. Pauline Koner in the midst of a group of dancers from the Leograft Physical Culture Institute, Leningrad, 1936. Photograph, Pauline Koner Papers, 1905–2000. Credit: Jerome Robbins Dance Division, New York Public Library for the Performing Arts, Astor, Lenox and Tilden Foundations.

Figure 7.3. Pauline Koner performing an improvisational dance on a beach in Leningrad (now St. Petersburg), Russia, 1936. Photograph, Pauline Koner Papers, 1905–2000, New York Public Library for the Performing Arts. Credit: Jerome Robbins Dance Division, New York Public Library for the Performing Arts, Astor, Lenox and Tilden Foundations.

As suggested above, the position at the Lesgaft Institute for Physical Culture had placed Koner squarely within the only accepted arena for what might be called "modern dance" in the Soviet Union. Named for the "father" of physical education in Russia, Pyotre Lesgaft, a biologist, social reformer, and education theorist who gave special attention to sport as a vehicle for "women's social emancipation," the institute's program embodied the hybrid projects of physical culture and women's empowerment under Stalin. In the Stalin era, a principal aim of Lesgaft's institute was to determine ways to "utilize physical exercise rationally to improve productivity," a project that evolved to encompass physical culture's emphasis, by the mid-1930s, on military preparation.[53] Physical culture was simultaneously a tool for cultivating "an individual with the harmonious development of mental and bodily strengths," an instrument of building workers' labor capacity, and a means of inculcating discipline and fitness for battle.[54] These were projects that many young Soviet women of the 1930s internalized as their own.[55]

Dance taught under the rubric of "physical culture" was to be collective, vigorous, and easily intelligible to the masses; these ideas inspired elements of the revolutionary dance movement in the United States but also echoed totalitarian mass dances of Nazi Germany, which converted *ausdruckstanz* into National Socialist spectacles.[56] In the Soviet Union, mass spectacles became increasingly commonplace, as a "new outbreak of festivity" accompanied intensification of "the purges and political repression of the Soviet elite" and as "most of the Soviet population struggled with poverty and deprivation."[57] But we would be wrong to assume that the massive demonstrations of collective unity under Stalin were entirely orchestrated by Soviet authorities without the consent of those performing. Recent scholarship on "Soviet subjectivities" emphasizes the ways in which Stalinism "gave common people [in the Soviet Union] an uncommon opportunity to reflect on themselves and constitute their identities and a sense of subjectivity."[58] This had particular importance for women. As suggested earlier, Stalinism produced a hybrid identity for young women growing up in the mid-1930s—that is, for the young women who would have been Koner's pupils and her inspiration. On the one hand, women at this time were encouraged to embrace motherhood and marriage; on the other hand, stories of women's successes—in such varied fields as "aviation, defense, agriculture, industry, and sports"—served "as a gendered justification of the modernity of the regime" but also held meaning for many young women, whose displays of strength, agility, flexibility, and rhythm in Physical Culture parades can be seen as scripted but authentic performances of attempts to embody the new Soviet woman.[59]

Koner's memoir barely says anything about the actual performance of her "Dance of the New Youth," and her Russian diary ends before the performance, stopping with the struggle she faced over the "ideological correctness" of having the dancers create a star formation. "I felt it symbolized the force [of] the new generation. . . . But everyone was extremely wary of chancing criticism," she lamented in her memoir. She came up with an alternative that consisted, she said, of "just some brilliant movement that would catch the eye."[60] There are a couple of news clippings in Koner's scrapbook with photographs that made me wonder what, exactly, the performance entailed. One article in particular has a startling headline, recognizable even to someone whose Russian skills leave much to be desired. The Leningrad sports newspaper *Spartak* featured a photo of the Lesgaft students' performance beneath Stalin's famous words, now evoked only as an ironic reminder of his regime's hypocrisy: "Life has become better comrades. Life has become joyful."

Спартак

ОРГАН ЛЕНИНГРАДСКОГО ОБЛАСТНОГО СОВЕТА ФИЗИЧЕСКОЙ КУЛЬТУРЫ

„Жить стало лучше, товарищи. Жить стало веселее" И. В. СТАЛИН

ЛЕНИНГРАДСКАЯ ПРАВДА

Figure 7.4. News clipping showing Koner's students performing in Leningrad physical culture parade, on front page of sports paper, *Spartak*, under statement by Stalin: "Life has become better, comrades. Life has become joyful." September 12, 1936. Pauline Koner Papers, 1905–2000, New York Public Library for the Performing Arts. Credit: Jerome Robbins Dance Division, New York Public Library for the Performing Arts, Astor, Lenox and Tilden Foundations.

Koner's scrapbook also contains a clipping from *Pravda*. The date in the scrapbook is wrong, so at first I did not realize it described the 1936 Leningrad parade and her students' performance, "Dance of the New Youth," until I found the same clipping on microfilm as I was trying to find out more about the performance. Translating the article proved revealing. *Pravda* describes the dancers in their white, blue, yellow, orange, and red jerseys, whirling and then freezing in place on a giant Soviet emblem (the shape of the emblem is unspecified in the article). The performance is said to take on "new power" as Koner herself joined the Lesgaft students:

> On the square rose a border pole. Suddenly there arrives a detachment of defenders of the Soviet borders. Unexpectedly, from an enclosure jumps a saboteur unit. With baited breath, all of the square expressed, through bayonets, the fervent courage of Soviet border guards. Here already gathered a handful of brave souls. The saboteurs rush the Soviet territory, but the new detachment of border guards turns out to cruelly resist them. The enemy is beaten. His pathetic remnants flee, etc. The victorious thunder "Oora!"[61]

Contrary to my own romantic impression of Koner and her students forming organic *tableaux vivants* on the Leningrad beach, I suddenly had to acknowledge and come to terms with the fact that Koner had choreographed and participated in a militaristic spectacle showing defenders of the Soviet borders crushing supposed saboteurs. "I had heard rumors that there were political trials going on, but knew very little about them," Koner wrote in her memoir about her final months in Russia, in words that suggest her dissociation from Soviet political machinations. Later in her memoir, she mentions the "Stalin purge." Nowhere does she describe the dance she choreographed for the parade, nor does her memoir mention that Stalin and other Bolshevik leaders were in the audience. All she says is that "the performance on the great Palace Square was quite a spectacle, and the newspaper reviews were excellent."[62]

Koner left the Soviet Union immediately after the Physical Culture parade. She had been invited to continue her work at Lesgaft and had purchased a round-trip ticket with plans to return after a two-month visit with her family in the United States. But when it came time to go back, foreigners were no longer being admitted to the Soviet Union. Koner was disappointed, but she recognized that the real draw for her was Pudovkin, who could never fully give himself to her, for he still loved his wife.

As with many of the people Alan Wald has written about, Koner is not usually remembered as having any affiliation with the Left. The Federal Bureau of Investigation kept a file on her but noted only a handful of performances she gave in the late 1930s and early 1940s in the United States supporting the Soviet Union or Spain. But her "Russian days" clearly made their mark on her. She is open in her memoir about having had positive experiences in the Soviet Union and the cover of her popular dance technique textbook shows a picture of Koner dancing, seemingly hanging midair, against the backdrop of the Leningrad beach (see figure 7.3).[63] The implication would seem to be that this place and this moment represented the culmination of Koner's technical development.

What, then, do we make of the massive performance for Stalin, Molotov, etc., that Koner choreographed or her desire to create the "New Soviet Dance"? Perhaps this entire project was, for her, another ethnographic act, an experiment performing another persona, undertaken not as an expression of faith but as a chance for "interesting work" that would advance an ambitious, talented young woman's career. Or maybe, at least for a moment, she found something of the Stalinist project actually inspiring. As David Hoffman notes, while being "among the most repressive and violent [regimes] in all human history," the

Soviet Union "sought to cultivate educated, cultured citizens who would transcend petty-bourgeois instincts and contribute willingly to a harmonious social order."[64] Couple this with the image of the Soviet "superwoman," and for an outsider who was young and not fully cognizant of Stalinism's terrible costs, dancing for Stalin could have been thrilling.[65]

Koner's experiences point to the Soviet Union as a space of possibility for American women at a particular historical moment. But they also point to the limits of that possibility. Koner's self-development as well as her professional development in the Soviet Union are ultimately inseparable from the fact that she made a conscious choice to choreograph and perform in ways that explicitly expressed support for an ethos that consolidated and rationalized repressive state power and unfathomable violence. In this context, Koner's gravity-defying leaps on the Leningrad beach must be understood as likewise denying the weight of the history they embodied.

Notes

1. Pauline Koner, "Working with Doris Humphrey," *Dance Chronicle* 7, no. 3 (1984): 235.
2. Isadora Duncan, *My Life* (New York: Norton, 1995), 119; Pauline Koner, Russia diary, December 16, 1934, Pauline Koner Papers, New York Public Library for the Performing Arts (hereafter Koner Diary). Transcriptions from the diary retain their original punctuation.
3. Koner Diary, December 16, 1934.
4. Isadora Duncan, *My Life* (1927; reprint, New York: Norton, 1995), 119. In fact, Duncan arrived in St. Petersburg earlier (there are reviews in her papers of performances she gave in December 1904, and the massacre did not occur until January). See review in *Novoya Vremya* [New Times] (St. Peterburg), December 15, 1904, 13–14, translated by Natalia Roslaveva, Irma Duncan Collection of Isadora Duncan Materials, New York Public Library for the Performing Arts.
5. Matthew E. Lenoe, *The Kirov Murder and Soviet History,* translations by Matthew E. Lenoe, documents compiled by Mikhael Prozumenschikov (New Haven, CT: Yale University Press, 2010). There is great debate among scholars concerning the number of people affected by the Great Terror. On the high end, Robert Conquest estimated that 20 million people were arrested, imprisoned, or killed. See Robert Conquest, *The Great Terror: A Reassessment,* 40th anniversary ed. (Oxford: Oxford University Press, 2008), 485–86. Recent work based on archival evidence suggests that numbers were considerably lower though still very high: about 2.5 million people were arrested or imprisoned during the Great Terror (for both political and nonpolitical reasons), and nearly 700,000 were executed. Combined, 1.5 million people were either shot or died in prison or exile. Wendy Z. Goldman, *Terror and Democracy in the Age of Stalin: The Social Dynamics of Repression* (Cambridge: Cambridge University Press, 2007), 5. I am especially indebted to Lisa Kirschenbaum, "Making Sense of Stalinism: Coercion and Enthusiasm," in

Russia's Long Twentieth Century: Contested Voices, Memories, and Perspectives, edited by Choi Chatterjee, Deborah Field and Lisa Kirschenbaum (New York: Routledge, forthcoming). Kirschenbaum referred me to the seminal article, J. Arch Getty, Gabor T. Rittersporn, and Victor N. Zemskov, "Victims of the Soviet Penal System in the Pre-War Years: A First Approach on the Basis of Archival Evidence," *American Historical Review* 98, no. 4 (October 1993): 1017–49.

6. On Duncan's years in postrevolutionary Russia, see Irma Duncan and Allan Ross Macdougall, *Isadora Duncan's Russian Days and Her Last Years in France* (New York: Covici Friede, 1929); Ilya Schneider, *Isadora Duncan: The Russian Years,* translated by David Magarshack (New York: Harcourt, Brace & World, 1968). On Duncan's reception in Russia, especially in the early years, see Elizabeth Souritz, "Isadora Duncan's Influence on Dance in Russia," *Dance Chronicle* 18, no. 2 (1995): 281–91; T.S Kasatkina, E.IA. Surits, *Aisedora: Gastroli v Rossii* (Moskva: Izd-vo Artist, Rezhisser, Teatr, 1992).
7. Duncan and Macdougall, *Isadora Duncan's Russian Days.* The most scathing reviews of Duncan's performances are from the prominent Soviet critic V. Iving. See, for example, "Revolutionary Dances" (1924?), (manuscript), RGALI, f. 2694, op. 1, d. 4, Moscow. Translation by Andrey Bredstein.
8. Koner Diary, May 1–31, 1935.
9. She choreographed her first dance in Russia in December 1935, thinking specifically about creating "the New Soviet dance." Koner Diary, December 24, 1935.
10. Koner Diary, May 1–31, 1935.
11. Isadora Duncan, "Moscow Impressions," in *The Art of the Dance,* edited by Sheldon Cheney (New York: Theatre Arts, 1928), 110, 109. See also in the same volume Isadora Duncan, "The Dance of the Future," 54–63, and Isadora Duncan, "Dancing in Relation to Religion and Love," 121–27.
12. Little has been written on American women's romance with revolutionary Russia. See Choi Chatterjee, "'Odds and Ends of the Russian Revolution,' 1917–1920: Gender and American Travel Narratives," *Journal of Women's History* 20, no. 4 (2008): 10–33. On suffragists, see Julia L. Mickenberg, "Suffragettes and Soviets: American Feminists and the Specter of Revolutionary Russia," *Journal of American History* 100, no. 4 (March 2014): 1021–51. For a more fleshed-out discussion, see Julia L. Mickenberg, *The New Woman Tries on Red: Russia in the American Feminist Imagination, 1905–1945* (Chicago: University of Chicago Press, forthcoming).
13. Christine Stansell describes revolutionary Russia as "a momentous fact" for the bohemian avant-garde in downtown New York and notes of these "Moderns" that "many poured their considerable faculties into endowing the new Soviet Union with an imaginative democracy that stretched across the world to include them." Christine Stansell, *American Moderns: Bohemian New York and the Creation of a New Century* (New York: Metropolitan Books, 2000), 321.
14. Conquest, *The Great Terror,* 3–22; Tim Tzouliadis, *The Forsaken: An American Tragedy in Stalin's Russia* (New York: Penguin, 2008).
15. Milly Bennett, letter to "Florence," January 27, 1932, Milly Bennett Papers, box 2, folder 1 (unidentified correspondence, 1932–1933), Hoover Library, Palo Alto, California.
16. Alan M. Wald, *The New York Intellectuals: The Rise and Decline of the Anti-Stalinist Left from the 1930s to the 1980s* (Chapel Hill: University of North Carolina Press, 1987), 147. The relevant scholarship on the anti-Stalinist debate with Popular Front

leftists is too large to recount, but see, for example, William L. O'Neill, *A Better World: The Great Schism; Stalinism and American Intellectuals* (New York: Simon and Schuster, 1982); Judy Kutulas, *The Long War: The Intellectual People's Front and Anti-Stalinism, 1930–1940* (Durham, NC: Duke University Press, 1995). See also Eugene Lyons, *The Red Decade: The Stalinist Penetration of America* (New York: Bobbs-Merrill, 1941).

17. David L. Hoffman, "Introduction: Interpretations of Stalinism," in *Stalinism: The Essential Readings,* edited by David L. Hoffman (Malvern, MA, and Oxford, UK: Blackwell, 2003), 2.

18. Sheila Fitzpatrick, *Everyday Stalinism: Ordinary Life in Extraordinary Times; Soviet Russia in the 1930s* (New York: Oxford University Press, 1999). There are a number of sources discussing American travelers to the Soviet Union in the 1920s and 1930s. See, for example, Sylvia Margulies, *The Pilgrimage to Russia: The Soviet Union and the Treatment of Foreigners, 1924–1937* (Madison: University of Wisconsin Press, 1968); Lewis S. Feuer, "American Travelers to the Soviet Union, 1917–1932: The Formation of a Component of New Deal Ideology," *American Quarterly* 24 (Summer 1962), 119–49; Paul Hollander, *Political Pilgrims: Western Intellectuals in Search of the Good Society* (New Brunswick, NJ: Transaction Publishers, 1998); Ludmilla Stern, *Western Intellectuals and the Soviet Union, 1920–1940: From Red Square to the Left Bank* (New York: Routledge, 2007); Michael David-Fox, *Showcasing the Great Experiment: Cultural Diplomacy and Western Visitors to the Soviet Union* (New York: Oxford University Press, 2011).

19. Koner Diary, December 24, 1935, and January 30, 1935.

20. Roger D. Markwick and Euridice Charon Cardona, *Soviet Women on the Frontlines during the Second World War* (London: Palgrave Macmillan, 2012), 8.

21. Ibid.

22. Ted Shawn, *Every Little Movement* (Brooklyn, NY: Dance Horizons, 1963); Genevieve Stebbens, *Delsarte System of Expression* (New York: E. S. Werner, 1887). On Delsarte's influence, see Hillel Schwartz, "Torque: The New Kinesthetic of the Twentieth Century," in *Incorporations,* edited by Jonathan Crary and Sanford Kwinter, 71–126 (New York: Zone, 1992).

23. John Martin, "Dance as a Means of Communication" (1946), in *What Is Dance: Readings in Theory and Criticism,* edited by Roger Copeland (New York: Oxford University Press, 1983), 146.

24. David L. Hoffman, "Bodies of Knowledge: Physical Culture and the New Soviet Man," in *Language and Revolution: Making Modern Political Identities,* edited by Igal Halfin (New York: Routledge, 1992), 231.

25. Ibid., 230.

26. Pauline Koner, *Solitary Song* (Durham, NC: Duke University Press, 1989), 145–46. Duncan's final dances in Russia were more in this style as well. See Ann Daly, "The Continuing Beauty of the Curve: Isadora Duncan and Her Last Compositions," *Ballet International* 13, no. 8 (August 1990): 10–15. Even so, Duncanism was by this time firmly understood as "wave-like movements for girls in tunics." Irina Sirotkina, "Dance-*Plyaska* in Russia of the Silver Age," *Dance Research* 28, no. 2 (2010): 146.

27. David L. Hoffman, *Cultivating the Masses: Modern State Practices and Soviet Socialism, 1914–1939* (Ithaca, NY: Cornell University Press, 2011), 110.

28. On the proletarian or revolutionary dance movement and Duncan's influence

on young Jewish dancers, see Ellen Graff, *Stepping Left: Dance and Politics in New York City, 1928–1932* (Durham, NC: Duke University Press, 1997), 18; Mark Franko, *Dancing Modernism/Performing Politics* (Bloomington: Indiana University Press, 1995), 25–26, 109–44. Also on Duncan's influence, see Edith Segal Oral History, Edith Segal Papers, New York Public Library for the Performing Arts. For commentary about dance in the Soviet Union, see, for example, Leonard Dal Negro, "Return from Moscow: An Interview with Anna Sokolow," *New Theatre* (December 1934): 27.

29. Koner performed at a Lenin-Liebknecht-Luxemburg memorial sponsored by the Young Communist League on January 15, 1937 (Graff, *Stepping Left,* 48). Koner discusses her "socially conscious" dances in *Solitary Song,* where she recalls a costume her mother made for her as a child, "a little chiffon tunic trimmed with rosebuds, and a little wreath for my hair." Wearing that costume, Koner "would do these dances that now, I realize, were very close to the Duncan style. It was called 'interpretive dancing.' But I just did free movement that came out from the inside" (114). One of her great regrets, in fact, was that she never got to see Duncan actually dance: as child Koner saw a poster of Duncan, and her mother promised to take her to one of Duncan's concerts when she was next in the United States, but Duncan never came back. Pauline Koner Oral History with Peter Conway, 1975, Pauline Koner Papers. Koner's papers contain a file devoted to Isadora Duncan.

30. Koner, *Solitary Song,* 2.

31. Ibid., 18, 23–55. On Ito, see the Michio Ito Foundation, http://www.michioito.org/. On Nimura, "Inventory of the Yeichi Nimura and Lisan Kay Nimura Papers, 1903–2006," New York Public Library, http://www.nypl.org/sites/default/files/archivalcollections/pdf/Nimura_1.pdf.

32. Koner, *Solitary Song,* 68.

33. Rebecca Rossen, "Hasidic Drag: Jewishness and Transvestism in the Modern Dances of Pauline Koner and Hadassah," *Feminist Studies* 37, no. 2 (Summer 2011): 340. Koner did perform an anti-Hitler dance in 1933 and frequently performed at events sponsored by Jewish groups. See "Pauline Koner, Brilliant 21-Year-Old Dancer, Greatly Incensed at Adolf," *Jewish Examiner,* June 1933.

34. Claude McKay, *A Long Way from Home,* edited by Gene Andrew Jarrett (New Brunswick, NJ: Rutgers University Press, 2007), 118. The phrase "magic pilgrimage" comes from McKay's description of his 1922 trip to the Soviet Union, and the phrase "new people" is a rough translation of the popular Soviet ideal of a *novy sovetsky chelovek,* or new Soviet person. For further discussion, see Kate A. Baldwin, *Beyond the Color Line and the Iron Curtain: Reading Encounters between Black and Red, 1922–1963* (Durham, NC: Duke University Press, 2002), 18.

35. Daniel Soyer, "Back to the Future: American Jews Visit the Soviet Union in the 1920s and 1930s," *Jewish Social Studies* 6, no. 3 (2000): 125.

36. Ibid.; Koner, *Solitary Song,* 94. She mentions seeing King Lear at the Jewish State Theater in her diary (and being impressed with it), Koner Diary, March 4, 1935. Photographs suggest that she may have also performed one of her "Jewish dances" in Russia, although she does not mention this in her diary or memoir.

37. Beatrice King, *Changing Man: The Education System of the U.S.S.R* (London: V. Gollancz, 1936).

38. Koner, *Solitary Song,* 80.

39. Koner Diary, January 27, 1935.

40. Ibid., February 3, 1935.
41. Ibid., May 1, 1935.
42. Ibid., March 8, 1935.
43. Ibid., December 24, 1935.
44. Ibid., December 24, 1935.
45. Ibid., January 21, 1935.
46. Ibid., February 1, 1935.
47. Ibid.
48. Ibid., February 1, 1935.
49. Mikhail Yampolsky, "Kuleshov's Experiments and the New Anthropology of the Actor," in *Inside the Film Factory,* edited by Richard Taylor, 31–34 (New York: Taylor and Francis, 1994). For Pudovkin's writing on the role of gymnastics and movement in film, see Vsevolod Pudovkin, "The Internal and the External in an Actor's Training" (1938), in *The Film Factory,* edited by Richard Taylor, 393–97 (London: Routledge, 1988).
50. Paul Babitsky and John Rimberg, *The Soviet Film Industry* (New York: Praeger, 1955), 122, qtd. in Amy Sargeant, *Vsevolod Pudovkin: Classic Films of the Soviet Avant Garde* (London: Tauris, 2000), vii. An undated letter (1935 or 1936) from Pudovkin to Koner emphasizes the importance of dance ("dance is the most immediate the most inartificial art"), and urges Koner to "view the new victory as your own victory." Pudovkin to Koner, n.d. (folder labeled ca. 1935–1936), Koner Papers, box 3, folder 8.
51. Karen Petrone, *Life Has Become More Joyous Comrades: Celebrations in the Time of Stalin* (Princeton, NJ: Princeton University Press, 2000), 1.
52. Koner Diary, April 9, 1936.
53. James Riordan, *Sport in Soviet Society: Development of Sport and Physical Education in Russia and the USSR* (Cambridge: Cambridge University Press, 1977), 20, 53, 146.
54. Hoffman, *Cultivating the Masses,* 115.
55. Ibid., 10–24.
56. Mary Anne Santos Newhall, "Uniform Bodies: Mass Movement and Modern Totalitarianism," *Dance Research Journal* 34, no. 1 (Summer 2002): 27–50.
57. Petrone, *Life Has Become More Joyous Comrades,* 1. See also Jane Dudley, "The Mass Dance," *New Theatre* (December 1934): 17–18; Graff, *Stepping Left;* Erika Fischer-Lichte, *Theatre, Sacrifice, Ritual: Exploring Forms of Political Theatre* (New York: Routledge, 2005); Susan Manning, *Ecstasy and the Demon: The Dances of Mary Wigman* (Minneapolis: University of Minnesota Press, 2006); Hoffman, *Cultivating the Masses*.
58. Choi Chatterjee and Karen Petrone, "Models of Selfhood and Subjectivity: The Soviet Case in Historical Perspective," *Slavic Review* 67, no. 4 (2008): 978. Chatterjee and Petrone are here referring particularly to the work of Igor Halfin and Jochen Hellbeck, who draw on Foucault's concept of the self.
59. Choi Chatterjee, *Celebrating Women: Gender, Festival Culture, and Bolshevik Ideology, 1910–1939,* Pitt Series in Russian and East European Studies (Pittsburgh: University of Pittsburgh Press, 2002), 140.

60. Koner Diary, n.d. (but under the April 9, 1936, entry, final entry in diary); Koner, *Solitary Song*, 107.
61. "Fizikyltyriy Parad v Leningrade," *Pravda*, July 13, 1936, 1 (my translation).
62. Koner, *Solitary Song*, 108, 110.
63. Pauline Koner, *Elements of Performance: A Guide for Performers in Dance, Theatre, and Opera*, Choreography and Dance Studies (Chur, Switzerland, and Langhorne, PA: Harwood Academic, 1993).
64. Hoffman, *Cultivating the Masses*, 1.
65. On the Soviet "superwoman" see Markwick and Cardona, *Soviet Women on the Frontlines during the Second World War*, 33.

[8]

The Revolutionary Meets the Capitalist: Robert Cantwell's Nonfiction Novel about Boston Magnate E. A. Filene

T. V. Reed

Writer Robert Cantwell is widely regarded as one of the two or three best novelists to emerge from the proletarian literary movement in the 1930s. He published one fine novel, *Laugh and Lie Down* (1931), and a second brilliant one, *The Land of Plenty* (1934), but then disappeared from the literary scene. What happened to this extremely talented young writer? Why was his fiction career cut short? The answer to such questions is always complex and multifaceted, but one strange twist in his situation played a significant role in what became a spiral away from fiction writing for the young writer from the Northwest. In a 1950 letter to Ernest Hemingway, Cantwell wrote that he had finished *The Land of Plenty* at "forced draft" in order that he might begin work on a new, very different project: the biography of millionaire department store magnate Edward A. Filene.[1] The proposed biography, commissioned by Filene himself and supervised by muckraking journalist Lincoln Steffens, occupied Cantwell from late 1933 until early 1935. The work was never published and is largely unknown even to those with an interest in Cantwell's fiction. Extant fragments of his manuscript in his papers at the University of Oregon Knight Library describe a fascinating encounter between the aging progressive capitalist and his extremely hostile biographer, an encounter that the latter transformed into a symbolic struggle between reformism and revolution.[2]

Late in 1933, Filene, who had made his fortune by expanding the idea of the "bargain basement" into a multimillion-dollar merchandising operation in the city of Boston, felt that it was time to have the story of his long career recorded for posterity.[3] As the apostle of enlightened self-interest among American capitalists, he had championed a number of progressive causes unpopular with his robber baron peers but aimed at bettering the lot of the masses upon whose purchasing power he felt the continued success of capitalism depended. The story he putatively wanted to tell was one not only of success but also of the failure to create a more progressive form of capitalism. Claiming to detest the familiar testimonials of other millionaires, Filene hired an old friend but a stern critic, Lincoln Steffens, to oversee the writing of his biography.[4]

Steffens, then in his late sixties and in poor health, set about in November 1933 to find a younger writer to bear the major burden of composing the projected work. He first sought the services of Whittaker Chambers, whose short stories in the *New Masses* he had admired for being both "proletarian and literary."[5] But Chambers declined his offer, and Steffens turned next to Cantwell, apparently on Chambers's recommendation. Cantwell struggled with the decision. Some of his literary colleagues, including John Dos Passos and Meyer Schapiro, advised him to do it. Others, especially his then boss Malcolm Cowley, were set against it (in fact, Cowley later came to believe that it ruined Cantwell as a writer by distracting him from fiction in his prime). Pressed by his ever practical wife Betsy, lured by the offer of a substantially higher salary, and with the assurance that Filene would not interfere in the writing of his biography, Cantwell accepted, quit his job at the *New Republic,* and made plans to move his family into an apartment next door to Filene's Boston mansion.[6]

Steffens's reasons for selecting Cantwell are not clear, but given that Chambers had been his first choice, it is clear that the old muckraker's choice of a radical to write the millionaire's life story was an intentionally provocative one likely to lead to something less than harmonious cooperation. In their initial discussion, Steffens had told Cantwell that Filene's career could illustrate an important point: "in itself [it] proved that American business, that capitalism, could not be reformed or reform itself."[7] Such was surely not the lesson intended by Filene, who remained a dedicated progressive, and thus from its inception the proposed biography was a battleground of conflicting interests and conceptions.

When Cantwell was offered the role of biographer, his only knowledge of Filene was an exclamation by Vladimir Lenin he remembered from a biography of the Bolshevik revolutionary: "So, Mr. Filene! You believe that all the workers of all the world are fools!"[8] Why should a man who could elicit such an outburst from Lenin, Cantwell mused, wish to hire Steffens and himself, neither of whom, the latter noted with understatement, were "known for a particularly uncritical attitude towards the methods and practices of capitalists," to write the story of his life? Cantwell made discreet inquiries among friends and acquaintances of the elderly merchant and could elicit little but negative responses to questions about Filene's character—"pretentious bore," "self-centered," and "untrustworthy" being typical. But each description seemed to add complexity and contradiction and the "more Balzacian and cryptic Filene seemed," the more intrigued the novelist in Cantwell became.[9]

The manuscript of Cantwell's projected Filene biography actually consists of two separate and quite different works. One is a rather straightforward work originally cast as a biography but later transformed into a ghostwritten autobiography through the substitution of "I" for "he" at appropriate points throughout. But by far the more interesting work is a 250-page manuscript in which Cantwell interweaves the details of Filene's life with a description of the initial encounters between the capitalist and his "very Desperate Ambrose of a biographer."[10] (Cantwell refers to himself throughout in the third person as "the biographer" or "the author.") Over time, both Steffens and Cantwell came to see this second text as an extension of the latter's literary work, a text in essence anticipating what would later come to be known as the nonfiction novel. Early in the manuscript, "the biographer" notes that his aim, like that of Steffens, is to use Filene's life to reveal the impossibility of reforming capitalism. But to this he adds a second reason more suited to his skills as a political novelist: to discover how a millionaire's mind worked and particularly "how [capitalists] justified to themselves the exploitation on which their wealth was based."[11]

Like James Agee with whom he later worked, Cantwell detested patronizing studies of the poor and dispossessed, "those smug and dehumanized inquiries into the social customs of delinquent women, or slum dwellers, or foreign language groups, or Kentucky miners." Noting that at the time of "this writing" a monthly magazine was publishing a series of articles by a Smith College graduate who had gone to live among the miners of Pennsylvania, Cantwell suggested that he would prefer that "a striking miner . . . go to live among the girls of Smith College, and report on their practices and beliefs." In lieu of that study, he hoped that his report on the practices of a millionaire might offer a similar antidote to such "presumptuous social studies."[12]

But Cantwell's study of the habits and beliefs of a capitalist almost ended before it had begun. In December 1933, he met Filene for the first time (at the latter's home on Otis Place, a mansion formerly owned by Filene's lawyer and friend Louis Brandeis).[13] The first words the millionaire spoke to his would-be biographer informed him that Lincoln Steffens had recently suffered a stroke and that the project would probably be canceled (without Steffens's oversight, Filene would not approve the book). Upon hearing this, Cantwell grew secretly enraged that no one had bothered to inform him of this turn of events sooner. Had he been notified promptly he would "not have quit his job, or gone into debt, or moved his family to Boston."[14]

When Filene began asking a series of naive and seemingly unrelated questions, Cantwell's outrage turned to suspicion and defensiveness. "His [the author's] distrust of capitalists in general, and of Filene in particular, was so great that he was convinced" that the millionaire's inquiries were some kind of "test."[15] As the conversation progressed, Cantwell came to view it as a subtle game, a kind of chess match in which the future of American capitalism seemed somehow at stake: "Again and again the author thought he saw Filene drift into a line of thought, a logical associative sequence of ideas, which if steadily followed would have led to the approach of some invisible contradiction, draw back, or change the subject."[16]

Cantwell felt as though he had descended into Wonderland as he listened to Filene ramble on almost incoherently "like a Joycean interior monologue," "his sentences such a jumble of short-hand rhetoric, so full of non-sequiturs," that at times "his biographer thought him mad."[17] Filene's first "false move" was to confirm, amid one of these rambling discourses, Cantwell's suspicion that the National Recovery Administration, the Massachusetts branch of which Filene headed, had been established "in part to head off and dissipate a nationwide wave of strikes and in order to make possible suspension of anti-trust laws without provoking labor and farmer and progressive hostility."[18]

Cantwell noticed almost immediately that the old merchant seemed to be at pains to create an air of "busy-ness" about himself, and it soon dawned on the biographer that "the myth of the American business man, the great executive and hard practical organizer . . . had so burrowed into [Filene's] consciousness" that he felt a need to prove his own worth through manic activity. He wore the businessman's image, Cantwell writes, "in much the same spirit that some minor poet might wear a black cloak or a Byronic melancholy." Cantwell thus concluded that "the proper training for success in business is not economics or accounting, but a course in dramatic arts; and the successful executive puts on the appearance of doing something in a haggard endeavor to conceal from himself as well as from others the social uselessness of his life."[19]

Cantwell appreciated the "acting" of the millionaire because he had already come to view Filene less as a living human being than as a character in a novel, Cantwell's novel. After a second day with the old merchant, Cantwell was in a state of "imaginative excitement": "The author kept repeating to himself, with a kind of secret enthusiasm and delight, 'What a character!,' conscious of the fact that he had tried to imagine, for a work of fiction, a progressive capitalist and enlightened employer, [but] could not, could never, have thought of anyone who so completely fitted the part." Cantwell adds that "he would have preferred to study a bigger and more important millionaire than Filene; ideally he would have chosen Dupont or Mellon or Rockefeller, for their conspiracies would have thrown more light on the system as a whole. But with Filene he felt he could clearly detect other significant values—particularly the psychological punishment suffered by a millionaire who permitted himself to remain conscious—from the point of view of human welfare—of the weaknesses of the capitalist system."[20]

During his third visit to the millionaire's mansion, on New Year's Day 1934, Cantwell plunged into the thirty bound volumes of Filene's public speeches that occupied a prominent place on the bookshelves in the study. Most of the speeches, Cantwell quickly discovered, "were dull, and all of them were familiar; and many were hollow and hypocritical with that strained baccalaureate optimism that can only be attained, in times of crisis, by the amputation of great areas of experience."[21] But as Steffens had remarked, "the man is a bore, but not his life."[22] Cantwell found in Filene's speeches a "startling" picture of counterrevolutionary activity on the part of Progressive-era capitalists. Cantwell was surprised and delighted "to find a capitalist theoretician in Boston in 1904 urging two young capitalists to inaugurate reforms for the purpose of aiding socialists 'and the masses they influence' to see the folly of their ways; and it was startling to find two budding millionaires [Filene and his brother] so conscious of their counter-revolutionary aims." "No revolutionist," Cantwell remarks, "could have asked for a clearer statement of capitalist principle."[23]

After reading one volume of Filene's speeches, Cantwell concluded that his "character's" thought was "hopelessly involved in that social democratic dilemma . . . that inevitable perplexity of all reform. . . . How to discuss profit sharing with workers without 'leading to the idea' that all profits belong to the workers? How to strengthen the labor unions and yet be confident in maintaining control?" Cantwell discovered a "vast uneasiness, a sleepless preoccupation, a deep sense of the power of the masses" apparent, "however dimly," in Filene's speeches.[24]

On his fourth day in Boston, Cantwell paid a visit to Filene's store, with its vast company archive, to delve more deeply into his character's milieu. But upon returning to Filene's home that evening Cantwell's plans were quickly and totally demolished:

> [H]is character fired him, quietly, mysteriously, politely and finally and without explanation; and the writer, whose characters had never acted this way before, felt himself grow pale. Some of his characters had, in the past, acted queerly—in one novel . . . a leading character had a way of dropping out of the story entirely—but never before had one attempted to dispense with his service as an author.[25]

At first Cantwell was dazed and disbelieving. He had just read a speech in which Filene had spoken of the painful and difficult process of firing employees and he thought the ease with which the old merchant had revoked his commission must indicate that it was all a dream.

But when Filene's secretary confirmed that Cantwell had indeed been given three weeks' notice, his astonishment turned to rage and defiance:

> Slowly at first, but with gathering momentum and intensity, he began to develop a rich and luxurious hatred of this character whose moods were so unstable. . . . He began to tramp the streets of Boston, going mad . . . ; as he had no money, he did not have anything to eat for three days. . . . At this point all desire to write anything about capitalists left him. . . . He merely wanted—was determined to have—his revenge.[26]

When Filene returned from a business trip, on the fourth day of Cantwell's "going hungry," he invited his former biographer to a sumptuous venison dinner. As the old millionaire talked on glibly about his conversation with President Franklin Roosevelt, Cantwell's desire for vengeance peaked and he became determined to write the biography whether he was to be paid for it or not.

During the remaining three weeks of his contract, Cantwell labored "madly" and intently, managing to complete drafts of three chapters covering the first twenty-six years of Filene's life. Throughout he must have harbored the hope that the chapters presented as a fait accompli would convince Filene to change his mind. And in his "madness," he never lost sight of the larger goal that lay behind his vengeance, for during this period, he wrote to friend Newton Arvin that

> I'm ghost-writing a biography of Filene for Steffens, who hasn't enough energy left to do the book himself. It's . . . a biography of a failure, of a progressive capitalist who tried to reform business practices, tried to turn his store over to his employees, and an analysis, a social analysis, of the reasons for his failure. It is fascinating material, no less, and after my first week of examining the documents I feel that I've learned more about the way our society is controlled than I could have learned in any other way.[27]

The first chapters were good enough to convince Filene to retain Cantwell, but relations between the two were far from cordial.[28] In the meantime Steffens, who had hoped to use the Filene project to recoup some recent financial losses, was gradually but shakily recovering from his stroke. When more or less recovered, he proved to be a master diplomat, somehow succeeding in keeping both Cantwell and his old friend Filene happy. As Justin Kaplan expressed it in his biography of Steffens, "Caught between Cantwell's savagery and Filene's mercurial interventions, Steffens derived what humor he could from the situation."[29] "The situation," after all, was partly his fault for bringing the two unlikely individuals together and he understood Cantwell's financial plight even if Filene could not. Moreover, Steffens believed in Cantwell as a writer, particularly after *The Land of Plenty* was published, and he believed in the novel biography. When the young radical biographer wrote complaining that the Filene life was keeping him from his fiction, Steffens replied,

> Terrible! What do you think you are doing now? I think you are writing a novel now. You ought to think not only the same but that you are engaged upon the only work you ever have or ever are going to do.[30]

By offering similar reassurance to Filene, Steffens kept the rather dubious project alive.

As Cantwell probed into Filene's life, he discovered that "all through the [childhood] years that Filene described as poverty-stricken and miserable, the Filenes lived and traveled in a manner that seemed luxurious to a single son of the proletariat."[31] And as the months of research wore on, Cantwell met a good many more capitalists possessed of a similar need to mythicize their pasts. He also found that like Filene, these wealthy men all strained to create an air of busyness to camouflage "the social uselessness of their lives."[32]

Alerted by Filene's distortions, Cantwell began to scrutinize every word and deed of the capitalists he met or read about. Again as a lover of words, he was startled to find himself in a "world dominated by a fearful abuse of words, by a criminal debauchery of their significance; and for the first time he felt that he understood what Lenin meant when he wrote of the 'shameful gap between bourgeois words and deeds.'"[33] In this, Cantwell himself may have exaggerated in the extent of the naïveté with which he had approached his subject. But he seems to have sincerely found his study of capitalists even more appalling than he had anticipated.

As he examined each of Filene's many schemes for humanizing the labor system, Cantwell also confirmed his belief that reform of capitalism was impossible. He was especially intrigued by Filene's advocacy of workers' credit unions that "the biographer" viewed as an even more insidious scheme for co-opting workers than profit sharing because it condescendingly kept workers from involvement in the unstable but often highly profitable stock market. But Filene's version of a credit union too proved a failure, and in the history of its failure, Cantwell discovered one of his favorite themes: "The record of credit unions effectively dramatized the differences between the workers' ability to manage and the hopeless incompetence and vicious deceptions of their employers."[34]

The single common thread that Cantwell discovered running through Filene's life was failure, and as Cantwell became more and more aware of this, his hatred turned toward (a highly qualified) pity. For Cantwell, a certain pathos emerged from the quixotic nature of Filene's efforts. He had tried to give his store to his workers, only to have it stolen from him by his own brother; he had helped to found the national and international Chambers of Commerce as citadels of enlightened capitalism, only to watch them turn thoroughly reactionary; he had even lost control of his own philanthropic endowment fund. And now Filene had lost control of his biography and just before his manuscript breaks off, Cantwell completed, or at least made explicit, the transformation of his "character's" life into a revolutionist's symbol:

> The biographer began to see [Filene], after a time, not merely as a capitalist, a millionaire, but as a kind of personification of American capitalism, not merely as a representative of his class, but an embodiment of it. Well-meaning, tasteless, awkward, shrewd, limited—he seemed to sum up a thousand capitalists whose personalities emerged dimly from behind the concealments of popular journalism. But most of all, he was old, and he concealed his age; he was weak and like capitalism itself he denied and concealed his weakness. The heart had gone out of him; and there was nothing left but the front.[35]

While fueling Cantwell's radicalism, his association with Filene also made it more difficult for him to function openly as a literary radical. Soon after Steffens hired him, Cantwell wrote to Newton Arvin about the problems that being in the employ of E. A. Filene were already causing him:

> I cannot work on the N[ew] M[asses] as a regular contributor without imperiling most of my income, the public announcement of my purpose would only make it more difficult for me to make a living. Yet I can contribute from time to time under my own name, and am submitting a short story under my own name for one of the first issues if the editors want it. I can do this under the limitations imposed on me by the people for whom I work. At the same time I am actively cooperating as a staff member under another name [Robert Simmons].[36]

In this letter, Cantwell seemed to have absorbed some of the passion for "secret" maneuvers he often attributed to his friend Whittaker Chambers, the rather paranoid, sometime member of the Communist underground who later became the most famous anticommunist of the 1950s. And Cantwell's duplicitous dealings with Filene encourage the speculation that Cantwell may have restrained public profession of the extent of his radicalism on other occasions for the same reason—to protect his job security.

Cantwell's work with Steffens on the Filene project was soon swept up into a series of larger political events that also came to play a role in his abandonment of fiction. There was a new urgency and stridency in Cantwell's public and private writings throughout 1934. In part this may have resulted from his intimate glimpse into the world of capitalist machinations, but the larger reason undoubtedly had to do with the course of political events during this year. Violent strikes led by radicals rocked New York City, Milwaukee, Philadelphia, San Francisco, and other cities and, coupled with the popularity of economic panaceas championed by such figures as Father Coughlin, Dr. Townsend, Huey Long, and Upton Sinclair, seemed to place Roosevelt's piecemeal reformism in jeopardy.[37] At the same time, the reorganization of the *New Masses* in January 1934 and then two months later the first appearance of *Partisan Review* suggested that a more subtle, sophisticated approach to Marxian aesthetics, one more closely matching Cantwell's position, was emerging. Cantwell had long argued that there was no conflict between literary quality and "propaganda" (as he increasingly called his fiction efforts), that the best radical fiction would use all the tools of "bourgeois" aesthetics to get at the complexities of social life and class struggle. He was therefore encouraged to sense more flexible critical standards and richer literary work developing in critiques of certain reductive approaches found among some leftist critics and writers in the early 1930s.

Amid these conditions Cantwell expressed understandable regret at being marooned in Boston, away from the action.[38] But he remained active despite his distance from New York and despite whatever "limitations" were "imposed" upon him by Filene and Steffens. In a letter to Newton Arvin, Cantwell made clear that he felt an urgent need to bring unity to the Literary Left and initiated an effort to do so:

> I have been corresponding with [Granville] Hicks, and the thought has kept coming up that a chance to discuss things might clarify critical and other problems a lot. Would you be interested in a quiet little conference sometime in the spring? We might be able to get [Malcolm] Cowley, [John] Chamberlain, perhaps [Edmund] Wilson, if it seemed advisable—or others who are thinking along common lines? I am thinking of a day or so of discussion of the actual cultural scene, of the people whose work is or promises to be important, of potential allies and how they can be won, of present and future enemies and how they can be disarmed. [N]o one of us can doubt that the next few years are going to bring terrible and violent changes, that the threats to everything we live for have never been so fearful. How are we going to act?[39]

The "threat" perceived here is incipient American fascism, and Cantwell's desire to unite these major figures of the Literary Left is clearly a deadly earnest response to a sense of deepening national crisis.

When the biographer's doubts grew severe amid the seemingly more important events unfolding all around the country, Steffens wrote to remind his young colleague that "the Thing you are writing is the great, modern American novel."[40] And when he had read the publisher's proofs of *The Land of Plenty* in late April, Steffens sent similar word to Filene, calling Cantwell's novel "an event in literature" and assuring his old friend that his biographer "is, in his line, what you are in yours: a leader."[41] Thus the project staggered on.

Throughout the spring, Steffens urged Cantwell to join him at his home in Carmel, California, and in the summer Cantwell accepted the invitation. The trip might in another time have been a vacation, for Steffens's home was situated in a lovely seaside resort setting, but both the difficult biography and turbulent events in nearby San Francisco and in Carmel itself made the visit far from a respite from the politics of the East Coast. In July, Cantwell was unexpectedly granted the opportunity to broaden the canvas of his counterpropaganda work when violence erupted in San Francisco and he was given the assignment of covering the events for the *New Republic.* A strike among Pacific coast stevedores led to a bloody clash on July 5, 1934, that quickly escalated into one of the great labor battles of the era, the San Francisco General Strike.[42]

The *New Republic* articles that Cantwell wrote about the strike stem from his deepest, most complex encounters with labor struggles in the age of the Congress of Industrial Organizations. Aptly, his reading matter while there included *The Eighteenth Brumaire of Napoleon Bonaparte,* one of Marx's most novelistic writings and a subtle analysis of the complex interactions of classes and class fractions during a political crisis. Cantwell met with all the major figures in the strike, including Harry Bridges, head of the International Longshoremen's Association, and Sam Darcy, head of the Communist-led Marine Workers' Union. Some of the important information that Cantwell drew upon for his *New Republic* articles had come from a clandestine meeting with Darcy arranged by Steffens's Communist Party-activist wife, Ella Winter. The meeting was held in secret because Darcy was in hiding after Communist Party and union offices in the city had been hit by a series of vicious raids by vigilantes (paid by the Shipowners' Association) and the San Francisco police.

Meanwhile in peaceful Carmel, a meeting of the local John Reed Club featuring Langston Hughes was attacked by the American Legion. The legion's attack must have brought up terrifying memories for Cantwell of the Wobblies beaten, castrated, and hanged by American Legion members in his home state of Washington during his youth. The events in San Francisco and Carmel deeply stirred Cantwell's literary imagination, and before the year was out he had begun to plan a new novel based on the general strike. In a letter written to friend T. S. Mathews, Cantwell hinted at some themes that his new novel would assay:

> The general strike in San Francisco was great and heartbreaking. They came so close to winning and were betrayed so shamelessly. The longshoremen and seamen could defeat the efforts of the employers to break the strike, the efforts of the government arbitrators, the city officials and police; they could, counting on help from other unions, have beaten the National Guard. But they hadn't clearly realized that they have got to beat the A.F. of L. officials just as much as the employers; there isn't any real distinction between them, but it wasn't so clear before. Meanwhile the patriots are busy driving the god damned reds into their holes....[But the radicals] have built up an organization that will be ready next time.[43]

In a letter to Dos Passos about that summer, Cantwell wrote that the planned new novel would imagine future struggles and help the masses see a clear path to change.[44] Armed with his now intimate knowledge of the capitalist mind, he imagined a panoramic work that would be a microcosm of America in class struggle. But events were moving faster than any young novelist could hope to absorb, and both his new strike novel and the biography of Filene were soon jeopardized by changing conditions in this country and abroad. The rise of Popular Front–era policies presented Cantwell with numerous difficulties, the first major one being doubts they cast on the fate of the Filene biography. The attack on Filene that Cantwell had begun at the height of his revolutionary enthusiasm was precisely the kind of effort being discouraged under the new Communist strategy of alliance with liberals. To assault verbally a leading progressive capitalist, one of the few prominent businesspersons to support Roosevelt's New Deal, was to run directly against the new spirit on the Left and might weaken the type of fragile coalition that Cantwell saw growing in California. It is therefore small wonder that the nonfiction novel was abandoned before reaching completion.

As for the ghostwritten "autobiography" version, Cantwell rushed to finish that manuscript in March 1935 so that he might begin a new, more lucrative job with *Time* magazine, but the results apparently did not meet with Filene's approval, for it too was never published.[45] Despite periodic attempts over the next several years to write his novel about the San Francisco general strike, Cantwell was never able to complete it (or any other work of fiction). He was pulled into the Henry Luce empire, and his fiction-writing career dissolved. As the decade ended, Cantwell was to find himself politically at sea, and 1942 found him in the midst of a severe psychological breakdown requiring months of hospitalization. His sojourn with the capitalist had proven in almost all ways a disaster for him and it not only provides insight into Cantwell's ideological whirlwinds but also reminds us of the quickly shifting winds that shaped and reshaped much of radical culture of the 1930s Left.

Cantwell has sometimes been portrayed as a writer of great potential destroyed by his association with the 1930s Left. Yet he produced one good novel, *Laugh and Lie Down* (1931), before his involvement with the Left and one great novel, *Land of Plenty* (1934), after his immersion in the Literary Left. The forces that undid him as a fiction writer were many, and not least of these was poverty. Many of his better-off colleagues sought to dissuade him from taking on the Filene project and later many more warned him against entering the Henry Luce publishing empire. But virtually all those urging him away from these more lucrative pursuits were far better off financially. Cantwell teetered on the edge of poverty throughout most of the 1930s, with not only a growing family of his own to provide for (including three children) but also a dependent set of relatives out West who often needed his financial assistance. Carving a space to write fiction under those circumstances proved immensely difficult. His heroic effort to turn the Filene project into what we would now call a nonfiction novel was an admirable effort to shape the documentary impulse that so fascinated the decade's cultural workers into something fitting his literary skills.

For Cantwell as for so many other leftists, the 1939 Nazi-Soviet Pact proved to be something like the last straw of disillusionment with the Communist Party USA, especially given that he had already come to share Luce's prointerventionist views (a decidedly minority view at *Time*). Cantwell began a slow drift to the right, reinforced by a deepening Anglican religiosity and association with an anticommunist clique at *Time* led by his longtime friend Whittaker Chamber. An inherently oversensitive nature, overwork, ideological stresses, and marital troubles all contributed to Cantwell's breakdown in 1942, an event from which he never fully recovered. After a harrowing time of insulin and electroshock, he never again succeeded in writing fiction or in engaging any direct form of political action. Instead, he contented himself with a safer route as a journalist writing about natural history and sports (he was an editor at *Sports Illustrated* for the last years of his career). But at the time of his death in 1978, Cantwell had again turned his mind to a nonfiction novel. This time it would be the story, informed in part by the thousands of pages of his Federal Bureau of Investigation (FBI) file obtained through the then new Freedom of Information Act, of the crazy arc of his 1930s career. That culminated, as Cantwell saw it, with the treachery of being dragged by implication into the Red witch-hunting whirlwind in the 1950s courtesy of his former friend turned anticommunist-in-chief, Whittaker Chambers. Whether or not Cantwell "named names" is unclear, but his closeness to Chambers meant that it was assumed by Cantwell's comrades that he had. He came to feel isolated from both his friends who remained on the Left and those who became anticommunist zealots.

The first version, given the working title *Privacy,* was imagined, à la the Filene manuscript, as a kind of nonfiction novel. As Cantwell outlined it, it would begin in the reading room of the FBI building in Washington, D.C., where he had in fact gone to look at those putative twenty thousand pages of files devoted to him. He apparently never got beyond this opening scene, but he intended it to be at once factually based in the documentary evidence and complex enough to show the inadequacy of such evidence and the treachery of memory.

The second version that Cantwell outlined was to be narrated in the voice of his first wife, Betsy Cantwell, noting that to do so would put the book in the voice of a "woman not interested in politics," one "who'd offer a clear-eyed view of highly literate people sometimes deluded by self-importance." Writing in his wife's voice, he speculated, bolstered by documentary footnotes, would perhaps allow a perspective different from the overly knowing, often treacherously self-justifying views he found in memoirs filled with what he called the "genuine peril involved in retractions" of writers' former leftist views (he mentioned the autobiographical writings of Malcolm Cowley, Matthew Josephson, Erskine Caldwell, Edmund Wilson, Mary McCarthy, Dwight Macdonald, and

Alger Hiss). "The book," he noted, "is not long. It is condensed and intense, chapter by chapter, sentence by sentence, quiet in tone, deceptively cool and unemotional, evolving slowly into melodrama before one is aware of the violence latent from the beginning." The story would start amid the narrator's southern girlhood, then introduce her cousin, Lyle Saxon, a homosexual bohemian writer whose New York literary connections eventually led her to her future husband, Robert Cantwell. By chapter 3, the narrator and her husband would be thrown into the whirlwind of literary politics, with Malcolm Cowley, Edmund Wilson, John Dos Passos, Erskine Caldwell, Matthew Josephson, Lincoln Steffens, and E. A. Filene making their appearances. But soon it becomes clear that "the center of the book is [the] recollection of Whittaker Chambers." That portrait would show Chambers as a character "whose need for being exceptional in a curious and self-impressed way leads to persistence and ruin," a man whose "conviction of his own rightness leaves wreckage all around him." Among that wreckage, apparently, was to be the sanity of the narrator's husband, Robert Cantwell, and the "conclusion would necessarily it seems to me [be] in the [mental] hospital."[46] A mental hospital is a sad place indeed to leave one of the most talented fiction writers of the proletarian literary movement, but from the moment of the revolutionist's encounter with the merchant capitalist, that was the telos of Cantwell's career in the 1930s. In circling back to the 1930s at the end of his life and in imagining a new nonfiction novel, Robert Cantwell seemed to at least tacitly realize that the encounter between his young revolutionary self and the self-important "merchant of Boston" had begun a profound transformation of trajectory that led him away from a potentially far richer literary legacy.

Notes

1. Cantwell to Ernest Hemingway, October 21, 1950, Robert Cantwell Papers, Coll 020, Special Collections & University Archives, University of Oregon Libraries, Eugene, Oregon (hereafter Robert Cantwell Papers). This essay is excerpted in part from T. V. Reed, *Robert Cantwell and the Literary Left: A Northwest Writer Reworks American Fiction* (Seattle: University of Washington Press, 2014). My book is a biocritical study focusing primarily on Cantwell's time as a literary leftist. For a more traditional biography of Cantwell, see Per Seyersted, *Robert Cantwell: An American Thirties Radical Writer and His Apostasy* (Oslo: Novus, 2004), an exhaustively researched and richly detailed book from which I have occasionally drawn (though most of my book was written before the publication of Seyersted's). While the detailed coverage is admirable, the book is theoretically

and interpretively thin, neither sympathetic to nor comprehending of Cantwell's complicated aesthetic and political positions in the 1930s.

2. Cantwell, "The Merchant of Boston" [biography of E. A. Filene], unpublished manuscript, Robert Cantwell Papers.

3. Filene's role in the history of retailing and worker management is a significant one, as brilliantly contextualized in Meg Jacobs, *Pocketbook Politics: Economic Citizenship in Twentieth-Century America* (Princeton, NJ: Princeton University Press, 2006).

4. Steffens met Filene in 1908 when the latter hired the journalist to rake the muck of Boston on behalf of the city's Good Government Association. As the two reformers summered together at Marblehead and floated about on Filene's yacht, they formed a lifelong friendship that even weathered Steffens's move to the Far Left in the 1930s. See Justin Kaplan, *Lincoln Steffens* (New York: Simon and Schuster, 1974), 166–67, 171, 174–75, 314, 316.

5. Ibid., 314.

6. Cantwell, "The Merchant of Boston," 8.

7. Ibid., 5.

8. Cantwell, "The Merchant of Boston," 8. Allegedly from Lenin's "An Open Letter to E. A. Filene and the Progressive Capitalists."

9. Cantwell, "The Merchant of Boston," 14.

10. All previous and subsequent citations refer to the second of the named versions of the manuscript. I have corrected obvious typographical errors in his manuscript. In drawing from Cantwell's unpublished archive, I share the attitude and goals expressed by Wald in these terms: "To reintroduce the individualized [context] of the writer's singular being and consciousness is not to become a biographer but to restore the self-activity of Left cultural workers as well as supply some neglected mediations in the creative act—especially the mentality of the artist and the force field of the institutions within which he or she worked." Alan Wald, *Exiles from a Future Time* (Chapel Hill: University of North Carolina Press, 2002), xvi.

11. Cantwell, "The Merchant of Boston," 7–8.

12. Ibid., 9.

13. Kaplan, *Lincoln Steffens,* 166; Cantwell, "The Merchant of Boston," 128.

14. Cantwell, "The Merchant of Boston," 17.

15. Ibid., 20.

16. Ibid., 45.

17. Ibid., 40.

18. Ibid., 22.

19. Ibid., 30.

20. Ibid., 47.

21. Ibid., 86.

22. Quoted in Kaplan, *Lincoln Steffens,* 314.

23. Cantwell, "The Merchant of Boston," 75, 86.

24. Ibid., 86.

25. Ibid., 110.

26. Ibid., 112.
27. Cantwell to Newton Arvin, January 14, 1934, Robert Cantwell Papers.
28. Cantwell, "The Merchant of Boston," 186.
29. Kaplan, *Lincoln Steffens*, 316.
30. *The Letters of Lincoln Steffens*, Vol. 2, *1920–1936*, edited with introductory notes by Ella Winter and Granville Hicks (New York, 1938), 976.
31. Cantwell, "The Merchant of Boston," 125. Cantwell can be accused of mythicizing his own past a bit here as well.
32. Ibid., 139–41.
33. Ibid., 215–16.
34. Ibid., 223.
35. Ibid., 140.
36. Cantwell to Newton Arvin, November 15, 1933, Robert Cantwell Papers. Evidence from other letters makes it clear that "N.M." refers to the *New Masses*. The short story he alludes to was probably "Hills around Centralia," his story about the Centralia "massacre" of Industrial Workers of the World members, later published in *Proletarian Literature in the United States* (1935), edited by Hicks, Joseph Freeman, and other members of the *New Masses* staff.
37. William Leuchtenberg, *Franklin D. Roosevelt and the New Deal, 1932–1940* (New York: Harper, 1973), argues that 1934 was the peak of radical enthusiasm. See chapter 5, "Waiting for Lefty."
38. Cantwell to Newton Arvin, January 31, 1934, Robert Cantwell Papers.
39. Ibid.
40. *The Letters of Lincoln Steffens*, 977.
41. Ibid., 982.
42. See Irving Bernstein's classic account, *The Turbulent Years: A History of the American Worker, 1933–1941* (Boston: Houghton Mifflin, 1970), and Charles P. Larrowe, *Harry Bridges* (Chicago: Lawrence Hill, 1977).
43. Cantwell to T. S. Mathews, n.d., Robert Cantwell Papers.
44. Cantwell to John Dos Passos, n.d. Robert Cantwell Papers.
45. Cantwell to Ernest Hemingway, October 21, 1950, Robert Cantwell Papers.
46. ["Privacy"] manuscript, Robert Cantwell Papers.

[9]

Red Feminists and Methodist Missionaries: Dorothy McConnell and the Other Afterlife of the Popular Front

Chris Vials

Founded in 1933, the American League against War and Fascism was among the most successful organizations launched by the Communist Party USA (CPUSA) during the Great Depression. Its achievement was not in the size of its dues-paying membership, which was relatively small, but in its role in shaping public debates over fascism. The rallies, congresses, and roundtables organized by the league received wide coverage in print and broadcast media and enjoyed the sponsorship of US congressmen, state governors, and city mayors. By the end of the decade, it had become the coordinating body for the antifascist activities of 1,023 affiliate organizations representing over 7 million people. For affiliates, the league served as an information clearinghouse, furnishing its biweekly bulletin *Facts and Figures* and disseminating over a million booklets, pamphlets, and newspapers in 1938 alone.[1] Its periodical, *Fight against War and Fascism* (hereafter *Fight*), provides a clue as to why so many organizations came together under its banner: arranged under the heading of "the fight against fascism" were a wide array of characteristically leftist and liberal campaigns including union building, lobbying for social democratic legislation, antiracism, anti-imperialism, the struggle for women's equality, and the drive to eliminate militarism in American culture. Most league activists were not CPUSA members, though whatever their affiliation, they used antifascism to conceptually link seemingly disparate demands and apparently distinct sites of struggle. Yet such a broad-based organization, while generative of intersectional politics and transformative coalitions, inevitably drew into its orbit—even into its leadership circles—individuals whose mobilizing passions were deeply complicit in the dominant order, a fact that has been undertheorized in scholarship on the American Left.

The class-conscious feminist Dorothy McConnell (1900–1980) was one of the central figures in this organization and provides a telling case study. Her entrance and exit from the league explains much about the kinds of individuals who were drawn to the radical Left in the 1930s but did not stay there. McConnell wrote a regular feminist column in *Fight* titled "As to Women" and served on its national executive board. *Fight* featured more bylines by women than any other communist-inspired publication, apart from those explicitly devoted to "the woman question." In the early 1930s, McConnell and other female writers merely highlighted the contributions of women to the antifascist struggle, but by the end of the decade they used the magazine as a forum to agitate for feminist workplace demands, placing "the woman question" at the center of broader issues of democracy.[2] The capacious nature of antifascism in the 1930s allowed a space for women activists to forge what is now called intersectional feminism, keenly aware of the hierarchies of race and class through which patriarchy is reproduced and constituted. In the pages of *Fight* and through their activism in the league, McConnell and her cohort created what Kate Weigand and Carol Boyce Davies trace in their studies of early postwar feminists: a class- and racially conscious brand of feminism crafted by the midcentury Left, one that transmitted influential tactics and concepts to the next generation of feminists.[3]

Yet this is not the end of the story. Alan Wald's recent trilogy on the midcentury Left concludes that what consistently drew intellectuals into "pro-Communist" circles was not a shared background in the working class but rather some kind of outsider status as people of color, gays and lesbians, "race traitors," Jews, or bohemians.[4] McConnell was certainly a nonconformist in her own right, but paradoxically, what drove her into the orbit of the Communist Party was her background in a quintessentially insider movement: the white Methodist missionary movement in Asia, which was deeply implicated in the history of US imperialism. Influential procommunist feminists such as Mary Inman and Claudia

Jones—who remained active in the Left their entire lives—were essentially reared in the culture of socialist and communist parties, aligning with them in their teenage years.[5] McConnell got involved with such organizations in her thirties and came to them from a different route. She was the privileged daughter of a nationally known Methodist bishop—Francis John McConnell—and was groomed for missionary work from an early age. For young Dorothy McConnell, like so many other women of her generation, the missionary world was an accepted sphere of public engagement that allowed a degree of freedom from a highly circumscribed role. After she joined the league, her writing for missionary publications dropped off considerably, though not entirely. McConnell authored league-sponsored, socialist-feminist tracts such as *Women, War, and Fascism* (1935) at the very same time she published missionary education materials such as *Friends in Nippon* (1934). The CPUSA's turn to the Popular Front in the latter years of the decade allowed her a space to more openly acknowledge her missionary commitments in the secular left-wing press. In her column in *Fight* from November 1937, she praised the women missionaries who stayed on to care for the wounded during the Japanese invasion of China and wrote that "No matter what you may think of missionary work, it is responsible for breaking down the 'America for Americans' feeling—at least, so far as China is concerned."[6]

McConnell felt comfortable expressing such positions in *Fight* precisely because, perhaps unexpectedly, Christian missionaries were no strangers to the American League against War and Fascism in the late 1930s. With the Japanese invasion of mainland China in the summer of 1937, the voices of missionaries became much louder in the organization's magazine. Most of these were women's voices, and they often took the form of reportage from the war zone in what was now a major front in the global struggle against fascism. Dr. Stewart Kunkle chronicled the medical aid and other services for refugees offered by the missions in China and proudly reported that "the missionaries have been helping in every way they could to lessen the suffering and to stand by their Chinese friends in the defense of their country."[7] Missionaries found a home in the league because their commitment to causes of the Left was not new. The Methodist Episcopal Church had a class-conscious and even radical strand dating back to the early twentieth century and the national chairman of the league—a Methodist minister named Harry F. Ward—emerged from this radical tradition.

Fight's Christian missionaries in China offer another kind of international brigade than that usually celebrated in the annals of the Left. The contributions by McConnell and others in the pages of the magazine suggest that missionary work in China during the occupation was politically transformative for many young white women, deepening their critiques of American foreign policy, their sense of women's place, and even their understanding of capitalism in general. Yet while it is unlikely that these critiques simply evaporated after World War II, the case of Dorothy McConnell suggests that this brief yet significant site of women's involvement in the antifascist movement did not go on to directly build the postwar anti-imperialist feminism described by Weigand and Davies. The culture of the white Methodist missionaries, while it came from a socialist tradition that intersected with the cause of antifascism in the 1930s, was not as resistant to the historical shifts of the Cold War, precisely because it never shed its deep roots in the history of Western imperialism. Indeed, McConnell went on to participate in the kind of Cold War people-to-people projects traced by Christina Klein, in which Americans created affective, universalist narratives that ultimately enlisted them in US empire building abroad.[8] As such, her retrofitting of antifascist globalism to Cold War ends tells us something about the Popular Front constituencies that did *not* continue to build the Left, a phenomenon far less examined in the scholarship on midcentury radicalism. Scholars continue to debate what can be called "the afterlife of the Popular Front," some arguing that its brand of internationalism and racial pluralism anticipated Cold War logics, while others suggesting that it created essential discourses, activist experiences, and institutional bases that would be quite fruitful for the Left in future decades.[9] However, the method of the in-depth individual case study, so finely developed by Alan Wald, allows us to see how *both* of these afterlife scenarios hold explanatory power. Clearly, some constituencies of the Popular Front went on to build Cold War liberalism, while others continued to build the Left: what is critical is the nature of one's embeddedness in multiple communities simultaneously—and the amenability of each of these various networks to co-optation by capital and empire.

To be sure, missionary work was not the entrée of most female participants in the American antifascist movement, nor was it the only avenue of women's participation in the American League against War and Fascism. In the summer of 1934, the league also formed a permanent Women's Division, which was quite active.[10] At its Third Congress in 1936, the Women's Committee, chaired by Margaret Forsyth, had subcommittees representing farm women, trade union women, and business and professional women. Together they collectively endorsed the fight against a clause in the Federal Economy Act that restricted employment opportunities for married women in the civil service. Forsyth admonished those at the congress to oppose fascism at home and abroad, as it relegated women to the status of "cheap labor."[11] Yet there were limits to the organization's feminism. Its early programs called out "to enlist for our program the women in industry and in the home," yet from 1933 to 1939 while its key statements of purpose explicitly addressed race prejudice, lynching, and attacks on the rights of labor, none addressed male dominance (despite the violent misogyny upon which fascism depended).[12] While the league sometimes failed to acknowledge the specificity of women's struggles, it should come as no surprise that so many women became involved in an organization devoted to fighting war and fascism. In the United States, the peace movement was an established (if not fully accepted) space of women's activity by the 1930s, having gained particular visibility through the Women's International League for Peace and Freedom, founded in 1915.[13] The status of the American League against War and Fascism as an antiwar movement likely drew many women to what they knew to be a relatively viable space for their activism.

During the CPUSA's turn to the Popular Front in the second half of the decade, women writers in *Fight* increasingly used antifascism to show the centrality of "the woman question" to democratic transformation. As McConnell wrote in her pamphlet *Women, War, and Fascism* (1935), "The defeat of any discriminatory law or act against women is a direct thrust at fascism."[14] As part of a broader and largely successful shift in CPUSA strategy to appeal to women during the Popular Front period, *Fight* began featuring articles about gendered wage inequalities in the United States and emphasized the pivotal role of women in shaping the antifascist resistance struggle abroad.[15] During this time, McConnell assumed her prominence in the magazine. In April 1937, *Fight* began a protofeminist column titled "As to Women," written by McConnell, that theorized the relationship between antifascism and the women's movement.

McConnell's writings for league publications reveal how antifascism in the Popular Front Left could function as a site of intersectional feminist analysis. To varying degrees of sophistication, CPUSA-oriented antifascists argued throughout the decade that hierarchies of class, race, and gender created discontent that could be exploited by fascist demagogues who appealed to the masses' desire for relief from suffering. Over time, they insisted, deepening structural inequalities created by ingrained modes of thinking among the people prevented the lateral unity (often class unity) necessary to oppose the social degeneration toward fascism and war. McConnell's analysis of the divisions among American women factory workers in her booklet *Women, War, and Fascism* (1935) reflects this view. As she wrote, "The married women, who have been most discriminated against, are afraid of the young girls replacing them. The young girls are resentful of the married women who hold jobs that might otherwise be theirs. The workers are criss-crossed with deep and bitter antagonisms. The state is thus less threatened." She argued that the root of the whole problem was that of "less wages for women. . . . Woman, as a cheap source of labor, is a danger to man. He resents her as a threat to his economic security." McConnell subsequently stressed that such gendered exploitation at the point of production, left unaddressed by the labor movement, was critical to the fascist project of military expansion.[16] What becomes clear in this line of McConnell's argumentation, as with so much antifascist writing in the 1930s, is that "fascism" is almost ancillary to her social analysis. For her, "fascism" was less a concrete regime in Germany or Italy and more a vehicle to conceive the *connectedness* of seemingly divergent struggles. In McConnell's case, as with many other women in the league, this sense of "connectedness" developed into a class-conscious feminism that Kate Wiegand described as a broad phenomenon among this generation of women activists.[17]

But what of the other Dorothy McConnell, the one who defended Christian missionaries abroad even as she espoused a radical brand of feminism and who, in 1937, attended a luncheon of the Women's Foreign Missionary Society of the Methodist Church to honor those who spread the New Testament to China, India, Korea, and Africa?[18] And how could someone so ensconced in the missionary movement wind up in the American League against War and Fascism in the first place? The involvement of devout Christians in the league was not a cynical case of bait and switch on the part of the CPUSA. The Methodists in particular had their own tradition of class-conscious political activism, and many sought out the league and other left-wing organizations as a seamless extension of their own histories of social justice work. Harry Ward, Dorothy McConnell, and her father Francis John McConnell all came into the Popular Front from a history of Methodist radicalism dating to the first decade of the twentieth century, one that Doug Rossinow calls "the left-wing of the social gospel." In the 1920s and 1930s, even official Methodist gatherings denounced the evils of "profitism" and the inequities of a society based on market values.[19]

These individuals had direct access to the American League against War and Fascism through its national chairman—Harry F. Ward—a Methodist minister who, in his leadership role in the Methodist Federation for Social Service (MFSS), brought this organization and his other coreligionists into the league. Founded in 1907, the MFSS was led for decades by Harry Ward and Francis John McConnell and it took a more radical turn after 1919. Long before the Popular Front, Ward and others in the MFSS had become seasoned coalition builders as they broke out of the established structures of the church to work with secular activist organizations.[20] Ward's status as a clergyman in no way dampened his procommunist commitments. He visited the Soviet Union in the 1920s, as did many other Protestant clergymen, and came back a true believer. Though he never joined the CPUSA, he closely mirrored the various shifts in its line in his public statements, more so than most contributors to *Fight.*[21]

McConnell emerged from this milieu and thus gleaned her leftist politics well before she came into contact with the American League against War and Fascism or the Popular Front.[22] From her sparse papers at Drew University, we learn that she was born in Ipswich, Massachusetts, in 1900 and that from her youth, her family and closest friends called her "Dot." She earned a BA from Ohio Wesleyan University and then went on to receive an MA at Columbia University in 1922. While at Ohio Wesleyan, a Methodist college that her father also attended, she was drawn to study English and history and took classes on missionary work. As a student she was already displaying a sharp critical voice, such as when she complained in a letter to her father that her teacher for "Missions" was a fool.[23] After graduating from Columbia, she stayed in New York to become editor of *World Service News,* the periodical of the World Service Agencies of the Methodist Episcopal Church, which organized missions throughout the world. (This organization, it should be noted, was not the radical MFSS of her father and as such was even closer to the Methodist Church establishment.) In this role, McConnell was credited as being a very effective editor, praised for an "impudent tone" that increased the circulation of the magazine in the United States and at missions overseas. Despite her promotion of missionary work in China and India, her editorials in the mid-1920s earned her a reputation as a rabble-rouser on issues of labor and racial equality. A number of readers objected to her stance on the race question, but she appears to have received more praise than condemnation. In 1926, for instance, a minister in Jersey City lauded her transformation of *World Service News:* "It will wake up a lot of brethren that need waking up, and occasionally seems to run the risk of encouraging the religious Bolsheviki, of which I am one."[24]

While McConnell was certainly more left-wing than her father, especially by the 1930s, they shared the same political temperament. Bishop Francis John McConnell had earned the ire of conservatives for his vehement support of the steel strike of 1919, and from that time into the 1930s, he promoted the kind of economy commonly touted by those aligned with the Popular Front, what Michael Denning called a "'moral economy' that would temper the ravages of capitalism."[25] Speaking at a gala in honor of his life's work at Carnegie Hall in 1937, Bishop McConnell stated that "The Marxian principles as to human values, the equitable distribution of wealth, the classless society are today recognized, virtually throughout Christendom, as substantially Christian aims—though not as to be introduced by Marxian methods" (by which he meant revolution). Dorothy's father also endorsed the American League against War and Fascism's Fifth Congress in 1939. With good reason, left-leaning Methodists were referred to as "McConnell Methodists" in some circles during the 1930s.[26]

Secular Communists and radical missionaries were ideologically and institutionally aligned in critical ways during the Popular Front: what they shared was a rejection of hard nationalism, promoting instead the idea of a unity of peoples across borders to be created through a softening of class hierarchies within and between nations. Yet the Methodists clearly felt the need to defend their global vision in their writings for the secular left-wing press. Missionary contributors to *Fight* showed an awareness of their complicity in US imperialism and made a case to secular left-wing readers for a fresh start. As Stewart Kunkle wrote in 1938, "It was the fashion some years ago to think of the missionary as the advance agent of Big Business. The missionary broke the way and the Standard Oil Company followed. Whatever the sequence of the events may have been, this was never a conscious policy of missions."[27] Likewise, McConnell urged leftist and liberal readers to see missionary work as transforming provincial women into antifascist internationalists. In her column from November 1937, she wrote that "There is hardly a town in the Middle West that is not supporting some part of the missionary work in China. Women missionaries return to the little towns and tell of their experiences. It is not unusual to hear women who have never been farther from home than the county seat tell of the situation in some remote school in West China. It is familiar to them."[28]

Yet the phrase "it is familiar to them" reveals a crack in these defenses of missionaries, which later helped to decisively split McConnell from the Left. There is something unsettling about *Fight*'s heroic tales of white middle-class missionaries in Asia, even though these narratives overwhelmingly praised the contributions of women. Unlike Agnes Smedley's reportage from the war zones in China, which stressed the agency and heroism of the Chinese people (and Chinese women in particular), in *Fight*, the missionary Dr. Kunkle focused on the hard work and dedication of the white missionaries—their care for the wounded, their continuing work as schoolteachers, and their services for refugees. This reflected a running motif in *World Service News* that was even more pronounced in its successor, *World Outlook,* which McConnell also edited. (Indeed, she also penned articles in this vein.)[29] The asymmetrical relations of power between the Americans and the Chinese come through quite clearly in one refrain by the missionaries in *Fight:* that for them, "China felt like home." At a time when the Chinese Exclusion Act prohibited Chinese people from migrating to the United States or claiming citizenship, Dorothy McConnell approvingly quoted a missionary in China who stated that "I always felt that China was a part of home," and Kunkle likewise cited an American woman who reported "that she feels almost as if the war had come to her own country."[30] Such affective claims to citizenship—which could never go in reverse from China to the United States—worked to annex and assimilate China within an American sentimental project.

As such, *Fight*'s white missionary contributors, including McConnell, did not shed the baggage of US imperialism that historically undergirded the missionary movement. Though there was certainly a social justice orientation to *World Service News* under McConnell's editorship in the 1920s, there was a pronounced undercurrent of racial and cultural homogenization that guided its project even then. While the bulletin clearly stood against the nativist spirit of the Johnson Reed Act (1924), it touted domestic missionary work among immigrants as a mode of economic development governed by an ethno-racial project of "Americanization." One article from 1925, for instance, praised missionaries working among Mexican migrant workers in California who taught their charges "lessons in American citizenship, Christian living, sanitation, [and] personal and social hygiene."[31] This spirit was echoed in a contemporaneous children's book authored by McConnell. Titled *Uncle Sam's Family* (1924), it consisted of a series of short tales, largely centered on nonwhite children in the United States, who move from ignorance or chaos in their ethnic enclaves to an assimilated life of Protestantism, education, clean living, and middle-class living standards. In this regard, the cultures of the World Service Agencies and the Board of Foreign Missions—formative for McConnell—were informed by middle-class, turn-of-the-century progressivism and were thus further from the Left than the MFSS and its publication *Social Questions.*

McConnell's papers shed no light on her shifting politics in the years after 1939, when the CPUSA abruptly pulled its support from the American League against War and Fascism as a result of the Molotov-Ribbentrop Pact. As such, they do not provide us with a clear sense of when she broke from the radical Left or with the nature of the break. She was certainly disregarding its positions; in December 1940, she signed a petition calling for armaments and aid to be given freely by the United States to Great Britain, the kind of gesture decried as "war-mongering" and "imperialist" in the Communist press at the time.[32] That same year, she resumed her work as an editor for the Methodist missionary press, editing *The World Outlook* from 1940 through the 1960s. While ostensibly prolabor, under her tenure, *World Outlook* showed little of the vexed radicalism of her *World Service News* of the 1920s. *World Outlook* gauged the Chinese Communist Revolution almost solely on the degree to which it allowed missionaries to continue their work in country, persistently touting Chiang Kai-shek and crediting missionaries for single-handedly guiding Chinese development.[33] After 1939, there is no record of McConnell's involvement with any other secular left-wing organization, even though she remained in Manhattan, the site of her former league activities, up until the last year of her life, when she moved back to Ohio. Yet long before her physical move, she had "gone home"—not to the Ohio of her youth but to the social world of the Methodist Church, where she remained quite active for the rest of her days. She was a prominent national leader in this regard, heading the one and a half million–member Women's Division of the church from 1964 to 1968 and serving on the national board of the YWCA.[34]

McConnell wrote and published quite actively in the 1950s and 1960s and she was still engaged in social action that bore the echoes of her former activities but with none of the radical trappings. During the Cold War, she traveled extensively to missions in Africa, East Asia, and the Middle East. She did not explicitly emphasize the communist menace in her later writings, but a dramatic reversal is clear. In 1936, McConnell, the class-conscious feminist, had criticized Roosevelt's Good Neighbor policy with Latin America as not going far enough to redress a history of Monroe Doctrine–driven imperialism.[35] But by 1952, in her book *Along the African Path,* she offered standard colonialist fare. A travelogue of her visits to Methodist missions in Angola, Liberia, Rhodesia, Congo, and South Africa, it tells the story of African primitivism and superstition receding before the light of Western medicine, religion, and rationality. To this end, the book fully embraces European and American economic development as a corollary to the missions. McConnell praises the Firestone Company for developing Liberia through its rubber plantations, noting that "whole villages are set up within the plantation in far more sanitary surroundings than the native villages were in the interior." (As a vestigial trace of her earlier politics, she looks sympathetically on a strike by the plantation workers.) She similarly praises the Belgian colonial government for irrigation projects, which "bring back into fertility Congo's starved fields" and feed its hungry people. In so doing, she argues, Belgium is preparing the Congolese for democracy, for which they are not yet ready.[36]

Yet for all its explicit embrace of US imperialism and European colonialism, McConnell's writing in *Along the African Path* is continuous, in one key regard, with an aspect of her political work, which had been part of the missionary project all along. Once again, she stresses the struggles of the white missionaries, whose individual stories are detailed in the book, while failing to mention a single African by name. She also approvingly quotes a white Harvard-educated missionary who refers to Liberia as "our country," repeating the symbolic annexation present in her and other missionaries' writings in *Fight* during the 1930s. McConnell had long promoted Christian missionary work as a facilitator of economic development among nonwhite peoples, an idea she repressed in her Popular Front years.[37] When she returned to this idea in the 1950s, her experience in Marxian antifascism deepened her ability to articulate it. The older McConnell looked on Africa with the eye of a sociologist and an organizer, describing economic conditions, the relations of forces in the field, the nuances of missionary organizational strategies, and the "the social distinctions which may divide groups" at the sites she visits. At the conclusion of the book, she calls for missionaries "skilled in knowledge of economics," revealing a lesson she learned in the Popular Front. Rather than culture singularly driving economics (as in *Uncle Sam's Family*), she now saw that a transformation of culture could not proceed without a concomitant change in the economic arena.[38]

Wald's recent trilogy on the midcentury Left, from *Exiles from a Future Time* to *American Night,* traces the lives of cultural producers over time, and the evidence it provides allows us to theorize the social forces that sustain the Left from generation to generation. In relation to Methodist missionaries and the American League against War and Fascism, his work suggests the following theoretical framework to think through the contradictions of a figure such as Dorothy McConnell and what separates her from a Mary Inman or a Claudia Jones. That is, in the postwar years, the various individuals and groups that participated in the Popular Front maintained their fidelity to their prewar alignments, based in part on the very cultural, experiential, and institutional influences that had initially made their interests converge with the procommunist Left. This is not to say that the afterlife of the Popular Front is merely an individual affair. Rather, it is to suggest that one's embeddedness within multiple social, cultural, and institutional matrices—inside and outside the Left—has something to do with the sustainability of left-wing commitments over time. The nature of this embeddedness, while it varies in its exact details from person to person, is always social in nature. Everyone who was a Methodist missionary did not become a Cold War liberal, nor did all radicals in the Congress of Industrial Organizations or in the Committee on African Affairs retain their radicalism after World War II. Rather, the common sense of the Left seeped into the marrow of these various social constellations unevenly. Since every individual is lodged in multiple social networks simultaneously, our politics over time arguably have much to do with the resilience of each of our various networks in maintaining oppositional or alternative values; this in turn has much to do with the ubiquity of oppositional discourses across the entire social field, which will inevitably be uneven.

Thus for McConnell, the prolabor politics and global vision crucial to her particular Methodist upbringing brought her into an alignment with the Popular Front that was politically transformative. Yet the contradictions of this upbringing, brought into collision with the contradictions of CPUSA-founded organizations such as the American League against War and Fascism, were not generative of oppositional politics once the historical terrain shifted. The imperial underpinnings of the Methodist missionary movement, so crucial to structuring McConnell's public and family life, never disappeared, making her investment in feminist and labor politics fragile. Moreover, in light of the Molotov-Ribbentrop Pact of 1939, the CPUSA revealed that it was not genuinely internationalist but was beholden to the foreign policy goals of a specific nation-state. As a result of this pact, the Party abruptly abandoned the league, an organization to which McConnell had devoted an incredible amount of energy. This sudden reversal, combined with the ubiquity of anticommunism after the war, would have made it quite easy for her to turn her back on what was a much shorter institutional relationship.

In this account of Dorothy McConnell, I do not intend to return to the narrative of the 1930s that Alan Wald has so persuasively helped to dispel: a story of betrayed fellow travelers caught up in a radical decade that ultimately left little impact on American culture. Rather, in decisively refuting this Cold War view, his work provides tools to assess the afterlife of the Popular Front as nonunitary in nature, prompting us to parse out its various players for the complex, sometimes contradictory commitments that their life worlds reveal. Such a view allows us to see that in order to properly evaluate the Left, one must recognize that those who participate in its parties and platforms often possess a privilege and a complicity in the dominant logics that makes their egalitarian commitments provisional and transitory. We would do well to remember that this complicity can be as instructive as their oppositional vision.

Notes

1. Fraser Ottanelli, *The Communist Party of the United States: From the Depression to World War II* (New Brunswick, NJ: Rutgers University Press, 1991), 174; *7½ Million Speak for Peace . . .* (New York: American League for Peace and Democracy, 1939), 36; American League for Peace and Democracy Papers, box 3, folder ALPD, 1939; "Report by Russell Thayer, Acting Executive Secretary," box 2, folder ALPD, 1938; *Proceedings: Third U.S. Congress against War and Fascism* (New York: American League against War and Fascism, 1936), 8; "Emergency Legislation for Peace and Democracy," box 1, folder ALAWF, 1937, *Call to Action: American Congress for Peace and Democracy,* box 3, folder ALPD, 1939; all in Swarthmore College, Peace Collection, Swarthmore, Pennsylvania.
2. Dorothy McConnell, "As to Women," *American League against War and Fascism,* September 1938, 24.
3. Kate Weigand, *Red Feminism: American Communism and the Making of Women's Liberation* (Baltimore: John Hopkins University Press, 2002); Carol Boyce Davies, *Left of Karl Marx: The Political Life of Black Communist Claudia Jones* (Durham, NC: Duke University Press, 2008).
4. Alan Wald, *American Night: The Literary Left in the Era of the Cold War* (Chapel Hill: University of North Carolina Press, 2012), 297.
5. Weigand, *Red Feminism,* 30, 102.
6. McConnell, "As to Women," *American League against War and Fascism,* November 1937, 24.
7. Dr. Stewart Kunkle, "The Missions in China," *American League against War and Fascism,* March 1938, 11.
8. Christina Klein, *Cold War Orientalism: Asia in the Middlebrow Imagination, 1945–1961* (Berkeley: University of California Press, 2003).
9. For the former tendency, see Klein, *Cold War Orientalism;* David Roediger, *Working toward Whiteness: How America's Immigrants Became White; The Strange Journey from Ellis Island to the Suburbs* (New York: Basic Books, 2005); and, to a more limited extent, Nikhil Pal Singh, *Black Is a Country: Race and the Unfinished Struggle for Democracy* (Cambridge, MA: Harvard University Press, 2004). For the latter tendency, see Michael Denning, *The Cultural Front: The Laboring of American Culture in the Twentieth Century* (London: Verso, 1998); Weigand, *Red Feminism;* Robin D. G. Kelley, *Hammer and Hoe: Alabama Communists during the Great Depression* (Chapel Hill: University of North Carolina Press, 1990); Penny von Eschen, *Race against Empire: Black Americans and Anticolonialism, 1937–1957* (Ithaca, NY: Cornell University Press, 1997).
10. Ida Dailes, "Building the League," *Fight,* August 1934, 15.
11. *Proceedings: Third U.S. Congress against War and Fascism* (New York: American League against War and Fascism, 1936), 7–8.
12. Box 1, folders ALAWF 1934 and ALAWF 1935; box 2, folders ALPD 1938 and ALAWF, 4th Congress; box 3, folder ALPD, 1939; all in American League for Peace and Democracy Papers (hereafter ALPD Papers).
13. Harriet Hyman Alonso, *Peace as a Women's Issue: A History of the U.S. Movement for World Peace and Women's Rights* (Syracuse, NY: Syracuse University Press, 1993).

14. Dorothy McConnell, *Women, War, and Fascism* (New York: American League against War and Fascism, 1935), 18.
15. Barbara Foley, *Radical Representations: Politics and Form in U.S. Proletarian Fiction* (Durham, NC: Duke University Press, 1933), 218–19; Weigand, *Red Feminism,* 23.
16. McConnell, *Women, War, and Fascism,* 4–6, 18.
17. Weigand, *Red Feminism,* 3.
18. "Methodist Women Prepare for a Fete," *New York Times,* April 7, 1937, 10.
19. Doug Rossinow, "The Radicalization of the Social Gospel: Harry F. Ward and the Search for a New Social Order, 1898–1936," *Religion and American Culture: A Journal of Interpretation* 15, no. 1 (2005): 63–106.
20. Ibid., 84. In 1948, the MFSS changed its name to the Methodist Federation for Social Action, under which it still operates today. The federation was heavily Red-baited during the McCarthy era, when its relationship with the Methodist Church became deeply strained.
21. David Nelson Duke, *In the Trenches with Jesus and Marx: Harry F. Ward and the Struggle for Social Justice* (Tuscaloosa: University of Alabama Press, 2003), 153; Harry Ward, *Fighting to Live* (New York: American League against War and Fascism, Publications Committee, 1934); *Proceedings: Third U.S. Congress against War and Fascism,* 14–17; Harold Ward, "The Middle Class Today and Tomorrow: Under Fascist Barbarism," *New Masses,* April 7, 1936, 33.
22. I should state here that the archive on Dorothy McConnell is thin—her papers at Drew University comprise only three file folders, and we learn nothing about her life from the collections of the American League against War and Fascism at Swarthmore. Moreover, any records of her life or work during the 1930s are conspicuously absent from her papers.
23. Letter from Dorothy McConnell to Francis John McConnell, January 29, 1919, Series: Family, Subseries: Dorothy McConnell, folder 2, Francis John McConnell Family Papers, United Methodist Archives and History Center, Madison, New Jersey (hereafter McConnell Family Papers).
24. Letter from Curtis Bayley Geyer, January 1, 1926, Series: Family, Subseries: Dorothy McConnell, folder 2, McConnell Family Papers. See also Letter from W. F. McDermott, April 25, 1925; Letter from N. Mueller, August 27, 1925; Letter from William Bernhardt, September 24, 1925; all in McConnell Family Papers.
25. Denning, *The Cultural Front,* 9.
26. *Twenty-Five Years of Religious Social Change* [pamphlet], 13, Series: Social Issues, folder Articles and Reports 1920–1976, McConnell Family Papers; "Church Labor Report Puts Fear in Senate Committee" (undated clipping, ca. 1922), folder Articles and Reports, 1920–1937, McConnell Family Papers; Letter to Allen Grobin, unauthored and undated, Series: Non-McConnell Records, Subseries: Correspondence, folder Correspondence, 1894–1978, McConnell Family Papers; Denning, *The Cultural Front,* 9; "Call to Action: American Congress for Peace and Democracy," box 3, folder ALPD, 1939, ALPD Papers.
27. Kunkle, "The Missions in China," 11.
28. McConnell, "As to Women," *American League against War and Fascism,* November 1937, 24.
29. For a few examples, see "Plan Weekly Clinics in Korean Outpoints," *World Service*

News, July 1925, 11; "It Is Good to Be Here," *World Outlook,* February 1942, 3; Dorothy McConnell, "India Today," *World Outlook,* March 1948, 5–7.

30. Kunkle, "The Missions in China," 10; Dorothy McConnell, "India Today," *World Outlook,* March 1948, 5–7; McConnell, "As to Women," 24.
31. "Summer in the Migrant Camps," *World Service News,* May 1925, 5.
32. "3 Faiths' Leaders Plead for Britain," *New York Times,* December 29, 1940, 14.
33. Gerald Winfield, "Will Communism Destroy Christianity in China?," *World Outlook,* March 1949, 11.
34. Obituary, "Dorothy McConnell, 90, Editor and Author," *New York Times,* October 11, 1989, D27.
35. Dorothy McConnell, "Pan-America," *American League against War and Fascism,* December 1936, 14.
36. Dorothy McConnell, *Along the African Path* (New York: Board of Missions and Church Extension of the Methodist Church, 1952), 26, 43, 59.
37. Ibid., 22. McConnell's contributions to the missionary press dropped off considerably during the 1930s, the years when she was most active in the secular Left. Even her one significant missionary publication during these years, *Friends in Nippon,* emphasizes mutual understanding and Japanese agency.
38. McConnell, *Along the African Path,* 32, 100.

[PART III]

Novels

[10]

The Crab Cannery Ship Boom, Amamiya Karin, and the Precariat: Dance Dance Revolution?

Heather Bowen-Struyk

In 2008, a nearly eighty-year-old proletarian novella became an overnight best seller in Japan. The magnum opus of Kobayashi Takiji (1903–1933), *The Crab Cannery Ship* (*Kani kōsen,* 1929), is a story about workers aboard a ship organizing against dehumanizing labor conditions. It is a work that all well-educated people in Japan had heard of but few had actually read. In Japan, as in throughout what we used to call the First World, research on proletarian literature during the Cold War was often met with incredulity if not outright scorn, but dedicated scholars kept the field going, and Takiji's oeuvre, and this work in particular, came metonymically to represent the entire movement.[1] In concert with the boom, a new English translation of *The Crab Cannery Ship* is now available after being out of print for a couple of decades.[2] That the boom happened was stunning, even to those of us working on proletarian literature, but even more remarkable was the way that the boom seemed to speak to and for a generation of youths known as "the lost generation."[3]

Figure 10.1. Four manga (graphic novel) versions of *The Crab Cannery Ship*.

Annual sales of *The Crab Cannery Ship* are typically about five thousand copies per year. In 2008 that number jumped to over five hundred thousand, and that does not include sales of the four manga (graphic novel) versions that reached many more readers.[4] Media attention to the boom was characterized by surprise followed by interest in how this might affect youths. A segment from *Super News Anchor,* a morning news program that aired in 2008 when the *The Crab Cannery Ship* became an overnight best seller, illustrates these points.

Figure 10.2. "Nearly 4000 sales by May," *Super News Anchor*, May 2008, http://www.youtube.com/watch?v=PipKkwlq_ps.

In the Kinokuniya store in downtown Osaka highlighted in this news clip, sales in May 2008 reached nearly four thousand copies. By the autumn of 2008, the *The Crab Cannery Ship* boom was being discussed everywhere in Japan, including women's fashion magazines, *Playboy,* television news, highbrow journals, and the blogosphere. New phrases were coined, including the verb "to do 'crab cannery'" (*kani kō' suru,* meaning to do degrading labor), and the lamentation "this is just like *The Crab Cannery*!"[5] In May and June 2009, one stage adaptation of this work and another play about its author were produced in Tokyo, and in the summer of 2009, blockbuster director SABU released a major motion picture with innovations for a new generation: the handsome Matsuda Ryūhei in the lead, the class-traitor superintendent of operations remade as a straight-from-anime villain complete with scar and cane, and a closing theme song by boy-band Nico Touches the Walls in an ending that rocks.[6]

In 2002, Douglas McGray famously declared that postindustrial Japan may not make any*thing* anymore, but it does make *cool,* referring to the growing international interest in Japanese popular culture such as anime, manga, video games, television dramas, and pop music.[7] Calling this "gross national cool," McGray wondered whether and how Japan would be able to cash in on this new form of soft power. It is perhaps premature to say that Japan is postindustrial, given, for example, the renewed focus on dire work conditions among those employed in manufacturing being highlighted in a much discussed NHK (national broadcast) documentary, *Freeters Adrift.*[8] But there has been a discernible shift from manufacturing to flexible, immaterial labor, so McGray's formulation struck a nerve. In response, Kukhee Choo writes that "the Japanese government shifted its focus from a century-long practice of promoting traditional arts to supporting the popular culture industry under the banner 'Cool Japan.'"[9] In 2004, the Content Industry Promotion Law was passed to further promote already profitable popular culture.

While it has not been as economically successful as hoped, Cool Japan has been much celebrated as a successful national rebranding. But Cool Japan embodies the central contradiction associated with youths. On the one hand, Cool Japan represents the rich entertainment industry of young people. On the other hand, young people are bearing the brunt of the now quarter-century-long recession that has badly injured the Japan Inc. brand of the high growth years and, along with it, its social hallmarks: family, school, and corporation. Early in the recession, the neologism "freeter" (made of the English "free" and German *arbeiter,* or "worker") emerged to describe young educated people who opted out of corporate society, choosing instead part-time or contract work to allow them to live a supposedly freer life. Much criticism was directed at freeters for failing to grow up and assume the adult responsibilities that would supposedly have saved Japan from the ongoing recession. But the discussion has changed and it is now widely recognized that those former good jobs have disappeared.

In Anne Allison's choice formulation, "So, when such a construct of youth sells commodities, it is claimed as 'gross national cool.' But when real youth fail to get steady jobs or reproduce, as did their parents, they are castigated for not assuring Japan's future—what gets rendered as a crisis in reproduction."[10] Allison contrasts the "enterprise society" of the economic bubble period held up by "the three pillars of school, family and corporation" with the neoliberal flexible economy based on service, asking with earnestness what new "pillars" might take their place.[11] As possibilities, Allison identifies emergent freeter unions (unions that can be joined by anyone, regardless of workplace), nonprofit organizations, and the kind of antipoverty activism practiced by participants in an emerging precariat movement. "Precariat," a neologism combining "precarious" and "proletariat," was first used in the 1980s by French sociologists, but with decades of intervening neoliberalization and the 2008 economic crisis, it has gained new traction. Guy Standing sees the precariat as a global phenomenon, consisting of people who lack labor-related security including labor-market security, employment security, job security (within one's employment), work security (protection against harm at work), skill reproduction security, income security, and representation security.[12] While this is inflected differently in different cultures, there are several key features of the global precariat: "it consists of people who have minimal trust relationships with capital or the state, making it quite unlike the salariat. And it has none of the social contract relationships of the proletariat, whereby labour securities were provided in exchange for subordination and contingent loyalty."[13] The securities sought by postwar social democrats, labor parties, and trades unions have been diminished by the transformations wrought by a flexible economy, a reliance on temporary workers, a turn to migrant labor, and the resultant loss of social support.

Within this matrix in 2008, a dusty communist novella became a best seller in Japan, inviting us to think about how the literature of the proletarian movement is being reconceived as culture of, by, and for the precariat. Although there is a precariat movement, as of yet it lacks the strength of the leftist proletarian movement of the 1920s and 1930s. Moreover, the blockbuster film based on *The Crab Cannery Ship* was hardly a product of the precariat movement but has much in common with it. Perhaps it represents a beginning culture of the movement: new catchphrases, manga, blockbuster film—disenfranchised youths embracing a proletarian novella in the vernacular of popular culture? In short, that the boom happened at all was breathtaking, but what really got people talking (which in turn fueled the boom) was the way it was reportedly being consumed and remade by youths. So, beyond the *why* was the tantalizing question: Did this portend a developing consciousness among a young generation known as the lost generation? And if so, what kind of consciousness and how different from the proletarian novella is it?

The Crab Cannery Ship, Russia, and the Making of the Boom

This 1929 novella describes a motley crew of seasonal workers who fish for crabs and then can them aboard ship. The ship's superintendent charts a course to the treacherous waters between Russia and northern Japan, subjecting the contract workers to brutal treatment. As the ship sets sail ceremoniously, the fishing company's manager descends down into the hold: "The fisherman's shit-hole was lit by feeble electric lights. Its air was thick with tobacco smoke and the odor of crowded human bodies; the entire cabin stank like a toilet. People moving about in their bunks looked like squirming maggots."[14] The superintendent spits on the littered floor and declares:

> Needless to say, as some of you may know, this crab cannery ship's business is not just to make lots of money for the corporation but is actually a matter of the greatest international importance. This is a one-on-one fight between us, citizens of a great empire, and the Russkies, a battle to find out which one of us is greater—them or us. Now just supposing you lose—this could never happen, but if it did—all Japanese men and boys who've got any balls [XX] at all would slit their bellies and jump into the sea off Kamchatka. You may be small in size but that doesn't mean you'll let those stupid Russkies beat you.[15]

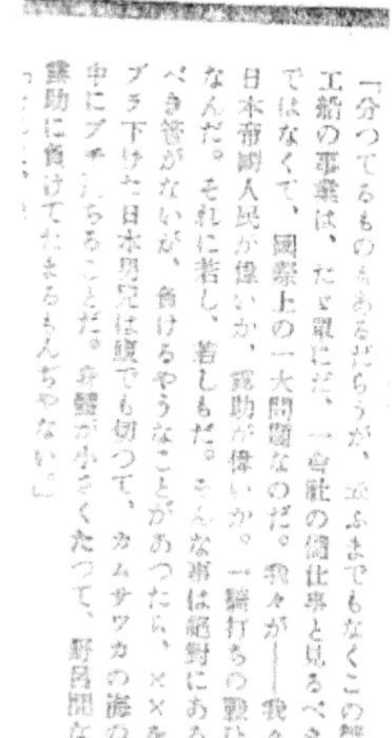
「分つてるものもあるだらうが、云ふまでもなくこの蟹工船の事業は、たゞ單に、一會社の儲仕事と見るべきではなくて、國際上の一大問題なのだ。我々が――我々日本帝國人民が偉いか、露助が偉いか。一騎打ちの戰ひなんだ。それに若し、若しもだ。そんな事は絶對にあるべき筈がないが、負けるやうなことがあつたら、××をブラ下げた日本男兒は腹でも切つて、カムサツカの海の中にブチ落ちることだ。身體が小さくたつて、野呂間な露助に負けてたまるもんぢやない。」

Figure 10.3. Excerpt from the original publication of *The Crab Cannery Ship*, in *Senki* [Battleflag], May 1929.

The original publication, shown in figure 10.3, includes a double X ("XX") six lines from the right near the bottom.[16] These are characters used by authors and/or editors to avoid words or phrases that would have provoked the censors and led to banning and fines. This is a minor example, and the XX—"balls"—would at a glance be comprehensible without violating obscenity rules. It was not uncommon in proletarian literature for entire sentences to be replaced with X's or ellipses, but this was published in *Senki* (Battleflag), the organ of the largest proletarian arts organization Nippon Artista Proleta Federacio, which took greater chances, often provoking the censors.[17] In fact, the second installment, in which factory hands say they hope the emperor gets stomach cramps after eating the crab, caused the June 1929 issue to be banned. Writer Ibuse Masuji (1898–1993) recalled having heard from a female clerk at the Kinokuniya book store that in the late 1920s and early 1930s, *Senki* would be placed on the front counter and sell a hundred copies in the first day because savvy customers knew to buy it before it was banned the following day.[18] To summarize the rest of the story: Amid unbearable work conditions, a fishing trawler that embarked from the cannery ship accidentally washes up on shore in Russia. A kind Russian family takes the fishermen in, and they receive a rudimentary introduction to communism pantomimed by a Chinese interpreter speaking in broken Japanese:

> "Boss do nothing, get rich. Proletariat always this." (He showed a person being choked.) "This, no good! Proletariat, all you, one, two, three . . . hundred, thousand, fifty thousand, hundred thousand, all, all, this." (He imitated children joining hands) "Get strong. All right!" (He slapped his arm.) "No lose, nobody. Understand?"[19]

If some in the proletarian movement could be accused of using theoretical language that was inaccessible to the general working class, here was the message made plain and simple. The interpreter pantomimes the "rich man boss" fleeing and Japan becoming a "good country" with "all working people."[20] It is important to notice that the goal is a country of working people.

A couple of days later when the storm calms down, the shipwrecked men return and share their experience. Meanwhile, two major events leave those on board alternately hopeless and angry. First, the superintendent decides not to go to the aid of a nearby ship signaling SOS because it would have meant losing a week of work, so 425 men die. The men aboard the crab cannery ship realize that the other ship is insured for more than it is worth, so the ship's demise is profitable. Then, the death of a coworker by the superintendent's neglect and abuse makes the workers realize that none of their lives is valuable, despite the rhetoric often employed by the manager that they belong to the great empire of Japan.

So they organize and strike. And just when they might be successful, the navy destroyer that has accompanied them all along—to protect them from the Russians, they were told—sends soldiers aboard to arrest the leaders of the strike. Crestfallen, the men realize that they have lost. But as they are packing the crab meant for the emperor and making the objectionable comment about how they hope it gives him cramps that is not replaced with X's or ellipses, they suddenly understand that they could win if they all stood together rather than letting the leaders be arrested—the lesson learned from the trip to Russia. The threats to their lives and well-being occur on the ship, but the insight into how to combat them is gained from that accidental trip. The novella ends famously: "'Well, let's do it again, one more time!' And so they rose. One more time!"[21] The story is followed by a postscript about how the second strike was successful even though they all end up getting arrested. But after being released, the men spread out to various sectors of labor to continue organizing. The key points: the lesson about worker solidarity is learned from Russians, and the emphasis is on creating more humane working conditions.

How and why does this become relevant in the neoliberal twenty-first century? On the one hand, there were material factors that laid the groundwork. First, Communist organizations have maintained Kobayashi Takiji's legacy by keeping his works in print, promoting scholarship, and honoring him with a graveside ceremony on the anniversary of his death as well as evening remembrances that include scholarly talks and musical and theatrical performances celebrated throughout Japan, such as the 2009 graveside ceremony. With a special focus on remembrance and legacy, these events highlight Takiji's commitment to fight against Japan's nationalist-imperialist project as well as the tragic circumstances of his death: arrested on the street on February 20, 1933, Takiji was subjected to brutal torture and killed while under interrogation.

Figure 10.4. Graveside ceremony to honor Kobayashi Takiji, February 2009, Otaru, Japan, https://www.youtube.com/watch?v=8eDJ-vDPCcwhttps://www.youtube.com/watch?v=8eDJ-vDPCcw.

Second, the Takiji Library was established in 2003 and maintained until 2008 by Mr. Sano Chikara, retired president of Oracle in Japan, who channeled his considerable energy and wealth toward the promotion of new scholarship, hiring committed scholar and curator Satō Saburō to build the library, sponsoring four symposia, and sponsoring the publication of ten books, including a new manga version of *The Crab Cannery Ship*.[22] Sano's extraordinary zeal for promoting Takiji took a hit with the economic crisis of 2008, but by then he had accomplished his goal: to bring Takiji's works back to the public's attention. Having graduated from Takiji's alma mater, Sano was motivated by school and civic pride, as he explained, and he spoke with conviction about how important it was for young people to learn the lessons in Takiji's literature—although I was left wondering how far he would be willing to take that.[23]

But there were also the strange workings of chance: a young, precariously employed paperback stocker at a bookstore read an article about the relevance of *The Crab Cannery Ship* to contemporary workers by a new breed of public intellectual-activist, Amamiya Karin; ordered 150 copies; and handwrote a note encouraging the working poor to read it. And the final whimsy, a news story about the boom in early May was written before the boom was real. But the story itself circulated, and as it did, it became real. Norma Field described these developments:

> Two liberal newspaper articles, an initial book order of 150 copies, then a conservative newspaper article turned the trickle of interest into a flood. Finding a story that sells is of course a central preoccupation of the media, with the hoped-for outcome being a cascade of sales. The aura of newsworthiness prompted publishers to reprint more copies, bookstores to provide more space, provoking further media attention, then more copies reprinted.[24]

In a turn of phrase that invites us to keep thinking, Field calls the boom "a miraculous meeting of pure contingency and absolute necessity, of commercial appetite and human need."[25]

Amamiya Karin and *The Crab Cannery Ship*

The match that lit the fire of the *The Crab Cannery Ship* boom was a transcribed discussion between author-activist Amamiya Karin and author Takahashi Gen'ichiro that appeared in the *Mainichi Daily Newspaper* on January 8, 2008.[26] Amamiya remarked that she had recently read the novella and was struck by how it seemed to be describing the current state of freeters. Takahashi responded that he had just recently taught the work in a university seminar and that while he had planned on teaching the students about the idea of the proletariat, he was surprised to have them tell him that they already got it and that it was just like their lives.

Amamiya Karin (b. 1975) has emerged as an author, activist, and advocate for the precariat. She debuted in a 1999 documentary *The New God* (*Atarashii kamisama*) by leftist filmmaker Tsuchiya Yutaka. Twenty-four-year-old Amamiya was lead vocalist of an ultranationalist punk rock band, The Revolutionary Truth, when she was invited by the Japanese Red Army (a controversial communist group) on a trip to Pyongyang, in the Democratic People's Republic of Korea.[27] Tsuchiya gave her a camera and asked her to record a video diary, which she did with great emotional candor. The documentary progresses as a three-way conversation between Amamiya, her bandmate Itō Hidehito, and the filmmaker (who also appears onscreen) as the three discuss politics and Amamiya struggles to confront the source of recessionary Japanese suffering.

Amamiya has since developed into an extremely prolific and topical speaker and writer. She tackles issues related to not only youths in poverty, including bullying, social withdrawal, and suicide, but also NATO, the G8, and the problems associated with nuclear power and weapons. Amamiya resists being called a leftist, not least because she is committed to thinking compassionately about those on the right, and she recalls with gratitude how it was the right wing that first gave her a sense of community and opportunities to think about the relation between individual suffering and social structure. She writes that "It is an opposition movement against the fact that people all over the world are forced into instability because of neo-liberalism, which is advancing globalization."[28]

Articulate and self-aware, Amamiya speaks for and to a generation of youths who feel disenfranchised from economic power. Her fashion sense is deliberately youthy and provocative: from Lolita goth to faux schoolgirl to a frilly white baby-doll dress, she presents herself as a representative of youth. She is sensitive to the media mix of popular culture, producing music, film, blog, tweets, fiction, nonfiction, and demonstrations in a style that combines a well-rehearsed emotional vulnerability with a hard-core defiance. Part of the appeal of Amamiya as a spokesperson-mascot for the precariat is the way she appears to function independently not only of all the organizations—including family, school (she withdrew), and corporations—that have been contaminated by association with Japan Inc., but also, interestingly, of old-school organized politics. Working within the same culture generative of capital represented by Cool Japan, Amamiya's affective labor insists on affirming nonproductivity.[29] Undoubtedly, she profits from her productivity; still, she parlays that into an appeal for those without the same benefits.

Figure 10.5. Amamiya Karin, Indies May Day March, Tokyo, May 3, 2012. Credit: Heather Bowen-Struyk.

Even Amamiya was surprised to find out about the boom. She recalls that on May 2, 2008, at the Indies May Day in Gifu, she was with a bunch of twenty-something students, freeters, regular employees, and Internet café employees all talking about work conditions when someone said, "Isn't it just like *Kani kō*?" "Unfortunately," writes Amamiya, "I was drinking, so I don't exactly remember what was just like *Kani kō*."[30] She reflects:

> *Kani kōsen* [*The Crab Cannery Ship*] turned into *Kani kō* [*Crab Cannery*], and it was appreciated as "my story" by the 21st century precariat—freeters and others forced to do precarious temp work, but also including those regular employees who are management in name only and the unemployed. That would surely surprise Kobayashi Takiji.[31]

Most often, leftist literature is reissued by publishers sympathetic to the entreaties of scholars who insist that there is, or at least *ought* to be, a reading public. But in this case, the nearly eighty-year-old communist novella was already available in print by a mainstream publisher, when, anticipating increased market demand and the celebrity appeal of an afterword by Amamiya, the leftist press Kin'yōbi issued a new edition in response to the boom. In her essay, she meticulously details how *The Crab Cannery Ship* describes work conditions that are remarkably similar to the precarious work situations faced by irregular workers in Japan today. Amamiya insists that labor conditions in *The Crab Cannery Ship* are not remote at all, although they may seem remote to those with the wherewithal to purchase the book. She focuses on those doing manual labor (in contrast to contemporary scholars who focus on immaterial labor) and, moreover, focuses on those whose working conditions are as harsh and precarious as the fishermen and canners aboard Takiji's ship. To give just one example, Amamiya explains that contemporary employers are hiring workers as "contract" (*ukeoi*) workers, but the laws regarding these contracts are even less regulated than the much-discussed "temp" or "dispatch" (*haken*) workers, enabling even greater exploitation just as the sailors and factory hands aboard Takiji's factory ship face greater exploitation in the unsupervised waters of Kamchatka. Not subject to labor laws or even "temp" regulations, there is little supervision, and there is also unfair firing. All of the big companies that represent Japan—Hitachi, Tōshiba, Canon, Toyota, and so on—use this contract labor system, it was revealed in 2006.[32] *The Crab Cannery Ship* therefore is not remote: "In this tale overflowing with depictions of an exceedingly 'cruel' workplace, there are many uncanny similarities to the lives of young people living in the 21st century."[33]

Figure 10.6. Cover of the 2008 edition of *The Crab Cannery Ship* (Kin'yōbi Press), with essay by Amamiya Karin.

Moreover, Amamiya explains that like the workers on the ship, atomized workers in Japan are all floating along isolated from each other and she never imagined that they would be able to unite. But then, she writes, it happened: "Labor unions like Goodwill, Full Cast, M. Crew were formed one after another at companies with daily dispatch (temp) workers, breeding grounds for the working poor, and now, all over Japan independent labor unions are being formed in which anyone—whether a freeter or just an individual—can join."[34] New labor unions—especially freeter unions—have arisen to try to bring together disparate individuals: "Young people who have been divided, made to compete with each other, yelled at and fired for demanding rights while living in such uncertain times, have begun to stand up for themselves like the workers in *The Crab Cannery Ship*."[35] In conclusion, she refers to the Indies May Day March, which connected freeters and others, wondering whether *The Crab Cannery Ship* could possibly be a catalyst for youths in the way that Russians are within the novella; yet in so doing she removes the significance of Soviet Russia altogether.[36]

Dance Dance Revolution?

SABU's blockbuster adaptation follows Takiji's storyline more or less, with a twenty-first-century style makeover that is also a substance makeover. One of the most significant changes SABU made in adapting the film was the transformation of the Russia scene; instead of being stranded on shore in actual Russia, the fishermen are picked up by a Russian transport ship, and this entire scene is filmed with filters that suggest the fantastic.

Figure 10.7. The "happy dance party," from the film *Kani kōsen* (directed by SABU, 2009), http://www.youtube.com/watch?v=I7RSAYTjJ5w.

With a carnivalesque dance party in the background, a Chinese interpreter dressed as a joker explains the truth of the ship to the men in enigmatic broken Japanese: it is their own fault that their labor conditions are so bad, he says—they just need to decide for themselves what they want and then act on it.

Figure 10.8. "Each is important," from the film *Kani kōsen* (directed by SABU, 2009), http://www.youtube.com/watch?v=FQ8KGOjqus4.

With no talk of the rich getting richer off of working people's labor, this wisdom from the joker sounds less like a lesson in communism and more like the kind of neobourgeois advice routinely dispensed by adults in Japan to the "lost generation" as it has grown up in recessionary Japan. Although Japan famously has had a low unemployment rate, "one-third of all workers, but half of all young workers between the ages of 15 and 24, are irregularly employed. . . . Without steady employment, fewer youth are marrying, having children or leaving parental homes. Moving from job to job and getting stuck in time without the means to become 'adults,' youth are futureless—a state they also get blamed for."[37]

SABU's film quotes imagery from two film classics (Sergei Eisenstein's 1925 *Battleship Potemkin* and Charlie Chaplin's 1936 *Modern Times*), combining the two into a tragicomic indictment of industrial capitalism for a postindustrial youth audience. At the end of the film, the workers organize and present a list of their demands to the manager. The navy boards the ship and shoots Shinjo (idol Matsuda Ryūhei, one of the two fellows who went to the Russian ship); the men then become despondent and go back to work as usual, having failed, until they spontaneously come to the same realization (that they should have banded together), and they walk off the job together with blood-splattered flag flying and an energetic theme song appropriate for a video game.

In contrast to the novella, it is not entirely clear what comes next for the workers in the film. In one of the scenes showing their organizing, Shinjo—reflecting the neobourgeois ideology learned on the Russian ship—asks the group what they want to be. And they answer variously:

a doctor, a teacher, an architect, a singer says the only man on this ship not attractive enough to be a pop star. But the point is that no one wants to be a factory worker, because in 2008 "*kani kō' suru*" (to do "crab cannery") briefly became a new verb, meaning to do degrading labor. The film leaves it unclear whether there is the possibility of factory labor with dignity or whether the only answer is to get a better job and move into the bourgeoisie, a solution that would have disgusted radicals in the 1920s and 1930s.

To return to the Russian boat scene, the two protagonists turn to each other, saying "we were wrong" to think they could not change things. Then Shinjo asks Shiota "What do you want to do?" and the answer is "I want to dance up a storm." This is the coming-into-consciousness moment when Shinjo and Shiota realize that they must act in order to effect change, so why is this represented by a dance party? Doesn't anyone on this Russian transport ship work? Like the popular arcade game Dance Dance Revolution (DDR), the revolution itself is effaced by its invocation. On this Russian transport ship, the superintendent is cool, joining in the dance party and affirming the superiority of the Russian way—but where is the revolutionary message? Russia no longer offers the specter of Communism but rather a phantasmic dance party. In the next scene, the two are returned to the ship, exhausted but also energized and inspired.

Figure 10.9. "I want to dance," from the film *Kani kōsen* (directed by SABU, 2009), http://www.youtube.com/watch?v=-iu0CH8_lac.

When I invoke DDR, I am not just being frivolous: I want to think more about how the lost generation forms communities and projects aspirations for the future. SABU's reformulation of the Russia scene as a phantasmic dance party speaks to the recession generation's (lost generation's) ambivalence about labor. DDR is a wildly popular arcade game introduced to Japan in 1998 in which players follow prompts on a video screen and step on motion-sensitive squares to score points. While the promotion of Cool Japan is intended to strengthen Japan's economy and its gross national cool, popular culture is also blamed for the failures of youths, including outbreaks of violence. Since 1989—when it was discovered that the one responsible for kidnapping, sexually abusing, and killing young girls (Miyazaki Tsutomu) had a large collection of horror films and anime—there has been a moral panic regarding certain aspects of popular culture referred to as "otaku" culture. In Japan, the connoisseurs of video games, manga, anime, collectible figurines, and so forth are unflatteringly referred to as "otaku" (although a positive self-appropriation of the term is also apparent). Otaku are considered to be socially maladjusted and to prefer dwelling in virtual reality. Media attention to otaku habits in each new shocking instance of youth-initiated violence adds to the panic about pop culture as the problem. More recently, in 2013 in the United States, it was revealed that the shooter (Adam Lanza) responsible for the deaths of twenty-six people at the Sandy Hook Elementary School was an avid fan of DDR, prompting a similar panic about popular culture.

As in any cultural subgroup, there may be those with mental illness who need treatment or those with the wherewithal to be cruel, but it is hard to fathom why DDR could be considered the cause of a murderous frenzy. Practicing psychoanalyst Saitō Tamaki insists that although he identifies otaku as those [men] who use female anime characters as masturbation aids, he also insists that this perversion (in the psychoanalytic and thus not pejorative sense) in the imaginary realm does not interfere with their daily lives because sane people can tell the difference between the two. Tamaki adds that "This is another way in which Miyazaki Tsutomu was entirely exceptional."[38]

Popular culture is glorified when it leads to economic growth but is blamed for the failures of youths and a contradiction emerges when the recession generation uses the vernacular of popular culture to remake images of revolutionary authority. For Miriam Hansen and others, "vernacular modernism" describes the ways Hollywood cinema grappled with modernity through popular culture, dignifying it as a means to diversify agency. What if we also read otaku culture, like DDR and manga, as part of the process by which the recession generation makes sense of precarity rather than as a cause of decline?[39] SABU's creative introduction of the "happy dance party" scene is important, because this is where the two "lost" Japanese workers are ideologically reoriented in an atmosphere that is carnivalesque and notably lacking in labor. The revolutionary message to be learned from the Russians is to dance dance, with a revolution yet to be determined. DDR, as an example of

Cool Japan, represents the successful promotion of commodity culture, but it also rhymes with the way youths are themselves rethinking and remaking political activism.

May Day, Mayday! M'aidez!

In 2012, I joined the Freedom and Life May Day March in Tokyo. The march was in its ninth year (the sixth since Amamiya joined), so it had started to acquire its own sense of historical mission, one that grows and changes from year to year. It is an independent May Day demonstration, organized in conjunction with the All-Japan Freeter Union (not affiliated with any political party or old-school labor unions). Throughout the world, May Day is commemorated as an international day of labor. May 1 is an official labor holiday in over eighty countries, and in many more, the day is marked with marches and demonstrations. In Japan, May Day is not an official holiday, but it falls during Golden Week, a string a four official holidays: April 29, Showa Day; May 3, Constitution Day; May 4, Greenery Day; and May 5, Children's Day. As a result, many aspire to take the entire week off. During the period of high economic growth, Golden Week was associated with luxury, including overseas vacations for those who could afford them.

May Day has been celebrated in Japan since 1920 after the formation of the Socialist League and continues to be observed in Tokyo and elsewhere by organized labor. But the Indies' Freedom and Life May Day is an attempt to redefine May Day by organizers at the All-Freeter Union—a union that allows anyone, regardless of employment, to join and therefore initiate new forms of community. The Freedom and Life May Day 2012 Planning Committee was responsible for a well-organized march and a two-page list of "slogans." Corralled into a single lane by police, the 2012 march moved energetically in a circuit through the busy streets of Shinjuku (despite a downpour that began midway) as Amamiya Karin issued call-and-response slogans such as "Liberate Shinjuku!" and "Let's make some noise in the streets!" with a danceable, syncopated rhythm. Headed by a sound car with a live DJ and a banner that read "Dance is not a Crime," this was not your parents' May Day march. It represents both the transformation in protest culture and the consciousness of the recession generation.

Figure 10.10. Amamiya Karin, Indies May Day March, Tokyo, May 3, 2012. Credit: Heather Bowen-Struyk.

According to the Twitter buzz, police estimated 300 participants, while the organizers estimated 170.[40] Widely recognized as the busiest train station in Tokyo (and therefore Japan), Shinjuku teems with people, especially east of the station in the plaza in front of the landmark Alta Studio, where demonstrations like this are held precisely because of the many passersby. At any given point, there were at least as many spectators as marchers (many recording it with portable devices) and seemingly almost as many police. The numbers may have been relatively small, but the march more than made up for that in spectacle: dance beat, sound car, the photogenic Amamiya wearing a lacy white baby-doll dress and carrying a bullhorn, several participants in cosplay (costume play) giant animal costumes, and a general celebration of nonconformity hardly dampened by the rain.

In figure 10.11, Amamiya has the bullhorn amid the lively crowd. The theme of the 2012 march was "The aspirations of a motley crew," which focused on respecting diversity of background, nationality, sexuality, and schooling. First, the dance car led the march with a giant yellow sign on the back reading "DANCE IS NOT A CRIME." Several dozen participants near the car danced rhythmically and sang along—sometimes to the DJ and sometimes to Amamiya's calls. Chants included the danceable "Us Guys Don't Just Do What We're Told," from the song by ECD.[41]

Figure 10.11. "Liberate Shinjuku!" "Liberate the streets!" Indies May Day March, Tokyo, 2012, http://www.youtube.com/watch?v=K6x_esZ3zhM.

Amamiya called out "We oppose labor" within a string of phrases beginning with "We oppose" that also included "We oppose overtime," "We oppose sexual harassment," and, tellingly, "We oppose getting up early." In fact, this resistance to labor is characteristic of the precariat. Guy Standing writes that "Besides labour insecurity and insecure social income, those in the precariat lack a work-based identity. When employed, they are in career-less jobs, without traditions of social memory, a feeling they belong to an occupational community steeped in stable practice, codes of ethics and norms of behaviors, reciprocity and fraternity."[42] In a 2011 book on the rising freeter union movement in Japan, sociologist Hashiguchi Shōji (b. 1977) describes the movement in terms of the contradiction between "let us work" and "we won't work."[43]

Is it a coincidence that SABU's remake of the Russia scene and the Indies' May Day protests both suggest DDR? It may be. Street protests in Japan continue to transform in the vernacular of youth culture as documented by sociologist Mōri Yoshitaka (e.g., incorporating music and live DJs).[44] Takiji's 1929 novella ends with considerable optimism despite the severe government crackdown and widespread arrest of leftists in March 1928 and April 1929. A 1953 film version ends with members of the imperial navy boarding the ship and gunning down everyone in an atrocious bloodbath, a critique of the tragic consequences of militarization still fresh in the early postwar period. Rereading—and rewriting and rescripting—*The Crab Cannery Ship* in twenty-first-century recessionary Japan allows for new endings, as the story is itself unfinished and requires the reader to imagine its continuation vis-à-vis the postscript. In 1929, Russia played a crucial role in the coming into consciousness of the workers in *The Crab Cannery Ship*. By contrast, in the way that the novella is reimagined for a twenty-first-century youth audience, Russia becomes phantasmic, if not entirely replaceable. In 1929, what was being affirmed was the possibility of a worker's revolution. Now there is nostalgia for those jobs associated with preneoliberal security; at the same time, there are emerging forms of protest that oppose, among other things, labor itself. This 2009 film has an ambiguous ending. The men organize and learn the skills necessary to unionize and demand humane working conditions (we assume, for the viewers are not actually shown the demands). At the same time, the neobourgeois ideology of individual choice and individual action is also emphasized, suggesting a paternalistic intervention into the precariat's apathy toward labor.

Notes

1. I follow the Japanese language practice of putting the family name, Kobayashi, before his personal name, Takiji. Also, following the literary practice in Japan, I call him Takiji.
2. The first partial translation appeared shortly after the author's death by torture while under interrogation in 1933 in *The Cannery Boat by Kobayashi Takiji and Other Japanese Short Stories,* translation anonymous [Max Bickerton] (New York: International Publishers, 1933). A second English translation was published in 1973: *"The Factory Ship" and "The Absentee Landlord,"* translated by Frank Motofuji (Seattle: University of Washington Press, 1973). Both of these earlier translations are out of print, but a new 2013 translation has brought it back into print in English: *The Crab Cannery Ship and Other Novels of Struggle,* translated by Željko Cipriš (Honolulu: University of Hawai'i Press, 2013). In addition to Cipriš's translation, which includes two additional novellas by Takiji, there are six more of his pieces forthcoming in a volume coedited by Heather Bowen-Struyk and Norma Field, *For Dignity, Justice, and Revolution: An Anthology of Japanese Proletarian Literature* (Chicago: University of Chicago Press, 2015).
3. For an excellent account of the boom, see Norma Field, "Commercial Appetite and Human Need: The Accidental and Fated Revival of Kobayashi Takiji's *Cannery Ship,*" *Asia-Pacific Journal,* February 22, 2009, http://www.japanfocus.org/-norma-field/3058. The seeds of my essay can be found in my early reflections on *The Crab Cannery Ship* boom in Heather Bowen-Struyk, "Why a Boom in Proletarian Literature in Japan? The Kobayashi Takiji Memorial and the Factory Ship," *Asia-Pacific Journal,* June 29, 2009, http://japanfocus.org/-Heather-Bowen_Struyk/3180.
4. The four manga versions are all graphic novels: Yes Koike, *Gekiga kani kōsen: Haō no fune* [The Graphic Novel *Crab Cannery Ship*: A Ship Ruled by Force] (Tokyo: Takarajimasha, 2008); Variety Art Works, *Kani kōsen: Manga de dokuha* [*The Crab Cannery Ship*: Read It All in Manga] (Tokyo: East Press, 2007); Hara Keiichirō, *Kani kōsen* [The Crab Cannery Ship] (Tokyo: Shinchōsha, 2008); and Fujio Gō, *Manga kani kōsen: 30 pun de yomeru . . . daigakusei no tame no* [The Manga Crab Cannery Ship: For College Students to Read in 30 Minutes] (Tokyo: Shirakaba Bungakukan Takiji Raiburarī, 2006).
5. "Keikyō: 'Kani kōsuru' 'Maru de kani kō da na' . . . Hiseikikoyō no wakamono

ga nageku kakushakai" [The Situation: "To Do Crab Cannery" and "This Is Just like *The Crab Cannery*!"—Irregularly Employed Youth Cry Out against the Divided Society], *Okinawa Times,* December 5, 2008, http://anchorage.2ch.net/test/read.cgi/bizplus/1228460670/.

6. SABU (aka Tanaka Hiroyuki), dir. *Kani kōsen* [The Crab Cannery Ship] (Tōei Video, 2009), DVD. The Japanese trailer is available at YouTube, http://www.youtube.com/watch?v=qmJ6DCXIM40.
7. Douglas McGray, "Japan's Gross National Cool," *Foreign Policy,* May 1, 2002, http://www.foreignpolicy.com/articles/2002/05/01/japans_gross_national_cool
8. *Furiita hyōrū: Monotsukuri no genba de* [Freeters Adrift: Where Things Are Made], NHK documentary, first broadcast February 5, 2005.
9. Kukhee Choo, "Nationalizing 'Cool': Japan's Global Promotion of the Content Industry," in *Popular Culture and the State in East and Southeast Asia,* edited by Nissin Otmazgin and Eyal Ben-Ari (London: Routledge, 2012), 85.
10. Anne Allison, "The Cool Brand, Affective Activism and Japanese Youth," *Theory Culture & Society* 26, nos. 2–3 (March–May 2009): 91.
11. Ibid., 90.
12. Guy Standing, *The Precariat: The New Dangerous Class* (London: Bloomsbury Academic, 2011), 10.
13. Ibid., 8.
14. Translations from Takiji Kobayashi, *The Crab Cannery Ship and Other Novels of Struggle,* translated by Željko Cipriš (Honolulu: University of Hawai'i Press, 2013), 25–26.
15. Ibid., 26.
16. "Kani kōsen" [The Crab Cannery Ship], *Senki* (May 1929): 141–88 and (June 1929): 128–57.
17. For more on censorship and redaction, see Jonathon Abel, *Redacted: The Archives of Censorship in Transwar Japan* (Berkeley: University of California Press, 2012).
18. "Since 1927: Kinokuniya shoten no ayumi" [Kinokuniya company history from 1927], Kinokuniya Web Store,http://www.kinokuniya.co.jp/company/history.html.
19. Kobayashi, *The Crab Cannery Ship and Other Novels of Struggle,* 46.
20. Ibid., 46.
21. Ibid., 95.
22. Takiji Library, http://www.takiji-library.jp.
23. Sano Chikara, "Go-aisatsu" [Greetings], in *2008 Okkusufodo Kobayashi Takiji kinen shinpojiumu ronbunshu: Takiji no shiten kara mita shintai chiiki kyoiku* [Report of the 2008 Kobayashi Takiji Memorial Symposium at Oxford: Body, Region, and Education], 3–4 (Otaru: Otaru University of Commerce and Kinokuniya, 2009).
24. Norma Field, *"Commercial Appetite and Human Need: The Accidental and Fated Revival of Kobayashi Takiji's* Cannery Ship," *Asia-Pacific Journal,* February 22, 2009, http://www.japanfocus.org/-norma-field/3058.
25. Ibid.
26. Amamiya Karin and Takahashi Gen'ichirō, "Kakusa shakai: 08nen no kibō o tou; Takahashi Gen'ichirō-san—Amamiya Karin-san taidan" [Income Disparity

Society: Exploring the Aspirations of '08; A Dialogue between Takahashi Gen'ichirō and Amamiya Karin], *Mainichi Shimbun* [News], Tokyo asakan [morning edition] (January 8, 2008).

27. *Atarashii kamisama* [The New God], directed by Tsuchiya Yutaka, DVD, 1999.

28. Amamiya Karin, "Suffering Forces Us to Think beyond the Right-Left Barrier," translated by Jodie Beck, in *Mechademia 5: Fanthropologies* (Minneapolis and London: University of Minnesota Press, 2010), 254. Original publication: Amamiya Karin, "Ikitzurasa ga koesaseru 'sayū' no kakine: Baburu no hōkaigo no 'yakenohara' nite," *Migi to hidari wa te o musuberu ka* [Can the Left and Right Join Hands?], special issue of *Rosujene/Lost Generation* (May 2008): 44–53.

29. See Allison, "The Cool Brand"; Michael Hardt, "Affective Labour," Generation Online, 2008, http://www.generation-online.org/p/fp_affectivelabour.htm.

30. Amamiya Karin, "Kaisetsu: Gendai ni kaerisaku *Kani kōsen* no sakebi" [Essay: The Cry of *The Crab Cannery Ship's* Revival], in Kobayashi Takiji, *Kani kōsen* (Tokyo: Kin'yōbi, 2008), 146. Translations are mine.

31. Ibid., 147.

32. Ibid., 153.

33. Ibid., 151.

34. Ibid., 161.

35. Ibid., 161.

36. Ibid., 162.

37. Allison, "The Cool Brand," 90.

38. Saitō Tamaki, *Beautiful Fighting Girl*, translated by J. Keith Vincent and Dawn Lawson (Minneapolis: University of Minnesota Press, 2011), 30.

39. Miriam Bratu Hansen, "The Mass Production of the Senses: Classical Cinema as Vernacular Modernism," *Modernism/Modernity* 6 (April 1999): 59–77.

40. Tweet by @radiomikan, May 3, 2012.

41. For more on this song and rave demo culture in Tokyo, see Sharon Hayashi and Anne McKnight, "Good-bye Kitty, Hello War: The Tactics of Spectacle and New Youth Movements in Urban Japan," *positions: east asia cultures critique* 13, no. 1 (Spring 2005): 87–113.

42. Standing, *The Precariat*, 12.

43. Hashiguchi Shōji, *Wakamono no rōdō undō: "Hatarakaserō" to "Hataranakai" no shakaigaku* [Labor Movements of the Youth: Sociology of "Let Us Work" and "We Do Not Work"] (Tokyo: Seikatsu Shoin, 2011).

44. Mōri Yoshitaka, *Sutoriito no shisō: tenkanki to shite no 1990 nendai* [Theory of the Streets: The 1990s as an Age of Transformation] (Tokyo: NHK Books: 2009).

[11]

Richard Wright's Poetic Marxism

Konstantina M. Karageorgos

Marx, a Poet?

The final question of an interview with Richard Wright for *France-U.S.A.* in September 1960, asked by translator and journalist Annie Brierre, was "Do you read a lot?"[1] Replying to this standard, even banal, question for a famously voracious reader, Wright began his answer rather mechanically, listing novelists for whom he had long expressed admiration. The names offered—Sherwood Anderson, Mark Twain, James T. Farrell, Nelson Algren, Thomas Hardy, Guy de Maupassant, Marcel Proust, and Fyodor Dostoyevsky—are unsurprising, as is Wright's emendation that he would "give them all up for a book by Dreiser" who "encompasses them all."[2] But in the very moment that we are prepared, as no doubt Brierre was as well, to learn nothing new from this practiced recitation, Wright chose to disrupt his rote. After a full stop, he noted separately, "And I should like to add that I am fond of Freud and Marx, not from a political angle but because they are poets."[3] Wright's Delphic response piqued Brierre, who immediately attempted to secure a future interview on this idea of Karl Marx as poet. Although that interview never materialized—Wright died of a heart attack two months later—this line survives as the most explicit if interpretively oblique expression of Wright's engagement with the form of Marx's writing. Offering a new lens through which to read and understand Wright's complex relationship to Marxism throughout his writing career, Wright's recasting of Marx as poet is of special importance to critics and readers of Wright's postwar fiction, a body of work that, due in no small part to Wright's departure from the Communist Party in 1942, has been stripped of its Marxist valences.

What was Wright trying to communicate through this provocative recasting of Marx as a poet? The subject here is not poetry, neither Wright's nor Marx's, but a method of reading. In reading Marx as a poet, Wright expands the interpretive possibilities engendered by a traditional reading of Marx. No longer the author of a fixed discourse known as Marxism, Marx is transformed into a "founder of discursivity."[4] Although this distinction between Marx and Marxism comes from "What Is an Author," Michel Foucault's 1969 essay in which he explains his relationship to Marx's thought as structural rather than conceptual or political, the import of Wright's critical act must not be subsumed by Foucault's more concentrated explanation. While the deliberate ambiguity of Wright's statement is powerfully reinforced by the precision of Foucault's theoretical language and its comparative familiarity to postwar theoretical revisions of Marx, Wright's dialectical reading of Marx prefigures and, as will become clear, far exceeds the parameters established by Foucault.

Nevertheless, Foucault's reclassification of Marxian discursivity offers crucial support to a topic—Wright's Marxism—overdetermined (and routinely distorted) by methodologies that align Wright's support for Marx with positive representations of the Communist Party USA (CPUSA).[5] Under Foucault's rubric, the test of conceptual allegiance—wherein a work's Marxist potency is determined by the degree to which it appropriates and deploys a content that has been vetted as properly Marxist—is proven not only insufficient but also theoretically (and ultimately politically) impotent. It is not enough for a discursive field to generate new ideas and discoveries; whether a work is praised for the ease or for the complexity of its appropriation does not matter if the discursive field itself is left unchanged. What distinguishes Marx (and Sigmund Freud) from other "initiators of discourse"—including Aristotle, Ferdinand de Saussure, Galileo, and Isaac Newton—is a formal quality that communicates an active resistance to such imitation and orthodoxy.[6] Thus, while the study of either historical materialism or psychoanalysis necessitates a "return to the origin"—to Marx or Freud—the product of this return is not delimited in advance by the initiator's original findings.[7] The endgame, then, is neither revision nor supplementation. No matter how potentially useful to the host discipline, such additive practices, which deny the principle of historical contingency, affirm their own discursive stagnation.

My primary motive for integrating Foucault is terminological. Foucault's systematic critique of the discursive limits of contemporary Marxism, buttressed by his revision of Marx as a "founder of discursivity," carries intellectual resonance with my present inquiry.[8] Significantly, though, the points at which Foucault and Wright overlap—their shared resistance to allegedly pious readings of Marx, including both the motivated distillation of Marx's thought into isolated propagandistic mandates (e.g., "the philosophers have only interpreted the world, in various ways; the point is to change it") and its codification into a comprehensive system (as with Stalinist diamat, or dialectic materialism)—are balanced by different and ultimately incommensurate understandings of form.[9] Foucault's explicit disinterest in "the totality of Marx's thought," combined with his public "shun[ning]" of "all things related to the dialectic,"[10] reveals the limits of his formal interest in Marx and as such distinguishes his project from Wright's.[11] Additionally, Wright's primary aim—to "locate [in Marx] the rules that formed a certain number of concepts and theoretical relationships"—affirms his as a structural and disciplinary (philosophical) approach to Marxian discursivity.[12] Wright's re-creation of Marx as poet stands as a direct challenge to such systematized methods of reading. Rather than reading for rules in order to establish structural patterns in Marx's thought, Wright reestablishes Marx's writings as a guiding but ultimately unrealizable aesthetic—as poetry—locating the revolutionary potential of Marx's thought in its formal qualities, those that cannot be easily lifted for political or philosophical appropriation.[13] Poetry, neither "the name for a [restrictive] form of writing made by poets" nor a generalized "metonym for the arts," becomes for Wright a way of coding what he identifies as a structural imperative in the specific context of Marx's thought.[14]

Wright Reads Burke

Wright's understanding of the poetic quality of Marx's thought was likely influenced, albeit rather quietly and ultimately very critically, by Kenneth Burke's aborted project, beginning in *Permanence and Change: An Anatomy of Purpose* (1938), to render Marxist aesthetics—and specifically Communist practice—poetic.[15] It is through Burke rather than the Russian formalists (whose works Wright neither owned nor read) that Wright was first introduced to a politicized understanding of poetics undetermined by the generic limitations of race and even class-specific forms of linguistic or narrative transgression.[16]

Burke's theory of poetic action, his move away from the study of static symbols in literature, poetry, and criticism in order to develop a vocabulary that could represent the hidden movement, or action, of dialectical thought, resonated with Wright, who was struggling, after sentimental reviews of *Uncle Tom's Children* (1938), to develop a mode of expression that exceeded existing forms of literary radicalism.[17] However formative to his development as a writer, the guiding principles of proletarian fiction—to represent the revolutionary potential of the laboring classes—had by this time run their course. Rather than continue to create literature designed for the "cauldron of the Revolution" as specified by CPUSA literati,[18] Wright, at the height of his celebrity as the "Party's most illustrious proletarian author," began to amend his narrative principles.[19]

Given the increase in CPUSA suspicion toward unorthodox approaches to Marx's thought, particularly those practiced by its African American members, Wright's new interest was at risk of intellectual atrophy.[20] Left with few viable theoretical models, Wright turned to Kenneth Burke. Although Wright had encountered Burke three years earlier at the First American Writer's Congress—Burke's iconoclastic speech "Revolutionary Symbolism in America" would have been all but impossible to miss—he was not moved to further inquiry until late 1937, the year that the *New Masses* published Burke's scathing critique of Jacques Barzun's *Race: A Study in Modern Superstition* (1937). The review, which was printed on the same page as Wright's "Between Laughter and Tears," a similarly critical analysis of the retrograde race writing of Walter Edward Turpin and Zora Neale Hurston, confirmed the special interest in race of these leading Marxists (and the journal in which they published).[21] The final lines of Burke's "The Science of Race Thinking" proved to be an ideal preface to Wright's own article:

> This book [Barzun's *Race: A Study in Modern Superstition*] should also be read by Marxists because it indicates how both class and regional divisions can in naïve hands lead to a schematization of psychological traits that is hardly other than a concealed variant of the same oversimplified patterns as prevail in race thinking. On Marx's own testimony, a theory of purely economic classification must be subtilized when one is analyzing the expressions of any specific individual.[22]

Burke's recourse to Marx in the context of naive theorizations about race and racialized psychology would have appealed to Wright, who had been forced to neglect the very subject that had inspired his interest in the Party due to his heavy workload as the Harlem bureau's editor of the *Daily Worker.* Even more, it would have *surprised* him. Wright considered contemporary Marxism's interest in the psychology of the oppressed a recent phenomenon, one he attributed to Stalin's *Marxism and the National and Colonial Question* (1934) rather than to Marx himself.

The timing of Burke's words combined with their proximity to Wright's own review was nothing short of serendipitous. Prior to this reading encounter, Wright had identified the primary function of Marx's thought—the demystification of the logic of capital—as a *content* to be *transcended* by the black literary vanguard. Now less than three years later, Wright began to reconsider his "blueprint." No longer did he believe that Marx's "capacity to lay bare the skeleton of society" was an end unto itself.[23] He was now in search of a vocabulary to support his thinking.

Wright records his thoughts on Burke's *Permanence and Change* in "Writing from the Left." A generically strange and infrequently cited piece of writing with a mysterious publication history, "Writing from the Left" documents Wright's thoughts on emerging theories of the relationship between Marxism and aesthetic practice. He offers the following précis of *Permanence and Change:* Kenneth Burke, in *Permanence and Change,* sought to frame a definition of Marxist aesthetics in terms of a poetry of action; from Burke's point of view, Communism becomes a poetic conception of life, of men unfolding their personalities through action.[24] Insofar as Wright's reading was guided by his dissatisfaction with the aesthetic parameters of committed art as it was then defined in American Marxist-inflected literature, Wright was particularly attracted to Burke's more capacious understanding of poetics in narrative. Burke criticized the necessity of singular "ideals" in narrative, proposing instead that writers work toward a more gestural ethic to be advanced through a complex dialogue among expository (or semantic) and hortatory (or poetic) forms of expression. No longer limited to the representation of specific (and existing) forms of liberation, the function of committed art was to instill a revolutionary sensibility, a sense of futurity, of the not-known. An author would "not merely give the names and addresses of events" in his work "but would," through the form of his prose, "also suggest exhortations for the promotion of better names and addresses."[25] For Burke, this new, prospective vocabulary was a necessary translation of Comintern materialism for American Marxists. Burke knew that the unmediated importing of the core of Soviet discourse—its promise to deliver "jobs for all"—would have a limited shelf life for Americans as they gained greater distance from Depression life. In order to "make revolutionaries out of people who were used to easy living," a "shift in nomenclature" was needed.[26] If, Burke mused in an unsent letter to Malcolm Cowley, the word "leisure" replaced the word "unemployment," American Marxists would be forced to admit that the abolishment of class required a signifying turn, or, as he would write in *The Philosophy of Literary Form,* the cultivation of a "strenuous cult of style."[27]

While the hortatory quality of Burke's understanding of poetic meaning-making stayed with Wright, informing the most significant of Wright's major revisions of the first draft of *Native Son,* other aspects of Burke's theoretical musings did not. Although Burke's intentionally incongruous approach to both Marx's thought and Communist practice makes concision difficult, there exists a thetic moment in *Permanence and Change* that communicates at once the ideological constraints of Burke's appropriation of Marxist thought and also the limits of his influence on Wright. In what initiates the complete reversal of his premise—that Marx's thought demonstrates a poetic quality ignored by doctrinaire interpretations—Burke suggests that the "highly humanistic or poetic nature" of communism is concealed *due to a conceptual and symbolic rigidity in Marx's thought.*[28] According to Burke, the "homogeneity" of Marx's "emphasis on one unifying ideology" can only be corrected by "exorcising" from the Marxist repertoire not only its many "misnomers," with which Wright would have agreed, but its "signifying logic" as well.[29]

In a lengthy passage, one of many cut from the first (1935) edition of *Permanence and Change,* Burke further explains the limits of his Marxist affiliation. In brief, Burke suggests that although communism, "by whatever name it may finally prevail," constitutes "the only coherent and organized movement" in existence, "a philosophical corrective to its technological rationalization" was needed. Replacement of the term "Communism" was first on Burke's list of revisions. Burke mistrusted the term's echoes of the word "communicant," which he identified as "the key term about which the entire religious rationalization of the West was constructed."[30] Burke insisted that unless Marxists wished to abandon their aims to build a "new rationalization" unfettered by oppressive precepts (Burke suggested that communism also invoked the language of "competition"), the word "cooperative" must overtake communism as the key term around which Marxist/communistic activity was organized.[31]

While both the sentiment and its rhetorical packaging are unsurprising—Burke was not shy about his desire to "convert [Communism] to [his] own vocabulary," expressing this publicly in "My Approach to Communism," published in the March 19, 1934, issue of the *New Masses* and privately in various letters to Malcolm Cowley throughout the 1930s—his efforts to translate Communism's "pivotal terms" amounted to a critique of Marx rather than a critique of contemporary Communist interpretations of Marx.[32] According to Burke, Communism, as a political ethic, was being held back by a terminological allegiance to Marx:

> I am not a joiner of societies. I am a literary man. I can only welcome Communism by converting it into my own vocabulary. I am, in the deepest sense, a translator. I go on translating even if I must but translate English into English. My book [*Permanence and Change*] will have the Communist objectives, and the Communist tenor, but the approach will be the approach that seems significant to me.[33]

Burke writes of the "Marxian method" and "Communist doctrine" as if they were exchangeable terms. In the same letter to Cowley, Burke admits that his endorsement of Communism required a complete overhaul of the "Marxian method," a process he refers to as his "personal manipulation of Marxian doctrine."[34]

What began as a traditional, even conservative form of study due to its principally affirmative relationship between writer (Burke) and reader (Wright) had by the monograph's end shifted to criticism. Wright had expected a poetic rendering of Marx outside CPUSA constraints and received its opposite, a poetic translation of Communist terminology supported by a displaced rhetorical critique of Marx's conceptual rigidity. As a generous but discerning reader, Wright did not discount Burke entirely but appropriated what he knew to be useful, the idea of a poetic Marx, in order to return to a stalled process of revision. Ironically, Burke's theoretical imprecision, his conflation of "Marxian logic" with "Communist doctrine," brought Wright out of what had seemed an impassable quandary.

Wright's Poetic Revision of *Native Son*

Wright's revised approach to Marx's thought, shaped by his reading of *Permanence and Change,* appears in the developmental notes for his first completed draft of *Native Son.*[35] In a direct challenge to Burke's deployment of the term, Wright uses "poetic" as a metonym for a form of Marxist overwriting or revision that exceeds simple conversion or replacement. Going beyond individual metaphors and symbols, as is the case for a poetics based on either word or image-specific substitution (such as Burke's), Wright, under the heading "POETIC MOTIFS TO BE WOVEN INTO FINAL SCENE," composed a list of seven principles to follow in his revision of the novel's end:

> POETIC MOTIFS TO BE WOVEN INTO FINAL SCENE:

> I. A sense of others striving to wrench the world away from a few and remold it to a truer shape of desire.
> II. A sense of that world in concrete form, buildings, earth, sunshine, snow still unmelted upon roofs.
> III. A [*sic*] up and surge of self-confidence, "What I killed for I am."
> IV. The realization that he is tried wrongly.
> V. Realize in flow of time the nearing goal of death, making him more feverish and feeling more what is in him to be emptied.
> VI. A storm of passion of remorse and regret—then a quiet curiosity about what is to come—and a pride enough to walk to death.
> VII. Most important of all poetic motifs is that of life being a deep, exciting and enthralling adventure; that is the note on which the book should end to carry over the premise and feeling of something which must happen in the future.
> I MUST SPEAK IN POETIC TERMS OF THIS . . .[36]

At once diagnostic and proleptic, the above criteria, embedded in nearly one thousand pages of a heavily worked-over draft, served as a guide for Wright's revision. Although he had already submitted his manuscript to trusted readers as all but done, Wright's heavy annotations reveal a persistent anxiety about the novel's reception. He had learned from the lachrymose response to *Uncle Tom's Children* that to write a novel for which tears could be no consolation, he would have to create less sympathetic characters and pay greater attention to form. With *Native Son*, he set out to do both, focusing less on the novel's plotline, for which he appropriated stories from the *Chicago Tribune*, and more on narrative structure and depth of character. In "How Bigger Was Born" (1941), Wright's retrospective on the process of writing *Native Son*, he explains his reason for relying so heavily on local news stories:

> Life had made the plot over and over again, to the extent that I knew it by heart. So frequently do these acts recur that when I was halfway through the first draft of *Native Son* a case paralleling Bigger's flared forth in the newspapers of Chicago. Many of the newspaper items and some of the incidents in *Native Son* are but fictionalized versions of the Robert Nixon case and rewrites of news stories from the *Chicago Tribune*.[37]

It was not for lack of imagination that Wright relied on news stories for the plot of *Native Son*. He believed that a quotidian plot would force readers to focus their attention elsewhere; the dramatic action that he hoped to relay was located not in the novel's basic plotline constituted by Bigger's murder of Mary and his subsequent trial but instead in the governing structures that made such a story so known, so acceptable, and so *inevitable*. It was this latter quality of inevitability that Wright hoped would shock the reader out of political submission.

Wright's apprehension was especially concentrated around the novel's final scene, which had "Bigger going smack to the electric chair."[38] Wright's concern lay with the finality of this act, which he feared too closely resembled the narrative logic of *Uncle Tom's Children.*[39] Unable to reconcile the scene's regressive qualities—particularly its emphasis on immediate (and symbolic) corporeal violence—with his burgeoning aesthetic and political vision, Wright cut the ending entirely. Rather than depicting Bigger's death, which would reinforce a reading of *Native Son* as yet another story of racial oppression focused on the retributive aspects of the "catastrophically damaged" American justice system, Wright began a process of revision designed to confront the methods through which political and ethical judgments are made.[40]

Although his marginalia indicate that he was under immense pressure to complete the novel, Wright refashioned the final scene as a conversation between Max and Bigger. Far more than a superficial endorsement of a more democratic ethos, Wright redeveloped the form of the novel's end to reflect the structural nuance of his own position between the Marxism endorsed by the Party and his own understanding of the emancipatory potential of Marx's thought. No longer convinced of the inevitability of deliverance by a communistic social order, Wright denied his readership the emotional and psychological relief of a fully drawn conclusion. The satisfaction of a positive political message, whether it was mandated by the Communist Party (Max) or articulated by a lumpen figure (Bigger), directly contradicted Wright's burgeoning understanding of the utopian quality of historical materialism. As with Theodor Adorno and Ernst Bloch, for whom there could be no "positive conception or vision of utopia," Wright identified the utopian as a *prospective* cognitive and material condition that evades fixed signification.[41]

Toward this end, Wright strove to create a narrative structure that would formally reinforce the irreducibility of the novel's political content. Therefore, the bottom line was characterization. Knowing that the tendency to interpret a single character as an isolated political symbol was something of a cultural compulsion, Wright fashioned Bigger as a figure of radical disidentification. Neither the proletarian rebel of traditional 1930s protest fiction (including his own) nor a reprisal of the culturally deft drifter (emblematic is Claude McKay's Lincoln Agrippa Daily in *Banjo,* 1929), Bigger is a figure undefined by either work or play. Although the consequences of race and class oppression have marked his life, his precarious status *within* rather than *outside* his political and cultural milieu have kept him impervious to traditional Marxist revolutionary appeals.

Dramatized subtly throughout the novel, Wright reinforces Bigger's recalcitrance to the period's supreme form of organized Marxism—the CPUSA—in the novel's final, revised scene. In an appeal designed to reveal Bigger's suppressed political consciousness—a space where one might expect his humanity to dwell—the unsubtly named Boris Max uses Bigger's death sentence to advance a polemic on the inextricability of race and class:

> Bigger, the people who hate you feel just as you feel, only they're on the other side of the fence. You're black, but that's only a part of it. Your being black, as I told you before, makes it easy for them to single you out. . . . They rule and regulate life. They have things arranged so that they can do those things and the people can't fight back. They do that to black people more than others because they say that black people are inferior. But, Bigger, they say that *all* people who work are inferior. And the rich people don't want to change things; they'll lose too much. But deep down in them they feel like you feel, Bigger, and in order to keep what they've got, they make themselves believe that men who work are not quite human. They do like you did, Bigger, when you refused to feel sorry for Mary. But on both sides men want to live; men are fighting for life. Who will win? Well the side that feels life most, the side with the most humanity and the most men.[42]

However sobering and emotionally potent to readers, Max's rather paternalistic explanation—he goes so far as to call Bigger "son"—inspires laughter in Bigger. Further convinced of his righteousness, Bigger, who had been silenced by Max's authoritative presence, finally gains the confidence to speak. Bigger's initial acceptance of his subordinate status, supported by his "trust" that "the sound of his voice rather than the sense of his words [would] carry his meaning" to Max's empathetic ear, is reversed by Max's speech.[43] Breaking his silence by shouting "I'm glad I got to know you before I go," Bigger, who had felt the shock of Max's depersonalized speech as he would a slap, proceeds to explain to Max the limits of his—and by extension the CPUSA Marxism's—revolutionary approach.[44]

Wright uses Bigger's silence to reaffirm the structural inequity between Max and Bigger. In doing so, Wright illuminates a major problem in Communist dissemination of Marx's thought: Party regulation of Marxist interpretation. Wright dramatizes the CPUSA's comparative neglect of cognitive development by emphasizing Bigger's automatic recourse to black nationalist appeals. A warning rather than an endorsement, Wright's intermittent return to black nationalist rhetoric through Bigger calls forth Marcus Garvey's imagined community of black nationalists, "The Bigger Brotherhood." When Max first enters Bigger's cell, Bigger feels too intimidated to speak. Though Bigger had much to communicate, he is repeatedly silenced by Max's presence, who leaves him without language; we are repeatedly told that he "could not speak" and "sighed" rather than spoke "an answer."[45] Through the exchange between Max and Bigger and the structural reversal between the two—first it is Bigger but ultimately it is Max who is without language and understanding—Wright reveals the limitations of CPUSA unity with African Americans and their struggle for liberation.

Wright's focus on the limitations of the historically revolutionary relationship forged between the Communist Party and disenfranchised African Americans does not eliminate the radical import of Communist-fostered Marxism altogether. Bigger owes the emergence of his *structural* awareness of social and political destitution to Max, whose preliminary interview with Bigger was the first meaningful interpersonal connection of his life. Bigger reminds Max of this during their final meeting: "You asked me questions nobody ever asked me before. You knew that I was a murderer two times over, but you treated me like a man."[46] Bigger's reference back to their first meeting resuscitates—in what could otherwise prove a singularly damning critical moment—the revolutionary foundation of African American and CPUSA relations. Max's broader indictment of capitalism as a system that thrives on the compulsory dehumanization of the laboring classes appeals to Bigger, whose insight into capitalist machinery, communicated by his grim utterance "all I know is that they hate *me*," is expanded by Max's sociological unmasking of class oppression.[47]

Significantly, it is the question of form rather than the particular content of Max's conversation that Bigger identifies as emancipatory. While Max's questions inspired Bigger "to think," the fruits of Bigger's cognitive labor shocked and even disappointed his lawyer, who, as it turns out, finds himself in the position of identifying and even empathizing with the slain Mary Dalton. Horrified by the extent of Bigger's disgust with Mary's touristic interest in the "the way Negroes live," Max attempts to overcorrect Bigger, refusing him the rhetorical space to disagree.[48] Despite his rhetorical savvy, Max's attempt to frame Mary's queries as "kindnesses" falls flat, as Bigger refuses to interpret Mary's condescension as a humane gesture. Able to sense the hypocrisy of Max's qualification that Mary "was acting toward [him] only as she knew how," Bigger confronts Max with his regressive logic. In a direct challenge to Max's interpretation of Mary's social transgression, Bigger reminds Max that he too was "acting toward her," a rich white woman, "only as *he* knew how."[49] With only his "feelings as a guide," Bigger recognizes that his vulnerability in the culturally overdetermined situation is ignored. Max's revolutionary fervor is tempered by his liberal generosity to Bigger's oppressor.[50] At this point in the conversation (and in the novel), we are meant to see that Bigger rather than Boris Max possesses the more sophisticated structural critique.

What begins as a straightforward juxtaposition of Bigger's revolutionary rawness with Max's political sophistication quickly becomes a staged confrontation between Bigger's extralinguistic understanding of structural oppression and Max's command of basic Marxist concepts mediated by the interpretive constraints of his association with the CPUSA. Yet rather than privilege Bigger's undisciplined political unconscious over Max's doctrinaire pedantry, Wright uses the conflict to demonstrate the *limits* of each. Bigger's insights may be used to emphasize Max's comparative naïveté, but Wright is far from offering Bigger as a Marxist exemplar. While Wright describes Bigger, in "How Bigger Was Born," as a "meaningful and prophetic symbol," his subsequent description makes his intent very clear.[51] Wright identifies Bigger as an unequivocally destructive harbinger of the future, a figure amenable to Nazi logic:

> When the Nazis spoke of the necessity of a highly ritualized and symbolized life, I could hear Bigger Thomas on Chicago's South Side saying: "Man, what we need is a leader like Marcus Garvey. We need a nation, a flag, an army of our own. We colored folks ought to organize into groups and have generals, captains, lieutenants, and so forth. We ought to take Africa and have a national home."[52]

Wright's confirmation of Bigger as a figure *psychologically* attracted to fascist rather than communist leadership serves as a warning to Marxist pedagogues, specifically those within the Party, to rethink not only their recruitment practices but their own approach to Marx's thought. The inclusion of this latter critique is essential to understanding the full importance of Wright's appraisal of contemporary Marxism. The novel was more than a "cynical reduction of the party" conveyed through the mouthpieces of the novel's Communist characters, as it was so often characterized.[53] Instead, *Native Son*'s defiance of narrative and ethical expectations dramatizes Wright's personal struggle with existing models of Marxist thought.

Notes

1. Annie Brierre, "R. Wright: America Is Not Conformist: It Renews Itself Endlessly," translated by Michel Fabre, in *Conversations with Richard Wright*, edited by Michel Fabre and Keneth Kinnamon (Jackson: University of Mississippi Press, 1993), 210.
2. Brierre, "R. Wright," 210. To this list, Wright occasionally included Anton

Chekhov, Joseph Conrad, James Joyce, and Henry James. On even fewer occasions, Wright included Gertrude Stein and Meridel Le Sueur.

3. Ibid.

4. Michel Foucault, "What Is an Author?," in *Language, Counter-Memory, Practice: Selected Essays and Interviews by Michel Foucault,* edited by Donald F. Bouchard (Ithaca, NY: Cornell University Press, 1996), 131.

5. The majority of studies of the US Literary Left, especially the Marxist Left, employ the usage of procommunist representation to determine a literary work's engagement with Marxism. It is generally not enough that a work of art include some aspect of the necessity for the destruction and restructuring of the economic system.

6. Foucault, "What Is an Author?," 131.

7. Ibid.

8. Ibid., 118.

9. Karl Marx, "Theses on Feuerbach," in *Marx/Engels Selected Works, Volume One* (Moscow: Progress Publishers, 1969), 10–11.

10. Foucault, "What Is an Author?," 118.

11. Etienne Balibar, "Foucault and Marx: The Question of Nominalism," in *Michel Foucault, Philosopher,* translated and edited by Timothy J. Armstrong (New York: Routledge, 1993), 39, 55–56.

12. Foucault, "What Is an Author?," 131.

13. My language here (until paragraph's end) is strongly influenced by Christopher Nealon's theorization of the "poetic case" in his article of the same name. The language supporting my argument is taken directly from the following sentence: "Poetry is not 'the name for a kind of thing made by poets—either literal writers of poems or artists generally' but a name for an aesthetic that pushes its reader to 'think' about aesthetic experience as marking a kind of human capacity, whether or not it produces traditionally aesthetic objects." Christopher Nealon, "The Poetic Case," *Critical Inquiry* 33 (Summer 2007): 868.

14. Ibid.

15. Eugene Miller has also developed a theory of Wright's poetics based on Burke. In doing so, Miller has *eliminated* any trace of Marx's thought from both Burke's concept of poetics and Wright's appropriation. Thus, Miller has not only depoliticized but de-historicized the work (and processes) of both. Eugene Miller, *Voice of a Native Son: The Poetics of Richard Wright* (Jackson: University of Mississippi, 2010).

16. Michel Fabre's annotated listing of Wright's library in *Richard Wright: Books and Writers* does not include any titles by members of the Society for the Study of Poetic Language, nor do his notes include indexical reference to Boris Eichenbaum, Viktor Shklovksy, Yury Tynyanov, or affiliated members Vladimir Propp and Roman Jakobson. Michel Fabre, *Richard Wright: Books and Writers* (Jackson: University of Mississippi, 2008).

17. Wright discusses the relationship between sentimental reviews of *Uncle Tom's Children* and the production of *Native Son* in "How Bigger Was Born": "The second event that spurred me to write of Bigger was more personal and subtle. I had written a book of short stories which was published under the title of *Uncle Tom's Children.* When the reviews of that book began to appear, I realized I had made

an awfully naive mistake. I found that I had written a book which even bankers' daughters could read and weep over and feel good about. I swore to myself that if I ever wrote another book, no one would weep over it; that it would be so hard and deep that they would have to face it without the consolation of tears. It was this that made me get to work in dead earnest." Richard Wright, "How Bigger Was Born." *Saturday Review.* June 1940, 16.

18. Mike Gold, "Towards Proletarian Art," in *Mike Gold: A Literary Anthology,* edited by Michael Folsom (New York: International Publishers, 1972), 62.

19. Daniel Aaron, *Writers on the Left: Episodes in American Literary Communism* (New York: Columbia University Press, 1991), 21.

20. While the extent of such suspicion and regulation remains contentious among Left scholars, there is an increasing amount of empirical evidence to support the fact that anxiety among nonorthodox black Marxists was prevalent as early the mid-1930s. For a recent example, see Lawrence Jackson, *The Indignant Generation: A Narrative History of African American Writers and Critics, 1934–1960* (Princeton, NJ: Princeton University Press, 2011). Jackson credits Marian Minus for providing "one of the earliest pieces of evidence" that "gets at" the theoretical complications for African Americans whose commitment to Marxism was compromised by various CPUSA mandates (60). In 1936, Minus declared with aplomb the ideological limitations of the Communist Party as the default organization for black Marxist expression. In fact, we learn from Jackson that it was Minus who first identified—and defended—Wright's preference for noncommunist forms of Marxist expression. Jackson quotes from a letter between Minus and Dorothy West:

> Someone just rushed to tell me that Dick Wright is a Trotskyite. If only you could have seen the horror in her face! I must talk to Dick because I think he's going through the same thing which I am just recovering from. The Party is, of course, embittered because Dick was the Communist front in literature so far as Negroes are concerned. Now he will always have a message because he has always been proletarian. But thank heaven he won't be forced to type out shibboleths just because he is a Communist. They should have seen long ago that he was beyond that stage and was crying to be allowed to let his mature work be born. (60)

21. For a visual image of this spatial juxtaposition, see "The New Masses, October 5, 1937 Issue PDF," UNZ.org, http://www.unz.org/Pub/NewMasses-1937oct05.

22. Anthony Dawahare, *Nationalism, Marxism, and Interwar African American Literature: A New Pandora's Box* (Oxford, MS: University Press of Mississippi, 2003), 8.

23. Richard Wright, "Blueprint for Negro Writing," *New Challenge* (1937), 11.

24. It is unknown how widely, or if at all, "Writing from the Left" was circulated. This excerpt is taken from Michel Fabre's annotation of the essay in *Richard Wright: Books and Writers* (19–20), but it is neither dated nor otherwise annotated.

25. Kenneth Burke, "Semantic and Poetic Meaning," in *Philosophy of Literary Form* (Berkeley: University of California Press, 1971), 127.

26. Ann George and Jack Selzer, *Kenneth Burke in the 1930s* (Columbia: University of South Carolina Press, 2007), 85.

27. Kenneth Burke, *Permanence and Change: An Anatomy of Purpose.* (Berkeley: University of California Press, 1971), 161.

28. Ibid., 93.

29. Ibid., 93, 134.
30. Ibid., 93.
31. Ibid.
32. See Paul Jay, ed., *The Selected Correspondence of Kenneth Burke and Malcolm Cowley, 1915–1981,* 3rd ed. (New York: Penguin, 1988), 22–23.
33. Letter from Burke to Malcolm Cowley (June 4, 1932), in Jay, *The Selected Correspondence of Kenneth Burke and Malcolm Cowley,* 202.
34. See Stacey Sheriff, "Resituating Kenneth Burke's 'My Approach to Communism,'" *Rhetorica: A Journal of the History of Rhetoric* 23, no. 3 (Summer 2005): 281–96.
35. See Keneth Kinnamon, ed., *New Essays on Native Son* (Cambridge: Cambridge University Press, 1990), 10.
36. Ibid.
37. Wright, "How Bigger Was Born," 16.
38. Ibid.
39. This is particularly true of "Big Boy Leaves Home" and "Bright and Morning Star." Both stories end with the torture and death of black youths.
40. The phrase "catastrophically damaged" comes from Jonathan Elmer, "Spectacle and Event in *Native Son,*" *American Literature* 70 (December 1998): 772.
41. Ernst Bloch, *The Utopian Function of Art and Literature: Selected Essays,* translated by Jack Zipes and Frank Mecklenburg, Studies in Contemporary German Social Thought (Cambridge, MA: MIT Press, 1989), 198.
42. Ibid., 421.
43. Ibid., 422.
44. Ibid., 416.
45. Ibid., 421.
46. Ibid., 424.
47. Ibid., 322 (my emphasis).
48. Ibid., 350. See the following sentence for an example of the coercive structure of Max's appeal: "But Bigger, you don't hate people for that. She was being kind to you."
49. Ibid. (my emphasis)
50. Dawahare, *Nationalism, Marxism, and Interwar African American Literature,* 8.
51. Wright. "How Bigger Was Born," 441.
52. Ibid., 445.
53. Barbara Foley, *Radical Representations: Politics and Form in U.S. Proletarian Fiction, 1929–1949* (Durham, NC: Duke University Press, 1994), 209.

[12]

Writing Brotherhood: The Utopian Politics of Ralph Ellison's *Invisible Man*

Nathaniel Mills

Ralph Ellison's *Invisible Man* has long been criticized from the Left for its apparent commitment to Cold War Americanism. Such critiques read the novel's Brotherhood as a misrepresentation, constructed through nonreferential representational strategies and informed by anticommunist stereotypes, of the 1930s and 1940s Communist Party USA (CPUSA). In 1952, Lloyd Brown wrote that *Invisible Man* foregrounds "the central design of American Century literature—anti-Communism," using the Brotherhood as a "euphemism" for the CPUSA and a surrealist aesthetic to construct an "anti-Communist lie."[1] Barbara Foley has recently argued that Ellison began writing *Invisible Man* as a proletarian novel but gradually revised it into an anticommunist expression of "existential ambivalence" and "vital center patriotism." Making the Brotherhood an authoritarian caricature of the CPUSA helped Ellison "depoliticize the novel's historical context and facilitate its critique of the left." In the final text, "reference bows down to rhetoric" as history—particularly the history of the Left—is obscured within a nonreferential aesthetic.[2]

But the assumption that the Brotherhood is really the CPUSA lets the distinction between text and history, and Ellison's reasons for maintaining the distinction, go unexamined. To quote Foley: "We wink and nod when Ellison identifies his leftists as the 'Brotherhood,' just as we previously winked and nodded at his dissociation of the Founder from Booker T. Washington and of the campus . . . from Tuskegee."[3] But distinguishing the Brotherhood from the CPUSA as literary and extraliterary objects, respectively, allows us to reconsider the political valences of the novel's aesthetic features.

John Callahan and Christopher Hobson have argued that *Invisible Man*'s representational agenda facilitates productive political significations that a realistic or strictly referential approach wouldn't permit. For Callahan, the novel's institutions, characters, and plot twists are archetypal objects bearing only historical "connotation," through which Ellison depicts general patterns of African American experience.[4] Hobson argues that *Invisible Man*'s ahistorical aesthetic "universalizes" the "double V" rhetoric of the World War II–era black Left, situating it within "an already existing African American tradition of struggle."[5] Ellison insisted in 1969 that the Brotherhood "never existed. . . . I did not want to describe an existing Socialist or Communist or Marxist political group, primarily because it would have allowed the reader to escape confronting certain political patterns, patterns which still exist and of which our two major political parties are guilty in their relationships to Negro Americans."[6]

Following Ellison, I read *Invisible Man* as a general theory of politics, institutions, and utopia informed by Marxism's transformative ethos. By politics, I refer to practical action directed toward the transcendence of present, oppressive sociopolitical arrangements. Politics is distinguished in the novel from the category of history, the key term of Brotherhood rhetoric and, for Ellison, a discourse of teleological determinism that undermines action in the present. Ellison's critique of this model of history is less a rejection of Marxism than a prioritizing of action over the inaction induced by investment in the inevitability of large-scale, long-term change.[7] Politics proper is committed to the achievement of brotherhood, a utopian ideal of human collectivity unrepresentable from within a present defined by power and hierarchy. Ellison's concept of utopia is thus construed negatively, as a future alternative to a present defined by divisive social hierarchies that are the opposites of brotherhood. Institutions such as the Brotherhood, because they are located within the sociopolitical order of the present, tend toward self-preservation and end up containing political change in order to maintain their own stable place within the inequitable present.

Invisible Man advances this theory and the problems it articulates through economies of symbolic implication that rely on preserving the distinction between literature and history. I trace this aesthetic strategy to Ellison's likely influence by certain literary debates within the Depression- and World War II-era Left. Then, through a reading that resists historicizing *Invisible Man* and charting references to the discursive and political parameters of the postwar moment, I delineate the novel's theorization of the general dynamics of political struggle itself. I do so in order to argue that the subject of *Invisible Man* is conceptual and thus potentially applicable within a range of specific periods and situations.[8]

Left Antecedents of *Invisible Man*

The strategy of foregoing accurate or literal historical reference in order to expand rather than suppress radical critique was discussed in Communist Left literary debates after the publication of Richard Wright's *Native Son* in 1940 and John Steinbeck's *The Moon Is Down* in 1942. As a Communist writer and literary critic in the 1930s and early 1940s, Ellison followed each controversy, and these debates can be read as alternative antecedents for the political and aesthetic maneuvers of *Invisible Man.*

Leftist debates over *Native Son* often raised the issue of the novel's referential accuracy. In a generally adulatory *Sunday Worker* review, Ben Davis, Jr. nevertheless found that Wright omits the "great historic fact" of black participation in Communist activism, whitewashing the CPUSA as "something 'foreign' to the Negro people."[9] Furthermore, the Communist characters "are not typical" and "reflect distorted ideas" about the Party, Boris Max's "distorted" courtroom speech does not reflect Communist legal strategy, Bigger Thomas's mother is not "a strong woman typical of Negro womanhood of today," and Bigger fails as "a symbol of the whole Negro people" because neither he nor any black character reflects the actual "constructive power of the Negro masses."[10]

Wright's defenders argued, however, that the novel should not be judged according to how accurately it references historical reality. Mike Gold defended *Native Son* with a certain sense of the relative autonomy of literary form. Because of literature's concern with individual characters, Gold holds, proletarian literature cannot be referentially typical: "no one worker's story can ever be the story of all of them—not if they are living characters. Each is an individual." The whole truth of the proletariat and the class struggle emerges only from "the great total of proletarian literature." In *Native Son,* Bigger's "individual psychology" is less representative than conceptual, serving as a mechanism for analyzing, "in a masterly and universal manner," the roles race and class play in shaping individual experience.[11] In a subsequent essay on *Native Son,* Gold compared literary form to painting. Painting and literature are not evaluated by "fidelity to the strict facts." Rather, the painter or novelist "can invent, improvise, re-arrange reality" in order to "convey the emotion behind the facts," an object underlying the empirical surfaces of reality. Facts may be distorted or occluded so as to bring this object of representation into focus.[12] Samuel Sillen made similar claims in the *New Masses,* writing that Bigger is a symbol of something archetypal: the revolutionary desire of the oppressed for action, "the deep urge to live and create which no exploitative society can permanently subdue."[13]

Gold and Sillen imply that limiting oneself to accurate documentation of specific historical situations might constrict an author's ability to think the underlying, general dynamics of such situations. A close friend of Wright's in 1940, Ellison admired *Native Son* and defended it to other leftists.[14] The debate over *Native Son* raises a particular aesthetic dilemma relevant to *Invisible Man:* how can an author seeking to theorize transhistorical, sociopolitical processes avoid the appearance of documenting a discrete historical reality? *Invisible Man*'s withdrawal from historical objects (the CPUSA, Tuskegee) to fictional objects (the nameless narrator, the Brotherhood, the College) shifts focus from the historical to the archetypal, from chronologically specific black political experiences toward an examination of politics in general.

Invisible Man's answer was predated by John Steinbeck. *The Moon Is Down* describes the occupation of a small town in an unspecified country by invaders from another unspecified country, governed by a dictator, in the course of an unspecified war. The invasion has no nationalist or ideological motive: the invaders compel the townspeople to extract needed coal from a local mine, and the occupation is only "a business venture," according to their commander.[15] The townspeople, however, possess a commitment to democracy that cannot be suppressed and their covert resistance gradually erodes the psychological and martial strength of the invaders. Published in 1942, the novel is obviously applicable to the struggles of Nazi-occupied Europe: the invaders are also at war with Britain and America, and their nation fought two decades earlier in France and Belgium. But this is as much concrete detail as Steinbeck provides and the lack of literal reference expands the novel's epistemological ambit, situating World War II as one instance of a historically recurring conflict between democracy and economic exploitation. Steinbeck is therefore able to theorize the dynamics of modern popular resistance itself, attributing it in the text to a triangulation of factors: irrepressible human agency, the decentered organization of the masses, and modern technological developments. *The Moon Is Down* thus explicates World War II and, potentially, other historical instances of mass struggle.

Because of the CPUSA's support for the Allied cause after 1941, leftist critics were uneasy with the novel's referential opacity. Louis Budenz argued that Steinbeck "[e]rrs [a]gainst [r]eality" by not literally or accurately depicting historical details, such as the facts of World War II, the specific contours of Nazism, and the working-class nature of anti-Nazi resistance. Therefore, Steinbeck's invaders are "unrealistic," and the town's resistance is distorted, driven not by the specific "character of this war" but by a "vague and almost mystical desire for 'freedom.'"[16] Stanley Edgar Hyman argued instead that such criteria—"Is the book true to Nazi conquest? and, Does it aid in the anti-Nazi struggle?"—neglect the specificity of Steinbeck's intentions. Because few details are provided that would definitively link the novel's world to the situation in contemporary Europe, Hyman argued that there is sufficient representational distance between the novel and World War II to direct critical attention away from matters of reference. Instead, Hyman reads the text for Steinbeck's figurative suppression of the tendency of his earlier works to retreat from social engagement into apolitical individualism. As Sillen and Gold did with *Native Son,* Hyman treats the subject of Steinbeck's novel as a general one: the problem of authorship and political responsibility itself.

Furthermore, Hyman's attention to Steinbeck's "naming and absence of naming" may illuminate Ellison's creation of the College and Brotherhood. Noting that terms such as "German" and "Nazi" never appear in *The Moon Is Down,* Hyman compares this lack to how Steinbeck "never uses the word Communist" to name the strike leaders in *In Dubious Battle* (1936).[17] Hyman doesn't develop this observation, but he nonetheless frames the mis- or nonnaming of historical agents as a potentially purposive literary strategy, letting us analyze *Invisible Man*'s own "absence of naming" as more than a curiously euphemistic style. Ellison admired Hyman's essay and began corresponding with Hyman shortly after its publication; the two would become close friends.[18] Gold, Sillen, and Hyman offer hermeneutic grounds for an alternative understanding of *Invisible Man,* one derived from the Literary Left rather than from Cold War reaction.

Invisible Man: Politics, Institutions, and Utopia

Invisible Man theorizes the relationship of politics, institutions, and utopia through a symbolic design of rags, papers, and monuments. By alluding to the history of the production of paper from discarded cloth, rags and paper figure the manner in which political needs and energy are both given articulation by and controlled within institutions. The move from rags *to* paper—connoting the move from passive material destitution to active institutional leadership, from amorphous political desire to specific programs—figures the institutional appropriation of politics, which tends to betray the transformative, future-oriented trajectory of political desire and action. Papers thus operate in the novel as mechanisms not for political change but instead for the preservation of institutional authority.

By codifying the practical, situationally contingent work of politics into dogmatic truths—by turning the possibilities inherent in the materiality of the wornout rag into finalized papers—institutions monumentalize their place as durable features of the present. Ellison's use of the monument to both conceptualize and figure the conservative dynamics of institutions is illustrated by the statue of the Founder at the College. By enshrining the Founder as *either* lifting the veil of ignorance from the slave or lowering it "more firmly in place," the statue symbolizes the dialectic of institutional form in which the transformative vision of politics is preserved, but only as empty rhetoric in the service of calcifying, or monumentalizing, the institution.[19] This monument illustrates how the College's ostensible goal—the education and civic empowerment of the black community—is subordinated to the College's self-preservation within the racist power structures of the nation. When a political institution assumes monumental form, its discourse of a better sociopolitical order shifts in function from the task of *transcending* the present toward internal discipline and self-reinforcement *within* the present.

Invisible Man in this manner addresses what Alain Badiou identifies as "the great enigma of the century: why does the subsumption of politics . . . ultimately give rise to bureaucratic submission and the cult of the State?"[20] For Badiou, emergent, radically destabilizing political movements always risk being ordered by and contained within statist forms. The question of how transformative politics is possible in the face of this risk drives *Invisible Man*. The novel proceeds with the conviction that practical contingency and situated reinvention keep politics from institutional stasis. As invisible man puts it, "the mind that has conceived a plan of living must never lose sight of the chaos against which that pattern was conceived."[21] This conviction is not simply an accession to a Cold War liberalism that validated ambiguity as the antidote to politics. Rather, such improvisation is Ellison's formulation of the strategic opportunism that Vladimir Lenin identifies with politics: "It is necessary to link the strictest devotion to the ideas of communism with the ability to effect all the necessary practical compromises, tacks, conciliatory manoeuvres, zigzags, retreats and so on."[22]

The novel's institutional critique is introduced in the College section.

In invisible man's dream, his scholarship is revealed as an "engraved document," sent from the whites of his town, ordering the College to "Keep This Nigger-Boy Running."[23] Despite its ideals of racial betterment, the College serves the present state of white rule. Dr. Bledsoe typifies this shift from future-directed progressive politics to present-directed institutional authority. He came to the College as "a barefoot boy who in his fervor for education had trudged with his bundle of ragged clothing across two states."[24] In the symbolic patterning of Bledsoe, his initial raggedness—suggestive of the material destitution that the College claims to address—has been reproduced as the letters of recommendation he gives invisible man. The letters have a general significance as papers that purport to advance black needs but, below the surface, discipline black individuals. The College's true purpose is to maintain itself by reinforcing racial and capitalist rule in America. "When you buck against me," Bledsoe warns invisible man, "you're bucking against power, rich white folk's power, the nation's power—which means government power!"[25] Bledsoe's "old leg shackle from slavery," which he calls a "symbol of our progress," echoes the significance of the Founder's statue: the College's discourse of "progress" merely masks its efforts to reenslave African Americans.[26] Or, as Mr. Norton tells invisible man, the College is a "monument" to Norton's daughter, herself a figure for the ideological sanctity of whiteness.[27]

Reverend Homer Barbee's speech further explicates Ellison's critique. Barbee recounts an incident when the Founder, speaking before a black audience and keeping his listeners "within the gentle palm of his eloquence," was interrupted by "a snowy-headed man" who demanded action rather than rhetoric. "Tell us what is to be done, sir! For God's sake, tell us! Tell us in the name of the son they snatched from me last week!" Unable to answer, "his eyes spilling his great emotion," the Founder collapses. The elderly man (a likely former slave) testifies to the persistence of racial oppression that black institutional leadership has failed to change. Bledsoe steps in to preserve the authority of that leadership. Amid the "turmoil" in the audience, Bledsoe's "voice ring[s] out whip-like with authority," leading the crowd in "a song of hope" while the Founder is treated.[28] The Founder recognizes the desire for political action but is unable to speak to or for it, as the questioner has revealed the limits of the Founder's vision for realizing structural change through nonradical means. The Founder thus has no answer to the paradigmatic Leninist political question "what is to be done?" Bledsoe embodies the institution's simultaneous appropriation and suppression of politics. When the need for transformative politics is expressed, institutional authority reinforces the enslavement of the African American masses through the reiteration of a discourse that, despite its forward-looking and hopeful content, actually defuses politics. Barbee praises Bledsoe as he "who with his singing of the old familiar melodies soothed the doubts and fears of the multitude; he who had rallied the ignorant, the fearful and suspicious, those still wrapped in the rags of slavery."[29] Those rags signify political desire stemming from historically persistent subjugation; Bledsoe co-opts that desire, and the "rags" of persistent slavery become the papers, texts, and codified rhetoric through which the College reproduces the status quo.

When invisible man encounters the Brotherhood in New York, he encounters a more intricate institutional undermining of politics. The Brotherhood is certainly inflected by Ellison's experience with the CPUSA, but the novel obscures connections between the Brotherhood and the Party. Brother Jack offers invisible man only a general explanation of Brotherhood principles: "we are working for a better world for all people." He adds that in this better world, "the joy of labor shall have been restored," but that's as close as the Brotherhood gets to any specific Marxist principle.[30] The Brotherhood privileges "history" but fetishizes it as a force beyond human control, and the leaders deploy this self-serving understanding of history to stifle politics. For the Brotherhood, history is not linked to the active transformation of reality but instead is an alienated ontology of reality that its leaders invoke against practical agency while disempowering the masses. Late in the novel when Brother Hambro justifies the Brotherhood's "sacrifice" of the political needs of Harlem to its own institutional needs, he invokes such an ontology: "All of us must sacrifice for the good of the whole. Change is achieved through sacrifice. We follow the laws of reality, so we make sacrifices."[31]

Ellison suggests that the Brotherhood's theory of history is in fact anti-Marxist. At the Chthonian, Jack describes the Founder of the College as someone who "lies outside history." He intends this pejoratively, adding that Booker T. Washington "is still a living force," and when the masses revolt, they resurrect for inspiration "all the old heroes" of their history. Jack invites invisible man to consider himself as such a resurrection, "the new Booker T. Washington."[32] Jack echoes Marx's analysis of revolutions in *The Eighteenth Brumaire of Louis Bonaparte* but revises that analysis. For Marx, bourgeois revolutions resurrect the heroes of past revolutions in part because they're limited as revolutions: they reinscribe the familiar rule of history—class exploitation—in new guises. But proletarian revolution rejects previous historical representations, because the terms of its transformation constitute a real break from history.[33] Invisible man similarly rejects Washington and opts for the Founder as his political role model, thus defining politics as the move beyond or "outside" history rather than as the reproduction of the same while resisting Brotherhood authority by resisting the full institutional submission that its theory of history works to ensure. "I would do the work but I would be no one except myself—whoever I was. I would pattern my life on that of the Founder."[34] In this statement, he links dissent from institutional control to the "work" of a progressive politics keyed to moving beyond history into futurity. As we saw in Barbee's speech, the death of the Founder marked the moment when political desire became captured and quelled by Bledsoe, the representative of institutional authority: Barbee describes the Founder's corpse as "already a bronzed statue."[35] The College, as a fixed monument to an unjust present, is erected on the death of the Founder's transformative, if strategically flawed, vision. By modeling his leadership on the Founder's, invisible man gestures toward a sense of politics exceeding finite historical location or institutional definition.

As for positive indications of the Brotherhood's identity, we know that it claims to stand for brotherhood: universal fraternity freed from hierarchy and difference. Hence, it represents African Americans in nonracial terms as human brothers. Despite the progressive intent of this outlook and the critique of racism that it affords, it often leads the Brotherhood to downplay the significance of race in structuring both the present situation and the particular needs of the black community. At one point, Jack rails at invisible man, "Why do you fellows always talk in terms of race!"[36] Color blindness enables the Brotherhood to eventually abandon its Harlem activism on the grounds that "the interests of one group of brothers must be sacrificed to that of the whole."[37] By distancing the Brotherhood from the CPUSA and its theory from Marxism, Ellison can measure the possibilities and limitations of any institution offering postracial radical solutions to black political needs.

Initially, invisible man is influenced by the Brotherhood to the extent that he correlates action and brotherhood as trans-racial needs. As he waits to take the stage at the arena where he will give his first speech for the Brotherhood, he recalls the ruins of an arena from his youth, a "hole" that "was used for dumping, and after a rain it stank with stagnant water." This hole was located near "a Hooverville shanty" by the railroad tracks. He recalls a man "[s]tooped and dark and sprouting rags from his shoes, hat and sleeves," "a syphilitic who lived alone in the shanty between the hole and the railroad yard, coming up to the street only to beg money for food and disinfectant with which to soak his rags." In this memory, the syphilitic beckons to him: "I saw him stretching out a hand from which the fingers had been eaten away and I ran—back to the dark, and the cold and the present."[38] The syphilitic's socioeconomic nonlocation and abjection are figured through the transience of the Hooverville and the refuse of the hole. And while the Hooverville gestures toward the Depression period, the syphilitic's organic destitution—he is "sprouting" rags—indicates the transhistorical persistence of the political need he embodies. As an unclassed and racially indeterminate embodiment of that need, he demands brotherhood.

Invisible man's speech thus disregards "the correct words and phrases from the pamphlets" for "the old down-to-earth, I'm-sick-and-tired-of-the-way-they've-been-treating-us approach."[39] His subsequent rebuke by the leaders for offering a "wild, hysterical, politically irresponsible and dangerous" and "*incorrect*" speech indicates the Brotherhood's true commitment not to political action, not to achieving brotherhood, but to its own preservation and control over the masses.[40] Invisible man is then trained in the specifics of Brotherhood discourse, an architectonic "science" that "recognized no loose ends."[41] He comes to believe that "[n]othing lay outside the scheme of our ideology, there was a policy on everything."[42] Ellison critiques not the content of this discourse—that content is only sketchily described—but its claim to finality. The Brotherhood, possessed with "a policy on everything," cannot discover new practices of politics and is thus calcified by its own "science."

Invisible man discovers the political stasis of that finality after Tod Clifton's murder, when he descends into the subway, encountering "[b]its of paper whirled up" by passing trains.[43] The trope indicates that his immersion in institutional discourse—the paper texts and pamphlets of the Brotherhood's policies on everything—is about to be disrupted. On the platform, he encounters a group of zoot-suited black men who prompt him to consider that the specific political needs and resources of urban African Americans might not fit within the Brotherhood's paradigm. The cultural style of the men—reflecting the abrupt transition that blacks have made from the rural South to the industrial North—offers a tenuous sense of possibility: "who knew but that they were the saviors, the true leaders, the bearers of something precious?" If these men offer some specific cultural resource for politics that the Brotherhood cannot access, then maybe there are limits to the Brotherhood's epistemological certainty. Furthermore, they indicate that history might be not an objective force but rather an enabling ground for subjective action. "What if history was a gambler, instead of a force in a laboratory experiment, and the boys his ace in the hole?"[44] The Brotherhood, he realizes, fails to promote action and has thus done little to help Harlem: "no great change had been made."[45] He is later rebuked by Jack, who reveals that strategically implementing black resources for a politics of brotherhood is not the Brotherhood's purpose any more than it was the College's. "We do not shape our policies to the mistaken and infantile notions of the man in the street. Our job is not to *ask* them what they think but to *tell* them!"[46]

In Rinehart, invisible man discovers a potential alternative model for politics. Rinehart plays multiple roles (pimp, preacher, numbers runner, etc.) because he grasps how his invisibility—the refusal of society to recognize and place him as an individual—cancels any restraints or responsibilities when it comes to performing identity. Unable to imagine "organizing a splinter movement" outside the Brotherhood, invisible man decides instead to exploit his own invisibility within the Brotherhood as "a means of destroying them."[47] He adopts "Rinehart methods," performing accession to institutional discipline while secretly working against it.[48] But by doing so, he appears to unwittingly advance a Brotherhood plan to abandon Harlem, leaving it at the mercy of racial and economic tensions that are sure to lead to rioting. Despite the practical opportunism suggested by Rinehart's name and lifestyle, he is not a viable model for politics. His name indicates not an ability to strategically differentiate "rind" from "heart"—apparent conformity from actual subversion—but the identity of rind and heart: unguided by a plan for social change and a positive commitment to futurity, invisible man's subversive actions end up conforming to the Brotherhood's institutional needs in the present. Similarly, during the climactic riot, invisible man encounters rioters preparing to burn their tenement and thinks that he has found a spontaneous, mass alternative to institutions. Institutions invest in preserving themselves as part of the present, but the rioters are destroying their own home, not building monuments. But not only does this action destroy the present without creating a better future, it is neither mass nor spontaneous. The destruction of the tenement is organized by Dupre, whose name reiterates how institutional leadership "dupes" the masses. Phonetically ("do pray"), it mandates submission and Dupre uses a gun to quell any "arguments" from the tenement's residents about the wisdom of burning their home.[49]

The novel's solution to the problem of politics and institutions is ultimately a hermeneutic practice. Early in the New York section, invisible man encounters a black man who calls himself Peter Wheatstraw and is singing the blues while pushing a cart filled with architectural blueprints that have been discarded "to make place for the new plans." "I got damn near enough to build me a house if I could live in a paper house like they do in Japan," Wheatstraw boasts. When a still naive invisible man insists that "[y]ou have to stick to the plan," Wheatstraw replies, "You kinda young."[50] By *not* sticking to the plan, one avoids building it into a monument. In Wheatstraw's salvaging, future-oriented potentialities, symbolized by the prospective status of the blueprint, are preserved without becoming concrete features of the present. Political action needs blueprints for transformation, and the political "plans" of various institutions need to be salvaged from those institutions and scrutinized for practical utility. Wheatstraw's fantasy of building a house *of* blueprints suggests that this practice might yield an institution that does not betray politics by turning blueprints into fixities—an institution whose papers carry no self-serving motives but one that realizes transformation as its very substance. Rinehart and Dupre indicate how a plan is necessary for politics, and that necessity mandates evaluating institutions by measuring their adequacy to their utopian aims, salvaging those aims for implementation in other plans. Peetie Wheatstraw was the persona of the 1930s African American blues singer William Bunch, but Ellison invokes Wheatstraw as a folk archetype rather than a specific person: "Peter Wheatstraw is a *mythological* figure that any number of people are *named* because they possess certain qualities," he explained in 1976.[51] Steven Tracy demonstrates how Bunch's lyrics defined Wheatstraw as an agent against African American racial and economic oppression.[52] Hence, the Wheatstraw archetype is, for Ellison, a usable figure for politics.

Invisible man practices Wheatstraw's hermeneutic in the epilogue, when he ventures to interpret his grandfather's deathbed injunction to handle white America by "yessing them to death and destruction."[53] He parses this advice as a style of reading: "he *must* have meant the principle, that we were to affirm the principle on which the country was built and not the men, or at least not the men who did the violence."[54] Transformation involves extricating the possibility of utopia from institutional co-option. The utopian "principle" of the nation must be distinguished from its betrayal by the state; one must salvage the plan from its manifestation as a monument of the status quo.

The utopian principle that the novel affirms is best described as *brotherhood:* human collectivity itself, an ideal betrayed by institutions such as the Brotherhood, the College, and the state. In 1957, Ellison used "brotherhood" as one signifier—along with "love," "democracy," and "the good life"—for an abstract possibility of communal fulfillment.[55] The term's utopianism also resonates within black political tradition: in *The Souls of Black Folk* (1903), W. E. B. Du Bois identified "the ideal of human brotherhood" across racial lines as the goal of African American sociocultural aspiration.[56] Ellison anticipates Fredric Jameson's argument about the dialectical imbrication of the ideological and the utopian. Jameson argues for a "positive hermeneutic" in Marxist dialectics, one that reads for the "Utopian impulse" within a text that otherwise "fulfills a demonstrably ideological function." That impulse is "a universal value inconsistent with the narrower limits of class privilege" that structure a given text.[57] Jameson's hermeneutic extricates this future-oriented impulse from the ideological (mis)definition in which it is packaged. To elaborate this argument, Jameson reverses Walter Benjamin's axiom that "there is no document of civilization which is not at one and the same time a document of barbarism," holding for a similar simultaneity of the "effectively ideological" and "necessarily Utopian."[58] *Invisible Man*'s statue of the Founder, signaling the preservation of the utopian impulse within its institutional suppression, can be read as a riff on this Benjaminian-inflected dialectic. Like Ellison, Jameson assigns the utopian impulse little content in order to associate it figuratively with a social collectivity to come, one in excess of historical institutional definition.

Ellison likely abstracted this dialectical reading practice from black political history. Before writing *Invisible Man,* he had read historian Benjamin Quarles's essay on the split between Frederick Douglass and William Lloyd Garrison. Garrison held that the US Constitution enshrined slavery as a national principle, and Ellison noted that this caused Garrison and his fellow abolitionists to refuse to work within the nation's political institutions. In 1851, Douglass argued that the progressive spirit of the Constitution's preamble was not, in fact, wholly cancelled by the remainder of the document. Extracting that spirit was practically enabling, allowing Douglass to, in Quarles's words, "use political as well as moral power for the overthrow of the slave system."[59] Douglass grasped the need to engage both the nation's ideological founding document and state institutions in order to extract and act on the utopian principle locked within yet betrayed by both. We can read *Invisible Man* similarly, extracting its theory of politics, institutions, and brotherhood from its institutionalization as a textual monument of Cold War ideology.

Acknowledgements

I would like to thank Paula Rabinowitz, Howard Brick, and Robbie Lieberman for their comments and suggestions on this essay; the College of Humanities Faculty Fellowship Program at California State University, Northridge; and Alan Wald, who supervised the dissertation from which this essay is derived and to whom I am greatly indebted for his guidance and encouragement.

Notes

1. Lloyd Brown, "The Deep Pit," *Masses & Mainstream* 5 (1952): 62, 64.
2. Barbara Foley, *Wrestling with the Left: The Making of Ralph Ellison's* Invisible Man (Durham, NC: Duke University Press, 2010), 1, 8, 324.
3. Ibid., 238.
4. John F. Callahan, "Chaos, Complexity, and Possibility: The Historical Frequencies of Ralph Waldo Ellison," in *Speaking for You: The Vision of Ralph Ellison,* edited by Kimberly W. Benston (Washington, DC: Howard University Press, 1987), 134.
5. Christopher Z. Hobson, "*Invisible Man* and African American Radicalism in World War II," *African American Review* 39, no. 3 (2005): 363.
6. Ralph Ellison, *The Collected Essays of Ralph Ellison,* edited by John F. Callahan (New York: Modern Library, 2003), 542.
7. Kimberly Benston argues that *Invisible Man* critiques a Hegelian Marxism wedded to "the concept of an *inevitable historical movement* leading through ever-changing antitheses to a teleological goal." The novel seeks instead "the *retrieval* . . . of history as a field of ambiguity and possibility." See Kimberly Benston, "Controlling the Dialectical Deacon: The Critique of Historicism in *Invisible Man,*" *Delta* 18 (1984): 92, 90. Benston clarifies the target of the novel's critique as not Marxism itself necessarily, but eschatological inheritances in Marxism. Ellison might be compared with Louis Althusser, who sought to purge Marxism of both Hegelian and orthodox Marxist determinative teleologies in order to make room for situated theoretical and political invention. To quote Gregory Elliott, for Althusser, "neither schema—economism or historicism/humanism—offered a viable basis for scrupulous scientific analysis of the real world, for an investigation and explanation of the complexities of concrete socio-historical processes—a theoretical demerit with practical, political implications." See Gregory Elliott, *Althusser: The Detour of Theory* (Chicago: Haymarket Books, 2009), 30.
8. For a constructive debate over historicizing interpretations of *Invisible Man,* see the following discussions of Foley's *Wrestling with the Left:* Nathaniel Mills, "Wrestling with Ralph Ellison," *Against the Current* 26, no. 2 (2011): 24–28; Paul M. Heideman, "Wrestling with Ellison," *Against the Current* 26, no. 5 (2011): 41–42; Nathaniel Mills, "History, Theory, Politics and *Invisible Man,*" *Against the Current* 26, no. 5 (2011): 43–44; and Joseph G. Ramsey, "Invisible Tragedies, Invisible Possibilities: Or, Re-Reading What's Left of a Great American (Anticommunist) Novel," *Cultural Logic* (2010): 1–28, http://clogic.eserver.org/2010/Ramsey_review.pdf.
9. Ben Davis Jr., "Richard Wright's 'Native Son' a Notable Achievement," *Sunday Worker,* April 14, 1940, 6.
10. Ibid., 4.
11. Mike Gold, "Some Reflections on Richard Wright's Novel, 'Native Son,'" *Daily Worker,* April 17, 1940, 7.
12. Mike Gold, "Still More Reflections on Richard Wright's Novel, 'Native Son,'" *Daily Worker,* April 29, 1940, 7.
13. Samuel Sillen, "The Meaning of Bigger Thomas," *New Masses,* April 30, 1940, 28.
14. Lawrence Jackson, *Ralph Ellison: Emergence of Genius* (Athens: University of Georgia Press, 2007), 226–29.

15. John Steinbeck, *The Moon Is Down* (New York: Penguin, 1995), 14.
16. Louis F. Budenz, "Steinbeck's 'Moon Is Down' Is Pioneering Work in War Novels of Present Day," *Daily Worker,* April 5, 1942, 4.
17. Stanley Edgar Hyman, "Some Notes on John Steinbeck," *Antioch Review* 2, no. 2 (1942): 185, 186.
18. Jackson, *Ralph Ellison,* 271.
19. Ralph Ellison, *Invisible Man* (New York: Vintage, 1995), 36.
20. Alain Badiou, *Metapolitics* (London: Verso, 2006), 70.
21. Ellison, *Invisible Man,* 580.
22. Vladimir Lenin, "'Left-Wing' Communism—An Infantile Disorder," in *The Lenin Anthology,* edited by Robert C. Tucker (New York: Norton, 1975), 610.
23. Ellison, *Invisible Man,* 33.
24. Ibid., 116.
25. Ibid., 142.
26. Ibid., 141.
27. Ibid., 43.
28. Ibid., 124–25.
29. Ibid., 129.
30. Ibid., 304.
31. Ibid., 502.
32. Ibid., 306–7.
33. Karl Marx, *The Eighteenth Brumaire of Louis Bonaparte* (New York: International Publishers, 1975), 15–18.
34. Ellison, *Invisible Man,* 311.
35. Ibid., 130.
36. Ibid., 292.
37. Ibid., 502.
38. Ibid., 336–37.
39. Ibid., 342.
40. Ibid., 349.
41. Ibid., 382.
42. Ibid., 407.
43. Ibid., 438.
44. Ibid., 441.
45. Ibid., 444.
46. Ibid., 473.
47. Ibid., 510.
48. Ibid., 512.
49. Ibid., 547.
50. Ibid., 175.

51. Ralph Ellison, *Living with Music: Ralph Ellison's Jazz Writings,* edited by Robert G. O'Meally (New York: Modern Library, 2002), 282.
52. Steven C. Tracy, "The Devil's Son-in-Law and *Invisible Man,*" *MELUS* 15, no. 3 (1988): 49–56.
53. Ellison, *Invisible Man,* 564.
54. Ibid., 574.
55. Ellison, *The Collected Essays of Ralph Ellison,* 705.
56. W. E. B. Du Bois, *The Souls of Black Folk* (New York: Norton, 1999), 16.
57. Fredric Jameson, *The Political Unconscious: Narrative as a Socially Symbolic Act* (Ithaca, NY: Cornell University Press, 1981), 286, 288.
58. Ibid., 286.
59. Benjamin Quarles, "The Breach between Douglass and Garrison," *Journal of Negro History* 23, no. 2 (1938): 150. For Ellison's notes on this article and subject, see Notes 1942–1950, box I:152, folder 7, Ralph Waldo Ellison Papers, Manuscript Division, Library of Congress, Washington, D.C. Referenced with permission of the Ralph Ellison literary estate.

[13]

"That Was One Goddamn Good Left Hook!" Rethinking the Limits of Mass Culture in Len Zinberg's *Walk Hard—Talk Loud*

Joseph G. Ramsey

Consider the "strange" career of Leonard (Len) Zinberg, one of the most widely read procommunist US writers of the twentieth century, albeit a strikingly unknown figure today. He is unknown not only because virtually all of his thirty-plus novels are out of print, but also because, of the twenty-eight million copies he sold worldwide before his death in 1968, almost all of them were published under the tough-guy pulp fiction pen name "Ed Lacy." If it were not for Alan Wald's painstaking research for *Trinity of Passion: The Literary Left and the Anti-Fascist Crusade,* the second volume of his epic trilogy, Zinberg might have been lost to us entirely.[1] In *Trinity,* after giving us an overview of this lost Harlem-based Jewish writer's life, Wald concentrates on the Ed Lacy detective fiction of the 1950s and 1960s, charting the covert career that followed Zinberg's public outing as a Communist in 1947.[2] For Wald, Ed Lacy becomes a kind of bridge between Old Left and New, using black detectives and private eyes to extend a Popular Front critique of racism, capitalism, and male chauvinism into the era of civil rights and Black Power.

Zinberg's first book, *Walk Hard—Talk Loud,* is only briefly discussed by Wald, who notes the novel's positive reception.[3] In this way, Wald denaturalizes and contests Zinberg's disappearance from American literary history—and reminds us of the early procommunist sympathies of reviewers such as Ralph Ellison—but fails to give much attention to the book that provoked the praise.[4] Emphasizing the continuity between the early and later Zinberg, Wald argues that "the shift from novels in the proletarian tradition to pulp fiction by Lacy was more a matter of entering a mass market than a change in his form or ideology. . . . In all phases of his career, Zinberg's disconcerting irony and multilayered perspectives challenged prevailing constructions of racial and ethnic identity, and especially white male pretensions to ultramasculinity."[5] More broadly, Wald sees Zinberg as capturing "the nervousness of the post-World War II and Cold War cultural climate," including nervousness about "participation in the mass culture industry which by its nature dilutes and compromises the radical sensibility he aspires to impart to his writing."[6]

Wald's insights are apt and enticing, and yet the emphasis on *continuity* between Zinberg's prewar "proletarian" fiction and his postwar "pulp" may lead us to overlook some important *differences,* eliding the question of what may have been lost (formally *and* ideologically) in the Cold War transition of Len Zinberg to "Ed Lacy." Similarly, focusing on the postwar pulp may lead us to neglect the novelty of Zinberg's early work as an intervention in 1940s mass culture. Addressing these and other questions, the present essay will offer a close examination of *Walk Hard—Talk Loud,* a work that Wald has helped to return to view but left for others to fully explicate. I do so, in part, by examining *Walk Hard—Talk Loud* as a Popular Front *boxing* novel, one that stretched the limits of this popular genre in some remarkable ways. By bringing together two complementary currents in contemporary American literary and cultural studies, I stage a missed encounter between Wald's own recovery of leftist writers and recent reconceptualizations of prewar US mass culture.

In his recent study, *Realism for the Masses,* Chris Vials describes boxing fiction of the Popular Front era as a "major popular genre of the movement," one that has been largely overlooked in radical scholarship of the period.[7] Working to correct this long-standing blind spot, Vials examines both the Hollywood boxing films of the time—there were twenty-eight produced between 1931 and 1948—as well as a number of plays and novels by Popular Front writers, such as Clifford Odets and Nelson Algren, who sought to capitalize on the genre's popularity and radical potential.[8] Vials also looks at the writings by Left-affiliated African American writers Richard Wright and Chester Himes, who, though they never published boxing fiction per se, devoted substantial attention to the question of boxing's political and social meaning during a period when an African American, Joe Louis, reigned as heavyweight champ.[9] *Realism for the Masses* thus provides a useful background against which to place Zinberg's 1940 boxing novel *Walk Hard—Talk Loud,* a book that is notable for the way it aligns with but also departs from important generic tendencies. Zinberg's contribution to the genre broke new ground in terms of its treatment of gender and race while exploring the class contradictions of mass culture in ways that echo but also complicate the reflections of contemporary black writers. Furthermore, this lost Zinberg work sketches a utopian dimension characteristic of prewar radical mass culture, one that would tend to fade in Ed Lacy's postwar pulp pages.

The Popular Front of Boxing Fiction

As Vials shows, Depression-era boxing narratives "bear the imprint of the era's oppositional politics," often painting a critical portrait of capitalism for a mass audience.[10] Typically in these popular stories, an ambitious male protagonist is seduced and preyed upon by unscrupulous managers, criminal syndicate bosses, and the moral corruptions of American consumer culture. Popular Front appropriations of the genre usher ethnically marked working-class underdogs through a melodramatic arc of success and disillusionment, exposing not only the corruptions and class structures that undercut the supposed meritocracy of the boxing ring but also the ideologies of individualism, consumerism, and would-be white American assimilation that propel the protagonist into the ring in the first place. The typical ending of these books sees the conscience-stricken hero turning against what has been exposed as a rigged game; he says good-bye to the corruptions of the ring so that he can (re)turn to some other, less tainted realm of social life. In the end, according to the boxing genre, "If the sport had value, it was in that the stakes of 'the fight' could be transformed and redirected toward a more meaningful, redemptive struggle, allowing audiences to enjoy the spectacle of boxing while removing from it the stench of capitalistic masculinity."[11]

Vials unpacks leftist appropriations of the genre as contesting both capitalism and white supremacy, in part by foregrounding the physical, social, and moral costs—to both the protagonist and those around him—of ethnic assimilation and materialistic individualism. Yet he also points to the ideological limits of the genre, in terms of its depiction of gender as well as race. "Despite its critical exploration of masculinity as a performance of class and race identity," Vials writes, "the representation of women within the Popular Front boxing narrative reveals its inability [to] extend that exploration to an interrogation of male dominance." Women in boxing fiction and film alike are largely confined to the roles of love interests: "either the innocent sweetheart or the temptress/jezebel," deriving their meaning narrowly from the romantic role they play in the life of the male boxer.[12]

The racial limitations that Vials tracks are subtler but nonetheless profound. At times, Popular Front boxing fiction and film do explore the special oppression of black people, in particular dramatizing how the working-class ethnic boxer's achievement of "white" American "success" requires complicity in the cheating and beating of African Americans. Yet even the most progressive of these narratives—here Vials's favorite is Abraham Polonsky and Robert Rossen's remarkable film *Body and Soul* (1947)—still cast blacks primarily as victims. Ironically, during a period when actual black boxers, such as heavy weight champ Joe Louis, were racking up victory after victory, dominating the white competition, black boxers' main role in (white-authored) boxing narratives was to lose fights, to fall victim, or even to die in such a way as to spur a white hero's conscience.

To these two limits we might add a third, namely that the melodramatic moral redemption offered by the genre's typical ending posits a social space safely beyond the reach of the corruptions and oppressions that characterize the boxing ring. These endings might be imagined as a return to the American countryside (as opposed to the corruptive city), the ethnic community (as opposed to white American assimilation), or high or folk culture (as opposed to the materialism and superficiality of consumer culture). While each offers a critique of tendencies within modern capitalism, they still suggest that it is possible to escape (rather than, say, confront, challenge, overturn, or transform) the corruptive forces they decry. The suggestion of a need for systemic social change (based in transformative collective action) thus tends to be displaced, while a will to individual social relocation takes center stage—not a particularly radical motif in a market society that has long prided itself on myths of personal social mobility.

Len Zinberg challenges all three of these limits, stretching the ropes of boxing narrative. He neither reduces women to innocents and jezebels nor casts black boxers as victimized stepping-stones to white ethnic self-transformation. Moreover, his final alternative to boxing is not an individual escape or a return to some incorruptible sphere of American society but instead is a traumatic (even emasculating) confrontation with the need for collective struggle in the face of racist and capitalist oppression: there is no outside to flee to. *Walk Hard—Talk Loud* suggests that the fighter can achieve redemption only by continuing the fight, not for championship money but for social revolution, not with his own two fists but as part of the people. Interestingly, women become the chief bearers of revolutionary consciousness in the text, while Zinberg's black boxer hero, Andy Whitman, likened to the "next Joe Louis," never loses a fight. Whitman emerges as a symbol not of black victimization but of a militant black resistance that poses a challenge both to the white bosses who dominate the ring and to the procommunist movement that seeks to forge a class-based political movement that opposes white supremacy.

Walk Hard—Talk Loud

The plot of *Walk Hard—Talk Loud* follows black Harlem youth Andy Whitman's emergence from shoeshine boy and street fighter to professional boxer, his rapid rise to championship prospect, his disillusionment at the "business-side" of the ring, and the sudden suppression of his career by racist syndicate boss and prominent New York capitalist Lou Ross.[13] The novel includes a number of expertly drawn boxing matches, yet its focus is also Whitman's intellectual and political development, inside and outside of the gym. Two Communist women, best friends Kate Grath (Irish) and Ruth Lawson (black), play central roles in this process of development—the latter as a romantic as well as an intellectual interest. Echoing yet departing from the typical ending of the genre, the slugfest climax of the novel comes when Whitman—frustrated by having been robbed of a bout victory at the hands of racist white judges—publicly confronts syndicate boss Lou Ross for calling him a "nigger," knocking the gangster out at his own exclusive "whites only" after-party. (Only the presence of prominent newspaper reporters saves Andy from quick murder by Ross's goons.) In the end, Andy is not killed but is instead blacklisted: Ross buys out his contract, quashing a once-promising boxing career with the stroke of a pen. Forcibly retired at the height of his powers but having finally felt the thrill of a fight that truly mattered, Andy Whitman is left saddened and shaken but not alone. Ruth comforts him and predicts that he will continue to fight but now as a part of the common people, not as an individual in search of money, escape, or championship glory.

As Wald has noted, prominent black critics praised the novel. Writing in the *New Masses,* Ralph Ellison, who would later explore the ironies of black prizefighting in his famous "Battle Royal" section of *Invisible Man,* lauded Zinberg for accomplishing a rare feat for a white writer: "successfully depict[ing] Negro character." Ellison attributed this success to the author's Marxist grasp of the economics structuring Negro life as well as to his shedding of racial stereotypes. He further praised Zinberg's use of "hard-boiled" techniques to capture the violence of Harlem life.[14] African American newspaper editor George Schuyler argued in the *Pittsburgh Courier* that *Walk Hard—Talk Loud* was "superior on several accounts to Richard Wright's *Native Son,*" the massively influential and controversial 1940 best seller. Zinberg's "superiority," as Schuyler notes, grew out of the fact that his black characters "are not caricatures as were Wrights [*sic*]. The red blood of authenticity pulsates through all of them." Specifically, Schuyler singled out Andy Whitman's "sweetheart," Ruth Lawson, as "one of the finest female Negro characters yet created . . . far above . . . the liquor sated Bessie of *Native Son.*"[15]

The Ruth Lawson praised by Schuyler is not just some innocent "sweetheart"; she is also the streetwise voice of Harlem Communism. Departing from the roles generally given to women in the boxing fiction of this era, the women in *Walk Hard—Talk Loud* represent more than sex objects or love interests; they call for conscious commitment to organized, collective politics, to interracial working-class struggle and solidarity. While Andy Whitman often resembles the classic hard-boiled lone rebel scrapping with his wits and fists against a cutthroat (and racist) world, Ruth Lawson—her name recalls longtime Hollywood Communist leader John Howard Lawson—is the committed "revolutionist," vowing not just to lash out at the violent world but to work patiently to change it.[16] Unlike those who tell him to mind his own business, make his money, and "do his fighting in the ring," these female comrades struggle against Andy's individualist and escapist tendencies (though not moralistically against boxing per se), specifically challenging his dream of making a quick fortune in the ring so he can move out of the country.

Ruth and Kate don't wait for Andy's own ideological development. Rather, the novel suggests that they have active social and political lives of their own, frequently putting Andy off to attend political meetings; at one point, Andy must track them down at the Harlem Workers Center. Nor are Zinberg's Red women Steinbeckian Ma Joad types with some natural link to the community or old-fashioned morality. Indeed, both Kate and Ruth are modern women: unmarried urban wage workers. Both a stenographer and a waitress who aspires to become a writer, Ruth is critical of conservative, domestic, maternal ideals, which she catalogs as among the many ways by which people flee the reality of the world for some "private realm." After speaking with her, Andy thinks how the Reds must *read* a lot.

While Andy's experiences in the ring, in the gym, and on the streets offer many insights into social class, race, and corruption (in keeping with the Popular Front boxing genre), Ruth and Kate play a crucial role in helping Andy—and the reader—to bring these antiracist and anticapitalist lessons to consciousness, extending local insights into a broader social critique. They allow *Walk Hard—Talk Loud* to pursue a pedagogical strategy akin to what Barbara Foley in *Radical Representations* calls a Leninist literary practice—bringing Marxist ideas into contact with more immediate working-class experiences.[17] Ruth especially offers wide-ranging explanations of racism, addressing its economic function as well as its psychological aspects, tracing the political tendencies and limitations of Harlem's competing social circles, and emphasizing the need for collective rather than individual action: "The only way we're going up is when all of us go up together. You can't run away from that....Discrimination is a result, you have to get at the bottom, fight the cause."[18] The cause at root for Ruth is "the pocketbook nerve...the backbone of the present setup....Everything boils down to dollars and cents....Everything from war and murder to a guy slapping his wife can be traced to money, lack of a job, or bum food, slums, and all the other delights of your funny friend—capitalism."[19] In this diagnosis, Ruth finds hopes for black people's struggle, for as she sees it, blacks "aren't alone":

> The poll tax hits the poor white too. Remember, they also lynch and murder whites—when they start kicking about conditions. Look at the Okies, the union men that get killed and slugged, read about the murder of Laura Law. . . . Our country is in a hell of a fix, and all because of the pocketbook nerve . . . a few people are going to make profits even though the rest of us starve. But it's all going to backfire—we don't need them but they must have workers.[20]

And yet at the same time that she waxes optimistic about the long-term emergence of working-class unity in what she calls "our country," Ruth agrees with Andy that sometimes the brutal racism of whites makes the idea of turning to retaliatory violence appealing.

In contrast to boxing narratives that cast blacks primarily as victims of white violence, Zinberg tends to validate black nationalistic militancy as an impulse even while criticizing it as a strategy. Reflecting on how "whites own all the damn stores and good jobs, even in Harlem," Andy himself indulges a violent fantasy:

> It would be something for all the black boys to march down Broadway and Fifth Avenue, all armed with machine guns. Would the whites be scared! We'd march into the hotels and restaurants and say, 'No more of this stuff about we can't eat here—you won't serve us. Some service and make it snappy before we shoot the living hell out of this joint! And then we'd take over a skyscraper and walk into those big companies and say, "How come you got a thousand stenos working here and not one colored girl. . . . Give

> out with jobs or we'll blow you full of holes!" And we'd get them damn jobs soon enough. . . . Boy no wonder the nationalists get rich, it's a good dream![21]

The strategic limits of the "good dream," however, are clear to Andy: "The next day the whites would get going and there must be near twenty whites to every one of us and they'd wipe us out. But not before one helluva fight."[22]

For Andy—and for Zinberg—such direct confrontation retains an undeniable appeal. Only a few chapters later, Andy and Kate Grath get harassed and followed by two drunken racists on the way back from walking Ruth to a political meeting. Whitman's desire to physically confront them quickly turns into a debate: Kate, the white Communist, wants to run to avoid the race riot that she fears a confrontation might provoke. "I thought you Reds fought this stuff!" Andy objects, prompting Kate to reply, "This isn't the way to fight. There's nothing I'd like better than to see you kill them, but it might start a riot. The papers would play it up wrong—you know the angles—and it would incite more riots and bad feelings."[23] Begrudgingly, Andy goes along for the moment, fleeing the thugs—past a smiling and complicit policeman—with tears of shame running down his face. But even as he escorts Kate to safety, he can't suppress his militant desire; he can't stop "thinking of those white stomachs, and how his fist would sink into them—brown against white. Couldn't even hurt your hand on a stomach like that. They were like the white, swollen, gassy stomachs of dead cats—a clean crack would almost rip them open." He criticizes Kate's caution: "Damn if she didn't sound like a conciliatory preacher telling the folks to be good niggers. Newspapers, hell, one good wallop."[24] At such moments, Andy Whitman represents an insurgent "hard-boiled" resistance to gradualism, paternalism, and the subordination of militant antiracism to long-term strategic concerns—and not just in theory.

Once he arrives with Kate to their destination, Andy feigns an excuse to leave the party, doubles back, and puts the two "bums" in the hospital with stomach hemorrhages. He then returns to the festivities, now in a jovial spirit, uncharacteristically asking Kate to dance. Though Kate and the partygoers do not know it, Whitman wages a covert struggle against the immediate face (or rather, the soft underbelly) of racism, even while making a place in their integrated class-based organization, with its media-savvy long-term strategy. In such moments, Zinberg suggests that the violent individualistic hard-boiled masculinity of the boxing ring might have a role to play in the street, while suggesting that the Communist Party needs to take more seriously the immediate demands of black people for direct antiracist action.[25]

In contrast to Kate, Ruth takes a more militant stance that is closer to Andy's. In the face of nasty looks on the city bus, Ruth stares down prejudiced whites, chastising one as a "patronizing bitch." The struggle over how to correctly deal with white racism, then, is depicted in *Walk Hard—Talk Loud* not as one that neatly pits party activists against independent radicals but instead as one that is taking place within and among Communist Party activists and fellow travelers alike. Unlike the canonical (and anticommunist) work of Ralph Ellison's *Invisible Man,* there is no sense of Communists' antiracism being inauthentic, let alone a deliberate ruse.[26] Kate remains a sincere comrade and Ruth's best friend, and Kate's concerns about white racist backlash are honest and understandable, even if Andy disagrees.

Moreover, both the virtues and the limits of Andy's violent, individualist, hard-boiled approach are made apparent after he beats boss Lou Ross to a pulp: though he "felt great" doing it, like he "can do anything," his action does little to undo Ross's economic, political, and social power.[27] Zinberg simultaneously offers readers the rare spectacle—not found anywhere else in US boxing fiction or film—of a black boxer KOing a white racist syndicate boss while suggesting that it is not enough to attack the flesh and bone of such figures. More collective and sophisticated ways of fighting are thus called for, even as the inspiration of Andy's flesh-and-blood fightback imbues that collective struggle with "guts" that it might otherwise lack. The symbolic victory of Andy smashing Lou Ross's face offers readers a tantalizing taste of what a revolutionary action might feel like, even while Zinberg's closing pages insist that we not delude ourselves into mistaking this symbolic victory for a real one.

Closing the novel, Ruth Lawson both praises Andy for his irrepressible instinct to fight back in the face of racism (contrary to financial sense that would have him stifle his integrity for the sake of monetary gain) while suggesting that his loss of a fight career can actually be turned into a gain of a different sort. "All that has happened is that your special little rose-colored bubble has busted," she tells Andy. "Now you're like the rest of us, like the people. You'll have to work and struggle, fight all your life, like every working person does—like your mother told you to. And when we win, you'll win too, but not by yourself."[28] In such moments, we can see how Zinberg's Red women not only break the conservative confines of the genre but also help the novel to develop discussions of race, class, and antiracist strategy that point beyond the boxing ring.

Grasping the Race and Class Contradictions of Mass Culture

In his essay "Black Intellectuals and the Sport of Prizefighting," Gerald Early reviews the ambivalent engagement of black writers with boxing during the period that black boxers such as Joe Louis were achieving dominance. For Richard Wright, for instance, Early finds that boxing represented the stored-up potential power of black folk culture. But it also is emblematic of the "tyrannical blandishments of American popular culture" that so manipulate and trap the likes of Bigger Thomas in *Native Son* through "emotionally crippling, self-destructive escapism."[29] As Early puts it, Wright's boxing articles, published in the *New Masses,* "reveal an essential ambivalence: Joe Louis is a product of American popular culture, its creation in effect, and therefore is nothing more than the convenient bread and circus invention of white American capitalists; but Joe Louis is [also] a hero of the black masses, a potential source of political mobilization because he can so deeply excite so many blacks."[30] Ralph Ellison's later fiction maintained an even more vexed relationship to black prizefighting, most famously exemplified by his blindfolded black-on-black "Battle Royal" that opens *Invisible Man.* "What Ellison emphasizes with the battle royal," Early points out, "is the paradoxical tension of white coercion on the one hand and the willing participation of the black boys on the other.... The fight is not possible... without the fighter himself seeing something of value in the ritual."[31] For Ellison, the all-black prizefight comes to suggest "the impossibility of human solidarity," within conditions of Jim Crow oppression.[32]

Zinberg's Andy Whitman to some degree embodies Wright's ambivalence toward the sport, dreaming of championship glory—as both a means to escape racism and a way to inspire other black people to fight their oppression—while registering the myriad ways that rich (and racist) whites hold the (pocketbook and puppet) strings behind the scenes.[33] *Walk Hard—Talk Loud* thus paints boxing as a simultaneously *mass* manipulating "puppet show" and *popular* phenomenon resonating with the oppressed people, indicating untapped stores of revolutionary energy. Complicating Wright and Ellison's outlooks, however, Zinberg explores the dynamics of a racially integrated sports workplace, suggesting the proletarian potential that is latent in the class structure of the boxing gym itself. Zinberg depicts the fight scene as a contradictory site: one that offers real potential for class-based solidarities that cut across racial lines and yet where such solidarities are continually compromised not just by capitalist control but also by racism inside and outside the ring. Zinberg's portrait of the sport suggests the possibility that sportsmanship and camaraderie—both between boxers and among true fans—could, if shorn of its capitalist structure and racist management, lay the basis for proletarian solidarities, creating the specter of a collective fighter with a left hook that no puppet master could control.

Boxing Bigotry with a Fast Left Hook

The novel opens with an unofficial boxing match, as Andy Whitman defends his shoe-shining turf with his fists against a white youth on a street corner just outside of Harlem. An ethnically diverse white crowd surrounds the combatants, more interested in the sport of the contest—and especially in the black boy's fighting prowess—than in the fight's racial character. After Andy knocks the white boy out, one observer exclaims, "By God, that was one goddam good left hook! Fast!" Watching the two sluggers banter after the fight, "Some of the people laughed and the colored boy smiled and walked through the crowd to his shine box. People made room for him."[34] The opening optimistically suggests that the working-class ethnic white community holds the rules of the street-boxing game above codes of racial exclusion; Andy's fast left hook earns their respect.

Yet when a white policeman arrives on the scene and demands to know what has happened, things change. One of the onlookers responds to the cop's inquiry, saying that "A nigger knocked down a white boy." Even in the face of the police nightstick, however, the white shoeshine closes ranks with Andy, telling the cop that his mouth is bleeding because "I got a hemorrhage when I saw you coming." The cop forces both "shines" to leave the area, calling Andy a "dinge" and telling him to "stay up in Harlem, where you belong. I got enough trouble with the Wops and Kikes without having you around."[35] Interestingly, here the trope of "shine"—a derogatory racial term often directed at African Americans—is used to refer to a class position, a line of work, one that unites the youths across racial lines. At the same time, Zinberg suggests the role that the state plays in enforcing racial segregation and in perpetuating racial violence by actively interpellating white subjects and threatening those who transgress racial lines. The white youth later tells Andy that "it wasn't because you're black [that he picked the fight]. I just don't want no competition around here. I chase all the shine guys, no matter what they are."[36] What first appears to be strictly antiblack hostility is explained as more about economic self-interest than racial bias. Yet even the shine-to-shine solidarity is complicated by Andy's subsequent doubts about whether "that kid [actually] chases the white kids too?"[37] Despite seeming to have earned his place, Andy remains uncertain about the potential of male boxing/bonding to truly break down racial lines.

Similarly, *Walk Hard—Talk Loud* represents the boxing gym itself as a class- and race-divided workplace, where the egalitarianism of the sport operates in contradiction to regimes of oppression and exploitation that seek to profit and police it. Notably, *Walk Hard—Talk Loud* focuses more on the training and socializing in the gym than on the fighting in the ring, presenting the gym as a place where racial discrimination—at least between boxers—appears less pervasive than in broader society. (Boss Lou Ross, of course, is another matter.) Andy is "surprised at the number of colored and Puerto Rican boys. . . . They all seemed to have an air of eagerness, of hope, like guys hanging around the employment agency for the first time."[38] Race hatred does rear its head in the gym too, especially when black and white fighters are pitted against one another or when racist audiences call for black blood. Yet at the same time, Whitman observes a commonality of struggle that lays the basis for a kind of pug-proletarian consciousness. As Andy observes, "The gym was hard and tough and crooked, but he liked it. The fighters—the boys—were all from his class, his kind of people, the poor; he felt this and was glad he was part, even a small part, of something at last. . . . Andy belonged in the gym. It was full of Negroes, Italians, Jews, Filipinos, Porto Ricans, Irish—all poor hard-working men. The fighters were hard-workers."[39]

And yet it seems clear that this is a working-class community without much of a future. Case in point: Andy's older white sparring partner, Happy, whose "legs were covered with a worm-like patchwork of dirty blue veins" and who wishes only that he could get a "regular job." Happy's "eyes don't look happy."[40] Happy's (or Andy's) possible future is represented to us by a blind "huge Negro heavyweight" Andy meets on the street outside the gym who is begging for change and holding a card proudly informing passersby that he is the "former sparring partner of [heavyweight champion] Primo Carnera and Ernie Schaff, and other fighters. . . . Kindly, please help me." Connecting these two victims of the sport is a young white fighter, about Andy's own age, employed as a sparring partner for a heavyweight contender. Referred to only as "the kid," he is repeatedly and mercilessly knocked to the canvas by the trainee, in part to impress the local media and generate press hype. The "kid" is beaten not only literally, out of his senses, but also, symbolically, out of his whiteness. As Whitman observes, "The kid was bleeding pretty badly from the mouth and nose, and his stomach was a dull red. . . . The lower part of the boy's white face was a bloody smear and part of his stomach was rash-red." When an onlooker expresses disgust at the bloody spectacle, a manager exclaims that "He's getting *paid* for taking it, ain't he?"[41] Another white fighter nearly loses an eye in order to pay back a twenty-dollar debt.

Such bloody snapshots call attention to the way in which an exploitative capitalism pushes even would-be *white* pug-proletarians into the *red,* suggesting the way that class exploitation creates common interest across racial lines even while racism constantly threatens to undercut such unity. These portraits of sparring partners bring to the foreground the human costs of producing the championship stars, the gory underside of boxing glory; for every champ, there is (and must be) a legion of burned-out tramps. Moreover, Zinberg explores how even championship contenders with access to the big money, like Andy's friend Bachelo, are systematically rendered dependent on their managers and syndicate bosses, in part through the lure of womanizing and conspicuous consumer spending. Andy overhears pug owners discussing how they keep fighters such as Bachelo under control by getting them to spend their money and thus keeping them broke, suggesting the role that consumerism plays in reproletarianizing even those stars whose success might otherwise allow them to challenge the current regime.

Nonetheless, though Whitman's experiences in and around the ring offer glimpses of hope and solidarity, the novel tends to suggest the stark limits of the scene as a site of politics. Fear, cynicism, and competition rule. When Lou Ross shows up, even the most wizened pug (Happy as well as Bachelo) shuts up. In this sense, Andy's blacklisting should seem like a kind of liberation. And as Ruth Lawson would have it, it is. Andy has been saved from the delusions of individualism and the deadly, blinding violence of the ring. Yet being blacklisted, Andy is cut off not only from his escapist/individualist dreams but also from this class-bound, interracial community of fighters. Ironically, even as he is ostensibly freed to begin fighting not for prize money but for social equality, he has been stripped of the sense of belonging to something bigger than himself. Whitman's proletarianization is thus a deeply ambivalent one: consciousness and comradeship coming at the cost of community. Though Andy has Ruth beside him—and though she represents clearly the prospect of a new and emergent communist collectivity—the novel ends with him in tears: "It was the first time he could remember crying—and he didn't like it."[42] Class consciousness arrives to Zinberg's proletarianized protagonist not as epiphany but as (emasculating) trauma. The hard-boiled hero mourns for what has been lost, even as Ruth reminds him, and us, that the setting of the sun on Andy's private dreams may represent in fact a communist horizon: a red sun rising even as another sets. "And if you were an office clerk, [rather than a boxer]," Ruth asks Andy earlier in the novel, as they flirt amid the bustle of the Workers Center, "What would you do then?"[43]

Notes

1. Alan Wald, *Trinity of Passion: The Literary Left and the Antifascist Crusade* (Chapel Hill: University of North Carolina Press, 2009), 1–11. Certainly, without Wald's work and his generous guidance, I would never have heard of this "strange" Communist, let alone made his fascinating 1940s fiction a centerpiece of my dissertation "Red Pulp: Radicalism and Repression in Mid-20th Century U.S. Genre Fiction," PhD dissertation, Tufts University, 2007.
2. Following his exposure as a "red" in the *New York Times,* Zinberg never published another book under his own name. See "Hargrove's Post Spurned by Legion," *New York Times,* September 13, 1946, 4.
3. Leonard Zinberg, *Walk Hard—Talk Loud* (New York: Lion Books, 1950).
4. Wald devotes a couple of paragraphs to reviewing Zinberg's 1948 novel *Hold with the Hares* and sees it as a kind of "psychobiography" for this forgotten writer.
5. Wald, *Trinity of Passion,* 9.
6. Ibid., 11.
7. Chris Vials, *Realism for the Masses: Aesthetics, Popular Front Pluralism, and U.S. Culture, 1935–1947* (Jackson: University of Mississippi, 2009), xxxix.
8. The industry virtually ceased making boxing films during World War II. Vials points out how often the novels and plays followed routes and models established first by the movies.
9. Richard Wright left unpublished a novel manuscript focusing on an African American boxer. It is available in the Wright Papers at the Beinecke Rare Book and Manuscript Library at Yale University.
10. Vials, *Realism for the Masses,* 17.
11. Ibid., 19. The Popular Front version of the genre is of course drastically different from later revisions of boxing narrative, from the *Rocky* series to *Cinderella Man,* that tend to affirm autonomous, competitive white hypermasculinity rather than to problematize it. For an insightful analysis of continuity and change within the boxing (and wrestling) film genre, see Benjamin Balthaser, "Re-Staging the Great Depression: Genre as Social Memory in Darren Aronofsky's The Wrestler" [review of Darren Aronofsky's *The Wrestler*], *Cultural Logic: An Electronic Journal of Marxist Theory and Practice*, 2010, http://clogic.eserver.org/2010/Balthaser.pdf.
12. Vials, *Realism for the Masses,* 35–36.
13. Interestingly, while Andy Whitman's last name invokes the progressive democratic icon of Walt Whitman—frequently referenced during the Popular Front period—his first name recalls Sailor Anderson, the slain black boxer featured in the 1939 film adaptation of Clifford Odets's popular play, *Golden Boy.* The main character in Zinberg's third novel, *Hold with the Hares* (1948), would be named Steve Anderson. Anderson too, like many a Zinberg/Lacy protagonist, has an instinct and a talent for swinging his fists in the face of injustice.
14. Ralph Ellison, "Negro Prize Fighter," *New Masses,* December 17, 1940, 26–27. Ellison first published "Battle Royal" as a short story in 1947.
15. George Schuyler, "Looks and Books," *Pittsburgh Courier,* December 28, 1940, 11. See also George Schuyler, "Looks and Books," *Pittsburgh Courier,* January 18, 1941, 6.
16. Even Andy's own rebelliousness, we learn from Andy's father Charlie, comes

from his late mother Hannah, a former laundry worker who is remembered as having quit jobs to protest the racism of her white employers. When Andy begins hanging out with "Reds," Charlie declares that he has his "mother's spirit in him" and implores him to "just do your fighting in the ring." Zinberg, *Walk Hard—Talk Loud,* 173.

17. Barbara Foley, *Radical Representations: Politics and Form in U.S. Proletarian Fiction, 1929–1941* (Durham, NC: Duke University Press, 1993), 99.
18. Zinberg, *Walk Hard—Talk Loud,* 134–35.
19. Ibid., 136.
20. Ibid., 204. A left-wing labor activist and Finnish immigrant, Laura Law was bludgeoned and stabbed to death with an ice pick in her Aberdeen, Washington, home on January 5, 1940. No one was ever tried for her murder.
21. Ibid., 129.
22. Ibid., 128–29.
23. Ibid., 189.
24. Ibid., 191.
25. It is worth noting, of course, that Harlem would erupt in a violent black rebellion (or so-called race riot) in 1943.
26. I discuss Nate Mills's thoughtful analysis of *Invisible Man* in my essay "Invisible Tragedies, Invisible Possibilities." Joseph G. Ramsey, "Invisible Tragedies, Invisible Possibilities," *Cultural Logic: An Electronic Journal of Marxist Theory and Practice,* 2010, http://clogic.eserver.org/2010/Ramsey_review.pdf.
27. Zinberg, *Walk Hard—Talk Loud,* 231–32.
28. Ibid., 255.
29. Gerald Early, *The Culture of Bruising: Essays on Prizefighting, Literature, and Modern American Culture* (New York: Ecco, 1994), 24.
30. Ibid.
31. Ibid., 28.
32. Ibid.
33. "[Andy] wondered if there would ever be a time when Harlem would be singing his name and people filling the streets like they did when Louis flattened Schmeling. . . . They fussed over Big Joe. What did it really get the people? Louis got all the money and cheers. Louis has a fine house and car, while the people still get nothing. But it did pep the people up, it sure did, one of *our* boys did something . . . our Joe is champ" (Zinberg, *Walk Hard—Talk Loud,* 114–15).
34. Ibid., 5–6.
35. Ibid., 6.
36. Ibid., 8.
37. Ibid., 6.
38. Ibid., 27.
39. Ibid., 43. Of course, the text qualifies that "Whatever equality there was stopped the moment they stepped out of the gym" (43). Andy's friendship with Bachelo, a cynical white heavyweight contender who is a staunch antiracist from his days working as a union longshoreman, concretizes this possibility of extending this

equality outside. Yet Bachelo also embodies a very problematic and over-the-top macho sexism, suggesting Zinberg's critique of violent white masculinity as alienated, anxious, and outright dangerous.

40. Ibid., 19.

41. Ibid., 33–34.

42. Ibid., 256.

43. Ibid., 130.

[14]

Benjamin Appel's *Fortress in the Rice*: Forging the Radical Conscience of the Empire

E. San Juan, Jr.

Benjamin Appel (1907–1977) may be the most neglected or forgotten radical-democratic novelist of the mid-twentieth-century in the United States.[1] The most recent incisive commentary on Appel appeared in Alan Wald's *Trinity of Passion: The Literary Left and the Anti-Fascist Crusade* (2007), which focused on *The Dark Stain* (1943), the last of a trilogy that began with *Brain Guy* (1934) and *The Power House* (1939). Those books became the basis for Appel's reputation as a novelist specializing in crime fiction set in a milieu of poverty and corruption, where "the morass of racial prejudice devours even those of good intentions."[2] Committed to Popular Front politics, Appel combined Leo Tolstoy's psychodrama with elements of Charles Dickens, Upton Sinclair, and Theodore Dreiser to describe, in hard-boiled fashion, an urban American race war as a protofascist environment. He was recognized at the time in *The New Yorker* and elsewhere as an authentic voice of the streets.[3]

Despite this notoriety, few remember that Appel also wrote about the raging anticolonial struggle and class war in a tropical archipelago, a territorial possession, more than eight thousand miles away from the continental United States. Within five years of publishing *The Dark Stain,* Appel turned his attention to "the misery and despair of Asia . . . shared by nearly all the nonwhite people of the world" and to those who struggled for a "bowl of rice"—the symbol of material existence indicating the common humanity of all.[4] As the Cold War expanded after 1945, Appel's sympathy for the underdog widened and deepened to embrace the brutalized peasants of the Philippines confronting Japanese, American, and native oppressors. His novel, based on firsthand experience, *Fortress in the Rice* (1951), showed his combination of realistic vision and empathic sensibility.

Trajectory of the Partisan Intelligence

Appel's early experiences brought him into contact with multiethnic constituencies. From 1935 to 1941, he was an active member of the left-wing League of American Writers, whose black members included Richard Wright, Langston Hughes, Ralph Ellison, and many others. The league also provided opportunities for delegates from other countries to participate in its meetings. Appel might have encountered the left-wing Filipino delegates who attended the league's third congress in June 1939, when anti-imperialist speeches inspired the committed audience.[5] Later as an officer of the league, he signed the 1942 "Call to the Writers Win-the-War Congress," which was intended to "articulate the will and desires of the people" and to remember and avenge the victims of Pearl Harbor, Lidice, and Stalingrad; using "words as weapons," league members advocated "the democratic integration in this people's war of the total energies of the Negro people, by fighting with them against discrimination in any form whether in civil life or in the armed forces."[6] Appel's radical-democratic stance was rooted in his conviction—like that of the critic Kenneth Burke—that the people as a whole (rather than a narrowly defined, proletarian class in itself) provided the transitional vehicle for moving beyond a class-divided polity toward a larger inclusive, egalitarian order.[7] In humanist-populist terms such as these, Appel would identify with *Hukbalahap* (People's Army against the Japanese), often called the Huks, the Communist-led peasant insurgency in the Philippines that continued after the defeat of Japan. For him, the Huks were an organic popular ensemble uniting all under the banner of grassroots democracy, popular justice, and socialist-internationalist solidarity.

In the last months of the war, Appel had worked in Washington, D.C., for the Office of War Mobilization and Conversion. Thereafter he was made a special assistant to the US high commissioner to the Philippines

Paul V. McNutt. In the Philippines from November 1945 to March 1946, Appel conducted field investigations of the social, political, and cultural conditions of the islands. His unusual insider's vantage point enabled him to scrutinize firsthand those crucial months of negotiations that followed the liberation of the country from Japanese occupation and led to formal independence. He described the painful, dangerous process of restoring normalcy to a society wracked with centuries of peonage, violent pauperization of millions, rampant injustice, and ferocious class antagonisms. Those deep-rooted social maladies emerged from a legacy of three hundred years of Spanish domination, four years of ruthless Japanese oppression, and over forty years of US white-supremacist ascendancy. In the brief, pivotal interregnum between the end of the war and Philippine independence (which in large part was a delusory cover for US neocolonialism), Appel directly encountered all the issues of wartime collaboration, agrarian conflict, military insubordination, diplomatic chicanery, and political opportunism that dominated the headlines of that period.

Appel's rich, data-filled letters to his family, collected in an unpublished "Manila Diary," provided the raw material for his two novels set in the Philippines. One of them, *Plunder* (1952), carried over some of the traits of his earlier work: it was a racially calibrated exposé of underworld racketeering in the war-ravaged Philippines, an interethnic drama involving American soldiers colluding with Filipinos, Chinese, and others to enrich themselves in piracy. *Fortress in the Rice* was more of a departure: by charting the vicissitudes of the Huk rebellion, it offered one of the most trenchant critiques of a racialized colonial ideology as it operated in the psyches of both masters and subalterns.

Appel described the education he gained in the Philippines in several letters to prospective publishers:

> After meeting Sergio Osmena [then president of the Philippine Commonwealth] and Manuel Roxas [elected first president of the Philippine Republic and exonerated by General Douglas MacArthur for his collaboration with the Japanese] etc., I became interested in the history of the dominant Nacionalista Party over half a century. After attending the trials of General Yamashita, I became interested in the Japanese policy during the occupation, particularly in its propaganda against the West. After meeting the guerilla leaders, both American and Filipino, I became interested in unraveling the feud between the Hukbalahaps and the American-led guerillas. I discovered that there was one common cord binding together such historical phenomena as the Nacionalista Party with its drive for independence from the United States, the Japanese occupation, the bitter feud between the guerilla groups: *who should own the land.* Landlord or peasant? Today, the land-rice revolt is continuing not only in the Philippines but throughout all Asia. In

> my opinion, it is the greatest historical fact of our times, involving the fate of half the world's population.[8]

Thus, Appel aimed to build his novel *Fortress in the Rice* on the "theme of the Asiatic peasant's struggle for rice and land" and added, in rhetoric still resonating with Popular Front ideals, that "my hero in this novel are the billion Asiatics, the common man across the Pacific who for all his differences is not too dissimilar from the common man of the big American cities."[9] This commonality was to be embodied in the two central and typical characters of the novel, the American David MacVey and the Filipino Manuel Careo. US colonial power and Filipino resistance to it would be fleshed out in these complicated personalities. In Appel's ethico-political imagination, their lives acquired meaning because they reacted to changing historical circumstances and the moral challenges posed by the pressures of their times.

Caught between Two Worlds

Knowledge of the Philippines as the only direct Southeast Asian colony of the United States has been, for the most part, obtuse and sparse. *The Reader's Companion to American History,* for example, makes quick work of it: citing the US defeat of Spain in 1898 and subsequent annexation of the Philippines, the book notes that "anti-imperialists opposed to taking over a foreign people without their consent and holding them in a colonial condition objected bitterly." Thereafter, we are told, the United States poured aid into the islands to pacify dissident groups and communities and in 1946 "granted the Philippines their independence, though still maintaining bases and political influence there."[10] Other historians, however, such as Howard Zinn, Stuart Creighton Miller, and Gabriel Kolko, have gone further, describing the unconscionable violence exercised by US forces in suppressing Filipino insurgents after 1899 by means of pacification campaigns running through the first three decades of the twentieth century. The US colonial administration granted concessions to win over the vacillating middle strata and petty bourgeois intelligentsia, but the majority of Filipinos did not benefit: over 80 percent of the toiling masses consisted of peasants and workers chained to peonage in the fields and mines, subjected to degrading conditions.[11]

US tutelage resulted in pauperization of the peasantry and immiseration of the working-class and indigenous communities, due chiefly to the polarization of land ownership. Historian Jonathan Fast found that "in 1903 [when the US administration claimed that the insurgency had been defeated] an estimated 81 per cent of all land holdings were worked on directly by their owners; by 1938 this figure had fallen to 49 per cent and in the post-war decade the rate of polarization increased further . . . [until] two thirds of all the rural population were landless."[12] On the eve of the Pacific War, deteriorating socioeconomic conditions, the increasing rate of land tenancy, heavy rural indebtedness, and massive pauperization spawned a movement of militant unions demanding land redistribution and the end of landlord control of the courts and the bureaucratic apparatus. Nonetheless, private landlord armies and vigilante groups controlled by the elite suppressed any agitation, however peaceful and legal.

World War II caused a rupture in the system of unequal relations between colonized subalterns and imperial lords together with their native overseers. The war released popular energies catalyzed by the people's stubborn resistance to Japanese brutality. The anti-Japanese Huk insurgency was composed of Socialists, Communists, and other nationalist forces. They fought not only the Japanese invaders but also their Filipino collaborators—the puppet government and its constabulary police and soldiers—who defended landlord property and oligarchic entitlements, those pillars of the iniquitous prewar status quo. The Huk insurgency was ultimately what Appel called "a battle for the land,"[13] for the radical transformation of the economic and political structures that entrenched a privileged propertied minority.[14] After establishing local governments, the armed peasantry organized by the Huks implemented land redistribution, uncompromising punishment (often by assassination) of collaborators, and the denial of rice supplies to the Japanese occupiers (the unique strategy of the Huks' "harvest struggles").

And so the struggle for land and freedom would arrive at a critical turning point. The Popular Front policies of the Huk movement saw the US-backed anti-Japanese guerrillas—known as United States Armed Forces in the Far East (USAFFE)—as allies. When the US colonial officials and their army returned in 1944, the Huks welcomed them as fellow comrades in the antifascist struggle. The Huk commanders carried out an initial voluntary demobilization in their regional and local guerrilla infrastructures. But instead of being recognized for their contribution to the destruction of Japanese forces in the major provinces of Luzon (the largest island), the Huks were disarmed. Huk leaders were hounded and persecuted. USAFFE guerrillas accused the Huks of all kinds of crimes and persuaded the US Counter-Intelligence Corps to arrest well-known Huk leaders such as Luis Taruc, Casto Alejandrino, and Silvestre Liwanag. Under the Commonwealth regime of Manuel Roxas, installed by General MacArthur, landlord-controlled military police kidnapped and murdered Huk leader Juan Feleo and labor militant Jose Joven. In a historic atrocity of February 5, 1945, Appel would find the episode he later rendered as the climax to his novel. That day, Huk Squadron 77 was waylaid by a Filipino colonel, Adonais Maclang. Maclang then killed 130 unarmed Huk guerrillas with the knowledge of the US Military Police and civilian administrators. Only one American official, Air Corps colonel Gwen Atkinson, protested the outrage. This event was also described in the Huk leader Luis Taruc's autobiography *Born of the People* (1953), which came out two years after the publication of Appel's *Fortress in the Rice.*[15] Here was incontrovertible evidence of the dominance of landlord-reactionary politicians and military chiefs who were then supported by Roxas and, by extension, his backer General MacArthur.[16]

In effect, American liberation of the islands spelled the return of the old order of mestizo elite exploitation of the majority of peasants and workers. The immediate postwar period of collaboration and MacArthur's subversion of principles proclaimed by President Franklin Delano Roosevelt and other American leaders (i.e., affirmation of national self-determination, human rights, and democratic liberties) were summed up by Filipino journalist Hernando Abaya in his 1947 commentary, *Betrayal in the Philippines.*[17] For Appel, that treachery was shocking; exposing it became the moral burden he bore in writing the novel. The betrayal was in fact completed, in the wake of formal independence, when the Bell Trade Act and the Military Bases Agreement of 1947 converted the territory into a neocolony. These and other measures preserved feudal landlord structures and the client-patron nexus of oligarchic power while carrying on the three hundred–year heritage of colonial subjugation under a new name.[18]

Lineaments of the Narrative Structure

The historical events covered by *Fortress in the Rice* begin with the bombing of Pearl Harbor and the Philippines on December 7, 1941, and span the subsequent defeats of American and Filipino defenders of Bataan and Corregidor as well as the guerrilla resistance mounted by the Huks and surviving USAFFE fighters, to conclude with the return in 1945 of General MacArthur's troops and his anticommunist agents. The novel's protagonist is an American bank clerk named David MacVey who joined USAFFE and was marooned in the countryside when the Japanese took the islands. Plunged into a complex social panorama of class and national conflicts, MacVey must work out his own salvation in what becomes a long narrative of learning and discovery. The novel describes

MacVey's apprenticeship as witness and bearer of testimony amid the ironic unfolding of history.

Four blocs of character types fill the stage. First, the Filipino *hacienderos* and oligarchs, with whom American business on the islands was historically linked, are represented by Narciso Ferrer, who flees his country home for Manila and becomes the minister of justice in the puppet regime established by the Japanese occupation. The American MacVey had found haven at Ferrer's estate, becoming the sweetheart of Ferrer's daughter Teresita. The second group consists of American USAFFE officials and the villainous soldier Joe Trent, a kind of double—or diabolic shadow emanation—of MacVey. The third group consists of the Filipino Huk guerrillas represented chiefly by Major Manuel Careo. Finally, situated between the Huks and the Japanese, we find an outlaw group led by a woman named Sisa, leader of the bandit group who retreats to a wilderness hideout in Dingalan Bay, and an opportunist USAFFE band led by Major Ortala and supported by landlords and fascist elements.

At the outset, we see the young, naive MacVey befriended by the hacienda overseer, Jacinto, who was left behind in charge of the estate when Ferrer fled to Manila. The first lesson in MacVey's education comes as peasants take their revenge for centuries-old humiliation by slaying Jacinto. With psychological acuity, Appel renders the impact of the oppressed's newly found power on the anguished white man, whose only refuge is to assert his national/racial identity:

> In this room become a slaughter pen Dave looked from the killers to the killed. On the overseer's hand—the hand that had an arm—he recognized his wrist watch and glimpsed his own murdered self, as if bound, indeed, to the Filipino. Jabbering, the killers walked to him, and although he shouted, "Don't kill me! I'm an American! *Amigo*! *Americano*!" there was a part of him that seemed as utterly dead as the overseer.[19]

MacVey's second lesson in self-examination comes from his association with Joe Trent as both of them journey toward the Huk headquarters at Lawang Kupang. Witnessing Trent's rape of a helpless native woman, MacVey vows to bear witness to this epitome of colonial/racial/sexist terrorism: "He could have wept for her and for himself. He could have wept for this evil thing Joe had done to her and to all Americans. But what was the use? In this hut who would care or understand? 'Joe,' he said, 'when we get to Lawang Kupang I'm turning you in, Joe. I'm telling Careo.'"[20] On reaching the camp of Huk leader Careo, MacVey is reunited with Teresita, who has broken with her father by joining the Huk rebels. MacVey's report of Trent's crime has no effect; both the Americans, MacVey and Trent, are dispatched to a USAFFE group commanded by

Colonel Ryker. They also spend an interlude together with Sisa's bandits at the remote Dingalan Bay. Further steps in MacVey's moral education emerge from the sojourn at Dingalan Bay, leading to the novel's denouement, when MacVey fully assumes his role as testimony-bearer and witness.

The Artist's Vocation: Historian and People's Tribune

MacVey's role as witness, of course, mirrored Appel's own status as an observer-cum-partisan, someone (as aide to McNutt) affiliated with the colonizer who discovers the US betrayal not only of the Philippines but also of the democratic ideals that Appel's Popular Front politics had identified with a genuine New Deal for the world. Appel saw himself as a historian-educator capable of conveying knowledge of a multidimensional sociohistorical totality in the form of a novel. His method followed Georg Lukács's understanding of the novel as a venture in interiority as well as Lukács's definition of realism as the invention of typical characters representing social categories, such as MacVey, Narciso Ferrer, Careo, etc.

Appel had no intention of achieving a kind of documentary pastiche that one associates today with Truman Capote's *In Cold Blood* or with the raw if now banal naturalism of Émile Zola and Frank Norris. Appel disclaimed being a political reporter or foreign correspondent. In a letter to the editor of Macmillan, Appel confessed that the novel is the "story of one American's education in the Far East—an education begun so long ago in an American schoolroom—and what he learned of the new colonialism so ominous for all the peoples of the world. It is the story of sixty days, a moment of history, that lost all Asia."[21] Later, Appel wrote that in 1945–46, he felt he was "living at the center of a typhoon"; it was "a year of momentous decisions when all Asia held its breath, waiting for the United States, the world's supreme power to point the way to the future. . . . And weren't the 1950s and the 1960s decades of wars and civil wars in Asia? And wasn't the United States itself torn apart by violent dissension?" Appel assumed a self-conscious, transnational perspective: "No sensitive person could have been in the Far East in 1945–46 without being aware that the American alternatives in Asia were limited. It was a choice between the mailed fist, a restoration of the pre-war status quo, or a recognition of the 'rice bowl' revolution. And my novel reflected what was to come."[22]

He wanted to report faithfully but also judge and evaluate what was happening. It is clear that he had been deeply moved by the epic struggle of the Filipino masses for genuine democracy and equality, encapsulated in his phrase "the rice bowl revolution of landless peasants," an epic struggle to which American "leadership at all levels is pathetically blind. . . . All colonialism is doomed but our leadership remains blind."[23] Appel's urgent task was to awaken not only the leaders but also the broad audience of his work about this ethico-political blindness, this willful ignorance, bred from a long history of colonial hauteur. His advantage over previous historians was that he happened to be a witness-participant at a turning point when the main contradiction between Japanese fascism and the Allied cause of free-enterprise democracy clashed head-on with the revolutionary tide in the Philippines. "To know, to understand and to act in the democratic tradition" was Appel's ethico-political motive, a duty as witness to testify to the truth and an obligation to incite the audience to action in order to prevent what was to come—the disasters and misfortunes of humanity, born from the reality of the unexamined benighted past.

As a socially responsible artist, Appel conceived his task as the traditional one of rendering into concrete dramatic scenes the meaning of what he witnessed, investing acts of misery and despair with pity, compassion, and love. The burden of artistic representation would center on constructing a narrative that would flesh out the manifold contradictions of that historic conjuncture. The artist would immerse himself in a specific milieu in which the conflicts of classes, races, and nations would assume an imaginative unity that would attain timelessness in and through the ephemeral circumstances of everyday life. He extracted from the Philippine geopolitical milieu a contrived plot of one young American's education (MacVey's experience) about the deceptive nature of the new colonialism, shown in the strife between the Huks and USAFFE right after the end of the war with the Japanese.

Apart from fidelity to a multifaceted actuality, the novel's realism is complicated by a need to profit from the hazardous journey of discovering the truth behind illusions both official and psychological, illusions about white supremacy and American "benevolent assimilation" (first proclaimed by President William McKinley upon annexing the islands in 1898). The sublimation of romantic ideals embedded in tradition and social conventions proceeds through love scenes, fantasies, and experiences of disappointment, anger, joy, and longing. What results is the ironic revelation of the limits of metaphysical hopes and idealist promises vis-à-vis the unyielding facticity of real life: Appel reroutes the classic burden of the bildungsroman, self-realization as an educational process of disillusion and learning, through syncopation with social satire and lyrical episodes of adventure beyond the humdrum routine of quotidian life. Appel's perspective—one of hindsight based on his Philippine experience turned into foresight about the disasters of US postwar policy in Southeast Asia—informs the novel's prophetic charge.

As Appel strove to reconcile his self-appointed roles as novelist, historian, and partisan, he sought to portray MacVey as a typical white middle-class American whose education involves a moral journey beyond racism, possessive individualism, and fatalism—all in the process of recognizing the humanistic aspirations of the Asian revolution. Even in passages describing MacVey's rapturous reunion with Teresita near the camp of Huk leader Careo that critics have faulted for purple prose, Appel's real aim was a suggestive invocation of moral development. Lyrical passages celebrate the loss of that narrow ego-centered mentality that underlays class, racial, and national divisions among humans. Losing ego in that sense harmonized with the transcendent cosmic rhythm of nature:

> Before them a dark slope lifted, and they listened to the mountain stream gurgling and tumbling over unseen pebbles. If the mountain slept, its voice was always babbling—of lovers' farewells and the passing of love, and of death. Down, down to the hills, the stream sang, down to the uplands, love passes, down into the green and golden rice, down to the plain, love passes and death awaits. . . . He kissed her gently on the lips, his eyes closing, and in the silence the stream still sang of love and death. "You're here, and I'm here!" he whispered. "The biggest fluke."[24]

That last slangy phrase borrows the language and tone of Appel's early tough-guy writing in order to defuse unduly romantic transports.

In the Huk camp, Major Careo marries MacVey and Teresita, and thus Careo becomes a father figure and teacher to the American. MacVey's inherited racism is evident as he willfully fantasizes that Teresita is Spanish, not Filipino; he admits his unease at the prospect of being the father of a "brown kid," a fatality "too remote for him to grasp."[25] Careo drives home the cathartic value of the process of self-examination as he tells MacVey, "You are ashamed of the prejudice. That is the first step, my friend. To admit your life as it has been, to understand your own past. Only then can a man begin to understand the lives of others different from him. Once we understand, we will have no use for prejudice." Complementing this self-enlightenment is a view that the past is not immutable, proof of which is the wedding of two persons representing seeming opposites, disparities, incommensurables: "You will open other doors, all the doors of your past, this prison that holds us and keeps us from being brothers."[26]

Learning and Teaching

That memorable exhortation rests on the trope of liberation from enclosing mind-sets and fixations. In the chapter that Appel titled "The First Liberation," the morality of decision is sharply enunciated as the antithesis of what is and what ought to be, a choice between resignation to the static actuality of everyday life and defiance in attempting to change the drift of things: "The way things are, Dave thought. . . . But what about the way things ought to be? Lifting against the chorus of the way things are, he seemed to hear voice after voice . . . for always there came a time of decision. Always a man has to raise his own voice or be still against the steady, repeated everlasting chorus of the way things are."[27] This classic philosophical contradiction between is and ought, what is dead (the past) and what ought to be vibrant (the future as present), axiomatically expresses the theme of the novel.

Yet MacVey has not yet fully embraced this lesson. Separated once again from Teresita—whom he learns later abandoned him for an opportunist USSAFE officer—MacVey indulges his sexual desires with the bandit leader Sisa, lover of Joe Trent as well. This triangular affair brings MacVey to a point of almost complete corruption before he resumes his emancipatory education. Imagining Dingalan Bay and Sisa's way of life as nearly idyllic, he is almost prepared to surrender all previous ties, obligations, and remorse. It is a moment of liberation from self-centered concerns, even an anarchistic moment of self-dissolution—of the wrong kind. After being assured that he has equal claims to Sisa in competition with Trent, MacVey begins to admire Sisa as a free agent, "a perverted female Robin Hood, loyal to her wine-stealing, raping bunch of *tulisans* [bandits]." Even "Caveman Joe Trent," as a man with no ties, has nearly been redeemed for MacVey. When, however, Sisa proves her utter indifference to the murder of a former lover by Trent, MacVey recoils. Sisa comes to represent amoral fatalism, and Joe represents the acquiescence to beastly impulses. At this point, MacVey's internal divisions can no longer be disguised or ignored. Fearing that he had been lulled into *becoming* his double, he "was tormented most by the feeling that he was Joe."[28] This epiphanic moment for MacVey ushers in his return to the role as witness and truth-bearer.

As MacVey breaks with the bandit camp and begins a long perilous trek back to USAFFE headquarters, he finds himself truly dispossessed. Having escaped the illusions of pleasurable abandon, he also comes to terms with the loss of Teresita, no longer claiming rights of ownership over her or anyone else. He reaches a stage, that is, when "need and enjoyment have lost their egoistic nature" (as Marx once envisaged)—his need for sexual enjoyment, for example—and when the complete emancipation of all the human senses and attributes occurs with "the supersession of private property," in this case, one woman's body treated as the husband's private possession.[29] In terms of the larger theme of imperial domination of other lands, the colony and its people can no longer be treated as possessions—the Filipinos and their natural resources are no longer the private property of American capitalist investors and businessmen. Not only has MacVey taken a step beyond petit bourgeois egoism; he has also assumed an anticolonial vocation. Appel sought to combine the techniques of the bildungsroman with the political critique of the neocolonial situation in Southeast Asia. He would resolve the contradiction between New Deal/Popular Front democratic ideals and authoritarian neocolonial reality by forcing the hero (David MacVey) to shift his concern from his romantic-personal misfortune to the moral obligation to defend human dignity, social justice, and civic responsibility for the victims of class wealth and racist power. The climax of MacVey's education—his graduation into becoming a reliable, full-fledged witness of the brutalities and self-deceptions of war—leads to the novel's denouement in the fate of the Huk rebellion.

In his fictionalized version of the massacre of Huk Squadron 77, Appel depicts the capture of Major Careo by pro-American guerrilla forces who accuse Careo and his men of opposing landlords as Communists and execute them on the spot. Ironically, the colony was freed from the Japanese by American liberators, only to be surrendered to the yoke of quislings, criminal opportunists, and the private armies of landlords and rich politicians and bureaucrats who had pandered to the Japanese and were now eager to prove their subservience to the returning US masters. MacVey comes upon the scene at the end of his long journey from Dingalan Bay. After seeing the corpses of Careo and his other erstwhile Huk comrades, MacVey is seized with "a paroxysm of grief and rage." Prying open Careo's knotted fist, MacVey finds a handful of palay (unhusked rice grains), symbolic of the noble ideals of the peasant resistance. He shouts at Major Ortala, the opportunist officer who carried out the execution to please the reactionary landlord-oligarchs:

> "You're not getting away with it! I'll tell what I know! Here! Back home! I'll tell the whole world the truth!" He spun around, looking down at the major who was a corpse. "Manuel, nobody'll stop me. Manuel, I swear in God's name, Manuel!" And he turned from Manuel, the first in the row of Hukbalahaps, as if even now in death he were leading them, toward Major Ortala and the sergeant and sentry. "You killed him! Killed all of them for the *haciendero*s! For the *haciendero* collaborators! You killed them, but they'll hang you!" And with the motion used in tossing a hand grenade, he drew back his arm, his fist opening, and into their faces he flung the rest of the palay.[30]

Thus, MacVey accepts responsibility for America's failures and hypocrisies.

Appel's metaphoric index of the hungry masses—the palay—is meant to overshadow MacVey's bitter disenchantment at the end with its dreadful aura of futility. The imagery and rhythm of the following passage exemplifies Appel's finely controlled rhetoric. His prose style here is neither overly optimistic nor cautiously genteel. The narrator inventories the polarized forces confronting each other in an imagined portrait of the coming future:

> (The design will be blood-red, and its words will spell out Law and Order. The smoke of burning Hukbalahap barrios will spell out Law and Order, a Law and Order of the hacienderos. . . . Mailed fists and rebellious land-hungry peoples on the march. Who will help them? They will help themselves. Who will hear their ancient cry for land and rice? They will hear themselves. America, great land, land of the free, will you help, will you hear? Will you understand that the revolution of Asia is a revolution of hunger and that the hungry are reaching for more than a bowl of rice? Reaching for the land that has never belonged to them, and for more than the land. Reaching for their own manhood, for dignity, for love. Yes, for love, as the revolution kills and burns in its march toward power. For the marching peasant soldier is the father who sold his daughter to keep the family from starvation; the marching peasant soldier is the son who watched the police torture his mother; the marching peasant soldier is the brother whom nobody called brother but the organizers and leaders of the revolution. America, you must understand that if the mailed fist is strong, American democracy is stronger, and only American democracy can win friends in Asia. Only democracy.)[31]

In this spirit, Appel's concluding pages produce mixed feelings of subdued hope, vigilance, and anger. Optimism and melancholy coalesce. Ultimately, MacVey takes up the challenge of broadcasting to the world the truth of colonialism and its deceptive masks. Although aware of human limitations and the inertia of institutions, Appel ardently believed in progress by stages. He reaffirmed his commitment to a Popular Front vision of the (betrayed) promise of a New Deal for the world. Thus, he reinvented his novelistic vocation by syncopating his usual realist method with a subtly allegorical, quasi-Brechtian pedagogical maneuver. *Fortress in the Rice* is the product of this process of renewal. Parallel to MacVey's passage from shock to understanding and engagement, the novelist's process of giving pleasure by resolving crises coincides with his pedagogical task. Although the accumulation of events overwhelms practically all the major characters, MacVey as well as Careo and others derive insight and wisdom from the difficulties of their individual predicaments. Appel's ethico-political objective of depicting the emergence of US neocolonial hegemony in the Philippines fuses with his artistic goal of mobilizing the novel form to serve both aesthetic and political ends.

Appel's narrative strategy of weaving individual fates within the fabric of international-local relations succeeded in synthesizing the complex motives of humans caught in a turbulent crisis. We are engaged here with the historic crisis of a system—monopoly capitalism in its highest stage, imperialism before World War II, and neocolonialism after it—that is inevitably dying, while the egalitarian future nourished in its womb, like the palay grains in the bloodied ground, is still struggling to be born. Careo's death and MacVey's new voice emblematize those moments. This ambitious task of historical clarification and complex symbolic representation is the message of *Fortress in the Rice,* a powerful artistic creation by this forgotten American chronicler of the ongoing Filipino revolution.

Notes

1. The lack of critical attention has not been altered by the republication of a half dozen early crime novels by Appel, since 2005, in paperback and Kindle editions.
2. "Appel, Benjamin, 1907–," SNAC: The Social Network and Archival Context Project, http://socialarchive.iath.virginia.edu/xtf/view?docId=appel-benjamin-1907—cr.xml.
3. Alan Wald, *Trinity of Passion: The Literary Left and the Anti-Fascist Crusade* (Chapel Hill: University of North Carolina Press, 2007), 143.
4. Benjamin Appel, *Fortress in the Rice* (New York: Bobbs-Merrill, 1951), 424.
5. Franklin Folsom, *Days of Anger, Days of Hope* (Niwot: University Press of Colorado, 1994), 254.
6. Ibid., 348.
7. See Kenneth Burke, "Revolutionary Symbolism in America," in *Communism in America: A History in Documents,* edited by Albert Fried, 278–80 (New York: Columbia University Press, 1997); Daniel Aaron, *Writers on the Left* (New York: Avon Books, 1961), 304–8.
8. Letter to Macmillan editor, circa 1949, box 7, folder 3, Benjamin Appel Papers (1920–1977), Harry Ransom Humanities Research Center, University of Texas, Austin (hereafter Benjamin Appel Papers).
9. Ibid. See also relevant materials in box 14, folders 1, 2, 3, and the typescript of "Manila Diary" in box 7, folders 1, 2, and 3, Benjamin Appel Papers.
10. Eric Foner and John A. Garraty, eds., *The Reader's Companion to American History* (Boston: Houghton Mifflin, 1991), 836.
11. Howard Zinn, *A People's History of the United States* (New York: Harper, 1980); Stuart Creighton Miller, *"Benevolent Assimilation": The American Conquest of the Philippines,*

1899–1903 (New Haven, CT: Yale University Press, 1982); Gabriel Kolko, *Main Currents in Modern American History* (New York: Pantheon, 1984).

12. Jonathan Fast, "Imperialism and Bourgeois Dictatorship in the Philippines," *New Left Review,* no. I/78 (March–April, 1973): 76. For updates, see James Putzel, *A Captive Land: The Politics of Agrarian Reform in the Philippines* (London: Catholic Institute for International Relations, 1992).
13. Letter to Macmillan editor, circa 1949, box 7, Benjamin Appel Papers.
14. Renato Constantino, *Neocolonial Identity and Counter-Consciousness* (New York: M. E. Sharpe, 1978); Mariano Miranda, Jr., "The Economics of Poverty and the Poverty of Economics," in *Land, Poverty, and Politics in the Philippines,* edited by Mamerto Canlas, Mariano Miranda, Jr., and James Putzel, 25–36 (London: Catholic Institute for International Relations, 1988); William Pomeroy, *The Philippines: Colonialism, Collaboration, and Resistance!* (New York: International Publishers, 1992).
15. See also Hernando Abaya, *Betrayal in the Philippines* (New York: A. A. Wyn, 1947).
16. Teodoro A. Agoncillo and Oscar M. Alfonso, *History of the Filipino People,* revised ed. (Quezon City: Malaya Books, 1967), 533–36.
17. See also Hernando Abaya, *The Making of a Subversive* (Quezon City: New Day Publishers, 1984). On McNutt's position regarding the collaboration issue, see David Joel Steinberg, *Philippine Collaboration in World War II* (Ann Arbor: University of Michigan Press, 1967).
18. E. San Juan, *U.S. Imperialism and Revolution in the Philippines* (New York: Palgrave, 2007).
19. Appel, *Fortress in the Rice,* 45.
20. Ibid., 105.
21. Letter to Macmillan editor, circa 1949, box 7, folder 3, Benjamin Appel Papers.
22. Ibid.
23. Ibid.
24. Appel, *Fortress in the Rice,* 239.
25. Ibid., 248–49.
26. Ibid., 197.
27. Ibid., 409–10.
28. Ibid., 355.
29. Karl Marx, *Early Writings,* translated by Rodney Livingstone and Gregor Benton (New York: Random House, 1975), 352.
30. Appel, *Fortress in the Rice,* 423.
31. Ibid., 395.

[PART IV]

Histories

[15]

Peasant Studies Meets the World System: Eric Wolf, Immanuel Wallerstein, and Visions of Global Capitalism

Howard Brick

In a widely read essay of 1984, literary critic Fredric Jameson argued that so-called postmodernism in the arts, much discussed in the 1970s, signaled the disorienting condition of life produced by a new stage in the "prodigious expansion" of "capitalism around the globe"—an experience marked by the difficulty (even the "impossibility") that individuals faced in grasping their place within "the as yet untheorized original space of some new 'world system' of multinational or late capitalism."[1] As he returned repeatedly to the notion of a "whole world system" and the need to find new ways of theorizing an order of things that lacked the legible experience of traditional class struggle, of assembled workers directly confronting the capitalist or exploitative boss (for how exactly was one to grasp the relation between the bids made by a bond trader in a London financial house and the impoverishment of a West African village?), Jameson may have signaled the very beginning of an enterprise—that is, describing a new kind of global capitalism—that gained steam in the 1990s and continues today in critiques of a so-called neoliberal order. All these attempts posit a new form presumably different from, and successor to, the mid-twentieth-century system of welfare-state capitalism. Curiously, Jameson made no reference to the social theory, just cresting at the time he wrote, that had pioneered the notion of capitalism as a "world system." The phrase was then, and has since been, most identified with the work of sociologist Immanuel Wallerstein (b. 1930), whose monumental *The Modern World-System* had appeared in its first two volumes (1974 and 1980). But others used the phrase as well, notably the anthropologist Eric Wolf (1923–99), whose 1982 book *Europe and the People without History* was greeted the following year by Philip Curtin, president of the American Historical Association, as a template for reinvigorating the study of "world history."[2]

Jameson echoed without citation the new discourse of "world system," relying instead on the work of Marxist economist Ernest Mandel in *Late Capitalism* to identify the basic contours of the "new expansion of multinational capital." Yet if Jameson had dimly perceived the emergence in his own time of a neoliberal global economy, his choice of Mandel's work as his touchstone was likely misplaced; at its original publication in 1972, *Late Capitalism* was the culmination of Mandel's long-running project, begun in the 1950s, of describing the midcentury order itself, not its successor.[3] Likewise for that matter, Wolf's and Wallerstein's work had evolved from a starting point soon after the end of World War II and reached fruition in the wake of the sharp radicalization that both of these authors identified with the year 1968. Each belonged to a cohort of social science scholars in the United States who entered the academy after the war with some affiliation to left-wing politics; their work matured through the years of the Cold War and the world politics of decolonization, fashioning by Jameson's time a language of global interconnectedness to which we are still largely indebted.

Indeed, I see a "world turn" in American social science and humanities scholarship taking place roughly from 1968 to the mid-1980s, when Jameson posed his challenge to discover new ways of "mapping" a bewildering global capitalist terrain.[4] The very idea of an interknit world in which the global frame contained a systemic order sui generis was for the most part a product of innovations worked out—largely by left-wing theorists—over a period stretching across the 1970s. In the wake of this world turn, scholars increasingly have sought to identify frameworks and processes of a large scale—transnational, regional, and even literally global—that condition events and trends in many particular milieus and draw those milieus into relation with each other. Historians so inclined now imagine world history as a whole greater or different than a sum of national histories (and distinct, by and large, from earlier Eurocentric traditions in which one region alone represented all that was grandly significant and "world-historical" in Hegel's sense). Literary scholars discern a "world republic of letters," and ethnomusicologists talk of "world music" (or musics).[5]

Charting the political and intellectual course taken by these two scholars, Wolf and Wallerstein, from the end of World War II to the turning point of 1968 and beyond, I understand this course to be a particular lineage of the American academic Left. Both men studied at Columbia University in the late 1940s and early 1950s, entering the social sciences through new channels of studying the non-Western world. Wolf began his work in a field that came to be called peasant studies, while Wallerstein brought general concepts regarding modernity (or modernization) to the study of the new states arising in Africa and elsewhere in decolonizing regions. Their political sensibilities differed, with Wolf maintaining a relatively far-Left affiliation with Marxist thought and Wallerstein attuned to a near-Left kind of social democracy bound by ambivalent ties to the American Cold War consensus, and in fact their intellectual paths hardly crossed at all until their work during the 1970s intersected—that is, when peasant studies met the world system. For both of them in any case, their work was in certain crucial ways markedly radicalized by the rebellious experience of 1968. Thus, they represent a peculiar, interstitial generation of intellectuals, traversing the span from the period of the decline of the Old Left (in its varieties) to the inception and high pitch of the New Left. Their work fashioning notions of a world system left an enduring mark on the "world" or "global" consciousness of intellectual life. The question nonetheless remains whether these distinctly 1968er visions of the world system provided effective means of taking up Jameson's challenge to map the neoliberal global order that emerged only after the heyday of New Left radicalism.

A Left Academy Undercover during the Cold War (1945–1955)

The development of Wolf's and Wallerstein's thinking began in 1945–55, when the drift from Allied victory over fascism to the Cold War generated crosscurrents in public discourse and academic life whose complexity is rarely recognized in one-dimensional views of a repressive Cold War university. Multiple dimensions of change—the new bipolar geopolitics, construction of the US-focused Bretton Woods world economic order, decolonization and national-liberation struggles yielding new states committed to autonomy and development, and the domestic struggle over the final form of the New Deal institutional settlement—were overlaid and intertwined in ways that pushed and pulled political and cultural actors in many different directions. The main political expression of this conjuncture in the United States, the Red Scare, resulted in putting the brakes on the industrial-union movement and consigning the loosely fashioned social-democratic political bloc around it to defeat.[6] The Red Scare also hit the universities, mainly from 1949 to 1954, though its effects there were somewhat less devastating. While anticommunist inquisitions excluded a substantial number of left-wing scholars and chilled debate, young intellectuals influenced by the radicalism of prior years also entered the academy and pursued research that kept dissenting views alive, however moderated or veiled.[7] In what might be called a Left academy under the radar, we can recognize currents of the far Left (holding residual loyalties to Marxism or other oppositional views) and the near Left (preserving social-democratic aspirations of the mid-1940s qualified by more or less ambivalent ties to Cold War anticommunism).

The postwar conjuncture led a number of young academics to turn outward, toward the wider world. Some answered the call to help fashion the intellectual resources of US world hegemony; others saw forces of "progressive" social transformaton abroad that were more vital than those in Cold War America. In many cases no doubt, an idiosyncratic combination of both those motives served to fashion a scholar's aims. Wolf and Wallerstein were, each in his own way, among the postwar cohort of inductees to the social sciences who gravitated toward the study of decolonization, the new states, and what would later come to be called Third World development. Prevailing over this range of issues by the late 1950s was the dominant social science current called "modernization theory." Historians have demonstrated that most US modernization theorists cleaved to visions of change that were elitist and positivist (in a Comtean sense): rooted in gradualist schemes of crescive development, geared to the maintenance of social order, resistant to social protest and upheaval, vested in the priority of scientific reason and technological determinism, committed to the vanguard role played by elite expertise, and fostered by the most "advanced" societies that showed to all others a course of change recapitulating a generalized sequence of stages.[8] Yet some intellectual innovations of the postwar academy addressing that emerging world stood apart from such standards and fashioned more nuanced visions of social, cultural, and political change in "modernizing" societies. Wolf and Wallerstein serve here as examples. Their journeys through the postwar academy, via innovative channels they cut through the disciplines of anthropology and sociology, respectively, tell two stories that converged over time in an emergent radical milieu that contributed in turn to global perspectives arising after 1968.

Born in Vienna to a secular Jewish family, Eric Wolf arrived with his parents in the United States as a teenaged refugee from Nazism in 1940. Although his father had been a business manager in the Sudetenland before their flight from Europe, the Wolfs' circumstances were modest. Eric attended Queens College, near his home in Jackson Heights, for a few years before entering the military and serving with the US Army's mountaineering corps in Europe. He relied on the GI Bill to continue his education after his return. It is unclear whether he had any definite affiliations (or party membership) on the Left in those years, though he read the *New International,* the Marxist theoretical journal of Max Shachtman's Workers Party in the early 1940s and Dwight Macdonald's *politics* after the war.[9] Not long after Wolf's arrival in the United States, he spent a summer volunteering at the Highlander Folk School in Tennessee, the labor-organizing center that later played a key role in training activists in the southern civil rights struggle, and he was intrigued by the work of C. L. R. James, both for James's account of the Haitian revolution, *Black Jacobins,* and his theory of the Soviet Union as a "state capitalist" order. In later recollections, Wolf linked his Highlander summer and his reading of James, both serving to awaken his sense of how popular movements could change history. According to his close friend Sidney Mintz, Wolf was something of a "Trotskyist," though many of his left-wing peers once he started graduate school at Columbia University in 1946 leaned instead toward Communist politics of the late Popular Front.[10] Wolf took a nondogmatic, nonsectarian stance on the far Left; he and Mintz, who hewed to the Progressive Party into the early 1950s, marched as veterans, in uniform, in postwar May Day parades.

Although Columbia's anthropology department had been the home of cultural pluralism as fashioned by Franz Boas (1858–1942), the department of the late 1940s was led by the anti-Boasian, neoevolutionist Julian Steward, part of a surge in American anthropology after the late 1930s to reinvoke ideas of sequential change in culture over time, shorn of the racialist hierarchies bound to evolutionism in the nineteenth century.[11] Moreover, as Steward's graduate students worked on a field study of Puerto Rico in 1948–49, concentrating on the differentiated forms of culture and economy across the island, they took part in a crucial shift of the discipline away from a nearly exclusive focus on "primitive" peoples (in the United States, on American Indian tribes) to new studies of "peasant" communities recognizably tied to the modern world. In the Puerto Rico fieldwork, there was also a turn toward more "materialist" conceptions of political economy and a distinctive kind of *historical* awareness that militated against conventional notions of culture as a static form. Hence, in the long book chapter that came out of Wolf's dissertation on the more or less "peasant" order of Puerto Rico's coffee lands, he argued that the stereotypical, grasping land hunger of the "peasant" was not a given, categorical trait but instead was a measure of stress due to the *decline* of the coffee economy there as American capital after 1898 redirected investment to sugar.

The outcome of the Steward group's study, *The People of Puerto Rico* (1956), explored the diverse "subcultures" of different agricultural regions—areas of small commercial farmers, "peasant" producers, haciendas, and wage laborers in cane fields—while looking for "developmental factors" in each, that is, changes understood as "differential local effects of the island's participation in world commerce."[12] Despite this dawning global perspective, Steward's team avoided explicit political issues of colonialism and anticolonialism in Puerto Rico. Within a few years, however, Wolf and others from the Columbia cohort—who had formed a discussion group, including Mintz, jovially known as the Mundial Upheaval Society (MUS)—offered more overt political judgments.[13] In 1959 Wolf published a dense cultural history of Mexico, ending with his view that the "institutionalized" revolution of the ruling party had failed to bring the country out of poverty. He warned that neither Cold War developmental model posited by Soviet or American policy offered an appealing future, and he hinted that there must be some kind of alternative path: "Will Middle America eventually find its own voice?"[14] A year or so later, MUS member Stanley Diamond, working in West Africa, made a similar point more explicitly: Diamond assailed US foreign policy for "echo[ing] the heritage of colonialism" as it turned hostile to the radical nationalist, Pan-African, and collectivist policies of new states such as Ghana while maneuvering against Congo's Patrice Lumumba on misguided anticommunist grounds.[15] "It could be a mistake," Diamond wrote to Steward, "to assume that certain processes which seem universal can*not* be modified, changed, or [rejected] by large enough groups of people so as to alter the structure which emerges. I am not at all certain about the 'inevitable' direction of West African society . . . [for] to assume that they all unroll toward Westernization or Sovietization is to play fast and loose with history."[16] In a world of upheaval, the MUS scholars wished to take their distance from conventional modernization theory.

The seven-year gap between Wolf's birth and Immanuel Wallerstein's made a great deal of difference: Wallerstein's war was to be cold, not hot. The son of a physician and an artist living in the Bronx, Wallerstein was precocious and relatively privileged. His mother intended to encourage a career in the arts: Wallerstein was a child actor who was enrolled in the experimental "Terman classes" for high-IQ children, established by Teachers College psychologists at P.S. 500 near Columbia University; the program involved instruction in French, a focus on the arts, and an innovative curriculum with Deweyan accents of "learning by doing."[17] The school also permitted Wallerstein time away from class to travel with theater troupes. This did not prevent him from skipping grades, so he was ready for college entrance in 1946, though Columbia College, overfull with returning veterans, put off his admission for a year.[18]

Political interests nurtured in his home life drew Wallerstein into a left-liberal milieu. His father held to a kind of left-wing Zionism that identified the emergence of a Jewish homeland in Palestine with the Indian independence movement, both ostensibly opposed to British colonialism. Wallerstein himself closely followed news of India, whose independence commenced shortly before his freshman year. At Columbia out of interest in political affairs, he attended local meetings of the American Veterans Committee (AVC), begun by liberal veterans as an alternative to the American Legion. The AVC was racially integrated and promoted black voter registration in the South; it allied with the Congress of Industrial Organizations (CIO) and campaigned against the Taft-Hartley Act, advocated international control of nuclear energy, called for granting greater peacemaking powers to the United Nations, and criticized US policies deemed militarily provocative, such as the Truman Doctrine.[19] Mostly composed of New Dealers, whose alliance with the CIO placed them within the mid-1940s social-democratic bloc, the AVC also attracted Communist Party and Progressive Party activists, growing to one hundred thousand members before splitting apart prior to the 1948 election, as the anticommunist New Deal wing, aligned with the new pro-Truman Americans for Democratic Action (ADA), combated left-wing Henry Wallace supporters. Wallerstein watched the acrimony grow, saying later that he agreed with what each of the rival camps, Communists and social democrats, said about the other. Out of the wreckage, however, Wallerstein discerned another pole of attraction: the World Federalist movement, which drew the allegiance of many liberal AVC members who promoted disarmament, sought to check the new superpower division of East and West camps, and advocated decolonization, which they charged the United Nations with delaying.[20]

United World Federalists (UWF), founded in 1947, became the focus of Wallerstein's youthful activism. The movement's roots lay in a heritage of peace advocacy, at least a half century old, that enrolled a range of activists and propagandists running from radical to ultrarespectable and including morally committed pacifists, elite "arbitrationists" devoted to nurturing international law, and assorted visionaries. An eminent journalist, Clarence Streit, gained public attention on the eve of World War II for promoting ideas of world federation modeled on the federal structure of the American union; it was a residual interwar vision of world peace then retooled to anticipate the aftermath of Allied victory. While UWF adherents could be sharp critics of the United Nations, a mere international organization with no supranational powers of the sort the UWF advocated, they were far from extreme in any of their proposals. They kept their distance from agitators such as Garry Davis, who made headlines by declaring himself a world citizen, renouncing his US citizenship and denouncing nationalism tout court. UWF adherents meant just what their name implied: established nation-states would remain, their citizenship valid, while they would cede limited powers devoted to world peacekeeping to a federation of states. At its founding, the UWF gained the support of numerous businessmen capable of philanthropic largesse and committed to building a deep-pocketed foundation to back a campaign focused on elites. The UWF quickly became a major national organization, claiming close to 50,000 members, an annual operating budget of half a million dollars, and the affiliation of public figures such as William O. Douglas, Jerry Voorhis, Alan Cranston, Oscar Hammerstein II, Albert Einstein, Carl and Mark Van Doren, Norman Cousins, and Harris Wofford. Vigorous chapters of Student Federalists resided at scores of colleges and universities, notably Yale, Stanford, the University of Chicago, and Columbia—which alone counted 165 members on campus in 1948.

Above all, the UWF faced the problem of navigating the shoals of intensifying Cold War politics while trying to maintain its internationalist ideals; in fact, as the world crisis mounted, the UWF adapted by gradations to US containment policy, while the Soviets as well as Communist activists in the United States and elsewhere denounced world federalism as a bourgeois utopia. While the UWF attracted some pacifists, its leadership strove to maintain a nonpartisan appeal to the major political parties along with a posture of realism and prudence; the organization chose not to oppose limited expenditures by nations on military defense while promoting other supranational agencies capable of restraining military conflicts between nations. UWF members differed among themselves on the question of a peacetime draft in the United States and generally opposed rearmament of West Germany, yet as the first spate of the Cold War climaxed in the formation of NATO, the UWF supported it with the mildest qualifications. The right wing of the movement went so far as to call for a limited federation of "Western" nations opposed to the Soviet bloc, while the UWF leadership officially upheld the goal of a genuinely universal federal pact. In the summer of 1950, however, the UWF unreservedly backed the United States in the Korean War.

All along, generational rifts compounded political tensions within the movement, and Immanuel Wallerstein—a national leader by 1949—was one of those who regarded the parent UWF as insufficiently daring. Student Federalists tended to embrace concrete programs with greater alacrity than the "adult" leadership, such as a proposed "peace force," to be armed and recruited internationally for deployment in ending conflicts. A more activist or movement-building disposition could lead the student wing into conflicts with the elite, nonpartisan disposition of the parent group: students at the University of Chicago endorsed the South Side state assembly campaign of a black United Auto Workers organizer running in a primary election against the Democratic Party machine before they were censured by UWF. Indeed, Student Federalists constituted a very mixed group, with a membership that included many with views decidedly more left wing than the UWF as a whole. As a representative of Student Federalists on UWF executive panels, Wallerstein champed at the bit, threatening to resign in the face of the UWF leadership's flagging commitment to world peace as Cold War tensions heightened. Others peeled away: the young veteran David Montgomery, who joined the executive council of the Student Federalists from his chapter at Swarthmore, resigned in early 1948—perhaps due to a Swarthmore-nurtured pacifism or a decision to go with the Henry Wallace campaign as a peace initiative; a few years later Montgomery would join the Communist Party as a union activist before embarking on a career as a labor historian. Other young Federalists such as Shane Mage, at the University of Chicago, and Peter Novick, who was active as a Jersey City high school student, found their way into the Shachmanite Young Socialist League by the mid-1950s. Wallerstein, however, rescinded his resignation while continuing to insist that Federalists needed to stir the imagination of the young as a genuine force for world peace. He called for the creation of a "federalist revolutionary world party" promoting the "end of racial discrimination, end of colonialism, [and] 'social security' (economic development)."[21] In Wallerstein's milieu, unusual signs of radicalism continued to crop up occasionally: at a 1950 Student Federalist conference, a young Argentine warned that exploitative US capital alienated many Latin Americans, while he hailed the "third world" (or the "middle world" as another speaker called it) as a force for peace—a few years before French demographer Albert Sauvy more famously coined that term.[22]

Through the Student Federalists, Wallerstein found his way to a career-defining affiliation that lasted through the 1950s and introduced a further political twist to his formative commitments. As he was finishing his college years at Columbia and about to commence military service, his conscription was delayed a month so he could represent an American contingent, ardently backed by Student Federalists, to the first American-hosted meeting of the World Assembly of Youth (WAY). The global orientation of this new international group clearly appealed to his federalist convictions, but on joining it Wallerstein could hardly avoid taking sides in the Cold War: WAY was first conceived in 1948 by Labour Party leaders in Britain's Foreign Office and established the next year in Belgium as a counter to the Soviet-backed World Federation of Democratic Youth (WFDY), known for its massive youth festivals in Eastern Europe and the pro-Soviet political resolutions issuing from them. At the founding convention of WAY, the French section, which was able to claim the support of delegations from the French colonial territories, determined the leadership (electing a Quebec student) and sought to deflect any impression that WAY was "a purely American creation."[23] Despite that claim, the organization received the bulk of its funding after 1951 from the Central Intelligence Agency (CIA).

Stationed in the Panama Canal Zone, Wallerstein used his free time to get "involved with the Panamanian youth organization to try to get them to join WAY."[24] After discharge from the army in 1952, he attended another WAY conference, in Dakar, Senegal, that introduced him to Africa as independence movements were growing.[25] Within a few years—while serving as an international vice president of WAY—he would make African independence the object of his graduate studies in sociology. During his graduate student years at Columbia, he straddled the growing political divide between the self-consciously radical intellectual C. Wright Mills and the anticommunist social democrat Daniel Bell. Neither of them, however, nor anyone else in Columbia sociology—given the discipline's formative commitment to analyzing "modern," presumably Western, societies—could mentor his studies of decolonizing Africa. If Wolf's anthropological turn toward the peasant in the modern world marked an innovation in his field, so too did Wallerstein's sociological turn to the non-Western world made him something of a pioneer.

But what did Wallerstein's Cold War affiliations through WAY mean for his politics? As one of WAY's international officers in the mid-1950s, Wallerstein may or may not have known of the CIA backing it received—though WAY's contest with the Soviet-backed WFDY was clear. His own apparent choice for the West did not, of course, connote conservative or right-wing principles. As a longtime observer of Indian affairs, he might have known that the Congress Party youths, who shared

Nehru's ostensible embrace of "socialist" development, had wrangled with Communist youths and joined WAY. Indeed, whatever the intent of the Western powers to retain colonial power, their youth delegations in WAY recognized decolonization as an ideal and competed with WFDY in affirming anticolonial principles in ways that carried Wallerstein's federalist convictions forward; in any case, he likely viewed WAY in 1951 as possessing an energy that United World Federalists by that point lacked. Moreover, CIA support of an anticolonialist (but anticommunist) WAY was of a piece with CIA funding of other liberal, left-leaning, or social democratic groups, such as the National Student Association in the United States, which the red-baiters of the 1950s regarded as "pink," or the Congress of Cultural Freedom (CCF), which enrolled any number of socialist and labor intellectuals in a transatlantic alliance.[26] The CIA's operatives in the cultural Cold War were thoroughly familiar and comfortable with left-liberal anticommunist currents, and many social democrats in turn were not averse to the handshake. Wallerstein's senior colleague at Columbia, Daniel Bell, moved prominently in CCF circles abroad, judging the intellectuals on the right-leaning end of the British Labour Party (or "right-wing social democracy" in European parlance) to represent the political center of gravity in CCF affairs; the social democratic and anticommunist newspaper Bell once edited, the *New Leader*, would also subsist on covert CIA funding, and that paper became the prime venue for Wallerstein's political journalism regarding the struggles of the new African states in the 1960s.[27] At the same time, Wallerstein's ardent endorsement of radical leadership in Africa as part of a worldwide anticolonial front (though outside the Soviet sphere) positioned him somewhat further to the left than most of the liberal anticommunist milieu. These were the coordinates of his near-Left posture in the field of American sociology.

The Emergence of the Third World and a New Left (1955–1969)

The new departures in American scholarship that engaged Wolf's and Wallerstein's attention in their early careers—"peasant studies" and "new states"—flowed from the given conditions of the postwar world coming into focus by the mid-1950s and from a new configuration of the political Left. The rise of anticolonial movements and independent, postcolonial states found emblematic expression in the 1955 Afro-Asian Conference in Bandung, Indonesia, convened by the nationalist leaders Sukarno, Nehru, and Gamal Abdel Nasser. "This is the first intercontinental conference of colored peoples in the history of mankind," Sukarno declared in his welcoming message. "Let a new Asia and a new

Africa be born," he said—as a world force in its own right—for in the face of nuclear-armed Cold War, Sukarno argued, "*We* can inject the voice of reason into world affairs. We can mobilize all the spiritual, all the moral, all the political strength of Asia and Africa on the side of peace."[28] The image of this new world as a peace bloc between and apart from the two superpowers had also been put forward three years earlier by the French demographer Albert Sauvy, who dubbed the emerging nations the *tiers-monde,* a term intended both to summon up the revolutionary heritage of the "third estate" and to tie this postcolonial force to the prospects for a *nouvelle gauche*—a "new left" imagined as a "third force" aside from the United States and the Soviet Union by Claude Bourdet, the editor of the newspaper that published Sauvy, *France-Observateur.*[29] The apparent neutralism and global consciousness of the Bandung meeting indeed appealed to a variety of independent leftists. The self-exiled former Communist Richard Wright traveled from his home in Paris (on a CCF grant) to Bandung and echoed the idea of stepping aside from the Cold War in his report tellingly called *The Color Curtain* (i.e., a different fault line of world politics from the Iron Curtain): "The despised, the insulted, the hurt, the dispossessed—in short the underdogs of the human race were meeting. Here were class and racial and religious consciousness on a global scale."[30] The American pacifist Homer Jack authored a pamphlet hailing the promise of Bandung for challenging the bipolar, armed world—even though Jack's ardent anticommunism suggested that he did not fully embrace a "neutralist" abstention from the Cold War.[31] Likewise Wright, whose anticolonial radicalism made him a familiar of the Parisian Left, from Jean-Paul Sartre to the proponents of "Negritude" around the journal, *Présence Africaine,* secretly volunteered to help the US embassy "offset Communist influence" at the 1956 international Congress of Negro Writers and Artists in Paris, called a "second Bandung" by its *Présence Africaine* sponsors.[32]

Indeed, the political sentiments swirling around the original Bandung conference were themselves ambiguous and ambivalent. One of the least romanticized and most clear-eyed reports on the actual politics of Bandung came from the American scholar George Kahin, whose anticolonial sentiments were stirred when he witnessed Indonesian independence firsthand in 1949 and who later devoted his career to building Southeast Asian studies at Cornell University. According to Kahin, Nehru, Sukarno, and their Ceylonese and Burmese collaborators were not only eager to deter US-Soviet rivalry from intruding on Asian politics but also hoped to encourage China to keep its distance from the Soviets and then help restrain the domestic Communist insurgencies that all of these leaders sought to contain or defeat.[33] The ambiguity between the neutralist declarations and the actual anticommunist politics of the conveners suggests a political stance congruent with the mixed politics of someone like Wallerstein, given his social democratic, Nehruvian sympathies and his association with the Cold War youth organization WAY. This ambiguity would run through the circles that Wallerstein frequented through the 1950s and his politics and scholarship as it developed in the 1960s. As he cultivated links with French West Africa—devoting his dissertation to the independence movement of Côte d'Ivoire (compared with that in Britain's Gold Coast)—and with associated Parisian intellectual currents, the awkward mix of militant anticolonialism and evident or quiet affiliations with Cold War anticommunism persisted.

The coordinates of Wolf's political experience in these years were somewhat different. Although never so much a joiner as Wallerstein, Wolf pursued the anthropological study of peasantries in ways that nonetheless linked his work to Third World stirrings as well.[34] Among the intellectual leaders of the neoevolutionist current in US anthropology was Robert Redfield—coincidentally, a prominent figure in world federalism—who pioneered work on "the peasant" as a "transitional" or "intermediary" figure, situated (in his view) "between" country and city, midway on the "rural-urban continuum," and hence a bellwether of social and cultural development moving toward modern civilization.[35] Redfield himself straddled a number of divides. As a Federalist, he was among the respectable elite of the movement, though one who resisted the drift toward Cold War allegiances; as a cultural theorist, he held to a variant of Spencerian views of linear (Eurocentric) evolution and yet recognized in his time that peasant-based groups—which he called variously an "external proletariat," "minority peoples," "imperialized folk," and "remade folk"—played a distinctive role in the contemporary world: "the East today is in revolt," he wrote in 1953, and "mankind is on the move again."[36] Indeed, it was hard not to confront the peasantry when examining the anticolonial revolt, and Wolf's own penchant—drawn from the Highlander Folk School and C. L. R. James—for recognizing the agency of popular groups fitted him well in this regard. The politics of the emerging Third World, of course, highlighted peasant movements. Sukarno claimed that his anticolonial, nationalist politics rested on the place of the poor peasant—the "Marhaen"—whose toil represented the "people" more than the "proletarian" figure promoted in Western socialist politics. In Frantz Fanon's theorizing of anticolonial revolution, peasants found pride of place, and both the Chinese and Vietnamese revolutions were famously rooted in peasant armies. Wolf eventually studied these phenomena, always with a degree of sympathy but also critical distance.[37] At the same time, his own political views stemmed from the 1940s Shachtmanite Marxism, whose sharp critique of both capitalism and Soviet communism held forth hope for an independent "third camp" in the world. That "third camp" perspective was precisely the view that Wolf avowed in his 1959 verdict on Mexico and was the basis of Diamond's resistance to the Cold War in Africa. It was a stance that from the start gave him a somewhat clearer independence of US world hegemony than Wallerstein's ambivalent Cold War anticolonialism.

In MUS, Wolf was the best educated in Marxist theory, and his early graduate writings brought Marxist approaches into anthropology in ways not limited to the orthodox embrace of Lewis Henry Morgan originally authorized by Frederick Engels. Wolf's avid correspondence through the 1950s with Sidney Mintz discussed ethnographic matters in historical materialist terms, focusing on histories of European settlement and slavery in the Caribbean and Mexico, along with matters of land use, property, labor, and more—without any dogmatic jargon of sectarian Marxism.[38] They must have understood that studying peasant society meant embarking on untrod soil in Marxism. Best known in this area were Marx and Engels's dismissive remarks on peasantry ("a sack of potatoes" incapable of autonomous political purpose) and the priority of *proletarian* labor and social movements in their understanding of capitalism. Much less was known at the time of Marx's more nuanced interventions in disputes over the peasant village among Russian "Marxists" and "populists" documented in letters between Marx and Vera Zasulich that Wolf had seen reprinted in a 1942 issue of Shachtman's *New International.*[39] (Marx actually leaned to the "populist" perspective, showing interest in the revolutionary promise of the residual peasant commune.) Much American literature about the Soviet Union in the 1930s and 1940s still held firmly to the simple, entrenched idea of peasant "backwardness."[40] Thus, to think seriously in historical-materialist terms about peasants meant breaking new ground. It also entailed a persistent emphasis on economic developments traversing regions of the globe, setting the stage for later, more explicit studies of world systems.

Mintz and Wolf began with a critique of Robert Redfield's work on peasants for its ahistorical character and reliance on static cultural types defined in conventional terms of "tradition" and "modernity." Indeed, the very term "peasant" was not entirely accurate in the settings that Redfield had considered sites of "folk culture." Writing in 1953, Mintz found it remarkable that Redfield's studies in the 1930s of the Yucatán ignored the place of plantations growing henequen, even though Redfield himself noted in passing that "henequen determines the role of Yucatan in the world economy."[41] As Mintz remarked, "since the seventeenth century the plantation has been the dominant method of European agricultural development in tropical regions," and its pattern of production relied on "landless, propertyless" workers.[42] What characterized a number of Yucatán towns was a "community" whose apparent unity was less a sign of inherited folk tradition than "an acquired cultural homogeneity."[43] In Mintz's view, "such communities are neither folk nor urban, nor are they syntheses of these classifications. . . . [They] are, rather, radically new reorganizations of culture and society, forming a distinctive type."[44]

Wolf joined Mintz in anatomizing variations in the historical development of rural life in an essay they nurtured carefully in exchanges running through the mid-1950s, "Haciendas and Plantations in Middle America and the Antilles" (1957). They distinguished "two kinds of social organization" that were "characteristically the products of the expansion of world economy, particularly since the fifteenth century," though each manifested a distinct ensemble of traits.[45] The hacienda typically was of smaller scale, more labor-intensive and less mechanized than the plantation, marked by more paternalistic authority and noneconomic means of "binding" poor laborers to it; crop production for sale on the estate coexisted with semi-independent subsistence farming carried on by its workforce in small plots. Even at this early point, Wolf and Mintz dissented from conventional thinking about modernization, for they rejected the idea of "necessary sequential stages in the development of modern agricultural organization"; rather, they wrote, "all social systems have histories," and the growth of markets, or changes in the constitution of workforces, typically took place "in differential involvement with other processes."[46] The plantation form was often situated in long-range links between "underdeveloped" and "developed" countries (the latter providing the capital), but it also figured in "dichotomized" relations between plantation regions and "marginal" areas, where poor peasant farming and haciendas might prevail, side by side. Thus "a quite uneven development" occurred.[47]

Their method here stemmed from a combination of Steward's neo-evolutionist guidelines with what Wolf and Mintz regarded as their more determinedly historical and "materialist" approach, rooted in Marxism and to some degree in Wolf's roughly Trotskyist bent—as indicated by reference to the theme, so central to Trotsky's analyses of Russian history and the colonial world, that is, of "combined and uneven development."[48] Steward's method started with the identification of a "social type" (in this case the hacienda or the plantation) that could be recognized as a form appearing in diverse times and places. Observing such a type change over time, given its embeddedness in various particular social environments, might reveal to the anthropologist certain discrete patterns of culture change, not in a universal-unilinear sense determining the course of all human history but rather in a "multi-linear" scenario of limited "evolutionary" sequences that appeared in various locales to be "cross-culturally recurrent."[49] The method was profoundly comparative. Thus in 1954, Wolf forecast a major study of change in "corporate peasant communities"—such as the Russian *mir* (precisely the object of the Marx-Zasulich correspondence) and the *musha'a* form in the Near East—as they were affected by "increasing commercialization," by the power of a "controlling group" or dominant class outside the commune, and by the place they occupied within the larger "social-political system."[50] China, Japan, East Africa, England, Mexico, Indonesia, and Russia offered the comparative cases.

Over time, however, and especially under the influence of the antiwar movement of the mid-1960s, Wolf's plan for a comparative study of peasant cultures turned into a work on comparative peasant revolutions. The work first outlined in 1954 came to fruition in Wolf's differently defined 1969 book, *Peasant Wars of the Twentieth Century,* which instantly became a magnetic work for younger anthropologists engaged in New Left antiwar activism. From Mexico in 1910 and Russia in 1917 to Algeria, Cuba, and Vietnam in his own time, Wolf analyzed social revolutions in which peasant grievances and peasant agency played central roles. His results were finely calibrated. From the start, his common definition of "peasant"—as a producer on the land, "existentially involved in cultivation" and possessing at least some prerogatives over "decisions regarding the process of cultivation"—admitted great variations (e.g., bound laborers also engaged in subsistence farming, freeholders partly shielded from mass markets and stratified in wealth, members of traditional communes or villages, tenants of absentee landlords, etc.).[51] Also assuming highly distinct forms were the large-scale social and political settings into which peasants of these differing sorts fitted. Peasant social and political relations were, he wrote in his characteristic vein, "variably conjugated in different situations and not exhausted in simple formulas."[52]

Wolf located some "cross-culturally recurrent" features. Perhaps influenced by his University of Michigan colleague (and fellow antiwar organizer) Marshall Sahlins, Wolf relied on the work of Karl Polanyi as he recounted the intrusion of capitalist norms and practices into noncapitalist and precapitalist social orders, rupturing customary social protections as land and labor were forcibly converted into saleable commodities. That intrusion yielded "skewed" societies where, in most of his case studies, poorly organized interest groups typically succumbed to some kind of Bonapartist government. When peasants' discontent gained traction, they fought against such central powers under the aegis of some "outside" force—a radicalized intelligentsia, banditry, an upstart party or army. Wolf's view of the concatenated frictions and shifting alliances in his cases was utterly disabused. His stories were often those of failure, certainly in the constitution of new overarching orders that disappointed those egalitarian and communal dreams that made "[middle] peasants in rebellion . . . natural anarchists."[53] If peasant rebellion lighted the spark turning an "already smoldering" society into the turmoil of revolution, the successes won by the supervening leaderships that put that force into gear made the "peasant's role . . . essentially tragic."[54] And yet it was "also [one] full of hope," he wrote at the conclusion of *Peasant Wars,* for his was a time when "human kind is moving toward a solution of the age-old problem of hunger and disease, and everywhere ancient monopolies of power and received wisdom are yielding to human effort to widen participation and knowledge."[55] This, he suggested, was the keynote of the modern anticolonial revolution, a prospect that compelled America, he wrote, to choose whether "to act in aid of human hope or to crush it."[56]

Wolf's group kept its distance from conventional modernization theory, while Wallerstein hewed more closely to it. His affiliation stemmed partly from his disciplinary roots—constitutively geared to the study of emergent modernity—and partly from the political object he chose to examine, the independence movements and "new states" of West Africa that offered cases of more or less peaceful transition and initial success. He initially studied the role of "voluntary associations" in the drive toward independence, a characteristic "civil society" approach to change, and he embraced the new governments as agents of national unification, centralized organization, technological development, economic growth, popular education, and civic participation—all hallmarks of modernity. As his counterpart in political science Ghana-observer David Apter put it as he looked back on his career in modernization theory, the goal that such reformers sought was "approximated in social welfare and social-democratic states."[57] Wallerstein too shared the mid-century view that mixed economies, with a significant role for government services and stimulus, held open a course of sustained growth that could distribute material resources broadly among a democratic populace. His long-standing attention to the politics of Nehru's Congress Party led him to see the independence governments as advocates of "socialist" state-led development. Moreover, Nehru and other Bandung leaders spoke in a democratic-populist idiom that Western reformers could champion. While often viewed in retrospect by its critics as a tool of American Cold War ambitions to dominate the world, modernization—at least as people such as Wallerstein and Apter understood it—was at first a natural fit for left-liberal or social democratic friends of the Third World.

Yet Wallerstein's modernization differed somewhat from the most conventional versions. From the start, he took his distance from those who saw only backwardness in the societies emerging into independence, and he embraced the politics of protest that accompanied the rising leaderships. The main thrust of Wallerstein's dissertation was simply that voluntary associations such as hometown leagues in the cities (comparable to Yiddish *landsmanschaften* or "native-place" societies in China) were not holdovers of "traditional" or "tribal" loyalties but mediators of adaptation to urban life. They represented a more modern notion of "ethnicity," one that could very well mesh with an even wider affiliation to "national integration."[58] Wallerstein pinned his early work on a challenge to an old worldview he ascribed to colonial administrators: that African societies remained rural and traditional, with the only large-scale organizing capacity lying with European influences "outside" African culture. The keynote of Wallerstein's work in this regard derived from French anthropologist Georges Balandier, part of the independent Left in France around the journal *L'Observateur* (successor to *France-Observateur,* where Sauvy had first identified the "third world"), who pioneered the concept of "the colonial situation": the colony (as an entity) had become the social and political frame in which contemporary Africans lived and acted, and hence the "nationalist" parties who aimed to take those state entities to independence were not, as their colonialist critics averred, illusory accretions on a congeries of tribal groups; instead, they represented an authentic political force in tune with current social change. Wallerstein recognized an analogue to Balandier's work in that of the British anthropologist Max Gluckman, whose circle at Manchester was likewise a home for left-wing scholars in Britain. From Wallerstein's point of view, both Balandier and Gluckman made the essential point that "the rulers of the colonial system, as those of all social systems, engaged in various practices for their own survival and fulfillment which simultaneously resulted in creating movements which in the long run undermined the system. In the case of the colonial situation, what emerged as a consequence of the social change wrought by the administration was a nationalist movement which eventually led a revolution and obtained independence."[59]

As a partisan of independence movements, Wallerstein reported on the new states in the anticommunist labor-liberal journal the *New Leader* through the 1960s, striving to allay US anxieties about radical leaderships ("Our Unfriendly African Friends," he called them in a phrase suggesting his wish to consider them, notwithstanding their radical rhetoric, aligned with "the West"), while he defended one-party systems arising in the Third World as a means of fostering a unified national identity. He championed Pan-Africanism, the ideology promoted by Kwame Nkrumah, Sekou Toure, and other radicals seeking "African unity." However, by the time of Wallerstein's second major book, *Africa: The Politics of Unity* (1967), the frustration of the initial hopes of the independence movements—by ethnic rivalries, political instability, coups, and sluggish economic growth—had pushed him toward a new kind of critique. In *The Politics of Unity,* he called upon older ideas of "unequal trade" (developed by Latin American scholars in the 1950s and 1960s) to explain the world context that put a great stumbling block in front of autonomous African economic development and secure political independence. The terms "core" and "periphery," understood as an exploitative linkage that hobbled the new states, took pride of place in his work at this time. (In his work of the 1970s, he would add the intervening category of the "semi-periphery.") Thus, it appeared that Wallerstein began formulating "world-systems analysis" at this point; actually, his radical departure from his initial "modernization" paradigm was yet to come.[60]

Toward World History (1968–82)

The year 1968 was the fulcrum in Wallerstein's development of a world system concept—a time of "world revolution," he has written, from Vietnam to Prague to Mexico City, "which I experienced directly at Columbia University [in the student protests and strike of that year], and which helped expunge from my thinking both the lingering illusions of liberalism and a rosy view of the antisystemic movements."[61] We might better take this as a "long 1968," that is, a shift (somewhat more distended than a simple volte-face) that accompanied the peak years of "New Left" radicalization from roughly 1967 to 1973.[62] Accepting the shorthand, however, how and why should we understand 1968 as such a generative moment? Was not Wallerstein well on his way to a radical worldview prior to 1968? He was among the first American intellectuals to study decolonization in Africa, had an early fascination with the Bandung leaders, had ties to Parisian circles that included Balandier as well as *Présence Africaine,* met the revolutionary Frantz Fanon personally at a WAY meeting in Ghana in 1960, hailed Pan-Africanism in 1962 as a protest movement of world significance, and warned by 1967 that core-periphery relations were blocking African development.[63] How then could 1968, as his later recollections suggest, have changed things for him so very dramatically? In particular, what did he mean by saying that "1968" forced him to surrender "the lingering illusions of liberalism and a rosy view of the antisystemic movements"? Wasn't the anticolonial revolution a key force in "antisystemic" challenges to the world system, that is, something he embraced rather than soured on?

To untangle and understand the intellectual conversion Wallerstein underwent, I look to his first published reflection on "1968," his book based on the Columbia University student strike, *University in Turmoil: The Politics of Change* (1969). It is a telling manifestation of a left-liberal social theorist caught midstream in a radicalizing turn, occasioned by acute estrangement from prior Cold War anticommunist affiliations. To start, *University in Turmoil* offers a conventional welfare state, "postindustrial" narrative positioning the university as a central institution of modern society, subject in many respects to sharper strains than those characterizing the world of mass production, where he thought that a pacified union-corporate accord prevailed. Race was the new fault line of social struggle, impinging on academic life as the university assumed a position in the urban power elite (as a major landlord and financial heavyweight) set against an impoverished black minority. Meanwhile, the university's combined tasks of fitting the young into given social roles and nurturing independent, critical thought came into conflict—especially as the liberal American intelligentsia, he explained, experienced a radical alienation. Here Wallerstein looked outward, beyond the postindustrial society, to a world in which the Soviet Union had "renounced" an oppositional role in order to help manage "political and economic matters"; now the former Cold War antagonists, he wrote, became the joint "center forces internationally," while the Third World in revolt fashioned a "new left-right dichotomy" as the "struggle between the developed world . . . and the underdeveloped world" assumed "central importance."[64] If this kind of Third Worldism suggested a vaguely Maoist perspective on the world, Wallerstein's aspirations at this point were as yet quite mild. He still thought that organizations of "structured opposition" such as those of the traditional labor movement might play a promising role in pushing forward the democratization of American social institutions, and he proposed that the "left" in American politics had the modest goal of "reinforc[ing]" the "separation in analysis and action of the American center from the American right," which was opened up by the dispute over the Vietnam War.[65] That is to say, a political center pulled slightly leftward, away from hardline cold warriors, might restrain an aggressive US world posture and provide Third World states some breathing room, a chance to develop and shift the balance of world resources by some degree in their direction.

In all of this there was only the slightest hint of a "world system" perspective, for when he used that phrase in *University in Turmoil,* it still clearly stood for a conventional notion of an "international" system of states; for Wallerstein at this point, the prospect of easing US pressures on the Third World still implied a hope for more successful "state-led development." Some further theoretical shift was yet to occur in Wallerstein's radicalization. What was most significant in *University in Turmoil,* however, was the way he voiced an acute sense of having been betrayed: "What many intellectuals . . . seemed to be saying with increasing raucousness . . . is, 'We have been duped. For twenty years you, our governments[,] . . . have asked us to do many distasteful things, to suppress many moralistic qualms, in the interests of the primacy of the moral struggle between the Western and Soviet worlds.'"[66] Seemingly, his own role as a left-leaning fellow traveler of the US Cold War consensus, having defended the "unfriendly African friends" of the West, played into his reflections: "During the Cold War the 'enemy' as defined in Western Europe and North America was Soviet expansionism and 'totalitarianism.' . . . If there were occasional reticences in Europe and North America, it was still the accepted norm that universities would collaborate with their governments against the 'enemy.' When, however, many intellectuals of Europe and North America began to feel that the 'enemy' of their governments was the underdeveloped world, they found it more difficult (for some it was impossible) to collaborate against such an enemy." Writing again as a ventriloquist of the estranged intellectual, he concluded that "'[Now] we say no. . . . We discover now the secret machinations of the past, which we knew about but never admitted we knew. . . . We reject such machinations as immoral.'"[67] This poignant expression of estrangement, of having felt duped, suggests one dimension of 1960s intellectual history obscured by the familiar story of Cold War liberals turning to "neoconservatives": the alternative story of left liberals shifting sharply to the far Left.

Wallerstein's theoretical approach to "world systems," however, must be understood as a distinct development yet to come. His real paradigmatic breakthrough came after the publication of *University in Turmoil* and in the wake of a year (1969–70) he spent in Palo Alto, California, intending to write a short book summing up a Columbia University course he taught on Third World modernization. At that point, he was still committed to what he called, with his collaborator Terence Hopkins, "the comparative study of national societies," indicating his sense of the object entity to be studied, as suggested already by the idea of "the colonial situation."[68] He began his Palo Alto project intending to compare contemporary "new states" with the "new states" of sixteenth- to seventeenth-century Europe. How had the latter reached success in national development, when the former (in the twentieth century) stumbled? At the suggestion of the economic historian Fernand Braudel—who became Wallerstein's second great French influence after Balandier—Wallerstein read the work of Polish economic historian Marian Malowist, which convinced him that the "comparative study of national societies" was, as he later recalled, a "bad idea." Only then did "world-systems analysis" beckon.

From Malowist, Wallerstein learned of the early modern economic relation between Western Europe as the lead sector of commercial growth and its East European hinterland, a source of raw materials—that is, a relatively backward "periphery" that fed supplies to a "core." In the wake of that discovery, Braudel's notion of a "world-economy" (not in the sense of traversing the entire globe but rather in constituting a relevant, constitutive framework of experience) provided the way of naming a single order comprising both poles of Malowist's unequal relation. Thus, Wallerstein undertook a dramatic revisioning of his "unit of analysis": the only relevant "social system" was the kind of totality in which multiple states coexisted within a single "world-economy" in Braudel's sense (the political and economic dimensions taken together comprised in the "modern world-system"). The "bad idea" birthed a "good" one. Wallerstein's brief book on Third World modernization—a paradigm he declared dead in 1976—turned into a multivolume monument: the first two volumes (1974 and 1980) sketched a process in which a template of unequal core-periphery relations between Western and Eastern Europe was transposed over time onto a larger frame, whereby regions such as Africa and South and East Asia that once lay outside the European system were drawn into it, converted from "external arenas" to new "peripheries."[69] The process began in the sixteenth century on the European gradient from West to East; later volumes in Wallerstein's series would argue that it was there and then that modern capitalism arose, and later transformations—the French revolution or "the industrial revolution"—were not at all crucial to capitalist development.[70] And thus for Wallerstein, things now made a new kind of sense: given the carapace of the modern world system, there was no opportunity for successful state-led development in the new states. His *University in Turmoil* strategy, counting on a left-influenced US center to liberalize conditions for *national* development abroad, was groundless, and the Bandung-style nationalist leaders he had earlier championed were to be dethroned.

Thus, he shed his prior "rosy view of the antisystemic movements" and found his political and theoretical worldview transformed.

And Wolf? The period that Wallerstein focused on—a long sixteenth century—was of course the first age of European expansion, dominated by Iberia, whose colonial American enterprise had long been a focus of Wolf's studies. Commenting on his comparative cases of peasant revolution, Wolf's 1969 book led to a final chapter on Cuba: "Where Russia, China, Viet Nam, Algiers, and Mexico have immemorial roots in an autochthonous Neolithic past, Cuba was created to answer the needs of the expanding European commercial system of the modern period. Within Europe, the hegemony of Spain proved short-lived, but Spanish expansion was nevertheless a significant phase in '*the creation of the world as a social system.*'"[71] Thus, the notion of "the world" *as* the frame of analysis came to the forefront also of Wolf's thought, to result more than a decade later in *Europe and the People without History.* Nonetheless, Wolf likewise credited "1968" as a watershed. "The project for this book," he wrote in the 1982 preface to *Europe and the People without History,* "emerged from the intellectual reassessments that marked the late 1960s."[72] What was it exactly that induced a shift, in a body of work already engaged in radically inspired studies of Third World peasant revolution, toward a new perspective on the world? The answer in Wolf's case appears to lie with increasingly sharp left-wing challenges to the integrity of his own discipline and the consequent call to "reinvent anthropology."[73]

Most notably, in an episode that Wolf found acutely wrenching, he confronted evidence of what he regarded as scandalous complicity by his own discipline with the US war in Southeast Asia. Provided information uncovered by student antiwar activists, Wolf coauthored a blockbuster report, "A Special Supplement: Anthropology on the Warpath in Thailand," that dominated the front page of the November 19, 1970, issue of the *New York Review of Books.* The conclusion to that essay was a stirring cry for political engagement *with* dominated peoples as opposed to collaboration with government agencies whose interests made those peoples "objects":

> Admittedly, anthropology was ambiguously conceived. Now, in our view, it must disengage itself from its connection with colonial aims or it will become intellectually trivial. The future of anthropology, its *credibility,* depends upon sustaining the dialectic between knowledge and experience. Anthropologists must be willing to testify in behalf of the oppressed peoples of the world, including those whom we professionally define as primitives and peasants.[74]

Along with his coauthor Joseph Jorgensen, who knew how academic studies of Thai villages were tapped by repressive forces to identify insurgent sympathizers, Wolf quoted his old Columbia colleague Stanley Diamond:

> In turning away from the implications of their knowledge, anthropologists . . . were not only false [to those they studied] but to themselves. The field is no longer safely enclosed . . . and it is precisely the objective study, the reified examination, which is proving to be an illusion. In this situation, there can be no more students of Man studying men as fixed specimens in fixed environments. This was a privilege that the Western world preserved for itself as a consequence of domination. There can only be men who learn to bear witness to each other. In the struggle for the creation of culture against collective and dehumanizing forces, no matter [what] their ideological pretension . . . there can only be partisans.[75]

This new sense of partisanship radicalized Wolf's political and intellectual sensibility by a crucial quantum. Wolf's move away from the *comparative* orientation of *Peasant Wars* to the profoundly *connective* approach in *Europe and the People without History* was a major theoretical development: after all, the very notion of wide-ranging interconnectedness was what made possible a "world system" concept.[76] Nonetheless, the distinctiveness of Wolf's work appears when it is contrasted with Wallerstein's.

The key contributions of Wallerstein's world-systems analysis were threefold: (1) to explicate processes that knitted diverse regions together in global capitalism and thereby created a colonial (and neocolonial) order viewed as the *heart* of capitalist dynamics; (2) to venture an explanation of how, exactly, the capitalist mode of production was "born" in, and unimaginable outside of, "the world market"; and (3) to offer a comprehensive view of the relation of political structures, namely the modern nation-state and the interactions among multiple states, to the overarching global economy of capitalist relations.[77] He offered an intriguing view of the profound unevenness embedded in global capitalist relations, such that the modern neocolonial order could be understood as analogous to the "advanced" and "backward" regions of early modern Europe. Wallerstein performed a neat trick on the old "recapitulationist" view of modernization theory (the notion that new states had only to follow again, at some delay, the same processes that yielded the prosperous nations of the North Atlantic), because the developmental disabilities of "peripheral" regions were already present at the origins, built in. West European-style growth was not recapitulated; rather, the disadvantage in the West-East, core-periphery relation was recapitulated in ways that the modernization theorists had not contemplated.

Wallerstein's accomplishments, however, came at a cost. To explain the manner in which the capitalist system is by its nature a creature *of* the world market, his work had the effect, as numerous critics have pointed out, of subsuming the notion of capitalism *into* the world market so that no difference is perceivable between worldwide trade as such and a modern capitalism based on the exploitation of labor. Wallerstein has rejected this charge, arguing that he always understood "capitalism" as a system of exploiting labor but that his innovation was to site the key "division of labor" on a *geographic* plane, depicting exploitation as the drain on labor in subordinate regions by accumulators in dominant regions.

For Wolf, by contrast, "dichotomies such as 'core-periphery' or 'metropolis-satellite'" are far too crude a lens for grasping the global terrain, not only because "capitalist development created peripheries within its very core" but also because those dichotomies obliterate "the heterogeneity of the different societies and subsocieties making up the [world] system" that was created *in the nineteenth century*.[78] Two issues arise here. First, while he covered a similar stretch of time as Wallerstein, starting with the expansion of Europe in the sixteenth century, Wolf's account sketched the process leading to the present in two distinct, successive phases: (1) the expansion of trade in spices, minerals, furs, and slaves that created a world market and (2) the advent of industrial capitalism that developed networks of exchange more intensively, increasingly relied on profits drawn from the use of wage labor rather than from exploiting differential prices in distant sites, and penetrated spaces well beyond the "stopping points" of coastal entrepôts, where earlier European mercantile trade had been forced to respect the political power of foreign (South and East Asian) sovereigns.

The qualitative leap made from one phase to the next also meant that capitalist systems and noncapitalist orders, previously segmented, were now complexly intertwined. Industrial capitalism, Wolf claimed, "grew through its own internal ability to reproduce itself on an ever-widening scale . . . [thus] entering into working arrangements with other modes [of production]"; it had an uncanny "ability to enter in temporary and shifting relations of symbiosis and competition with other modes." Thus "capitalism-in-production," Wolf wrote, "enveloped and penetrated" societies and settings built on other terms, resulting in "a complex hierarchical system controlled by the capitalist mode of production, but including a vast array of subsidiary regions that exhibited different combinations of the capitalist mode with other modes."[79] To an extent much greater than in Wallerstein's account, the keynote in Wolf's presentation of a world system is particularity, variation, and the complex "interdigitation" of structured social relations of different sorts. The world scene that ensued from Wolf's second stage of world development featured "commodity frontiers" and "labor frontiers": the first where merchants exchanged goods with precapitalist societies (which thereby gained a temporary second lease on life), and the second where laborers in newly opened reservoirs (such as nineteenth-century South China villages scouted by labor brokers) fell under varied kinds of duress, unlike the "free" individualistic contract relations of the US labor market. There was, in short, a new world under industrial capitalism of new "connections" but still a varied, serried arrangement whose very complications often created the sparks in the social crises that Wolf's *Peasant Wars* had related. Unevenness reigned throughout.

Second, Wolf saw Wallerstein concentrating on "how the core subjugated the periphery [but] not . . . the reactions of the micro-populations habitually investigated by anthropologists," who were predisposed to consider "the range and variety of such populations, of their modes of existence before European expansion and the advent of capitalism, and of the manner in which these modes were penetrated, subordinated, destroyed or absorbed." He added, "Without such an examination . . . the concept of 'periphery' remains as much of a cover term as 'traditional society'"—that is, a way of avoiding the historical particulars of complex social and cultural forms.[80] To be sure, Wolf's book included few portraits if any of episodes that historians today would recognize as instances of subaltern agency, but Wolf's approach was, in principle, attuned to those who kicked back. His ironic title not only mocked the Eurocentric notion that people outside Europe, who bowed to its superior civilization and power, lacked history; it also proposed a new kind of anthropology (which is, literally, the study of "people") that puts *history*—that is, processes of change and interaction over time—at the heart of the discipline. This, Wolf proposed, would overcome an ethnological romance of cultures, "primitive" or not, that could be grasped as enduring wholes of settled meaning and mores. In the "interdigitated" or "articulated" forms of world systemic relations, all the parts moved.

These two streams, Wolf's and Wallerstein's, help illuminate the intellectual-theoretical development I call "the world turn" that took hold in academic scholarship in a period from the late 1960s and early 1970s to the 1980s, a turn that has fostered a legacy in the current practice of history, the social sciences, and the humanities. Attuned to the embeddedness of local and national affairs in the world at large, or at least in broadly regional and transnational networks (such as "the Atlantic world"), scholars have come to perceive links, interactions, overlaps, interweavings, and comparisons that routinely cross boundaries of all sorts; they perceive wide-spanning, tangled relations making the world what it has been and is, past and present.

Aside from that scholarly bequest, the work of Wolf and Wallerstein had another decidedly political impact, providing the vocabulary with which Fredric Jameson posed his challenge in 1984 to devise a new mapping of the bewildering terrain of global capitalism. Yet the course of intellectual history is itself profoundly uneven. As these two writers recognized, their "world systems" work was a creature of "1968," the culminating high pitch of what in retrospect we recognize as the modern anticolonial revolt. By the time Jameson wrote, that revolt had essentially come to an end, besieged in Central America, mired in economic devastation in Africa, fractured by nation-state rivalries in the East (China, Vietnam, Cambodia)—and the New Left that had voiced solidarity with the Third World revolt was itself in steep decline. Jameson already inhabited a different world from that of the midcentury struggles that formed Wolf's and Wallerstein's work. In a sharp turn of history so soon after the peak radicalization of 1968, the inception a "long downturn" in the capitalist economy in the mid-1970s broke the mold of the midcentury welfare state order and sparked a long process of renovation that by the 1990s led to some new capitalist configuration typically called "globalized" and "neoliberal."[81]

Social analysis, like history, typically looks backward and reaches conclusions as the conditions to which it applies are ending—while Jameson's mapping project was prospective: it held to the principle guiding the work of Marx, which supposed that a theory of social relations as they exist might also illuminate the ways and means of future action to recast them profoundly. This made Jameson's challenge such a bold bid: what, if any, are the conditions that might render thinking, on behalf of a political movement aiming for social transformation, not only accurate for describing the past but also adequate to assess present results and prospects? In the face of such a daunting, perhaps impossible task, the innovative world systems thinking of "1968" provided a suggestive start in understanding global phenomena but one perhaps that the onrush of historical change quickly rendered outmoded.

Notes

1. Fredric Jameson, "Postmodernism, or the Cultural Logic of Late Capitalism," *New Left Review* 1, no. 146 (August 1984): 87–88.
2. Philip Curtin, "Depth, Span, and Relevance," *American Historical Review* 89 (1984): 1–9.
3. Ernest Mandel, *Late Capitalism*, trans. Joris de Bres (London: NLB, 1975), first published as *Der Spätkapitalismus* (Frankfurt: Suhrkamp Verlag, 1972).
4. Jameson, "Postmodernism," 89–91.
5. Georg Wilhelm Friedrich Hegel, *The Philosophy of History* (New York: Dover, 1956); Pascale Casanova, *The World Republic of Letters* (Cambridge, MA: Harvard University Press, 2004); Philip Vilas Bohlman, *World Music: A Very Short Introduction* (Oxford: Oxford University Press, 2002).
6. Nelson Lichtenstein, *A Contest of Ideas: Capital, Politics, and Labor* (Urbana: University of Illinois Press, 2013), 13–28, 45–106.
7. On the University of Michigan dismissals of Mark Nickerson and H. Chandler Davis, the latter honored by the naming of Alan Wald's H. Chandler Davis Collegiate Professorship in 2007, see Ellen Schrecker, *No Ivory Tower: McCarthyism and the Universities* (New York: Oxford University Press, 1986), 219–34.
8. On the liberal and elite/positivist cast of mainstream American modernization theory, see especially Nils Gilman, *Mandarins of the Future: Modernization Theory in Cold War America* (Baltimore: Johns Hopkins University Press, 2003).
9. David Price, *Threatening Anthropology: McCarthyism and the FBI's Surveillance of Activst Anthropologists* (Durham, NC: Duke University Press, 2004), 336. For Wolf's biography, see Eric Wolf, "Introduction: An Intellectual Autobiography," in *Pathways of Power: Building an Anthropology of the Modern World*, 1–10 (Berkeley: University of California Press, 1999); folder "Marxism Notes, 1939–1945" (box 1), Eric R. Wolf Papers, 1939–2011, Bentley Historical Library, University of Michigan (hereafter Wolf Papers); "Talk (autobiographical) at Yale, 1984" (box 1), Wolf Papers.
10. Author's interview with Sidney Mintz, Baltimore, Maryland, November 2006.
11. Howard Brick, "Neo-Evolutionist Anthropology, the Cold War, and the Beginnings of the World Turn in U.S. Scholarship," in *Cold War Social Science: Knowledge Production, Liberal Democracy, and Human Nature*, ed. Mark Solovey and Hamilton Cravens, 155–72 (New York: Palgrave Macmillan, 2012).
12. Julian H. Steward et al., *The People of Puerto Rico: A Study in Social Anthropology* (Urbana: University of Illinois Press, 1956), 2, 7.
13. Joan Vincent, *Anthropology and Politics: Visions, Traditions, and Trends* (Tucson: University of Arizona Press), 301.
14. Eric R. Wolf, *Sons of the Shaking Earth* (Chicago: University of Chicago Press, 1959), 256. On the Cold War as a contest between two different models (US and Soviet) of modernization, see Odd Arne Westad, *The Global Cold War: Third World Interventions and the Making of Our Times* (Cambridge: Cambridge University Press, 2007), 1–72.
15. Stanley Diamond, "Reflections on the Heritage of Colonialism: Ghana and Northern Nigeria," typescript, box 12, Julian Steward Papers, University of Illinois (hereafter Steward Papers).

16. Letter, Stanley Diamond to Julian Steward, September 18, 1962, box 13, Steward Papers; Letter, Diamond to Steward, February 1, 1961 [misdated 1960 on letterhead], box 9, Steward Papers.
17. Leta S. Hollingworth, "The Terman Classes at Public School 500," *Journal of Educational Sociology* 10, no. 2 (October 1936): 86–90.
18. Author's interview with Immanuel Wallerstein, New Haven, Connecticut, November 25, 2013.
19. Robert L. Tyler, "The American Veterans Committee: Out of a Hot War and into the Cold," *American Quarterly* 18, no. 3 (Autumn 1966): 419–36; Robert Francis Saxe, *Settling Down: World War II Veterans' Challenge to the Postwar Consensus* (New York: Palgrave Macmillan, 2007).
20. Joseph Preston Baratta, *The Politics of World Federation: The United Nations, U.N. Reform, Atomic Control* (Westport, CT: Praeger, 2004); Joseph Preston Baratta, *The Politics of World Federation: From World Federalism to World Governance* (Westport, CT: Praeger, 2004).
21. Wallerstein, "Some Personal Assumptions on (Student) Federalist Program," May 6, 1951, typed memo, box 73, folder "Student Convention 1951," United World Federalist Papers, Lilly Library, Indiana University.
22. Report on National Student Conference (St. Louis), June 1950, "Fourth Panel: The Middle World," box 73, folder "Student Council and Executive Minutes, 1947–1951," United World Federalist Papers.
23. Joël Kotek, *Students and the Cold War* (Houndmills, UK, and New York: Macmillan and St. Martin's, 1996), 172–73.
24. Author's interview with Immanuel Wallerstein, Yale University, November 25, 2013.
25. Immanuel Wallerstein, *The Essential Wallerstein* (New York: New Press, 2000), xvi.
26. Kotek, *Students and the Cold War,* 206.
27. Hugh Wilford, *The Mighty Wurlitzer: How the CIA Played America* (Cambridge, MA: Harvard University Press, 2008), 229–30.
28. Quoted in Anna Loewenhaupt Tsing, *Friction: The Ethnography of Global Connection* (Princeton, NJ: Princeton University Press, 2005), 81–85.
29. Vijay Prashad, *The Darker Nations: A People's History of the Third World* (New York: New Press, 2007), 6–7; Stuart Hall, "The 'First' New Left: Life and Times," in *Out of Apathy: Voices of the New Left Thirty Years On; Papers Based on the Conference Organized by the Oxford University Socialist Discussion Group,* ed. Robin Archer (London: Verso, 1989), 14–15; author's interview with Norman Birnbaum, Washington, D.C., December 10, 2013.
30. Richard Wright, *The Color Curtain: A Report on the Bandung Conference* (Cleveland, NY: World Publishing, 1956), 12.
31. Homer Jack, *Bandung: An On-the-Spot Description of the Asian-African Conference, Bandung, Indonesia, April 1955* (Chicago: Toward Freedom, 1955). On Jack's ardent anticommunism, see Robbie Lieberman, *The Strangest Dream: Communism, Anticommunism, and the U.S. Peace Movement, 1945–1963* (Syracuse, NY: Syracuse University Press, 2000), 129, 131, 169, 174.
32. Wilford, *Mighty Wurlitzer,* 197–205.
33. George McT. Kahin, *The Asian-African Conference, Bandung, Indonesia, April 1955*

(Ithaca, NY: Cornell University Press, 1956); George McT. Kahin, *Southeast Asia: A Testament* (London and New York: RoutledgeCurzon, 2003).

34. On Wolf not being a joiner, e-mail correspondence, Sidney W. Mintz to author, February 21, 2014.

35. Robert Redfield, *Tepoztlan, a Mexican Village: A Study of Folk Life* (Chicago: University of Chicago Press, 1930); Robert Redfield, *The Primitive World and Its Transformations* (Ithaca, NY: Cornell University Press, 1953).

36. Redfield, *The Primitive World and Its Transformations,* 2, 3, 15, 79, 136.

37. Soekarno, *Marhaen and Proletarian: Speech before the Indonesian Nationalist Party at the Party's Thirtieth Anniversary at Bandung, July 3rd 1957* (Ithaca, NY: Cornell University, 1960); Frantz Fanon, *The Wretched of the Earth* (New York: Grove, 1965); Immanuel Wallerstein, "Fanon and the Revolutionary Class," in *The Essential Wallerstein,* 14–31; Teodor Shanin, *Peasants and Peasant Societies: Selected Readings* (Harmondsworth, UK: Penguin, 1971).

38. On "building toward a unified picture of anthropology as a discipline with meaning for non-'primitive' research," see letter, Mintz to Wolf, May 5, 1952, box 2, folder "Mintz, Sidney, 1952–1965," Wolf Papers.

39. On later discussions regarding Marx's engagement with the "Russian question" of his day, see Teodor Shanin, *Late Marx and the Russian Road: Marx and "the Peripheries of Capitalism"; A Case* (New York: Monthly Review Press, 1983); Kevin Anderson, *Marx at the Margins: On Nationalism, Ethnicity, and Non-Western Societies* (Chicago: University of Chicago Press, 2010). Both of these focus on the letters exchanged between Marx and his Russian followers. A part of those exchanges was published as "The Marx-Zasulich Correspondence," *New International,* November 1942, 298–302, originals of which were collected in Wolf's personal papers and cited in Eric Wolf, *Europe and the People without History* (Berkeley: University of California Press, 1982), 303, 452.

40. David C. Engerman, *Modernization from the Other Shore: American Intellectuals and the Romance of Russian Development* (Cambridge, MA: Harvard University Press, 2003).

41. Redfield, quoted in Sidney Mintz, "The Folk-Urban Continuum and the Rural Proletarian Community," *American Journal of Sociology* 59 (September 1953): 138.

42. Ibid., 139.

43. Ibid., 141.

44. Ibid., 142.

45. Eric R. Wolf and Sidney W. Mintz, "Haciendas and Plantations in Middle America and the Antilles," *Social and Economic Studies* 6 (1957): 380, 384–85.

46. Ibid., 381–82, 409.

47. Ibid., 400.

48. Michael Löwy, *The Politics of Combined and Uneven Development: The Theory of Permanent Revolution* (London: NLB, 1981).

49. Julian H. Steward, Robert F. Murphy, and Eric Wolf, "Multilinear Evolution in Acculturation," typescript, box 9, Cross-Cultural Research Project (1953–55), Steward Papers. See also Julian Steward, *Theory of Culture Change: The Methodology of Multilinear Evolution* (Urbana: University of Illinois Press, 1955).

50. Eric R. Wolf, "Project for Research on Cross-Cultural Regularities: Progress

Report," December 3, 1954, including "Projected Research, 1954–55," box 9, folder "Eric Wolf, Peasant Research, 1954," Steward Papers.

51. Eric R. Wolf, *Peasant Wars of the Twentieth Century* (New York: Harper & Row, 1969), xiv–xv.
52. Ibid., 99.
53. Ibid., 260, 291–92, 295.
54. Ibid., 295, 301.
55. Ibid., 301–2.
56. Ibid., 302.
57. David E. Apter, *Rethinking Development: Modernization, Dependency, and Postmodern Politics* (Newbury Park, CA: Sage, 1987), 24.
58. On "ethnicity and national integration," see Wallerstein, *Essential Wallerstein,* 3–14.
59. Immanuel Wallerstein, ed., *Social Change: The Colonial Situation* (New York: Wiley, 1966), 7. On Gluckman, see Geoff Eley, *A Crooked Line: From Cultural History to the History of Society* (Ann Arbor: University of Michigan Press, 2005), 41.
60. Immanuel Wallerstein, *Africa: The Politics of Independence; an Interpretation of Modern African History* (New York: Vintage Books, 1961); Immanuel Wallerstein, *Africa: The Politics of Unity; an Analysis of a Contemporary Social Movement* (New York: Random House, 1967); Charles Ragin and Daniel Chirot, "World System of Immanuel Wallerstein: Sociology and Politics as History," in *Vision and Method in Historical Sociology,* ed. Theda Skocpol, 276–312 (New York: Cambridge University Press, 1984).
61. Wallerstein, *Essential Wallerstein,* xxii.
62. Daniel J. Sherman et al., eds., *The Long 1968: Revisions and New Perspectives* (Bloomington: Indiana University Press, 2013).
63. Wallerstein, "Pan-Africanism as Protest," in *The Revolution in World Politics,* edited by Morton A. Kaplan, 137–51 (New York: Wiley, 1962).
64. Immanuel Wallerstein, *University in Turmoil: The Politics of Change* (New York: Atheneum, 1969), 20, 26–27.
65. Ibid., 130, 112–13.
66. Ibid., 23.
67. Ibid., 28, 23–24.
68. Terence K. Hopkins and Immanuel Wallerstein, "The Comparative Study of National Societies," *Social Science Information* 6, no. 5 (October 1, 1967): 25–58 .
69. Immanuel Wallerstein, "Modernization: Requiescat in Pace," in *The Uses of Controversy in Sociology,* ed. Lewis A. Coser and Otto N. Larsen, 131–33 (New York: Free Press, 1976); Immanuel Wallerstein, *The Modern World-System I: Capitalist Agriculture and the Origins of the European World-Economy in the Sixteenth Century* (Berkeley: University of California Press, 2011); Immanuel Wallerstein, *The Modern World-System II: Mercantilism and the Consolidation of the European World-Economy, 1600–1750* (Berkeley: University of California Press, 2011).
70. Immanuel Wallerstein, *The Modern World-System III: The Second Era of Great Expansion of the Capitalist World-Economy, 1730's–1840's* (Berkeley: University of California Press, 2011).

71. Eric R. Wolf, *Peasant Wars of the Twentieth Century* (New York: Harper & Row, 1969), 251 (my emphasis).

72. Wolf, *Europe and the People without History,* x.

73. Dell H. Hymes, *Reinventing Anthropology* (New York: Pantheon Books, 1972).

74. Joseph G. Jorgensen and Eric R. Wolf, "A Special Supplement: Anthropology on the Warpath in Thailand," *New York Review of Books* 15, no. 9 (November 19, 1970), 34–35.

75. Ibid. The quotation from Stanley Diamond was taken from Betty Nickerson, ed., *Chi: Letters from Biafra,* preface by Stanley Diamond (Toronto: New Press, 1970), vii.

76. On the distinction of "comparative" and "connective" histories, see Victor Lieberman, "Introduction," *Modern Asian Studies* 31, no. 3 (July 1, 1997): 451; Victor B. Lieberman, *Strange Parallels: Southeast Asia in Global Context, c. 800–1830,* Vol. 1, *Integration of the Mainland* (New York: Cambridge University Press, 2003), 14.

77. The problem of relating capitalist production and a world market that is both its fount and its result was already posed by Marx. In a characteristic remark during a discussion of price fluctuations, the valuation of capital, and the ways that surplus value is converted into profit, Marx noted that "The phenomena under investigation . . . assume for their full development the credit system *and competition on the world market, the latter being the very basis and living atmosphere of the capitalist mode of production.*" Karl Marx, *Capital: A Critique of Political Economy,* Vol. 3, trans. David Fernbach (London: Penguin, New Left Review, 1981), 205 (emphasis added). Marx continued: "These concrete forms of capitalist production [i.e., the financial system and competition on the world market], however, can be comprehensively depicted only after the general nature of capital is understood; it is therefore outside the scope of this work to present them—they belong to a possible continuation" (205). Not only was volume 3 of *Capital* never completed, but the suggestion here of treating finance and the world market in concrete detail also, of course, never came to pass.

78. Wolf, *Europe and the People without History,* 295–97.

79. Ibid., 79, 206.

80. Ibid., 23.

81. Robert Brenner, *The Economics of Global Turbulence: The Advanced Capitalist Economies from Long Boom to Long Downturn, 1945–2005* (London and New York: Verso, 2006); Peter Gowan, *The Global Gamble: Washington's Faustian Bid for World Dominance* (London and New York: Verso, 1999); Giovanni Arrighi, *Adam Smith in Beijing: Lineages of the Twenty-First Century* (London and New York: Verso, 2007); Philip Mirowski, *Never Let a Serious Crisis Go to Waste: How Neoliberalism Survived the Financial Meltdown* (London: Verso, 2013).

[16]

Wrestling with the Legacy of Stalinism: Recent Scholarship on W. E. B. Du Bois and the Left

Bill V. Mullen

> In one sense, we know more about the French Revolution or the Stalinist reign of terror than those who were involved in them, because we know what they led to. With the privilege of hindsight, we can inscribe these events in a broader narrative, making more sense of them than Robespierre or Trotsky were ever able to do. . . .
>
> . . . It is up to us to ensure that Michelangelo and Thomas Mann, say, did not belong to a race that ended up destroying itself. They themselves, being dead, are powerless to prevent that tragic denouement, whereas we are not. We can make a difference to their stories. We cannot undo the fate of those in the past who fought for justice and were murdered for their pains. But we can rewrite their narratives by our own actions in the present, and even give them a classical happy ending.
>
> –Terry Eagleton, "Waking the Dead"[1]

In the summer of 2013, Italian autonomist Ferruccio Gambino published "Reading *Black Reconstruction* on the Eve of 1968" in a special issue of *South Atlantic Quarterly* dedicated to W. E. B. Du Bois's book. Gambino describes himself in the essay as a searching young activist of the 1960s European Left living in a world divided. The Cold War partition into "two Europes," separated with a "line of barbed wire from the Baltic to the Black Sea," was haunted by the specter of Hungary's 1956 failed workers' uprising against Stalinist rule, leaving a generation of leftists "even more divided and more closed in on themselves."[2] The malaise made it difficult for radicals in Europe to assess their relationship to events worlds away, including African and Asian decolonization struggles and a southern US civil rights movement whose religious orientation made it pallid to a generation of historical materialists.

In the spring of 1967, Gambino was a student in residence in the United States under the mentorship of historian George Rawick. As Gambino recounts, Rawick strongly advised him to read two books: Du Bois's *Black Reconstruction,* and C. L. R. James's *The Black Jacobins.* Suddenly, for Gambino, the "gray North Atlantic shroud of the early 1960s" was rent. "It was easy to see," wrote Gambino, "that *Black Reconstruction* cast a bright light on crucial developments that were scarcely known or completely negated in the history books. Du Bois's book put the slaves at center stage and sought to overturn the dominant opinion that continued racist prejudice and the consequent intellectual laziness."[3] More important for Gambino, Du Bois's book seemed to resolve a historical impasse plaguing his own political generation's capacity to relate to struggles beyond the pale of home. The recognition that American slaves in 1848 had protested the US invasion of Mexico became for a generation steeped in another European trajectory from that year, a global license to dream:

> Du Bois's move seemed to be in tune with the anticolonial revolts in Asia and Africa in the 1920s more than with the interclass politics of the popular fronts, the alliance with colonial powers, and the abandonment of the anticolonial struggles, positions officially adopted by the Third International in the same year as the publication of *Black Reconstruction.* In other words, Du Bois's book was a milestone of historiography for all those whose history had been denied or stolen.[4]

Gambino's potent account animates a recurring challenge for scholars and activists on the global Left, namely the influence of Stalinism on its political theory and practice. *Black Reconstruction*'s emphasis on black agency and self-determination redeems hopes for internationalist solidarity and for Gambino, hopes seemingly emptied out by years of "socialism in one country" policy in which the Soviet Union used strategies such as the Popular Front to defend the Soviet state at the cost of support for anticolonial and working-class struggles. The effects of Stalinization were felt across Europe for years to come. During France's war with Algeria, for example, the French Communist Party supported the French state, this after backing the Soviet intervention in Hungary in

1956. Like Terry Eagleton's reflection in the epigraph to this chapter, Gambino's memory also speaks to the inevitable relationship between thought and practice, historiography and history making. His identification of *Black Reconstruction* as a source of inspiration for a New Left's internationalist commitments animates the core radicalism of Du Bois's work long after its expiration date and demonstrates what Eagleton calls a capacity to "rewrite . . . narratives by our own actions in the present."[5]

Yet this moment of backward glance also indexes the roots of a recurring problem in Du Bois scholarship, or what might be called more broadly commemoration. George Rawick notwithstanding, 1968 was a low tide in public appreciation for Du Bois's legacy. That year Martin Luther King Jr. made a desperate, and futile, appeal to the American public to accept once and for all Du Bois's turn to communism and his decision to join the Communist Party in 1961. That turn culminated more than a decade of public support for Stalin and the Soviet Union by Du Bois, including his hagiographic tribute "On Stalin" published on the former's death in 1953. Public communist sympathies had cost Du Bois his role as a columnist at the *Chicago Defender* in 1946, his arrest in 1951 under the Smith Act, the cancellation of numerous speaking engagements, and an unofficial blacklisting of much of his writing. Were it not for the dogged efforts of Herbert Aptheker and International Publishers, it is possible that Du Bois's autobiography would not have seen the light of day in the United States in 1968, some six years *after* its international publication in the Soviet Union. In the same year Du Bois's book did appear, as Amy Bass has documented, a broad alliance of groups in Du Bois's hometown of Great Barrington, including the American Legion, the Knights of Columbus, and the Daughters of the American Revolution, worked actively to oppose an emergent campaign to construct a memorial in his honor.[6] Du Bois's letters, newspaper columns, and secondary writings—especially those published after his more open turn to socialist thought—appeared intermittently in collections, mostly by small leftist publishers and mostly shepherded single-handedly by the communist historian Herbert Aptheker, only in the 1970s and 1980s well after Du Bois's death. Until 1998, Du Bois's novel about the age of the Communist International (Comintern), *Dark Princess,* first published in 1928, remained out of print, virtually unread. Meanwhile, his blacklisted manuscript "Russia and America: An Interpretation" remains unpublished to this day.

It was also *this* "shroud" that was rent for Gambino by his chance encounter with Du Bois in 1967. Yet the rigid classification of Du Bois's career and thought persists. The benevolent and soulful early work and the later dogmatic period, the "scholarly" Du Bois and the "polemical"

Du Bois, the Du Bois of "racial uplift" and the "transnational" Du Bois, and the "humanist" Du Bois and the "Stalinist" Du Bois are categories themselves reflective of what Alan Wald has called the "polarized thinking" of scholarship and commemoration generated under the influence of the Cold War.[7] In the case of Du Bois, an obsessive conflation of Stalin and Stalinism with the *idea* of communism in the twentieth century is mirrored in an obsessive conflation of Du Bois with African American cultural and political history and an unnerving anxiety about too closely miscegenating the two. Great man narratives of both have helped hold in place simplistic analyses of communist internationalism (the general absence, for example, of Trotskyist scholarship on the US cultural and political Left) reflected in an unsubtle analysis of Du Bois's own broad and shifting relationship to Marxism and twentieth-century struggles for global justice.[8] This is true despite the fact that Du Bois articulated support for a wide range of anticolonial and communist struggles, from India's 1947 independence to China's 1949 revolution to Pan-Africanism to the Gold Coast's struggle to become Ghana in 1957.

In large part, the generation of scholars and memorializers of Du Bois born well after the Stalin era have begun that nuancing work. This scholarship is unified by its own revisionist impulse to create what Eagleton calls a "broader narrative" of history that throws into relief essential elements of the twentieth-century global Left's theory and practice beyond the narrow parameters of Soviet or Stalinist influence: cross-border solidarity, collaborative political struggle, autonomous battles against racism and sexism, and the struggle for a redemptive, and often revisionist, relationship to both Marxism and its practice. In general, this scholarship has confronted political successes and failures of the revolutionary Left in the twentieth century by detaching from what might be called Stalinized historiography. In the case of Du Bois, for example, Eric Porter argues that "we must avoid the problem of making leftist ideas and affinities overly determinative of his thought . . . in either positive or negative ways. Du Bois might have praised Stalin, for example, but he was not a Stalinist in any systematic way."[9] Porter's insights clear the way for his own study of Du Bois's late, more explicitly anticapitalist work. Porter's 2010 book *The Problem of the Future World: W. E. B. Du Bois and the Race Concept at Midcentury* undertakes a detailed study of Du Bois's thought in the latter third of his life often eschewed by scholars as his "decline" into Communist influence. While acknowledging Du Bois's denials of Stalinist crimes and atrocities, Porter perceives Du Bois's turn to socialism as part of a desire for a "cosmopolitan" perspective on world events beyond the borders of American anticommunism and nationalism. Socialism, he argues, provided a means of understanding what Du Bois called the "race concept" as part of a larger fight for economic and political justice. Porter's larger ambition in his book—much like Gambino's 1967 epiphany—is to animate Du Bois's ideas for our global moment. In the wake of the collapse of state capitalist Communism in the Soviet Union and China and in the face of current global neoliberal devastations to workers, social welfare, and the environment, Porter cites David Levering Lewis's caution that "it may be suggested that Du Bois was right to insist that to leave the solution of systemic social problems exclusively to the market was an agenda guaranteeing obscene economic inequality in the short run and irresoluble calamity in the long run."[10] Porter concludes his study by writing that "while the historically specific state socialist project through which Du Bois hoped his reconstruction of democracy would happen founders on the ruins of the Soviet Union and on Russia's and China's free market and imperialist adventures in the present, the project of transforming the state to better promote economic and racial justice remains a necessity."[11] For Porter, this does not necessarily mean giving the previous era or our own what Eagleton calls a "classical happy ending" as much as it means studying afresh the residual pastness of the present in order to change it.

Porter's book thus partially addresses a need for what Wald has called a "decolonization" of scholarship on the Left by creating new frameworks for understanding old political problems.[12] In recent years, scholars identifying with currents in postcolonial studies have done much to aid this "decolonization." This scholarship, all of it generated in the official aftermath of the Cold War, has tried to reimagine the global Left (and frequently Du Bois's place in it) by focusing on anticolonial liberation in Japan, China, India, Africa, and African America beyond the influence of Soviet and Stalinist policy. Among these are Yuichiro Onishi, author of *Transpacific Anti-Racism: Afro-Asian Solidarity in 20th Century Black America, Japan, and Okinawa;* Dora Ahmed, author of *Landscapes of Hope: Anti-Colonial Utopianism in America;* Nico Slate, author of *Colored Cosmopolitanisms: The Shared Struggle for Freedom in the United States and India;* and Etsuko Taketani, author of *The Black Pacific Narrative: Geographic Imaginings of Race and Empire between the Wars.*[13] Their studies are united by endeavors to reframe African American political and cultural history within two broader twentieth-century narratives: Asian anticolonial struggles and transnational solidarity. Among the significant and original aspects of Taketani's work, for example, is that it is one of the first to examine the Japan and China sections of Du Bois's unpublished manuscript "Russia and America," completed in 1950, in order to interpret Du Bois's efforts to support twentieth-century Asian national liberation struggles. Taketani demonstrates that Du Bois's writings on Asia show him seeking an independent theory of socialism influenced by Pan-Asianism. Slate and Ahmed, meanwhile, show how a range of African American activists across a broad political spectrum—including Du Bois—helped galvanize popular support for Indian decolonization. More broadly, these studies show an urge to recover a century of independent leftist political activism forged in collaboration between South and East Asian revolutionaries and African Americans in the West, a turn that Onishi calls "Du Bois's challenge" to scholars of the twenty-first century. In turn, each of these studies spans the globe to give a new name to this form of political radicalism: Dohra Ahmed calls it "anti-colonial utopianism," Onishi calls it "Colored Internationalism," Taketani names it a "Black Pacific Narrative," and Slate denotes it as "Colored Cosmopolitanism." Cumulatively, these studies represent an effort to create a "subaltern" history of US colonial and postcolonial history, a reminder of the efforts of subaltern studies scholarship from the 1980s South Asian Left by figures such as Partha Chatterjee, Dipesh Chakrabarty, Gayatri Spivak, and Ranajit Guha. As has been documented elsewhere, subaltern studies was an effort to wrestle with the victories and defeats of the Indian Left, itself much shaped by Stalinist influence.[14] The new simultaneity of this body of scholarship across the globe today can be understood as a function of shared twentieth-century victories and defeats: both anticolonial liberation at midcentury and the collapse of Stalinist Communism in 1989 have taken on the sweet and sour tang of historical necessity for reassessing both the present and the past in this work.

The decolonization of scholarship on the twentieth-century Left has also not surprisingly deposed conventional, and masculine, means of commemoration, helping to replace "great man" theories alluded to earlier. It has specifically brought renewed attention to the role of women in building the international Left and to their contributions to leftist debates about women's oppression. The recovery of Agnes Smedley's career in recent years is a good example. Smedley entered the world revolutionary Left via participation in anticolonial organizing by Indian nationalist expatriates to the United States in the World War I era. She later worked for the Comintern in China and supported the Communist Party of China even while criticizing Stalin's "United Front" strategy advocating alliance between the Party and the Kuomintang. Smedley also corresponded briefly with Du Bois in the 1920s and spoke with him at the 1948 National Conference on American Foreign Policy and the Far East, organized by the Communist Party. Smedley has been the subject of two biographies, by Ruth Price and Janice and Stephen MacKinnon.[15] Both provide unvarnished views of Smedley's romantic infatuation with the Chinese Communist Revolution and her role in the Comintern. Smedley's recovery and championing in the 1970s and 1980s by the late novelist and 1930s radical Tillie Olsen and living firebrand Alice Walker has also shown continuities between the Old Left and the civil rights era regarding the "woman question" and women's oppression.[16] By and large, these explorations of leftist influence have provided a balanced assessment of Smedley's tangled relationship to Stalinism.

In addition to Smedley, the recent biography by Barbara Ransby of longtime Left activist Eslanda Robeson (a strong public supporter of Soviet Communism), Carole Boyce Davies and Marika Sherwood's separate biographies of Trinidadian-born Communist Party member and feminist theorist Claudia Jones, and Gerald Horne's 2002 biography of Shirley Graham Du Bois are important for throwing into relief some of the most important women of the twentieth-century Left while providing a *subordinated* perspective on figures such as Du Bois and Stalin who connect to all of them.[17] These works have allowed scholars to see political influence on the Left as bidirectional, fusing anticolonial, antiracist struggles to the gender equity that these struggles strove to produce. In recent years, scholars such as Lise Vogel, Angela Davis, Martha Jimenez, Cinzia Arruzza, Sue Ferguson, David McNally, and Tithi Bhattacharya have also plumbed the line on the woman question back to the nineteenth and early twentieth centuries to extraordinary revisionist effect.[18] Debates on the Marxist Left about women's oppression and how to fight it have rarely been as robust as they are now.

Decolonizing scholarship on Du Bois and the US Left has also taken a lead from a vanguard of scholars who have filled a void in attention to black women's proletarian internationalism, itself both shaped by and resistant to Stalinist influence. Recent books by Cheryl Higashida, Dayo F. Gore, Carole Boyce Davies, Marika Sherwood, and Eric McDuffie constitute a generational recovery of this work, emphasizing women who worked with and proximate to Du Bois but developed their own independent body of political thought.[19] Higashida's study of First and Third World predominately working-class black women in the 1930s, 1940s, and 1950s demonstrates how an "impasse" on the communist Left regarding gender was resolved by rethinking the Leninist thesis on self-determination. While the figures in her book remained nominally committed to the Russian Revolution through 1953, hence to Stalinism, they also produced an independent body of thought that anticipated black feminism. Higashida has also mined more carefully than any scholar the lineage of Claudia Jones's "triple oppression" thesis regarding black women and connects it to later intersectionality theory—a critical linkage for connecting Old Left and New Left, mainstream and dissident revolutionary feminism in the twentieth century. As Higashida writes, Jones's feminism is "intersectional, but not in the sense espoused by cultural critics who value nonhierarchichal conjunctions of different modes of resistance. In specifically giving precedence to national liberation, Jones demonstrates that it is necessarily transformed by centering black women's struggles within it instead of focusing exclusively on men."[20]

Similarly, Eric McDuffie and Dayo F. Gore have significantly broadened our understanding of independent African American women on the US Left. McDuffie recounts Communist Williana Burroughs's ten-year stay in the Soviet Union, from 1935 to 1945, as an early point on a century-long trajectory of black female expatriatism that Gore punctuates with an account of the life of Vicki Garvin.[21] Garvin was drawn to leftist circles and the Du Boises in the 1950s. In 1961, she moved to Nigeria after an offer of employment from fellow leftist Thelma Dale Perkins. After experiencing what Garvin called two years of "neocolonialism-disillusionment," she moved to Ghana, meeting up briefly with Shirley and W.E.B. Du Bois, then in 1964, moved to China, where she lived in exile for six years.[22] Garvin was what Gore describes as a "behind-the-scenes" strategist in supporting both China's Cultural Revolution and black liberation, the two conjoined, however crudely, after Mao's 1963 declaration of support for Negro liberation. The experience of exile and affiliation caused Garvin to describe herself as both a "pan-Africanist" and a "proletarian, working-class, internationalist."[23] Though all of the women in these studies hewed to procommunist politics in the Stalin era, collectively these works also help give credence to Alan Wald's claim about the wider legacy of Stalinism for scholars treating the twentieth-century communist Left: "Despite its clarifying potential when used in a sophisticated manner to treat an ideology, social system or political organization," he writes, "Stalinism can be an oversimplifying lens through which to evaluate the thinking, personalities and life activities of diverse individuals, not to mention works of the artistic imagination."[24]

Likewise paradigmatic of this trend toward decolonization of scholarship is work on Claudia Jones by Sherwood and Boyce Davies. Jones was a cosignatory to the "We Charge Genocide" petition to the United Nations authored by Du Bois, William Patterson, and other members of the Communist Party to which she belonged. Both Sherwood and Davies offer self-consciously reflective accounts of Jones's life, including her largely uncritical support for Stalinism, by placing it in the context of her wide field of political activism and the politics of our own time. Sherwood's *Claudia Jones: A Life in Exile,* for example, consists of seven chapters based almost entirely on primary source documents excavated after her death and supplemented by transcripts of the 1996 Claudia

Jones Symposium in London organized by friends and former colleagues. The symposium includes sessions on four aspects of Jones's life: "My Friend Claudia," a roundtable discussion of personal reminiscences by among others Rajana Ash, who recounts Claudia's formation of the Committee of Afro-Asian and Caribbean Organizations; "The Political Activist," including reflections by former comrades in the British Communist Party; "The West Indian Gazette"; and "Carnival." Sherwood's book is the best extant account of Jones's place in the wider postwar British Left and the local activists who built it. The book's combination of scholarly interpretation and commemoration as historical process makes it an important model for understanding and applying the lessons of diasporic internationalism to our present. Similarly, Boyce Davies analyzes the repression, surveillance, and deportation that Jones suffered during the 1950s in the context of post-9/11 US homeland security laws. She compares the Smith Act and the McCarran-Walter Acts to the Illegal Immigration Reform and Immigrant Responsibility Act of 1996 and the USA Patriot Act of 2001, both of which increased deportation, surveillance, and the political demonization of dissidents and immigrants, especially from Arab states. Boyce Davies challenges romantic paradigms of transnational and diasporic scholarship to include deportation and involuntary migration (political refugees, for example) as a central category of "mobility." She demonstrates that for figures forced into exile or quarantined by state repression, "diaspora" often involved involuntary dialectics of state repression and revolution.[25]

Finally, the "decolonization" of twentieth-century scholarship is an ongoing project enabled in part by the de-Stalinization of the last century's archives. Many of these works have generated interpretations of the US and global Left made possible only by texts that have surfaced for public view in the wake of the post-1989 collapse of the Soviet Union. Ruth Price's biography of Agnes Smedley draws upon materials from Soviet archives to document her role in the Comintern. Kate Baldwin's *Beyond the Color Line and the Iron Curtain* (2003) was one of the first to take advantage of the Soviet archival openings to reinterpret the relationship of Du Bois, Paul Robeson, and Langston Hughes to the Soviet Union.[26] Baldwin also remains one of the few scholars to seriously engage Du Bois's unpublished manuscript "Russia and America." Another is Taketani, whose 2014 book also investigates documents related to Chinese suspicions that Hughes was operating as a Soviet Comintern agent in Shanghai during his time there in the 1930s (he was not). John Riddell's magnificent restoration of the transcripts of the 1922 Comintern, published in 2011 under the title *Toward the United*

Front, provides an indispensable record and interpretation of what C. L. R. James in 1935 called the "rise and fall" of the World Revolution.[27] Finally, Datta Gupta's 2006 study *Comintern and the Destiny of Communism in India, 1919–1943* draws on extensive Comintern archives to revise understanding of the relationship of the Indian communist Left to the Comintern. Gupta's first chapter, "Comintern: The New Historiography," is especially essential reading. These examples provide a tip of the iceberg as scholars continue to construct the global dynamics of what the Comintern called "World Revolution," the political horrors and errors of Stalinism, and the tendrils that connected many members of the diasporic international in a shared project. Collectively, this scholarship is also continuously motivated by political developments of the present. As Gupta writes, historical recovery of Comintern records is vital "because the Left in India is still heavily dominated by the spirit of Stalinism, the consequence of which has been the persistence of a fundamentalist mindset." His book, he writes, "is addressed to all those who are prepared to rethink the history of Indian communism by going back to the basics, with the openness to look back at what happened and consider what could have possibly happened."[28]

Postscript: On February 23, 1968, Martin Luther King Jr. delivered the Centennial Address at Carnegie Hall in New York City at an event commemorating the one hundredth anniversary of W. E. B. Du Bois's birth. Du Bois had died at age 95 the day before the historic March on Washington of August 28, 1963. In his 1968 address, King famously appealed to listeners to set aside Cold War prejudice against Du Bois's late-in-life decision to join the Communist Party USA. "It is time to cease muting the fact that Dr. Du Bois was a genius and chose to be a Communist," said King. "Our irrational obsessive anti-communism has led us into too many quagmires to be retained as if it were a mode of scientific thinking."[29] Of course, the quagmire to which King alluded was all too real—the US war in Vietnam, a war, King noted, that the anti-imperialist peace activist Du Bois would have opposed with life and limb were he still alive.

King posed the question of how a Du Bois of our time would respond to current events shaped by those of the past, such as recent US imperial wars in Iraq and the Persian Gulf; ongoing drone strikes in Afghanistan, Pakistan, Yemen, and Somalia; and the seemingly endless "war on terror" and Islamophobia that has helped to sustain it. The speech also raises the question of how scholars of our generation might continue to construct a Du Bois relevant to it. If, as David Blight has poignantly argued, "all memory is prelude,"[30] then we should be keen to Du Bois scholar Amy Bass's caution that the making of reputations and commemoration are often keynotes to our own political present. "As the Cold War becomes grounded in the past, the sentiments and actions it created slide almost seamlessly into the post-9/11 era," writes Bass. "Binaries of 'us versus them' exist in amorphous yet devastating ways: someone—on behalf of and for the good of the general public—is continually trying to figure out who the 'us' is, since the 'them' remains part of an imaginary state of emergency, albeit one with very real ramifications, as it continues to drive US foreign policy in much the same way that it did in the Vietnam era."[31] Bass helps us understand how Du Bois's 1951 status under the Smith Act as an "agent of a foreign government" can look a lot like post-9/11 designations of American citizens as "internal enemies" of their government for failing to rally around the flag of US empire. Thus, scholars interested in wholesale reappraisal of American empire today might do well to begin with a reassessment of W. E. B. Du Bois's own dissident relationship to that empire and also attend to his own idiosyncratic application of communist thought in his work. I have attempted to review some of the more recent scholarship that has begun that endeavor, much of it in the name of emancipatory political movements of the twentieth century that not only survived the legacy of Stalinism but also superseded many of its worst aspects. Building from it, we might then begin to explore anew Du Bois's own investments and assessments of some of the most important events generated by the revolutionary Left of his lifetime, such as the Russian Revolution, India's decolonization, the Chinese Communist Revolution, and even the conflict between Israel and the Palestinians, a topic seldom explored in his work. In all of these domains of political imagination and struggle, the legacy of Stalinism itself remains unfortunately central, a legacy whose own "decolonization" may allow us to turn the page toward both commemorating and building a better world.[32]

Notes

1. The epigraph is from Terry Eagleton, "Waking the Dead," *New Statesman,* November 12, 2009, http://www.newstatesman.com/ideas/2009/11/past-benjamin-future-obama.
2. Ferruccio Gambino, "Reading *Black Reconstruction* on the Eve of 1969," *South Atlantic Quarterly* 112, no. 3 (Summer 2013): 530.
3. Ibid., 531.
4. Ibid., 532.
5. Eagleton, "Waking the Dead."

6. Amy Bass, *Those about Him Remained Silent: The Battle over W. E. B. Du Bois* (Minneapolis: University of Minnesota Press, 2009), 47.
7. Alan Wald, "From 'Triple Oppression' to 'Freedom Dreams,'" *Against the Current* 162 (January–February 2013): 24.
8. Exceptions to scholarship that tends to "polarize" discussion of the twentieth-century Left along Cold War lines would include in addition to examples cited in this chapter among others, the scholarship of Paul LeBlanc, Scott McLemee, Robin D. G. Kelley, James Smethurst, Mark Naison, Rachel Rubin, William Maxwell, Paula Rabinowitz, Winston James, Keeanga Yamahtta-Taylor, Chris Vials, and Alan Wald. While some of these scholars such as LeBlanc, McLemee and Wald openly identify with Trotskyism, others here have generated important analyses of strengths and weaknesses of the American Left by carefully examining contradictions and difficulties of maintaining communist and socialist allegiance in the United States before and after the Cold War.
9. Eric Porter, *The Problem of the Future World: W. E. B. Du Bois and the Race Concept at Midcentury* (Durham, NC: Duke University Press, 2010), 10.
10. Ibid., 5. See also David Levering Lewis, *W. E. B. Du Bois: The Fight for Equality and the American Century, 1919–1963* (New York: Henry Holt, 2000), 570.
11. Porter, *The Problem of the Future World,* 178.
12. Wald, "From 'Triple Oppression' to Freedom Dreams," 24.
13. See Yuichiro Onishi, *Transpacific Antiracism: Afro-Asian Solidarity in 20th Century Black America, Japan, and Okinawa* (New York: New York University Press, 2013); Dohra Ahmed, *Landscapes of Hope: Anticolonial Utopianism in America* (Oxford: Oxford University Press, 2009); Nico Slate, *Colored Cosmopolitanisms: The Shared Struggle for Freedom in the United States and India* (Cambridge, MA: Harvard University Press, 2012); Etsuko Taketani, *The Black Pacific Narrative: Geographic Imaginings of Race and Empire between the World Wars* (Dartmouth, NH: Dartmouth College Press, 2014).
14. See, for example, Partha Chatterjee, *The Nation and Its Fragments: Colonial and Postcolonial Histories* (Princeton, NJ: Princeton University Press, 1993); Partha Chatterjee, *The Black Hole of Empire: History of a Global Practice of Power* (Princeton, NJ: Princeton University Press, 2012); Dipesh Chakrabarty, *Provincializing Europe: Postcolonial Thought and Historical Difference* (Princeton, NJ: Princeton University Press, 2000); Ranajit Guha, *Elementary Aspects of Peasant Insurgency in Colonial India* (Delhi: Oxford University Press, 1983); Gayatri Spivak, *A Critique of Postcolonial Reason: Toward a History of the Vanishing Present* (Cambridge, MA: Harvard University Press, 1999). Most recently, Vivek Chibber has challenged the politics of subaltern studies groups in his book *Postcolonial Theory and the Specter of Capital* (London: Verso, 2013). Chibber's criticism of subaltern studies, especially the work of Chakrabarty and Chatterjee, is in what he sees as misplaced hostility to Marxism as a "universalizing" body of thought. Chibber's arguments can also be understood in light of distortions done to Marxism in India owing to Stalinist control over the Communist Party of India dating to the 1920s.
15. See Janice R. MacKinnon and Steven R. MacKinnon, *Agnes Smedley: The Life and Times of an American Radical* (Berkeley: University of California Press, 1988); Ruth Price, *The Lives of Agnes Smedley* (Oxford: Oxford University Press, 2005).
16. Olsen, who joined the Young Communist League in 1931, was raised by socialist parents and charted working-class women's oppression in her fiction, was instrumental in the republication of Smedley's *Daughter of Earth,* according to

Feminist Press publisher Florence Howe. Howe wrote that Olsen "insisted" on the book's republication in 1971. Howe also said that no gesture other than Olsen's was "more significant" in the press's history, as it helped to spearhead the press's efforts to recover other women writers. See Florence Howe, "Preface," in *Almost Touching the Skies: Women's Coming of Age Stories,* ed. Florence Howe and Jean Casella (New York: Feminist Press, 2000), ix. See also Alice Walker, "Foreword," in Agnes Smedley, *Daughter of Earth,* 1–4 (New York: Feminist Press, 1987). Walker calls Smedley a "poor white woman who, all her life, continued to act, to write like one. I recognize in her a matriot of my own country" (4).

17. See Barbara Ransby, *Ella Baker and the Black Freedom Movement: A Radical Democratic Vision* (Chapel Hill: University of North Carolina Press, 2005); Barbara Ransby, *Eslanda: The Large and Unconventional Life of Mrs. Paul Robeson* (New Haven, CT: Yale University Press, 2013); Carole Boyce Davies, *Left of Karl Marx: The Political Life of Black Communist Claudia Jones* (Durham, NC: Duke University Press, 2007); Marika Sherwood, *Claudia Jones: A Life in Exile* (London: Lawrence and Wishart, 1999); Gerald Horne, *Race Woman: The Lives of Shirley Graham Du Bois* (New York: New York University Press, 2002).

18. See Lise Vogel, *Marxism and the Oppression of Women: Toward a Unitary Theory* (1983; reprint, Leiden: Brill, 2013); Angela Davis, *Women, Race and Class* (New York: Vintage, 1983); Martha Gimenez, "Global Capitalism and Women," in *Globalization and Third World Women: Exploitation, Coping and Resistance,* ed. Ligaya Lindio-McGovern and Isidor Wallimann, 35–48 (Farnham, UK: Ashgate, 2009); See Susan Ferguson and David McNally, "Introduction," in Lise Vogel, *Marxism and the Oppression of Women,* xvii–xxxi; Sue Ferguson, "Canadian Contributions to Social Reproduction Feminism, Race and Embodied Labor," *Race, Gender & Class* 15, no. 1–2 (2008): 42–57; Tithi Bhattacharya, "Explaining Gender Violence in the Neoliberal Era," *International Socialist Review* 91 (Fall 2013): 25–47.

19. See Cheryl Higashida, *Black Internationalist Feminism: Women Writers of the Black Left, 1955–1995* (Champaign: University of Illinois Press, 2013); Dayo F. Gore, *Radicalism at the Crossroads: African American Women Activists in the Cold War* (New York: New York University Press, 2012); Eric S. McDuffie, *Sojourning for Freedom: Black Women, American Communism and the Making of Black Left Feminism* (Durham, NC: Duke University Press, 2011); Carole Boyce Davies, *Left of the Color Line: The Political Life of Black Communist Claudia Jones* (Durham, NC: Duke University Press, 2007); Sherwood, *Claudia Jones.*

20. Higashida, *Black Feminist Internationalism,* 20.

21. McDuffie, *Sojourning for Freedom,* 151.

22. Gore, *Radicalism at the Crossroads,* 145.

23. Ibid., 151.

24. Wald, "From 'Triple Oppression' to 'Freedom Dreams,'" 24.

25. See chapter 4, "Deportation: The Other Politics of Diaspora," in Davies, *Left of the Color Line;* Sherwood, *Claudia Jones,* 178–215.

26. See Kate Baldwin, *Beyond the Color Line and the Iron Curtain: Reading Encounters between Black and Red, 1922–1963* (Durham, NC: Duke University Press, 2002).

27. See John Riddell, *Toward the United Front: Proceedings of the Fourth Congress of the Communist International, 1922* (Chicago: Haymarket Books, 2011).

28. Sobhanlal Datta Gupta, *Comintern and the Destiny of Communism in India, 1919–1943* (Kolkata: Seribaan, 2011).

29. Martin Luther King, Jr., "Honoring Dr. Du Bois, No. 2, 1968," in *Freedomways Reader: Prophets in Their Own Country,* ed. Esther Cooper Jackson (Boulder, CO: Westview, 2000), 37.

30. David W. Blight, *Race and Reunion: The Civil War in American Memory* (Cambridge, MA: Belknap, 2002), 397.

31. Bass, *Those about Him Remained Silent,* 159.

32. Material from chapter 16 also appears in "The Afterthought" in *Un-American: W.E.B. Du Bois and the Century of World Revolution* by Bill V. Mullen. ©2015 by Temple University.

[17]

Remembering Nat Turner: Black Artists, Radical History, and Radical Historiography, 1930–55

James Smethurst

From the early 1930s to the 1950s, radical black poets, novelists, painters, and playwrights associated with the Communist Party USA (CPUSA) and its cultural sphere combined the leftist imperative of uncovering a revolutionary/people's history of struggle in the United States generally with an older and more specifically black project of contesting the racist Bourbon and Dunning Schools that dominated the profession of history, rendering black people as objects instead of subjects, as acted upon rather than historical actors. These black radical artists aimed not only to retell and reframe mainstream historical accounts with black people at the center as activists and leaders in the struggle to determine their own destiny, but also to rethink how and why and for whom history is told. To trace the trajectory of African American expressive art in the twentieth century, then, is to rethink our understanding of radical artistic production in the United States in the 1930s, 1940s, and 1950s in terms of both periodization and regional centers of that production. For example, we might be surprised to discover the radical public art of John Biggers in Houston during the heyday of the McCarthy era or of Hale

Woodruff in Alabama in 1940 and adjust our ideas about the South and the history of radical expressive culture accordingly.

In the first half of the twentieth century, the field of US history was dominated by white males who were racist by either omission or commission. U. B. Phillips was the dean of historians of the antebellum South. His take on slavery was basically that the peculiar institution was regrettable, but once the kidnapped Africans were transported here, well, what were you going to do, because they were too helpless to have survived on their own. In his accounts, slavery was a relatively benign if financially impractical institution that would have faded away of its own volition without the violent and unnecessary upheaval of the American Civil War. William Dunning (one of Phillips's teachers) and the Dunning School of historians portrayed Reconstruction as a singularly corrupt and undemocratic regime forced on victimized white southerners by northern white carpetbaggers and treacherous southern white scalawags and their sometimes childlike, sometimes brutish African American lackeys. More liberal leading historians, such as Charles Beard and Frederick Jackson Turner, downplayed the importance of race and indeed slavery in the development of the United States, ceding that territory largely to Phillips, Dunning, and their ilk. The mainstream historians' organizations, notably the American Historical Association, were indifferent, when not actually hostile, to black (and radical) historians.[1] Despite some challenges to the Bourbon School of slavery and the Dunning School of Reconstruction by Howard Beale, this racist scholarship dominated the history profession and teaching on secondary and college levels at least until C. Vann Woodward's *The Strange Career of Jim Crow* (1955) and Kenneth Stampp's *The Peculiar Institution* (1956).

While African Americans were not precisely absent from the scholarship of these mainstream historians, they were present as a relatively static group on which historical actors (read: great white men) acted, whether in the eras of slavery, Reconstruction, or Jim Crow. There were, of course, black historians who contested the Bourbon School in the early twentieth century, most famously Carter G. Woodson and the Association for the Study of Negro Life and History (ASNLH), which established Negro History Week (now African American History Month) precisely to highlight African Americans as historical agents rather than a sort of inert social material. By the 1930s, the ASNLH and Negro History Week came to have some significant influence on the curriculum of black schools in the South but almost none in the academic world outside of historically black colleges and universities.

These circumstances often inspired in black artists a particular sense of obligation to present narratives and interpretations of historical events—be they Nat Turner's revolt, African American participation in the Civil War, Reconstruction, the Jim Crow counterrevolution, and so on—as interventions in the field of history. These interventions also served a historiographical function. They said something about what that field had been and was—and for what purpose, for what audience, and by what methods historical narrative had been recounted and interpreted. At the heart of these interventions was the desire to show African Americans as historical agents whose efforts were aimed specifically toward the liberation of black people in particular and the expansion of US democracy in general. One can see this history and historiographical imperative among black artists at least as far back as the late nineteenth century. Frances E. W. Harper's 1892 novel *Iola Leroy* was as much a black revision of the proto-Bourbon accounts of the slave era, the Civil War, and Reconstruction as it was a call for African American unity to defend the advances of Reconstruction in the face of the emergent system of Jim Crow segregation. Paul Laurence Dunbar's turn-of-the-twentieth-century poems about the Civil War and black soldiers, such as "The Colored Soldiers" and "W'en Dey 'Listed Colored Soldiers," argued for the maintenance and expansion of black citizenship through historical remembrance and interpretation, countering reconciliationist efforts to bring together white Union and Confederate veterans, both actually and symbolically, while excluding black veterans and avoiding the subject of slavery. African American historical pageants often presented broad panoplies of African-descended people in the United States. Particularly notable as a forerunner of black 1930s historical art is W. E. B. Du Bois's 1915 pageant *The Star of Ethiopia,* which included African American vernacular music (mostly the spirituals) and African-inspired music, anticipating Langston Hughes's *Don't You Want to Be Free?*[2]

This black imperative to set straight popular and scholarly histories of slavery, Reconstruction, and Jim Crow intersected with efforts by the CPUSA and its supporters to uncover and promote a decidedly nonbourgeois revolutionary tradition in the United States during the CPUSA's Third Period. The term "Third Period" refers to Stalin's prediction of a catastrophic worldwide capitalist crisis following an earlier crisis during and immediately after the Bolshevik Revolution and World War I (the First Period) and a relatively short span of economic stability during the 1920s (the Second Period). The onset of the Great Depression made Stalin seem prescient. One central tenet of Third Period ideology was that the international working class would look for radical solutions to the crisis. The danger, argued Stalin and the Comintern, was that they might be misled back into capitalism by various sorts of liberal and noncommunist leftist groups, especially the various social democratic groups. As a result, the world communist movement in the late 1920s emphasized the establishment of alternative workers' institutions that were formally, thematically, and institutionally distinct from bourgeois culture, whether conservative, liberal, or even social democratic. One prong of this countercultural proletarian effort was the projection of an indigenous revolutionary history and of matching radical cultural traditions in the United States that were emphatically not bourgeois or liberal.

Also associated with the Comintern and Third Period ideology was the so-called Black Belt Thesis formally adopted by the Comintern in 1928. This position proposed that African Americans constituted a "nation" in the South (with a significantly shared history, culture, psychology, territory, and so on) with the right to self-determination up to and including the right to form an independent republic in the southern "Black Belt" where African Americans formed an often-overwhelming majority of the population. The thesis also postulated black people in the urban North as a "national minority" that should be fully integrated socially, culturally, and economically. One crucial aspect of the Black Belt Thesis is that it put the "National Question" and "Negro Liberation" at the center of the work of the CPUSA. In part because of these notions of the centrality of Negro liberation and the black nation, the more militant manifestations of black rebellion against slavery, Jim Crow, and racism—notably the slave revolts led by Nat Turner, Denmark Vesey, Singbe Pieh (aka Joseph Cinqué), and Gabriel (sometimes known as Gabriel Prosser)—were seen as exemplars of the true revolutionary tradition in the United States. Consequently, articles and editorials about slave rebellions and other forms of black resistance to slavery appeared in major political and cultural organs of the CPUSA, such as the *Daily Worker* and *New Masses.*

African American slave revolts, black efforts to maintain and even extend Reconstruction, and early black direct-action opposition to Jim Crow continued to have iconic status within the Communist Left.[3] As has been much noted, the Popular Front era tended to emphasize a broad democratic contest with fascism and right-wing reaction over a strictly proletarian struggle. Though the official period of the Popular Front as an international Comintern strategy runs from about 1935 to the Hitler-Stalin Pact at the end of 1939, the Popular Front approach to political and cultural organization and aesthetics characterized the domestic work of the Communist Left in the United States far beyond 1939. One can see this approach in African American art in Paul Robeson's 1939 version of Earl Robinson and John Latouche's "Ballad for Americans" and in John Biggers's 1953 Houston mural *The Contribution of Negro Women to American Life and History.* Both works were important and radical in their ways, and Biggers's mural had a certain revolutionary side too. The revolutionary heroes Nat Turner, Gabriel, Harriet Tubman, and so on did not vanish during the Popular Front. In fact, it was in the work of black artists that the revolutionary historical strain most often persisted and reached much larger audiences through the growth of public art during the Popular Front era, a phenomenon connected to the Works Progress Administration (WPA) Federal Art Project (FAP) in writing, theater, the visual arts, and music. That strain persisted in African American public spaces including schools, colleges, universities, YMCAs, and libraries well after the end of the FAP, as can be seen by John Biggers's Houston murals in the 1950s and early 1960s.

The great black radical landmark in historical studies of the 1930s was W. E. B. Du Bois's 1935 *Black Reconstruction.* Du Bois examined Reconstruction as a failed proletarian revolution in which the impetus and leadership came not from the top down (from outside agitators, carpetbaggers, radical white Republicans, and so on) but instead from the radicalized black masses and indigenous southern black leadership who were able to assimilate various "outside" liberatory ideas and practices with their own. While the genesis of this study dated back at least to 1909 and a paper he delivered at the annual meeting of the American Historical Association, it differed from this earlier work in its efforts to assimilate Marxist ideas and methodologies, particularly Third International Leninist Marxism. Despite the influence of the Bolshevik Revolution on *Black Reconstruction,* Du Bois projected African Americans not simply as political actors or ideological recipients but also as formulators of a revolutionary tradition in the United States. In this account, the ability to take in useful formulations and concepts and make them their own again demonstrates not the influence of outside (read: white) manipulators but the intellectual capacity of the black masses and their organic leaders, much as in the European revolutionary traditions. After all, people seldom talked, or talk, of Karl Marx and Friedrich Engels as being under the influence of outside French socialist and British economic agitators. Despite the impact of Third International Marxism on *Black Reconstruction,* the CPUSA tended to be very critical of Du Bois's study, seeing it as misapplying historical materialist analysis—though the vehemence of this critique was likely as much due to lingering Third Period ideological distrust of Du Bois as a former liberal "misleader" as to actual ideological difference. Still, *Black Reconstruction* was a crucial event in the development of black Marxist history and historiography because the book is almost as much about the history profession as the actual historical record of Reconstruction.

Arna Bontemps's 1936 *Black Thunder,* a novel about Gabriel's failed turn-of-the-nineteenth-century slave revolt in Virginia, takes much the same stance as *Black Reconstruction.* Barbara Foley has very helpfully characterized the novel as a "proletarian social novel," which is a multiply yet collectively narrated dialogic chronicle of simultaneous and interconnected events.[4] Among other things, the novel engages the complexity of the African American community in the antebellum South, showing a range of classes, complexions, crafts, statuses (free or enslaved), and gender roles as ideological positions inflected by those differences. In part, we get a tutorial about the difficulties of making a revolution, with both the strengths and weaknesses of Gabriel and his lieutenants on display as well as what we might think of as a principled traitor and unprincipled traitors among the slaves. The novel is both a history and radical historiography. In other words, Bontemps is telling a story that is truer and more accurate than what passed for scholarship on slavery in the annual meeting of the American Historical Association. And that mattered a lot to him and to his readers.

It is also important how Bontemps represents the relationship of the rebels to revolutionary ideology. As always, the slaveowners and the state look for the outside agitators, the Jacobins, the foreign revolutionaries:

> "Talk, dog. You had the lists and the records. Who gave you those pamphlets."
>
> Then, with a jolt of surprise, Gabriel heard Mingo's voice.
>
> "We didn't read no pamphlets. Them pamphlets didn't have nothing to do with us. We was started long before—"
>
> "How many names have you listed? Why did you plan to spare the French residents? Why were *you* so active in the thing? You were free."
>
> "We was—"
>
> Gabriel raised his head abruptly.
>
> "Die like a free man, Mingo."[5]

In this case, there really is a foreign revolutionary in the form of the exiled French Jacobin printer Monsieur Creuzot as well as in the radical white "natural rights" advocate and lawyer Alexander Biddenhurst. And clearly the discussions of Creuzot and Biddenhurst are shown to have an impact on Gabriel and, by extension, his fellow rebels. However, it is also clear that Gabriel and company do not take on these ideas blindly but instead process them and make them their own, combining them with already existing ideas and practices of theirs—again, much as Marx did with non-German political theory and economics. By the end, it is clear that Creuzot and particularly Biddenhurst have gotten more from Gabriel and what is seen as the continuing black liberation struggle than Gabriel and company have gotten from them. As Alan Wald notes, it is the black revolutionaries and their ideological synthesis that guide the rebellion, not the white radicals, whose ideas prior to their engagement with the black revolution remain on the level of abstraction, at least in the United States.[6] In fact, these white radicals are in some senses ambivalent about this incipient revolution in which they and their ideas are not in the lead. However, they recognize that they must support, indeed follow, Gabriel and the other black rebels or be complicit in the counterrevolution of the slavocracy: "'We cannot escape it,' he said at length. 'There is a struggle that takes us in. It takes us against our will. There is no escape for men of conscience.'"[7]

The specter haunting the slavocracy is the nightmare suspicion that the outside agitator explanation does not in fact explain that the revolt is a black initiative, that black people are not malleable material. If there is a major inspiration for Gabriel's revolt that originates beyond the shores of the United States, its source is not in Europe but in the Americas, and it springs not from white or even mixed-race radicals but from unequivocally black revolutionaries. In short, the shadow of Haiti and its revolution, the subject of Bontemps's 1939 novel *Drums at Dusk,* hangs over them. The name of Toussaint L'Ouverture is a sort of mantra of fear (for most of the white characters) and hope (for the black and a few white characters) in *Black Thunder.* Thus, we get a vision of a US revolutionary history (and the US present of the Scottsboro case, Angelo Herndon, the Sharecroppers Union, and so on) in which not only black issues but also black leadership are at the center.

Those who are inclined to think of the Popular Front as a move away from revolutionary cultural politics might see *Black Thunder* as a product of the liminal moment between Third Period and Popular Front leftist ideologies, hence explaining its unabashedly revolutionary (or nationalist revolutionary) sentiments as a sort of residual proletarianism. Such people might be surprised to find much the same sentiments and framing of black struggle by artists in what we might think of as the high Popular Front era. Langston Hughes's 1938 "poetry-play" *Don't You Want to Be Free?* is a genre- and media-bending mash-up of drama, black music, and dance that, as the production notes say, endeavors "to capture within the space of an hour the entire scope of Negro history from Africa to America."[8] There was some precedent in African American expressive culture for this mixture of genre and media in the black pageant movement, notably in Du Bois's *The Star of Ethiopia.* Another example descended from the black pageant tradition were the score and libretto by Shirley Graham (later an important Left activist and dramatist herself) for the opera *Tom Tom: An Epic of Music and the Negro,* commissioned by the Stadium Opera Company, then the leading opera company of

Cleveland. The opera combined music, dance, and theatrical spectacle to represent the arc of African American experience from the Middle Passage to the present. It was performed twice in 1932 to large crowds in Cleveland but apparently was not performed again. There is no evidence that Hughes attended the opera, though given his ties to Cleveland and the mutual connection of Hughes and Graham through Cleveland's Karamu Theatre, it is hard to believe that he did not know of it. While Graham's opera was certainly in more of a high art modality, incorporating black folk and popular elements after the manner of composers R. Nathaniel Dett and William Grant Still, rather than trying to present them more directly as did Hughes, it did provide a model of which Hughes was likely aware.

As in his friend Bontemps's novel, Hughes projects a history of interracial struggle against oppression, linking racial or national oppression to class exploitation but with African Americans significantly in the lead, doing much to shape the struggle and, indeed, providing some of the most glorious episodes of that struggle from the slave era to the rise of the Congress of Industrial Organizations.[9] While Hughes names some of the "democratic" icons famously associated with the Popular Front—most notably perhaps Abraham Lincoln—many of the icons of the earlier "revolutionary" period, such as Nat Turner, Denmark Vesey, Harriet Tubman, and John Brown, are invoked as well. The tone of the play is more in the mode of the United States fulfilling its democratic potential or the aspirations of Hughes's "Let America Be America" than that, say, of the more starkly revolutionary poem "One More 'S' in the U.S.A." Yet it ends with a crowd of black and white workers showing "the power of the worker's might" and shouting, "Fight! Fight! Fight!"—directly echoing the finale of Hughes's unabashedly proletarian 1931 play *Scottsboro Limited,* where the audience joins with the Scottsboro defendants and black and white workers in shouting "Fight! Fight! Fight! Fight!"

Don't You Want to Be Free also engages the relationship between art and history, how history has been and might be told, and what counts as historical evidence. In other words, it is as much historiography as it is history. First, the play incorporates previously published poetry by Hughes, including poems that have not been generally seen as particularly historical, such as some of his signature blues pieces. These poems are contextualized in the play as illuminating a range of historical moments. In short, what is offered is a leftist historicist reading of Hughes's work (and, by extension, that of his black contemporaries) in which that work both illuminates and is illuminated by history. Second, the play's interpolation of black music (spirituals, work songs, blues, jazz, and gospel), storytelling, and dance as well as literature makes an argument for radically broadening notions of what constitutes (or should constitute) historical evidence in order to produce a true (or truer) account of African Americans in the United States. Given the centrality of ideas and hierarchies of race as well as the economic centrality of black labor in the founding and development of the United States, then, what one is talking about is a true (or truer) history of the United States generally as opposed to those often liberal historians who largely ignored race. Echoing Frederick Douglass's famous observations about the nature of slave music in his autobiographies and anticipating Amiri Baraka's more elaborated historical claims in *Blues People,* Hughes (a major influence on Baraka) suggests that black popular and folk art and forms encode within them an account and interpretation of historical events. Obviously, the use of such black cultural objects is a common, if still somewhat disputed, move in the history profession over the last thirty or so years but was far from standard operating procedure in the 1930s.

The play goes on to propose that beyond its role as evidence, art—particularly popular art—has a dialectical relationship with history and the history profession. Popular culture, whether in the readings of Reconstruction in, for example, the plantation stories of Thomas Nelson Page or D. W. Griffith's *Birth of a Nation* (with its combination of the plantation genre, coonery, black-face minstrelsy, and Lost Cause mythology) or Hughes's play, have had profound impacts on the public framing of history, even by professional scholars (whether Phillips, Woodson, or Du Bois) who, in turn, provided grist for these popular culture representations and recountings.

Something similar is at work in the visual artist Hale Woodruff's *Amistad* murals, which he painted at Talladega College, a historically black school in Alabama, during the late 1930s, publicly showing them in 1940.[10] Woodruff was the founder and head of the arts program at Atlanta University. He encouraged his students to unsentimentally focus on local black workers, small farmers, and sharecroppers, leading him and the circle of artists he mentored to become known as the "Outhouse School," due to their penchant for including outhouses in their rural landscapes. Woodruff's program was a major beachhead of the Popular Front in the South and made Atlanta a hub for black visual artists.

As with *Don't You Want to Be Free,* there is a certain way that one can see the *Amistad* murals as keeping with a popular democratic struggle strain of the Popular Front. However, it is also hard to look at the panel of the actual shipboard rebellion showing the captive Africans overpowering and preparing to slaughter the slave ship's crew and not see a militant action of revolutionary self-determination in the spirit, again, of the

Haitian Revolution. To paraphrase Robert F. Williams, one might retitle that panel "Mutiny on the Amistad" as "Negroes with Machetes."[11] It is certainly possible to see more of a popular democratic iconography in the subsequent court scene. Even here, though, it is important to note that it is Singbe who is in the forefront, with his arms implacably folded and a stern, proud expression on his face, unlike the faces of his white attorneys Lewis Tappan or John Quincy Adams, leaving no doubt about the real leader of the struggle. In short, one is presented with both a revolutionary history with black people (and black workers, one might add) in the leadership of a multiracial (and multiclass) alliance that provides to or provokes in its audience not only a certain historical knowledge and consciousness but also a way of examining and understanding the bases of how history is represented or written and to what ends that history is deployed. The mural also raises the question of what happens, to paraphrase Mary Helen Washington's 1997 presidential address at the American Studies Association's annual meeting, when you put African Americans at the center of the field of history.[12]

Like Woodruff, Elizabeth Catlett played an important role in the creation of what might be thought of as an artistic black Popular Front in the South, first at Dillard University in New Orleans and later at Hampton Institute in Virginia. While she never had the institutional power that Woodruff or her student John Biggers had, she nonetheless was an inspiring teacher and, indeed, an inspiration for African American artists working in a wide variety of media and genres from the 1930s until her death in the twenty-first century. She created "I Am the Negro Woman," a series of linoleum cuts, in 1946 and 1947 for the communist cultural journal *Masses and Mainstream* while in Mexico studying at the left-wing Taller de Gráfica Popular.[13] What is perhaps most obvious about the series is the presence of what one would now call an intersectional analysis in which we see black women as workers (both urban and rural), mothers, educators, and political leaders who face the triple oppression of race, class, and gender as articulated in theoretical writings by black women Communists, notably Claudia Jones, as well as in the work of both male and female black radical artists.[14]

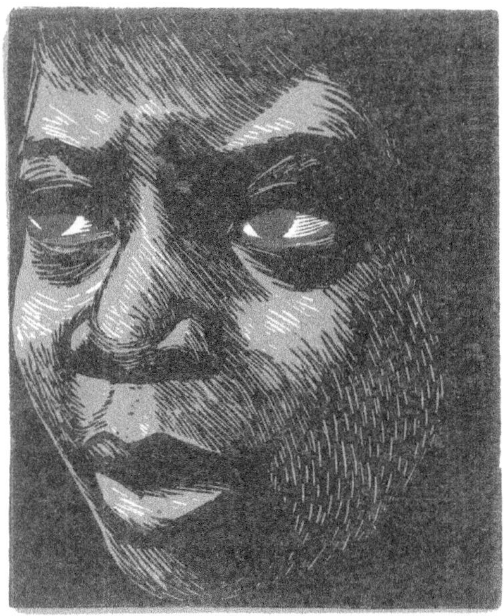

Figure 17.1. *I am the Negro Woman*, 1947, Elizabeth Catlett. Linocut on paper, 5½ x 5 in. Accession number 2011.1.172. Courtesy of the Pennsylvania Academy of the Fine Arts, Philadelphia. Art by Women Collection. Gift of Linda Lee Alter.

The series consists of fifteen linocuts: three featuring well-known historical figures (Phillis Wheatley, Harriet Tubman, and Sojourner Truth); eleven with unnamed black women who, among other things, labor, study, organize workers, suffer from Jim Crow in the South, endure gross discrimination in the North, and play music; and one with the full body of a black man who has been lynched (and the dangling legs of three other victims of lynching). She gives particular focus to the faces of the black women, often with one woman foregrounded in the company of other black women, creating a dynamic, one might say dialectical, relationship between the individual and the collective that characterizes the series as a whole. (In the one featuring lynched black men, titled "And a Special Fear for My Loved Ones," the focus is on the trunk of the body and on dangling legs, not the face.) As in Hughes's play and John Biggers's Houston murals, it would appear that the cuts are bifurcated into those that essentially document the present and others that represent a vision of the past, a history.

Figure 17.2. *In Phyllis Wheatley I proved intellectual equality in the midst of slavery*, 1946, Elizabeth Catlett. Linocut on paper, 9½ x 6½ in. Accession number 2011.1.120. Courtesy of the Pennsylvania Academy of the Fine Arts, Philadelphia. Art by Women Collection. Gift of Linda Lee Alter.

However, again, the presence of the overtly historical figures of Wheatley, Tubman, and Truth suggests that black women laboring in the present are historical actors in a continuum stretching back at least to the slave era. Again, as with Bontemps, the series not only suggests a counterhistory to that of the mainstream but also revisits and revises notions of what might count as historical evidence and which events might be significant. In doing so, it anticipates the new social history that would only gain real traction in the US academy under the pressure of black studies (and other manifestations of ethnic studies) and the culturally inflected labor history from below most closely associated with E. P. Thompson and such US devotees of Thompson as David Montgomery and Herbert Gutman (former Communists who never abandoned the Left). One might say that Catlett honors and invokes the revolutionary and Popular Front icons of Tubman and Truth (with the interesting inclusion of Wheatley, who is rarely present on lists of revolutionary black ancestors) while complicating what might be seen as a "great woman" theory of history. What one sees, then, is not simply a litany of heroines but a more dialectical relationship between leadership and the grass roots in which the familiar icons are placed in the context of, and on par with, everyday black women and in which there is a dynamic interplay between the individual and the collective.

Like Atlanta University, Hampton Institute in Virginia, where John Biggers enrolled in 1941, was a beachhead of the black Popular Front in the South. At Hampton, Biggers encountered and was deeply influenced by a leftist refugee from Nazism, Viktor Lowenfeld. Lowenfeld became Biggers's primary adviser, but Biggers was mentored as well by Charles White and Elizabeth Catlett, both closely connected to the Communist Party and sharing Woodruff's commitment to representing the struggles of urban and rural southern black communities as well as what might be considered the revolutionary tradition in African American history in public art. Lowenfeld, White, and Catlett encouraged Biggers to see his art not as individual expression but as voicing a collective African American culture of struggle: "I began to see art not primarily as an individual expression of talent, but as a responsibility to reflect the spirit and style of the Negro people."[15]

Biggers's amazing set of murals in public spaces and black institutions in Houston, which were commissioned from the early 1950s to the 1980s, display his journey from the Popular Front to the Black Arts Movement. The seeds of Black Arts, with a deep engagement to an African diasporic spirituality and sensibility, are clearly visible early on in Biggers's murals, while his Popular Front artistic origins, with the close linking of a local class-based perspective to the international, never really disappear.

Of course, to a considerable degree, the nature of each mural commission significantly influenced its content and ideological stance. One of Biggers's early commissions in Houston was the 1953 *The Contribution of Negro Women to American Life and Education* at the Blue Triangle YWCA. With a slightly cubist emphasis on planes and angles, it compresses a range of stories from slavery to the Jim Crow era into a historical mosaic, much as Diego Rivera did in his *Detroit Industry* murals. As in the work of Biggers's mentor Catlett, one sees the presence of the same intersectionality articulated by Claudia Jones and other black Communists and leftists in the late 1940s and 1950s. One also notices in Biggers's work, as in that of Catlett, Bontemps, and Hughes, the linkage of everyday people with more familiar icons, most prominently Harriet Tubman and Sojourner Truth (again, also featured in Catlett's *Negro Woman* series).

A commission from Local 872, a black local of the International Longshoremen's Association (ILA), is also clearly in the black Popular Front vein. While the national leadership and structure of the ILA was often corrupt and promoted the Jim Crow segregation of its locals, that arrangement allowed black stevedores in the South to run their own locals and promoted the growth of a progressive African American leadership of the ILA in the South that continues to this day. The 1957 mural that Biggers painted in the Local 872 union hall was, like Woodruff's Amistad series, clearly within the black Popular Front public art tradition in which Woodruff, Catlett, Charles Alston, Charles White, and Jacob Lawrence worked. Again, in a cubist-inflected mode, dignified and hardworking black longshoremen labor in the foreground of the mural while militant strikers are being urged on by a black orator in the background. One might find it hard to believe that such a militant black prostruggle mural could exist in a union hall in a conservative Jim Crow Texas city in the depths of the Cold War when northern-based radical black institutions, such as the National Negro Labor Council and the journal *Freedom,* had collapsed. But the mural's existence, in addition to creating a challenge to the practice of the mainstream profession of history before the appearance of Kenneth Stampp's 1956 *The Peculiar Institution,* might also cause us to rethink some of our assumptions about the disappearance of Left influence during the Cold War era, especially in the African American community.

As a result of a greater engagement with African culture, art, and politics, Biggers's work gradually moved away from his Popular Front social realist mode toward what might be thought of as an Africanist magical realism rooted in West African folklore and style. One example is his 1966 *Birth from the Sea,* commissioned in 1964 by a public library in the oldest black neighborhood in Houston. Even in *Birth from the Sea* one does not simply see a black Venus rising on a half shell, as might be predicted from the name. Instead, in many respects the mural is as organized around labor, particularly fishing and the processing of fish, as it is culture—though it is not likely that Biggers would separate labor and culture. In short, the Popular Front lingered. It is also worth noting that the seeds of this mythic rendering of black women dressed in white and emerging from water, which draws on black Christianity and the traditional African deities (particularly the Yoruba Yemoja), was already present in his *Sharecroppers* mural, which he painted in 1946 and 1947 at Penn State University.

To close, I circle back to the 1930s and the poem that gave the title to this essay, Sterling Brown's "Remembering Nat Turner." Brown's poem was part of his long unpublished collection *No Hidin' Place,* a volume that was finished in the mid-1930s but rejected by Harcourt, Brace, the publisher of his first book, *Southern Road.* The setting of the poem is Southampton County, Virginia, site of the uprising led by Turner. The speaker of the poem, whom the reader is led to identify with Brown, and some companions question local black and white people about Turner. The African Americans are unable to recall Turner, says the speaker:

The Negroes had only the faintest recollections:

"I ain't been here so long, I come from up roun' Newsome;
Yassah, a town a few miles up de road,
The old folks who coulda told you is all dead an' gone.
I heard something, sometime; I doan jis remember what.
'Pears lak I heard that name somewheres or other.
So he fought to be free. Well. You doan say."[16]

White people remember after a fashion but are in error about practically all the particulars—among other things, melding Turner's story with John Brown's:

An old white woman recalled exactly
How Nat crept down the steps, axe in his hand,
After murdering a woman and child in bed,
"Right in this here house at the head of these stairs"
(In a house built long after Nat was dead).
She pointed to a brick store where Nat was captured,
(Nat was taken in the swamp, three miles away)
With his men around him, shooting from the windows
(She was thinking of Harpers Ferry and old John Brown).[17]

The speaker "returns" to the site of Turner's rebellion, knowing the fact of Turner's rebellion, but also knowing, unlike the white people, of the need for local African American tenant farmers to remember Turner, to have an elaborated historical narrative to put themselves (and their ancestors, such as those who revolted) at the center of this history, and to understand the uses and abuses of historical representation.

This knowledge makes the revolutionary black artist a version of Antonio Gramsci's organic intellectual, perhaps an organic historian—that is to say, not simply one who is from the working class or an oppressed minority and has found a position in the mainstream intelligentsia while retaining some connection to her or his past but an intellectual-scholar-artist generated by the class, the oppressed people, to serve its needs and further its liberation—in this case through the generation of a history and methods of telling and defending histories that are truer and more in the interest of the African American people than what exists either in the mainstream profession or popular culture. This left-wing artistic practice of revolutionary history, which presented simultaneously both a new narrative and a methodological critique, remained an important feature of African American expressive culture through the late civil rights and Black Arts eras and beyond and marked, for example, Margaret Walker's 1966 novel *Jubilee* (a work begun in the Popular Front era by a onetime CPUSA member) and the black mural movement that began with the *Wall of Respect* painted in Chicago in 1967 (and was in part the brainchild of William Walker, a muralist who had a connection to Elizabeth Catlett through his mentor Samella Lewis, a former student of Catlett's). Revolutionary history appears as well in the post–Black Arts neoslave narratives, such as Sherley Ann Williams's *Dessa Rose* (1986), Toni Morrison's *Beloved* (1987), and Octavia Butler's *Kindred* (1979), that were such a large part of the explosion of writing by black women in the late 1970s and 1980s. In short, this line of radical black history and historiography marked an enduring influence of the Communist Left on US culture long after the institutional decline and isolation of the CPUSA.

Notes

1. W. E. B. Du Bois was invited to speak at the annual meeting of the American Historical Association in 1909. He delivered a paper that was a forerunner of what became *Black Reconstruction.* When the paper was published in the *American Historical Review,* the editor refused Du Bois's request that "Negro" be capitalized. The American Historical Association would not invite another black speaker until 1940. David Levering Lewis, *W. E. B. Du Bois: Biography of a Race, 1868–1919* (New York: Henry Holt, 1993), 249–51.
2. Soyica Colbert, *The African American Theatrical Body: Reception, Performance, and the Stage* (New York: Cambridge University Press, 2011), 63–76.
3. Quite a few white artists and intellectuals participated in this Popular Front effort to recover and reframe African American (and, by extension, US) history. Some examples of this sort of work include onetime *Southern Worker* editor and southern CPUSA leader James S. Allen's 1937 history *Reconstruction: The Battle for Democracy (1865–1876),* historian Herbert Aptheker's 1943 history *American Negro Slave Revolts* (a groundbreaking study of which portions had appeared in such communist-led journals as *New Masses* and *Science & Society* as early as the late 1930s), *New Masses* staffer (and former *Southern Worker* editor) Elizabeth Lawson's historical articles and fiction in the 1930s and 1940s, and Howard Fast's 1944 novel about Reconstruction, *Freedom Road.*
4. Barbara Foley, *Radical Representations: Politics and Form in U.S. Proletarian Fiction, 1929–1941* (Durham, NC: Duke University Press, 1993), 370.
5. Arna Bontemps, *Black Thunder: Gabriel's Revolt: Virginia, 1800* (1936; reprint, Boston: Beacon, 1992), 200.
6. Alan Wald, *Exiles from a Future Time: The Forging of the Mid-Twentieth-Century Literary Left* (Chapel Hill: University of North Carolina Press, 2001), 269.
7. Bontemps, *Black Thunder,* 142.
8. Langston Hughes, *The Collected Works of Langston Hughes: The Plays to 1942,* ed.

Leslie Catherine Sanders and Nancy Johnston (Columbia: University of Missouri Press, 2002), 570.

9. Hughes, too, was fascinated with the Haitian Revolution and published a play about it (*Emperor of Haiti*), albeit focusing on Jean-Jacques Dessalines rather than on L'Ouverture, a couple of years before the appearance of *Don't You Want to Be Free?*

10. Images and useful information about the murals may be found at "Amistad Murals," "Talladega College," www.talladega.edu/academics/amistad.asp.

11. Williams, a militant National Association for the Advancement of Colored People leader from Monroe, North Carolina, during the 1950s and early 1960s became a black radical hero for his advocacy of armed self-defense against the Ku Klux Klan and other racist white groups (and for his subsequent radio broadcasts and journalism from Cuba and China after being forced to flee the country). His most extended statement of his thought was the 1962 *Negroes with Guns,* published by the left-wing press Marzani and Munsell.

12. Mary Helen Washington, "Disturbing the Peace: What Happens to American Studies If You Put African American Studies at the Center?," *American Quarterly* 50, no. 1 (1998): 1–23.

13. Catlett initially studied at Taller de Gráfica Popular supported by a Rosenwald grant. She lived in Mexico for the rest of her life, in no small part to avoid political persecution during the McCarthy era. The series never ran in the journal due to some disputes between Catlett and editors. For a listing of all the linoleum cuts and reproductions of some of them, see "Elizabeth Catlett: The Negro Woman; Series of Fifteen Linoleum Cuts, 1946–1947," National Humanities Center, www.nationalhumanitiescenter.org/pds/maai3/segregation/text5/catlettnegrowoman.pdf.

14. Claudia Jones, "An End to the Neglect of the Problems of the Negro Woman!," *Political Affairs* 28, no. 6 (June 1949): 51–67. For an excellent, concise discussion of Jones's work and its relation to black feminism and black Left nationalism, see Cheryl Higashida, *Black Internationalist Feminism: Women Writers of the Black Left, 1945–1995* (Champaign: University of Illinois Press, 2011), 20–24.

15. Olive Jensen Theissen, *A Life on Paper: The Drawings and Lithographs of John Thomas Biggers* (Denton: University of North Texas Press), 13.

16. Sterling A. Brown, *The Collected Poems of Sterling A. Brown* (New York: Harper & Row, 1980), 209.

17. Ibid.

[18]

Marx, Stalin, and Derrida: The Continuing Tension among Marxist Theory, Soviet Communism, and the Poststructuralist Revolution

Cary Nelson

It should hardly be surprising that people's willingness to embrace Marxist terminology and insights is often dependent on their level of comfort with the patterns and consequences of late capitalism. Ideological and economic comfort often accompanies willingness to accept a given political order, especially in the vast, if decreasing, middle-class constituency. The brutally disadvantaged poor can be a source of articulate class-based anger, and the well educated and relatively well off are often enough capable of serious political critique. But revolutionary resistance requires not only definitive alienation but also appropriate political movements and mechanisms for action. In the United States, the poor often enough suffer definitive alienation but lack access to or awareness of political opportunities. Some segments of the middle class are involved in progressive political movements, but overall they lack sufficiently motivated alienation. We are left with class divisions facilitating stalemate.

Still, one waits for signs of change that are more than wishful thinking, despite so much evidence of pervasive injustice and heedless risk to everyone's common interests. The twenty-first century has been witness both to increasing evidence of planet-wide environmental degradation from unchecked industrialization pursued for profit without concern for consequences and to worldwide economic collapse based on commodification of the most illusory sort. When the bundled high-risk derivatives lost all their constructed value in 2008, it was clear that there really was nothing solid to melt into air, to adapt the famous phrase from the *Communist Manifesto*. Rather, their inherent emptiness, their hollow and willfully deceptive commodification, was merely revealed but at a huge social and economic cost.

And yet the last decade has also seen melt into air much that we thought more solid, as occupations have disappeared, communities have been financially or environmentally devastated, industrial unionization has been reduced to its weakest level since 1916, and industries such as higher education, once thought secure, have been wrenched into new (and not benign) shapes. We are in a period of accelerated change and social devastation driven by business interests. More broadly, we are surely in a new, and newly destructive, phase of late capitalism, with class disparities and inequities, at least in the United States, intensified and exaggerated. Income distribution is more unjust than it has been in decades, while the poor remain largely destined to pass on their poverty to their children. Democracy's fantasy of social mobility has been reduced to a handful of Horatio Alger stories cobbled together for the media. If it is true, as many observers claim, that most people will no longer have lifetime occupations, then the rate of social and economic change has risen dramatically. The economist Joseph Schumpeter argued that capitalism propels a "perennial gale of creative destruction," but except for rapid technological development and the creation of disproportionate centers of wealth, it is hard to see evidence of that part that is creative amid all that is destructive.[1]

When the University of Illinois's Unit for Criticism and Interpretive Theory launched "Marxism and the Interpretation of Culture" in 1983—a six-week series of summer courses followed by the conference, which was the basis of the book by that title—Lawrence Grossberg and I sought to demonstrate how Marxist economic and political analysis could be applied to every cultural domain. The developments of the last decade now seem to have offered belated evidence for the success of that project, even if some core Marxist insights now circulate in a decontextualized form, severed from their roots in or engagement with Marxism.

The Occupy Wall Street movement is the most obvious example. Marxist for some and merely anticapitalist out of humanist conviction or sympathy for others, it was even subject to criticism by those ready to decry the absence of a comprehensive anticapitalist economic and political analysis. Many observers, however, did recognize Occupy's implicit opposition to the American class system and its inventive forms of exploitation, commercialization, and proletarianization. Still, its revolutionary potential—if any—cannot be said to have been fulfilled. The movement's moment in the sun has passed, along with the fantasies temporarily invested in it. The working class did not rise up in revolution during the Great Depression and seems even less likely to do so now. And perhaps that is the price of grounding economic protest primarily in liberal humanism—especially a belief that equal opportunity and a redistribution of wealth are universal values—as if transformative change can take hold without fundamental alterations in the existing class system. Hope for progressive change can fall short of any meaningful goal when a more radical analysis and agenda are called for. Indeed, I am always haunted by my own practical interventions—most notably four decades of union organizing—that run the risk, as a Leninist critique has always maintained, of making people more tolerant of their relative exploitation if it is moderated.

The Left habitually celebrates some current—and ultimately fitful—avowedly protorevolutionary social movement as a sign of wonders to come, while yesterday's failed insurrection is relegated to nostalgia. Since whatever is actually happening now has obviously not yet come to an end, it can be invested with hope in cocktail party conversations, academic meetings, and progressive journalism alike. I heard many such conversations about Occupy Wall Street. But then events intrude, the wind drops from rhetorical sails, and the meek vigil begins again to await the next carrier of hope. There are certainly long-term potential triggers for mass discontent. Global warming could eventually jeopardize world food supplies and make coastal areas uninhabitable, and the resulting conflicts would have a class component. In the short run, however, even rising income inequality is unlikely to trigger a revolution.

Despite that, some real progress has been made in producing the theoretical insights we need to understand our current situation, even if we find it hard to turn that insight into momentum for fundamental change. I would like to reflect somewhat further on one such theoretical toolbox—the volume *Marxism and the Interpretation of Culture*—because I was involved in assembling it. At the same time, I want to disrupt any generalizable theoretical claims by using an assortment of anecdotes to insist on the contingency of both memory and the work of theory. My aim in what follows is to install a certain level of discomfort with—and necessary cynicism about—theoretical reflection.

The 1983 conference on Marxism and culture was conceived in the midst of the poststructuralist revolution in theory. We tried to grapple with what Stuart Hall called "Marxism without guarantees"—that is to say, we sought to confront the tension that still haunts efforts to integrate radical real-world irresolution with a discourse that hitherto had a significant teleological component. We also knew that a viable contemporary Marxism would have to engage directly with new social movements, integrate class analysis with issues of race and gender, abandon a rigid base/superstructure model, and credit cultural work with meaningful political agency. We assumed no small series of tasks, and we recognized them as interrelated. Yet reflecting on those several goals, we have reason to think either that they have been achieved or that the discussion surrounding them has matured.

No one now engaged with critical social and literary theory would doubt that new social movements play a role in social change, even if their results can be mixed. Like it or not, both revolutionary and progressive movements can include authoritarian or repressive components and potential. The work of Ernesto Laclau and Chantal Mouffe on new social movements, both within *Marxism and the Interpretation of Culture* and outside it, was central to the effort to credit their potential. We have also seen Stuart Hall's analysis of Thatcherism borne out in the American Right's social agenda more forcefully than any of us feared at the time. The theoretical links between class and race are now largely accepted and have certainly spread well beyond the academy. The base/superstructure model has lost almost all of its restrictive purchase on contemporary theory. And cultural work, partly by way of cultural studies, has universally acknowledged agency, even if its transformative powers are often ambiguous. The classical Marxist claim that economic interest immediately trumps cultural productivity hardly gets a hearing in the contemporary academy. And the popular press is altogether willing to speculate about the work that film, music, and other cultural forms can do.

If anything, the potential for modest social or aesthetic practices to imagine or realize resistant agency would be exaggerated within a few years after *Marxism and the Interpretation of Culture* appeared. Part of what Marxism is apparently necessary for is to draw political distinctions between various supposedly resistant practices. There is a great gulf between the resistance that Stuart Hall credited to black Jamaican Christianity and the resistance that John Fiske notoriously found in plastic flowers in a lower-class vase.[2] But perhaps no challenge was greater than the call to sever the link between analysis directed toward local political conditions and a set of overriding political convictions confident of eventual fulfillment.

Paradoxically, as a result of this interconnected agenda we were already engaged with a certain decoupling of some of Marxism's key concepts. As I suggest above, Marxism as a tool kit could embrace a critique of capitalism and empower class analysis without reducing cultural phenomena to economic analysis or overlaying the base/superstructure dogma on every cultural practice. The understanding of new social movements meant that it was no longer necessary to adhere to a belief in fixed class fractions. If the project was paradoxical, that is because on one level we were weakening Marxism as a necessarily interlocked body of concepts while simultaneously trying to make some of its components more influential. Yet Perry Anderson and Fredric Jameson, among others at the conference, insisted on Marxism's teleological truths. Without some confidence in Marxism's prediction of a workers' rising, they argued, Marxism really wasn't Marxism. Others, certainly including the organizers, had no faith in the capacity of any theory to make confident long-term historical predictions or even to adopt them as plausible goals. With poststructuralism very much part of my intellectual life before the conference began—and now long since thoroughly integrated into my DNA—it is only with a mix of incredulity and nostalgia that I can recall this as a positional struggle at the time, but it was. Some participants, I should add, notably Gaijo Petrovic (1927–93), sought to suture the conflicting impulses by integrating Marxist humanism with poststructuralist theory, thereby retaining at least a cluster of revolutionary impulses while casting them into doubt.

I had a certain fondness for Petrovic, in part because of his personal history. He was in the Yugoslavian resistance in World War II and was captured and tortured by the Nazis. When a group of feminist participants, still operating with purist 1970s motivations that not only conceived gender dichotomously but also gave the redress of wrongs against women absolute priority, protested his failure to address their concerns in his course, I called them into my office and asked them to grant him some quarter. Petrovic came to me the next day and said, rather to the point, "I'll take care of myself. If I told the Nazis nothing under torture, do you think I cannot handle some American students?" As might be expected on the basis of this anecdote, Petrovic's mutual interrogation (or dismantling) of Being and revolution, categories respectively philosophical and political, was altogether degendered. In other words, he played Being and revolution against one another without considering how gender might bear on either category. But that does not mean implications for the purchase gender has on social change cannot be read into his essay: "Are revolutions condensed fragments of social progress or are progress and revolution basically as different as the constant repetition of the improved old and the free creation of the qualitatively new . . . ?"[3] It is easy enough to insert feminism into this question, asking whether progress in gaining women's rights serves or undermines the revolutionary overhaul that the patriarchal gender system requires. In the frenzy of political conviction, we often demand that others make the same commitments we do, though there are other indirect ways of interrogating current politics. What some wanted Petrovic to do in his class, however, was to make an explicit act of witness, and that he was disinclined to do. In any case, at that time we were still in a moment in which some, including Jameson, could say that the effort to address feminist concerns would have to await the revolution.

Decades later, it is often assumed that poststructuralism and historical conviction or certainty have been sutured, with poststructuralist doubt dominant not only for feminism but also for deconstruction and other key bodies of recent theory. But in fact, a certain aporia all too often lodges itself in the space between two sets of assumptions in theorized political analysis today. There are reasonably practical and straightforward ways to avoid this, first of all by characterizing political advocacy as a choice and an act of contextually based will rather than as an application of reliable universal principles. But even that decision requires vigilance, as there will be no lack of inducements in both the academy and the public sphere to claim universal application for one's values.

Equally problematic—and an equal disavowal of poststructuralist principle—is a tendency to put one set of concepts under Derridean erasure and treat another set as unshakeable. Thus, in Marxist political readings of contemporaneity, a universalizing notion of justice for the poor, Third World populations, and the working classes will be set against pervasive deconstruction of First World capital and political power. *Marxism and the Interpretation of Culture* already put at least some implicit pressure on such tendencies by way of Spivak's conclusion—troubling to many—that there were many contexts in which the voices of oppressed peoples might indeed be silent or ineffective and in Hall's suggestion that despised concepts such as patriotism should not have their meanings ceded to the Right. Indeed, if the opponent's key terms and concepts could be rigorously deconstructed, they could also be repossessed and repurposed. Interestingly enough, Hall's provocation to rethink and rearticulate concepts such as patriotism, pretty thoroughly demonized on both the Marxist and non-Marxist Left, has never really been adopted.

Although in the book's introduction we acknowledged that self-reflexiveness about Marxist critical practice was a relatively recent phenomenon, we felt confident that poststructuralism had given Marxists "the vocabulary with which to begin theorizing their own determination."[4] Thus, we urged that "the very categories of power in Marxism—such as domination, class struggle, ruling and ruled classes—have to be rethought," and we cited essays in the book showing that process under way.[5] Marxism, we added, "cannot escape the critique of essentialism carried out by contemporary critical theory."[6] Unfortunately, we were either naive, optimistic, or simply wrong. One could plausibly argue that we have in fact lost some ground on that front in the intervening decades. In what now seems painfully understated, we warned that "questioning the relationship between criticism and its object is especially difficult for any body of theory that, like Marxism, is committed to political critique and opposition."[7] That said, it may be that a certain level of political passion generates reflexive blindness. Postcolonial scholars are often skeptical about Third World nationalism, whereas those who simple invoke postcolonial categories unreflexively may be unable to achieve the same distance.

A recent example of a poststructuralist project grounded in a Marxist attention to the dynamics of state power, relations between wealth and poverty, and avowedly fundamental issues of justice—and that purports to put these categories in the context of perhaps the single most charged contemporary political debate—gives us cold evidence of how far we have and have not come in realizing the self-reflexiveness we heralded nearly thirty years ago. The argument of the 2013 collection *Deconstructing Zionism: A Critique of Political Metaphysics,* edited by Gianni Vattimo and Michal Marder, is structured by all these fault lines. One key line of argument is that Zionism is an outdated movement because it is grounded in a nineteenth-century European model of the nation-state that has exhausted its efficacy. It is simply an act of faith on the part of the authors that nations as we know them, including the United States, are about to wither away: "What is known as the form nation-state is nearing its exhaustion."[8] At least on the theoretical level, nationalism would appear to be subjected to what is fundamentally a Marxist form of deconstruction. But the desirability of a Palestinian state running from the Mediterranean to the Jordan River is held out as an unimpeachable value, an unqualified manifestation of historical justice. Palestinians are to be granted justice, as the editors write, because they are "victims of the metaphysical, onto-theological, and neoliberal state machinery, invested in keeping its despised, destitute, denigrated Others stateless and hence traceless."[9] While the editors assert that "all metaphysically inspired ideologies deserve to be deconstructed," they do not honor the principle where the devotion to Palestinian rights and statehood are concerned.[10] They fault Zionism for claiming a connection to the land that is "transhistorical and unitary," but their vision of Palestinian statehood is no less transhistorical and metaphysical.[11]

The obvious problem that the editors and contributors to *Deconstructing Zionism* face is that the father of deconstruction, despite some ambivalence, appears overall to have been a Zionist. The solution, predictably, is to say that this was one thing Jacques Derrida got wrong. But the terms in which contributors fault Derrida are revealing. "Derrida does not," Christopher Wise writes, "deconstruct the Israeli 'Law of Return,' nor does he defend the Palestinian 'Right of Return.'"[12] Of course, deconstructing one and defending the other are hardly balanced enterprises from a rigorously deconstructive perspective, but the discrepancy is justified because justice is on the side of the Palestinians. "What makes Israel 'unacceptable' as a state is its racist-colonialist-anti-egalitarian original sin."[13] Contributors also fault Derrida for sympathizing with the religiously messianic tradition in Judaism, and they quite justifiably note how disturbing such convictions can be among West Bank settlers. But nowhere in the book is the equally disturbing messianic strain in Islamic jihad, or those Palestinians who subscribe to its ideology, taken to task. "To overcome the prison-house of religion, the nation, and the state is one of the most basic necessary conditions for resolving the Palestine/Israel conflict," writes Walter Mignolo, but religion, nationalism, and the commitment to statehood are central to both parties in the conflict.[14] The only contributor who seems to suspect that this may be both a philosophical and a political quandary is Judith Butler, though she does not register the awareness here. In *Parting Ways,* however, she makes it clear that she believes that Palestinian nationalist ambitions should be honored because, unlike Israelis, they have never had a state of their own. That is not, in my view, a compelling argument, but at least she realizes that there is a problem to address in suggesting that we need to evolve beyond commitment to the nation-state, which was then endorsing Palestinian nationalism.[15]

Interestingly enough, several of the contributors to *Deconstructing Zionism* are quite sound when they look at some of the major Western powers to lay out the dynamics of late capitalism. As Slavoj Žižek writes,

> After decades of the (promise of) a welfare state, when financial cuts were limited to short periods and sustained by a promise that things would soon return to normal, we are entering a new epoch in which the crisis—or, rather, a kind of economic state of emergency—with the need for all sorts of austerity measures (cutting benefits, diminishing free health and education ser-

> vices, making jobs more and more temporary, etc.) is permanent, becoming simply a way of life.[16]

Where Žižek fails, like so many of the other contributors, is when he places late capitalism in a dichotomous relationship with an oppressed or utopian Other. Then his judgments become either bizarre or unreliable, as when he asserts (inventing a category to prove that ethnic and racial othering is now capitalism's preeminent value) that "what is increasingly emerging as the central human right in late capitalist societies is *the right not to be harassed,* which is the right to be kept at a safe distance from others," or when he finds Israel guilty of "ethnic cleansing at its purest."[17] The desire not to be near other ethnicities, of course, does not obtain in his idealized multicultural Palestinian society. Meanwhile, one would have thought that the Bosnian Genocide of 1992–95 represents ethnic cleansing at its purest. We may conclude that key projects taken up *by Marxism and the Interpretation of Culture*—to encourage self-critique and a credible fusion of Marxism and poststructuralism—remain ongoing and is fundamentally incomplete.

The Modern Language Association's guide to graduate study called *Marxism and the Interpretation of Culture* "an epoch-creating book," and within a few years the American edition issued by the University of Illinois Press sold over thirty thousand copies. Macmillan published a separate British edition, but without the luminous red dust jacket and paperback cover, based on a special ink that had abalone shell mixed in it. The ink is a nightmare to apply, because it is sticky and the paper tends to lift up and stick to the print roller. It was something of a private joke—a vivid neo-Marxist red produced by an elaborate postmodern technology—though people who asked about the color (and many did) got the explanation. I frequently think of these things when picking up a copy of the book. As a physical object, the book testifies to the political context of its inception. Although the book was to be published by the University of Illinois Press, the contract we negotiated gave us responsibility for its design. Working with the designer David Colley, a colleague from the School of Art and Design, we adopted an insistent design that would help prevent readers from abstracting the book itself from material history. After a good deal of experimentation, we chose an industrial typeface and layout that might have been used for a 1950s Soviet five-year plan. The design thus forced a dialectic between contemporary theory and Soviet culture. Indeed, the book really does not look like any other book I know; the cover was distinctive enough so that its design won an award.

Within the progressive segment of humanities and social science disciplines, then, the book was influential, but sober political self-reflection would have forced a deflated view of what, if any, political impact the book or the other work of its contributors could have on the general political culture. This was brought home in the most dramatically inflated fantasy about the American establishment's likely response to the project when one of our speakers insisted that none of us would make it through the final conference weekend alive. The Central Intelligence Agency (CIA), she repeatedly announced, would kill us all with sniper fire. I got her to risk appearing on stage only after that session's moderator, my partner Paula Treichler, agreed to scan the audience for snipers nonstop. I never doubted that the CIA was in attendance; I just doubted that it felt so threatened by us. We were concluding two months of relentlessly taking ourselves seriously. This was not the only moment when we recognized that a reality check was necessary if politics was not to succumb to losing sight of reality. There were many others.

The only real local protest came when the janitors refused to clean the restrooms for a bunch of communists, a silent protest that was only revealed when I complained that the restrooms were filthy and piled with trash. I was reminded that this was, after all, the Midwest and that this was not the most self-evident venue for the subject matter. Indeed, there was an eerie disconnect every time we surfaced from our debates and remembered where we were. At least in the middle of Illinois, the working classes were neither ready to join the revolution nor eager for any advice we might offer. But this little demonstration of class resistance only amounted to a more overt (and chastening, if absurd) version of the attitude we could have found among working Americans almost anywhere in the midst of the Cold War. As we remarked in the book's introduction, radical politics remains vexed by the question of "whether the working class is to be the source of revolutionary struggle."[18] I was reminded of that again when Henri Lefebvre remarked, in what has remained my favorite line of the conference, that "I cannot believe what cheap wine these American Marxists drink." It was not a moment of solidarity with proletarian culture. Theory and culture were always intertwined, not infrequently with comic effect.

For me, the theoretical advances that the conference and the book brought into being will always be colored by these experiential moments. And I'm not sure it is different for anyone who has negotiated academic communities while advocating for a politically inflected viewpoint or has significant public activist engagement in his or her personal history. The possibility for civil rights progress for me is always set against my first and only experience of being on the Washington Mall among a decisively integrated mass audience: the August 1963 March on

Washington for Jobs and Freedom. In some ways, the experience of the crowd matters even more to me than Martin Luther King Jr.'s historic speech. In the same way, I cannot think of possibilities for the organized Left without testing them against a series of anti–Vietnam War demonstrations in Washington, D.C.

For me, even though the red ink has dried and even though the material evidence of organization for change has been more fitful, *Marxism and the Interpretation of Culture* retains both continuing relevance and a certain stickiness, its cultural arguments remaining entangled with what we used to call "actually existing socialism." It was often necessary at the time to claim a decisive separation between Soviet communism and Marxism, despite the fact that the possibility of real-world revolutionary change haunts even the most abstract application of Marxist theory. In order to help some African attendees get travel support to attend the events, for example, I had to generate letters of invitation that removed references to Marxism in the conference title and description. Jameson and Anderson would have asserted that a Marxism without totalizing historical convictions about the eventual triumph of the proletariat was not really Marxism at all. Jameson famously opened his presentation by declaring:

> During this Marxist conference I have frequently had the feeling that I am one of the few Marxists left. I take it I have a certain responsibility to restate what seems to me to be a few self-evident truths, but which you may see as quaint survivals of a religious, millenarian, salvational form of belief.[19]

And he concluded by insisting that "it seems unlikely that anyone who repudiates the concept of totality can have anything useful to say to us on this matter, since for such persons it is clear that the totalizing vision of socialism will not compute."[20] Nancy Fraser would soon fault Jameson for a "presentation of the question of totality, which seemed to me rather irresponsible," but Darko Suvin would applaud his "refusal to equate totality with totalitarianism," which of course alluded to the Soviet elephant in the room.[21] Jameson, to be sure, recognized both the contingent nature of progress and the destabilizing character of postmodern culture, but he also believed that a viable Marxism required both long-terms goals and a predictive confidence about their achievability. That said, all of us certainly felt the lesser need to imagine alternative futures and plot contemporary alliances that might facilitate fundamental change. Strategies to promote social, political, and economic goals, however, are often voided by emerging historical realities that their advocates do not anticipate. None of us would have predicted at the time that the teaching profession would be increasingly proletarianized on the long way to world revolution. And I think that imagining the fall of the Soviet Union and the reunification of Germany, even though 1991 was less than a decade away, was beyond any of us.

History is not always unpredictable. Many observers before 1939 saw World War II coming, even if they could not imagine the scale of death and destruction it would wreak, let alone the Holocaust. Yet most often history, even in the short run, surprises us. Thus, allowing a long-term utopian goal to color short- or medium-term expectations carries risks of irrational thinking. Hall's Marxism without guarantees enables local analysis without hitching it to predicted outcomes.

When the conference proposal was being reviewed by academic committees, I steadfastly refused any necessary relationship between Marxist theory and Soviet communism or any other privileged form of social organization. Indeed, I considered colleagues who challenged Marxist theory by citing oppressive Soviet, Cuban, or East German practices to be seriously mistaken about the nature of Marxism. And yet, I was not above exploiting the connection when necessary. The National Endowment for the Humanities (NEH) gave us a grant to cover tuition and expenses for faculty members from elsewhere attending the whole eight weeks. When a diminutive local administrator refused to sign off on the grant because the NEH didn't provide indirect costs, I lifted him up in the air and firmly declared, "We've invited some of the world's most remorseless revolutionaries here. Do you realize what's going to happen when I tell them you won't let them get reimbursed for their costs?" I set him down, and he signed.

The relationship between Soviet communism in particular and Marxist theory remains a burden, in some ways a more difficult one now than at earlier moments. This problematic relation was, of course, the historical topic that first brought Alan Wald a broad national reputation, due to his still-classic 1987 book, *The New York Intellectuals*, and its thoroughly researched study of the anti-Stalinist Left. In an ecumenical move that could not easily have been anticipated, Wald went on from there to become an impeccable authority on the creative work produced by Americans closely identified with the Communist Party. I refer of course to his magisterial trilogy *Exiles from a Future Time* (2002), *Trinity of Passion* (2007), and *American Night* (2012). The reach of those three books is still wider, to be sure, but they include subtle readings of writers whose political allegiances have not always seemed so subtle in retrospect.

Although the first fissures in Communist Party loyalty came in the 1920s, the more public defections came in the following decade. Like a surprising number of others in the international community, many Americans of varying political persuasions thought that the confessions accompanying the 1936–38 Moscow show trials were genuine and uncoerced. In 1939, Communist Party members justified the Nazi-Soviet Pact as a way to avoid involvement in a destructive imperialist war; later they saw it as necessary to buy time to prepare for German aggression, even though that required bracketing the brutal Soviet takeover of half of Poland and Eastern Europe, with its widespread murder of intellectuals and political activists. The later mortality numbers in the Gulag have generally been overshadowed by the Holocaust, in part because the Holocaust has for the last few decades been widely understood not only in terms of numbers but also by way of a great many stories and human testimonies that have helped shape public memory. Of course, it is also true that significant numbers of Gulag prisoners survived, whereas few who ended up in the Nazi camps did. And the industrialized and genocidal character of the Holocaust still sets it apart.

The victims of the Ukrainian famine in the 1930s, however, remained largely de-cathected numbers for many intellectuals, at least until Timothy Snyder's 2010 book *Bloodlands* documented the famine in gruesome detail and recounted the Soviet state's Orwellian arguments justifying its actions. That was surely Stalin's most ambitious mass murder project, despite the tiny fraternity of surviving members of the Stalinist Left who deny it. I had a conversation with a member of the Modern Language Association's Radical Caucus years ago in which that member complained that claims that Stalin murdered thirty million were horrendously and inexcusably inflated; he only killed twenty million. The implication seemed to be that this qualification pretty much let Stalin off the hook.

In March 2013, Radical Caucus leader Grover Furr sent an unsuccessful letter to the *New York Review of Books* asserting that "there was no 'intentional killing [by] starvation of millions of Ukrainians' by Stalin." I am quoting from the letter as he distributed it on listservs. This was, he continued, a "myth, which originated with pro-Nazi Ukrainian nationalists in the 1950s." Since Stalin established the policies and defended them when widespread starvation escalated, I suppose this argument hinges on splitting hairs about "intentional" and about Stalin's personal responsibility for the major initiatives of the Soviet state in general and Beria's People's Commissariat of Internal Affairs in particular. I suppose the same goes for Furr's claim that "Stalin did not 'attempt' to 'eliminate much of the Polish leadership,'" either in the 1940 Katyn forest massacre or at other points, where either "attempt" or "much" are the relevant hairs. As for myself, I find that I can no longer consider comparisons between Hitler and Stalin that treat them as equivalently totalitarian dictators to be bankrupt remnants of McCarthyism. That is not to deny that Nazi Germany and the Soviet Union were vastly different political systems, but it is to recognize that these two different regimes of terror share exceptional histories of mass murder—and thus to legitimize reflection on why that was the case.

I remain attracted to the romance of communism, as Vivian Gornick called it, in its founding decade, to the artistic outpouring within the Soviet Union during the 1920s, and to the utopian ambitions of American Communists in the 1920s and 1930s, but I can no longer argue that the distortions and depravities of Stalinism were simply consequences of capitalist antagonism and aggression toward the Soviet Union. That said, the communism in the heads of many American Communist Party members in the 1920s and 1930s was not the communism that all too soon took form under Stalin after 1927. Nor is the Marxism in the heads of late twentieth-century theorists, however haunted by history, fully congruent with the history that played out in Europe from the 1930s to the fall of the Soviet Union. And I should say clearly here that the basis of my attraction to Soviet communism from 1917 to 1927—and to the work that American communists did through the 1930s—is the evidence of the utopian "cognitive mapping" that artists did during that period, which is that same political-aesthetic investment that Jameson advocated in the 1983 conference.

We know from Communist Party USA (CPUSA) records discovered in Moscow after the fall of the Soviet Union that the Comintern was centrally controlled and that it sent its US affiliate rather explicit directives. But CPUSA members nonetheless to some degree made of these orders what they would—psychologically, motivationally, argumentatively, politically, and culturally. Many Communist Party members took possession of the practices that played out—as with the Party's emphasis on race—and made them their own. Thus, as Irwin Silber details in *Press Box Red,* the *Daily Worker* took it upon itself to be the only national paper tracking Negro League baseball scores.[22] And when disputes developed, they also acquired American inflections and cultural articulations.

Tracking that mix of theoretical commonality and differences in cultural practices remains a part of the negotiations that Marxism continues to have to undertake. We set it aside, however, in what we considered the next stage of the same intellectual project, a major conference and publication of its proceedings in *Cultural Studies.* That book was still more successful at over fifty thousand copies sold, but the project both lost and gained something from efforts to decouple political analysis from an explicit Marxist signifier. As a result, American cultural studies gained thousands more academics committed to it but became a far less politically incisive movement. If objections to mutually interrogating Marxist theory and communist history are designed to insist that Marxism can be a decontextualized philosophical theory, perfectible in the abstract, then the comparison between the two books stands largely in opposition to that claim. Gayatri Spivak's "Can the Subaltern Speak," certainly the most widely debated essay in *Marxism and the Interpretation of Culture,* comes to a theorized real-world conclusion that some found a betrayal of their utopian dreams about class identity, for in many contexts, she argues, the subaltern cannot speak.[23] Whatever its teleology, Marxist theory not only needs to be tested against contemporary realities and necessities but also needs to be reformulated in light of historical developments.

Some of the Marxist political options that were alive at earlier moments have now passed into the abyss of historical marginality. I think that both Alan Wald and I have had to confront this recognition, Alan in his definitive research into the anti-Stalinist Left and then into writers strongly identified with the Communist Party itself, and myself as I came to know many surviving members of the Abraham Lincoln Brigade. Being on the anti-Stalinist Left—perhaps with a Trotskyist identity—had political valence for a time. But in the United States, it is now largely an antiquarian interest. Maoism has some acolytes but, again, no broad cultural purchase, and China now pursues a rather different economic agenda. Cuban communism faces an uncertain future. So we are left with the shadow cast by the former Soviet Union, and perhaps with a conversation I long considered politically illegitimate.

The American veterans of the Spanish Civil War are now almost all dead, and their engagements with Stalinism and/or their disengagements from it varied. Some left the party in 1939, but many remained until Nikita Khrushchev's "Secret Speech" denouncing Stalin's purges at the Twentieth Party Congress in February 1956. Others remained loyal to the Party throughout their lives. None could forget that as they faced fascist troops in Spain, it was most likely a Soviet rifle they held in their hands.

When I first met Milt Wolff, the last commander of the Abraham Lincoln Brigade, in the 1990s, he leaned forward, put his hand on my knee, and asked, "Can you believe the terrible things they're saying about poor old Joe Stalin these days?" Indeed I could. And I couldn't tell if it was a taunt or a test. So I waffled and replied that I believed some of them. In his autobiographical Spanish Civil War novel *Another Hill,* Wolff has his own character summarily (without any military proceedings) execute an American deserter during the Ebro campaign in Spain in 1938. The man kept leaving the lines, leaving his comrades vulnerable, then returning and doing it over again. The question for me was whether it was really Wolff himself or someone else who had fired the fatal shot. When I questioned several vets who were nearby at the time, they all took responsibility: "I did it." I was witnessing a collective instance of personal and political loyalty that lasted more than half a century. There is, after all, no statute of limitations on murder. Even though the shooting took place in Spain, not in the United States, a certain solidarity and courage was on display.

Many veterans took their secrets with them to the grave. Despite the close personal friendships I had developed with them over years, there were some things about Spain they would not address. What did the security service really do or not do? Family members in the CPUSA at the time were equally closemouthed. I also came to know party members who followed orders and abandoned their families to go underground for years during the worst days of McCarthyism, seeking to keep some remnant of the Party alive. I have simply never met other people with this level of political discipline, sustained over half a century and more. So that is one part of the communist legacy that Marxist theory cannot easily cast aside. I have no reason to believe that a true revolution would require any less discipline or any less courage.

In the midst of the Great Depression, it was altogether possible to believe that capitalism was coming to an end—that its economic engine was broken and could not be fixed. It may be possible to believe this once again, though capitalism's death throes could yet outlive us. The most reliable short-term predictions would include a further concentration of wealth in the hands of a few and an increasing exploitation of working people. The possibility of vast population dislocations from environmental destruction looms as nature confronts us with prospects more apocalyptic than anything else in the modern era, yet the revolution is not at hand. Recognition of capitalism's capacity to eviscerate daily life may well increase. We will need Marxism to help inform that recognition and make it articulate, and thus the legacy of Marxist theory survives. Its methodologies remain useful, applicable, viable, and timely. But the political experience of the Red decade of the 1930s and its aftermath also has its lessons for us. We dismiss either the chastening or the inspiring ones at our peril.

Notes

1. Joseph A. Schumpeter, *Capitalism, Socialism, and Democracy,* 3rd ed. (New York: Harper and Brothers, 1950), 84.
2. See John Fiske, "Cultural Studies and the Culture of Everyday Life," in *Cultural*

Studies, ed. Lawrence Grossberg, Cary Nelson, and Paula A. Treichler, 154–73 (New York: Routledge, 1992).

3. Gajo Petrovic, "Philosophy and Revolution: Twenty Sheaves of Questions," in *Marxism and the Interpretation of Culture*, ed. Cary Nelson and Lawrence Grossberg (Urbana: University of Illinois Press, 1988), 237.
4. Lawrence Grossberg and Cary Nelson, "Introduction: The Territory of Marxism," in *Marxism and the Interpretation of Culture*, 7.
5. Ibid., 9.
6. Ibid., 11.
7. Ibid., 8.
8. Walter D. Mignolo, "Decolonizing the Nation-State: Zionism in the Colonial Horizon of Modernity," in *Deconstructing Zionism: A Critique of Political Metaphysics*, ed. Gianni Vattimo and Michael Marder (New York: Bloomsbury, 2013), 71.
9. Gianni Vattimo and Michael Marder, "Introduction: 'If Not Now, When?'," in *Deconstructing Zionism*, xiv.
10. Ibid., xv.
11. Ibid., xii.
12. Christopher Wise, "The Spirit of Zionism: Derrida, *Ruah*, and the Purloined Birthright," in *Deconstructing Zionism*, 125.
13. Gianni Vattimo, "How to Become an Anti-Zionist," in *Deconstructing Zionism*, 18.
14. Mignolo, "Decolonizing the Nation-State," 60.
15. Judith Butler, *Parting Ways: Jewishness and the Critique of Zionism* (New York: Columbia University Press, 2012).
16. Slavoj Žižek, "Anti-Semitism and Its Transformations," in *Deconstructing Zionism*, 10.
17. Ibid., 11, 7.
18. Grossberg and Nelson, "Introduction: The Territory of Marxism," 10.
19. Fredric Jameson, "Cognitive Mapping," in *Marxism and the Interpretation of Culture*, 347.
20. Ibid., 356.
21. Ibid., 358–59.
22. Irwin Silber, *Press Box Red: The Story of Lester Rodney, the Communist Who Helped Break the Color Line in American Sport* (Philadelphia: Temple University Press, 2003).
23. Gayatri Spivak, "Can the Subaltern Speak?" in *Marxism and the Interpretation of Culture*, 271–313.

[19]

Jewish Radical Intellectuals in Europe and the United States

Michael Löwy

"The bourgeois and clerical anti-Semites accuse the Jews of being revolutionaries. Let us work to deserve this accusation," wrote the French Jewish radical Bernard Lazare in an 1897 essay.[1] Clearly, some important Jewish radical intellectuals were active in the nineteenth century, particularly in Germany: Karl Marx, Heinrich Heine, Moses Hess, and Ferdinand Lassalle are among the best known. But after 1890 and throughout the twentieth century, a very large presence of Jewish red intellectuals in the political and cultural spheres, both in Europe and in the United States, was visible and influential. Anti-Semites tended to compound Judaism and radicalism: Henry Ford, in his influential book *The International Jew* (1920), forged the myth of "Judeo-Bolshevism," which was to become a central tenet in Nazi propaganda. Of course, the majority of Jewish intellectuals have been mild liberals. Nonetheless, it is true that a group of key Jewish intellectuals played a significant role in radical politics and culture, beginning with Rosa Luxemburg and Emma Goldman at the end of the nineteenth century and continuing through the twentieth century. This phenomenon has lasted until our own time, although after the extermination of European Jews during World War II and the creation of the State of Israel in 1948, Jewish radicalism declined in both

Europe (where few Jews remained) and the United States. That deradicalization was reinforced by the Israeli-Arab Six-Day War of 1967.

Who are leftist radical Jewish intellectuals? What does "radical" mean? The *Concise Oxford Dictionary* defines it as "affecting the foundation, going to the root." Radicals are those leftist intellectuals and activists who want to "go to the roots" of the perceived present social evils, that is, to suppress the capitalist system and/or the state. I will not attempt a definition of "Jew"; I doubt that such a thing is possible. But I can explain what I mean by "intellectual": intellectuals do not constitute a class but rather a *social category,* a group of individuals defined by extraeconomic criteria. In concrete terms, intellectuals constitute a social category composed of *producers of cultural goods,* as opposed to simple distributors, managers, or consumers of such goods. This criterion is quite large, but it is sufficient to distinguish the *creators* of symbolic objects, who are the intellectuals sensu stricto—for instance, writers, poets, artists, philosophers, scientists, theologians, certain kinds of lecturers, journalists, and students—from a much larger mass of intellectual laborers (as opposed to manual laborers), which includes the liberal professions, many technical or managerial employees, and most of the people working in education or the media. As a social category, intellectuals have a certain autonomy in relation to social classes, which explains their frequent social and political fluctuations. This is the reason why Alfred Weber and Karl Mannheim created the concept of *freischwebende Intelligenz,* or "free floating intelligentsia." This situation of uprootedness is particularly relevant for the Jewish intellectuals of the twentieth century—often exiled, nomadic, and reduced to a marginal, unstable, and precarious condition.

Obviously, Jewish intellectuals are not a bloc and have had very different conditions and cultural developments according to specific periods in time or concrete geographic-cultural areas. My own research is primarily concerned with the radical social and political commitment of Jewish intellectuals in Central Europe during the first half of the twentieth century, that is, before Auschwitz. But starting with this specific group, one can suggest some hypotheses, some comparative propositions, regarding both European and American radical Jewish intellectuals, including the romantic/messianic currents of Central European Judaism as opposed to the more rational/profane tendencies among West and East European Jewish radicals and the differences among these three political/cultural currents from Jewish radical culture in the United States. My hypothesis is that the historical and geographical as well as political and cultural contexts, as they shape the experiences of various generations, play a decisive role in the upsurge of specific forms of Jewish radicalism.

Jewish Radical Intellectuals in Europe

Central Europe

Mitteleuropa is a geographic but above all a cultural entity. Central European Jewish intellectuals thought and wrote in German, not only in Berlin and Vienna but also in Prague, Budapest, and even Czernowitz. Adjacent to the Yiddishland—Poland and Russia, where the Jewish language and culture were Yiddish—was a Deutsch-Jüdischland, the Jewish German culture of Central Europe, that persisted in the years that follow World War I in spite of the demise of the Austro-Hungarian Empire. The mid-nineteenth century to the 1930s witnessed an extraordinary upsurge of this German-speaking Jewish culture in all areas of cultural life: Heinrich Heine and Karl Marx, Sigmund Freud and Albert Einstein, Franz Kafka and Stefan Zweig, and Georg Lukács and Walter Benjamin are only a few among the best-known figures of this golden age, comparable only to the Jewish culture in Spain during the Middle Ages.

The social condition of Jewish German intellectuals in Central Europe was quite different from their counterparts in Western or Eastern Europe. In Western Europe (France and England) Jewish intellectuals were at least integrated into bourgeois society in appearance (consider the Dreyfus Affair!), while in Eastern Europe (Russia and Poland) they were excluded and treated as social pariahs. In Mitteleuropa, the situation was an intermediary one: with an ambience of exclusion, Jewish intellectuals felt themselves to be semipariahs, in spite of their desperate attempts at assimilation to the dominant (German) culture.

The concept of pariah intellectual has been discussed by Hannah Arendt. Her proposition, inspired by the brilliant insights of the French romantic socialist (anarchist) Bernard Lazare, distinguishes the Jewish pariah intellectual, bearer of a critical (Jewish) viewpoint, from the parvenu Jews, who denied their identity and adapted themselves to the social dominant forces.[2] In a remarkable essay on Jews and Germany, Enzo Traverso discusses these two ideal/typical figures as defined by Arendt: on one side, the lineage of the parvenus, the Jews who had grown rich, utterly conformist and craving for respectability, from Bismarck's banker Gerson Bleichröder and the Rothschilds to the businessman (and briefly foreign minister) Walter Rathenau; on the other side, the hidden tradition of the pariahs, excluded and persecuted, who rebelled against the bourgeois society, such as Heinrich Heine, Franz Kafka, and Rosa Luxemburg. Unlike Arendt, however, Traverso defines the rebel pariah by his social consciousness and not necessarily by a strong Jewish self-assertion.[3]

What were the differences among radical Jewish intellectuals in Central Europe? Rather than a classical political typology—anarchists, socialists, Communists, leftist Zionists, etc.—I propose a different approach, which begins by transcending these political distinctions. Radical Jewish intellectuals in Mitteleuropa were attracted by the two poles of German cultural life, epitomized by the two famous personae of Thomas Mann's novel *The Magic Mountain* (1922): "Settembrini," the liberal, democratic, and republican philanthropist—in part inspired by his own brother, Heinrich Mann—and "Naphta," the strange, romantic conservative and revolutionary Jewish Jesuit (!), probably inspired by Georg Lukács.

The first group consisted of Enlightened (*Aufklärer*) intellectuals—partisans of Western modernity and of rationalism, unreligious and believers in progress, whether they were social democrats, Marxists, or Communists: Eduard Bernstein, Paul Singer, Max Adler, Otto Bauer, Paul Levi, and Paul Frölich, among many other examples. Trying to understand why so many Jews supported socialism, Walter Laqueur wrote:

> They gravitated towards the left because it was the party of reason, progress and freedom, which had helped them to attain equal rights. The right, on the other hand, was in varying degrees anti-Semitic because it regarded the Jew as an alien element in the body politic. This attitude had been a basic fact of political life throughout the nineteenth century and it did not change during the first third of the twentieth.[4]

This hypothesis is certainly relevant, and it helps explain why so many Jews joined the Social Democrats in Germany, with even more in Austria. However, it is not an adequate understanding of the radicalization of the romantic Jewish generation, which distrusted rationalism, industrial progress, and liberalism and would be attracted by the anarchist utopia or by Communism rather than by Social Democracy.

The second main group, the romantics, shared a critical view of industrial/capitalist *Zivilisation,* the force they considered responsible for the disenchantment of the world. Their protest against bourgeois society was inspired by nostalgia for some aspects of the premodern past. Among the romantic radicals, the anarchist Gustav Landauer and the Marxist Ernst Bloch were perhaps the most influential.

In the specific context of Central European Judaism, a complex network of links—of *elective affinities,* to use a concept (*Wahlverwandtschaft*) borrowed from Johann Goethe by Max Weber in his sociology of religion—would be established between romanticism, Jewish messianism, antibourgeois cultural rebellion, and revolutionary (socialist and/or anarchist) utopias. This messianism was not the one of Jewish orthodoxy but a new highly political version, seen through the lens of German romanticism.

Within the romantic/messianic galaxy of the Central European radical Jewish culture were two poles. The first consisted of religious Jews with radical/utopian leanings: Rudolf Kayser, Martin Buber, Gershom Scholem, Hans Kohn, and the young Leo Löwenthal. The rejection of assimilation and the assertion of a religious and/or cultural Jewish identity was the dominant aspect of their thought. Most of them were Zionists but soon left the movement (Kohn and Löwenthal) or remained but were marginalized because of their antinationalist stance (Buber and Scholem). And all shared to varying degrees a universalist utopian perspective, a sort of libertarian (anarchist) socialism that they articulated with their messianic religious faith.

The other pole consisted of the assimilated, religious atheist Jews with anarchist and/or Marxist sympathies: Gustav Landauer, Ernst Bloch, Erich Fromm, the young Georg Lukács, Manès Sperber, and Walter Benjamin. Unlike the others, they distanced themselves from Judaism without breaking all the links, especially with its messianic tradition. The term "religious atheism," used by Lukács in reference to Feodor Dostoyevski, helps us understand this paradoxical spiritual figure, who seems to search, with the energy of despair, for the point of messianic convergence between the sacred and the profane. Some of those who represented this type received in their youth a religious Jewish education (Fromm and Sperber), but most of them discovered Judaism later in life. Apart from this individual trajectory, they had in common this strange and contradictory attitude that combined the rejection of traditional religious beliefs with a passionate interest in the mystical, heretical, and Chiliastic Jewish and Christian currents. They shared a messianic/revolutionary spirituality that wove together, in an inextricable way, the threads of religion and those of radical utopias. Sympathetic to the anarchist ideals during 1914–23, most would progressively be drawn to Marxism in the following years.

Eastern Europe

Three essential elements distinguish German radical Jewish intellectuals of Eastern Europe from those of German culture: Yiddish (instead of German) culture, a highly visible political leadership in radical movements, and the rejection of religion.

Within Eastern Europe a whole literature in Yiddish, deeply rooted in the life of the shtetl (the Jewish village) and of the Jewish communities, was widespread. Authors (most of them radicals of one kind or another) such as Mendel Moicher-Sforim, Sholem Aleichem, David Bergelson, I. L. Peretz, Moyshe Kulbak, and S. Ansky—and later in the United States Sholem Asch and Isaac Bashevis Singer—created a literary universe, at the same time both authentically Jewish and of general significance, that had no equivalent in Central or Western Europe. Jewish German writers such as Arnold Zweig and Franz Kafka were fascinated by this culture, though their own literature was of a quite different kind.

The participation of Jewish intellectuals in revolutionary movements was much more important in Eastern Europe—that is, in the Yiddishland, which included the whole space of the old czarist empire—than in Central or Western Europe; a very large section, if not the majority, of the intellectuals linked to the various anarchist or Marxist groups were Jewish.

The best known are only the visible peak of the iceberg: among the Marxists Lev D. Trotsky (Bronstein), Julius Martov (Tsederbaum), Raphael Abramovich, Lev Deutsch, Pavel Axelrod, Mark Liber (Goldman), Fiodor Dan (Gurvitch), Lev Kamenev (Rosenfeld), Karl Radek (Sobelsohn), Gregory Zinoviev (Radomilsky), Jakov Sverdlov, David Riazanov (Goldendach), Maxim Litvinov (Wallach), Adolphe Joffé, Michael Borodine (Grusenberg), Adolf Warszawski, and Isaac Deutscher, and among the anarchists Voline (Vsévolod Mikhaïlovitch Eichenbaum), Efim Yartchouk, Abba Gordin, Alexander Shapiro, Aron Baron, Senia Flechine, Olga Taratouta, and Emma Goldman.

In addition to this list, there are the intellectuals linked to specifically Jewish radical organizations, such as the Bund or the leftist Zionists, as well as the Jewish intellectuals from Eastern Europe who migrated to Germany and played an important role in its labor movement: Rosa Luxemburg, Leo Jogisches, Parvus (Israel Helphand), Arkadi Maslow (Isaac Tchereminski), August Kleine (Samuel Heifiz), and many others.

This massive commitment can be explained, at least partially, by the force and violence of anti-Semitism in the czarist empire and the much higher level of oppression and poverty among the Jewish communities—in a word, the *pariah* condition of the East European Jews, a favorable breeding ground for rebellion. A significant Jewish working class, moreover, played a pioneering role in the organization of the Russian labor movement.

These revolutionary intellectuals—whether Marxists or anarchists, Bundists or Communists, leftist Zionists or socialist internationalists—all rejected religion. The romantic current tempted by the reenchantment of the world, so important in Mitteleuropa, was practically absent among them. They held instead a rationalist, atheist, secular,

Aufklärer, materialist worldview. The Jewish religious tradition, in particular the mysticism of the Kabbala, Hasidism, and messianism, were, in their eyes, mere obscurantist survivals of the past—reactionary medieval ideologies that one should get rid of as soon as possible, with the help of science and the Enlightenment. When a radical Yiddish writer addressed messianism, such as Moyshe Kulbak in his novel *Monday* (1926), it was in order to denounce the sinister role of false Messiahs such as Jakob Frank, who carried along his disciples into catastrophe.[5]

Exceptions to this schema are rare: Nachman Syrkin (1868–1924), an outsider, socialist and Zionist, Marxist and populist, Yiddish and Hebrew speaker, considered both socialism and Zionism to be modern forms of Jewish messianism. Another example is the strange case of Nikolai Maximovksi Vilenkin, religious socialist, member of the philosophic-religious association of St. Petersburg, and editor of the socialist journal *Novaja Zizn* (New Life) published by Maxim Gorki, but Vilenkin converted to Orthodox Christianity, changed his name to N. M. Minski, and thereafter had no link to Judaism.[6]

Western Europe

The West European situation differed dramatically from the Jewish intellectual experience in the other two regions. Much more integrated in the established society, Western Jewish intellectuals were not often radicals. They generally supported the dominant culture in its liberal and democratic version. This orientation stemmed from the great bourgeois revolutions in those countries—Holland, England, and France—that emancipated the Jews and permitted their economic, social, and political participation in society.[7] Upsurges of anti-Semitism, such as the Dreyfus Affair, were considered by Western Jewish intellectuals as survivals of the past, doomed in last analysis to disappear.

For example, in France one could of course find Jewish French socialist intellectuals, but they were usually moderate social democrats such as Lucien Herr, the influential librarian of the École Normale; Léon Blum, the prime minister of the Popular Front (1936); or Victor Basch, the president of the League in Defense of Human Rights who was murdered by Nazi collaborators in 1944. Such figures were liberal rationalists, men of the Enlightenment, with no inclination for romanticism or messianic/revolutionary utopias. The historian Marc Bloch came from a similar background but during World War II joined a Communist-inspired resistance movement; he was arrested and shot by the Nazis.

An exception is the symbolist (i.e., romantic) writer and anarchist thinker Bernard Lazare (1865–1903), one of the main leaders of the campaign in defense of Alfred Dreyfus. Lazare's revolutionary ideas were rooted in romanticism, that is, the cultural protest against modern bourgeois/industrial civilization that spoke in the name of precapitalist communitarian values. He was radically antiauthoritarian, an enemy of the state in all its past, present, or future forms, and a libertarian romantic. Lazare was not religious, but he celebrated the libertarian and egalitarian value of the biblical prophetic tradition. As a consequence of this tradition, he wrote, "The Jews . . . not only believed that justice, liberty and equality could be sovereigns of the world, but they thought themselves especially entrusted with the mission of working for this reign. All the desires, all the hopes these three ideals gave birth to ended up crystallizing around one central idea: that of the Messianic times, of the coming of Messiah." It is no wonder that many Jews who were involved in every modern revolutionary movement, from Leo Frankel (the communard of 1871) to Heinrich Heine, Moses Hess, Ferdinand Lassalle, and Karl Marx, this "descendant of a long line of rabbis and teachers . . . inspired by that ancient Hebraic materialism."[8]

Of course, one can find in the first half of the twentieth century several other Jewish radical intellectuals in France (and other countries of Western Europe), but most of them were immigrants from Eastern or Central Europe. Some of these figures would play an important role in French leftist culture, mainly after World War II: Lucien Goldmann, creator of an innovative Marxist sociology of culture, and Georges Haupt, historian of internationalism, both from Romania; André Gorz (Gerhart Hirsch), born in Vienna and the founder of a socialist ecology; Joseph Gabel from Budapest, a sociologist of alienation; and Maxime Rodinson, the most important Marxist historian of Islam whose Russian Polish parents immigrated to Paris in the late nineteenth century.[9] There were also a few distinguished writers among French Jewish radicals, most notably Tristan Tzara (Samuel Rosenstock), the founder of Dadaism; Gherasim Luca, the surrealist poet; and Paul Celan, one of the greatest poets in German language—all three of Romanian origin.

After Bernard Lazare, one of the first native-born Jewish radicals in France, was the brilliant surrealist photographer and essayist Claude Cahun, descended from an old French Jewish family. A lesbian living with her half sister, Cahun began as a symbolist writer but soon developed radical ideas and Trotskyist sympathies. In 1934, she was the first to formulate the surrealist views on the relation between poetry and politics and became, during the 1940s, the key organizer of the anti-Nazi resistance on the island of Jersey.

It was mainly in the 1950s (during the struggle against the French colonial war in Algeria) and in the 1960s (around May 1968) that a new generation of French-born Jewish radicals emerged. The well-known historian Pierre Vidal-Naquet, descended from an old Jewish French republican family, was, together with his friend the mathematician Laurent Schwartz, one of the important anticolonial intellectuals in France during the years of the Algerian War. Some of central figures of the student rebellion of May 1968 were Jewish radicals, such as the anarchist Daniel Cohn-Bendit; the Trotskyists Daniel Bensaïd, Janette Habel, Alain Krivine, and Henri Weber; the Maoists Alain Geismar and Benny Levy; and the outsider Pierre Goldman. During the subsequent years, they would follow quite different courses: while many, such as Daniel Cohn-Bendit, deradicalized, others such as Benny Levy became Zionists and converted to Orthodox Judaism. Some, such as Daniel Bensaïd, remained faithful to their revolutionary ideas yet also became interested in heretical Jewish messianism (often by way of Walter Benjamin's work). Pierre Goldman, whose best seller *Memories of a Polish Jew Born in France* (1975) was written in prison, died at the hands of an unidentified fascist commando. There are few equivalent Jewish figures today. It should be noted, however, that a former Jewish resister and survivor from the concentration camp of Buchenwald, Stéphane Hessel, became an international icon of the recent radical youth movements against neoliberalism thanks to his booklet, *Indignez-vous!* (2010), which was translated into dozens of languages and sold millions of copies around the world.[10]

Jewish Radical Intellectuals in the United States

East and Central European Jewish immigrants to the United States (very few had definite West European roots) tended to develop political and cultural forms of radicalism similar to those characterizing their countries of origin. Thus, from the end of the 1890s to the 1920s, Jewish radicals—anarchists and socialists—emigrated from Eastern Europe. From the end of the 1920s to the 1940s, a specific "Jewish American" radicalism with Communist or Trotskyist sympathies based in the new American-born generation took hold. Then, after a period of deradicalization in part due to McCarthyism during the Cold War, another generation emerged in the 1960s and 1970s. After another ebb from the late 1970s until the 1990s, a fourth wave began as the latest cohort of Jewish American radicals grew in the wake of the mass demonstrations of 1999 in Seattle.[11]

The Immigrant Jewish Left

The first group of Jewish radicals in the United States was composed of immigrants, several of whom had already been social or political activists in their home countries and tried to continue in the American territory similar intellectual or militant activities. Coming from the Yiddishland, primarily Russia and Poland, they arrived at the end of the nineteenth century and the beginning of the twentieth century. Emma Goldman and Alexander Berkman are illustrious examples of this group, as is Isadore Wissotsky, born in Latvia and a committed organizer of the Industrial Workers of the World. Their way of thinking and their political culture remained to a large extent those of their original East European milieu. They may have tried to adapt their socialist or anarchist principles to the American context, but one can hardly speak of a specific Jewish American radical culture. Abraham Cahan and the intellectuals around the socialist *Forverts* (the most widely circulated Yiddish daily in the world) fit this pattern as well. The same can be said of another group emerging a few years later: Moyssaie Olgin and his friends around *Freiheit,* the Communist Yiddish daily, as well as the leftist Yiddish writers such as Shalom Asch and, following him, Isaac Bashevis Singer. Immigrant backgrounds also affected the next generation. As Alan Wald has argued, the high proportion of Jews in the radical Left and especially among Communists—some 50 percent of its intellectuals—"had a solid foundation in Eastern European Jewish immigrant families; they brought to their new country . . . working-class and socialist loyalties."[12]

One can develop a similar argument concerning the Central European immigrants entering the United States after 1933 as refugees from Nazism. Their residency may have been temporary—as in the cases of Theodor W. Adorno, Max Horkheimer, and Ernst Bloch—or permanent, for those who chose to stay in the United States after World War II such as Leo Löwenthal and Erich Fromm. In both cases, the culture, interests, and style of thinking that these figures manifested were those of German Judaism. This was true too for those such as Herbert Marcuse who tried to some extent to integrate themselves in American cultural and political life.

Communist and Trotskyist Milieus

It was only among the Jewish intellectuals born or educated in the United States that one could find specific American political/cultural manifestations and the constitution of a specifically Jewish American radical intellectual. This sort of radicalism bore some similarity to the East or West European types, but significant (perhaps obvious) differences also prevailed. While Jewish radicals have had a much greater *cultural* weight in the United States than in Western Europe, far fewer eminent revolutionary political leaders emerged among American Jews than was the case among East European Jews. The comparison to Central Europe is even more striking: the romantic, messianic, revolutionary Jewish culture of Mitteleuropa had very few equivalents among Jewish American radicals. Communist poet and writer Joseph Freeman was one of the rare exceptions in this regard. Born Yosef Yehuda Arye ben Yitzhak Aaron Halevy in Ukraine in 1897, Freeman was raised, after emigrating in 1904, in America. On March 1, 1951, many years after his exclusion from the Communist Party, he wrote a moving letter to his friend Floyd Dell. Discovered by Alan Wald, it contains a passage that Wald describes as "the clearest personal confession on record of the Jewish-American Messianic appropriation of Communism."[13] As a child, Freeman recalled, he had daydreams of the Messiah

> riding in his traditional white horse as he came to redeem us from exile and suffering. Eventually the Messiah did come for me; he came with hammer and sickle in hand to redeem the whole of mankind. But this savior, like all his predecessors, failed to leave behind him the promised land of universal justice and love. Nevertheless my verse continues to the chiliastic. . . . I cannot surrender my belief . . . that in the end man will free himself of evil and develop his godlike potentials to the full.[14]

This moving passage has obvious affinities with the Jewish "religious atheists" of Central Europe, such as Ernst Bloch and others. In contrast to them, however, Freeman's confession appeared in a strictly personal letter and not a public document that sought to develop a theoretical argument.

Yiddish culture or Jewish history may have been a source of inspiration for many Jewish American radicals, but very seldom did religion or messianism play that role. In a February 1930 article titled "Religion and the Good Life," Felix Morrow argued that the dynamic element in Judaism could be characterized more as an ethical tradition than a religion, and on this point he probably spoke for many of his generation's Jewish radical intellectuals.[15] Morrow's article appeared in the *Menorah Journal,* a remarkable Jewish journal begun in the 1920s that drew around it a brilliant group of leftist intellectuals: Elliot Cohen, Lionel Trilling, Herbert Solow, Felix Morrow (Mayorwitz), Clifton Fadiman, and Tess Slesinger. Most of these writers, who bore a cosmopolitan sensitivity, became Communists or Trotskyists during the 1930s. Comparing this group with the European Jewish intellectuals, Wald grasps in very precise terms the specific situation of the radical Jewish American intelligentsia:

> In the United States, the *Menorah Journal* writers and their contemporaries (usually second generation immigrants) were neither outcasts, as were the east Europeans, nor deeply integrated into the existing society and its established values, as were the English and French Jewish intelligentsia. The interwar years in the United States were marked by potentially radicalizing factors, such as the existence of a substantial Jewish working class and the persistence of a virulent anti-Semitism. Thus all wings of the radical movement in the United States experienced a considerable influx of Jewish intellectuals in the 1930s.[16]

Together with Phillip Rahv (Ivan Greenberg) and William Phillips (Litvinsky), some of the Jewish radicals from the *Menorah Journal* went on to create *Partisan Review,* which became increasingly sympathetic during the late 1930s to Leon Trotsky. The members of this group, the so-called New York Intellectuals, were perhaps the most "European" of the Jewish American radicals because of their admiration for the great European literary modernists: Marcel Proust, Franz Kafka, James Joyce, and even T. S. Eliot.

While Jewish religion was seldom relevant in their lives, American Jewish radicals, particularly (but not only) around the communist journal *New Masses,* demonstrated a certain romantic tendency not unlike that of the historic German Jewish community. An obvious example is the Communist writer Michael Gold, whose best work offered "a dazzling blend of proletarianism, bohemianism, [and] romanticism," Wald writes.[17] Unlike other Jewish Communists, who often were "non-Jewish Jews" as Isaac Deutscher identified the type, Gold was deeply immersed in Jewish (Yiddish) culture.[18] His celebrated novel *Jews without Money* (1930) is a direct reflection of his romantic/populist commitment to his community. The social and cultural critic Lewis Mumford, who met the young Gold before World War I, recalled years later that he was "a passionate, brilliant, vehement youth . . . a romantic and an anarchist, closer to Rousseau and Stirner than to Marx."[19] But even after his conversion to Communism, the romantic component remained alive—for instance in Michael Gold's enthusiastic endorsement of a quintessential American romantic poet, Walt Whitman, to whom he dedicated his 1935 "Ode to Walt Whitman."[20] There were also some messianic moments in Gold's writings. One of them is a tender but ironic reference to childish hopes: brutalized by an anti-Semitic gang, a Jewish boy dreams of the Messiah as a sort of Buffalo Bill, riding on a white horse and using his guns to defeat the enemies of the Jews! Gold's most important statement of secularized messianism, however, appeared as the conclusion of the first edition of *Jews without Money* (though it was suppressed in later editions): "O worker's Revolution, you have brought hope to me, a lonely, suicidal boy. You are the true Messiah. You will destroy the East Side when you come, and build there a garden for the human spirit."[21]

Antifascism, commitment to the Spanish Republic, and connection with socialist, Communist, or Trotskyist parties were common to most European and American Jewish radicals. Similarly, a range of varied literary techniques from social realism to modernist experimentation, which sometimes appeared in creative combination, tied them together. What most distinguished the Americans from their European counterparts was the primacy of literary intellectuals among Jewish radicals in the United States and their focus on American themes such as race.

Primacy of Literary Intellectuals

Mike Gold is just one example of a surprisingly large group of Jewish American radical writers. With far fewer radical political leaders in the United States than in Eastern Europe—with the exception of the small Trotskyist groups, where a great many Jews played important roles (Max Shachtman, George Breitman, George Novack, Albert Glotzer, Albert Goldman, Martin Abern, and many others)—most Jewish American radicals belonged to the realm of the literary and artistic culture. Unlike in Central Europe, however, there were few philosophers, with one exception being Sidney Hook.

Gifted writers among the Jewish American radicals included Nelson Algren (Nelson Abraham), Ben Barzman, Alvah Bessie, Vera Caspary, Guy Endore (Samuel Goldstein), Howard Fast, Kenneth Fearing, Michael Gold (Irwin Granich), Lillian Hellman, Norman Mailer, Arthur Miller, Clifford Odets (Gorodetsky), Tillie Olsen (Lerner), Dorothy Parker (Dorothy Rothschild), Abraham Polonsky, Muriel Rukeyser, John Sanford (Julian Shapiro), Irwin Shaw (Irwin Shamforoff), Budd Shulberg, Jo Sinclair (Ruth Seid), Tess Slesinger, and Nathanael West (Nathan Weinstein), among many others.[22] There is no equivalent list of Jewish radical writers in any European country.

Unlike most of their European counterparts, many of these authors were willing to participate in popular culture, writing detective novels, pulp fiction, or film scripts. The impressive presence of Jewish radicals in Hollywood as screenwriters and filmmakers is a chapter in itself, with no equivalent in Europe. Six of the so-called Hollywood Ten persecuted by McCarthyism in 1950—all gifted screenwriters—were Jews: Alva Bessie, Herbert Biberman, Lester Cole (born Lester Cohn), John Howard Lawson (Levy), Albert Maltz, and Samuel Ornitz.[23] Several blacklisted filmmakers would later be celebrated: Herbert Biberman for *The Salt of the Earth* (1954), about a miner's strike; Abraham Polonsky for *Tell Them*

Willie Boy Is Here (1969), a Western focused on Native Americans that Polonsky made into an allegory about racism, genocide, and persecution; and Martin Ritt for *The Front* (1975), a film about the television blacklist of the 1950s.

The American Themes

It should be emphasized that writers and artists were not the only Jews attracted to radical movements. Roughly 40 percent of Communist Party members in 1939 were Jewish, and one could perhaps find similar percentages among the smaller Trotskyist groups. Nonetheless, the field of cultural production in which Jewish American radicals flourished was further distinguished from the European scene by the specifically American topics that came to define their work. Paramount among these have been particular American heroes and positive American traditions—or, on the contrary, resistance to social injustice in American history, such as the extermination of the Native Americans and, above all, the oppression of African Americans by slavery and racism.

A striking example of a positive reception of American traditions by Jewish radicals is Noam Chomsky. He presents his anarchism, or libertarian socialism, as an ongoing pursuit of classical liberalism and Jeffersonian democracy. Like many other Jewish American radicals, Chomsky defines himself as a son of the Enlightenment, opposed to all forms of "irrational beliefs."[24] He claims that an important and visible red thread leads from Cartesian rationalism and the Enlightenment (Immanuel Kant, Alexander Humboldt, and even Adam Smith) to the anarchist ideas he espouses.[25] But Chomsky also insists—and this is less obvious—that criticism of the state is "as American as apple pie"; many representatives of the "old American tradition," such as Thomas Jefferson, denounced the "coercive power of the State," and it is not an accident that anarchist thinkers have often responded favorably to the American experience and to the Jeffersonian idea of democracy.[26]

Other Jewish radicals have chosen a different set of heroes: rebel African Americans. In addition to antiracism, a passionate identification with the suffering and struggles of African Americans has long been a strong component of this Jewish American radical culture. One of the reasons was certainly the association between antiblack racism and anti-Semitism—between the lynching of African Americans and pogroms against Jews in Europe (and Nazi anti-Jewish atrocities). Also, as Wald aptly observes, "the view that anti-Black racism was the symptom of an inegalitarian capitalist economic order that was dangerous for Jews and other oppressed groups" was reinforced in the wake of the Depression.[27]

Of course, Jews had no monopoly on American antiracism: internationalism and the solidarity with the oppressed were key elements of leftist culture generally. But the history of the Jews as a persecuted minority contributed to reinforcing this empathy, leading many Jewish radicals to write novels whose heroes were African American rebels. Indeed, this empathy was not one-sided but mutual: many leading African American radicals, such as W. E. B. Du Bois and Paul Robeson, not only denounced anti-Semitism but also showed an active sympathy with the Jewish minority. As Nicole Lapierre writes in her book on common struggles borne by blacks and Jews in the world, *empathy* was not humanitarian compassion but a solidarity based on respect and reciprocity.[28]

Some writers, such as Guy Endore, celebrated slave rebellions in their novels, such as *Babouk* (1934); John Sanford praised the antiracist revenge of an African American female protagonist in *The People from Heaven* (1943). Interestingly, both novels were criticized by Communist Party officials for being ultraleft and too influenced by black nationalism.[29] Many Jewish Communists—such as the poet Aaron Kramer, author of a pamphlet-poem, *Denmark Vesey* (1952), celebrating the hero of a Negro slave revolt—felt that they had a "Black soul," and not by accident; the founding editor of the famous African American magazine *Ebony* (1945) was a Jewish Communist, Ben Burns (Benjamin Bernstein).[30] Jewish radical poets such as Martha Millet and Eve Merriam wrote about African American struggles for Communist publications, and Ed Lacy (Len Zinberg) in his novel *Room to Swing* (1957) invented the first African American "private investigator," Toussaint Marcus Moore—an obvious homage to Toussaint L'Ouverture, the great leader of the Haitian slave rebellion.[31]

Many Jewish red writers, such as Earl Conrad (Earl Cohen), author of *Harriet Tubman: Negro Soldier and Abolitionist* (1942), created rebellious blacks as their spokespersons. A fellow traveler of the Communist Party, Conrad worked for the New York office of the African American newspaper *Chicago Defender* and published popular books excoriating racism, such as *Jim Crow America* (1947) and *Scottsboro Boy* (1950). Conrad never depicted Jewish characters in his novels nor wrote about Jewish matters in his other books. However, in his notes for the autobiography he was completing when he died in 1986 (discovered by Wald), Conrad started by referring to himself as "a Twentieth Century Abolitionist." He then made a startling statement, never appearing in any of his published writings: "My interest in the 'underdog,' the submerged or oppressed, in particular the blacks, had Judaic origins." Wald adds the following insightful commentary:

> Conrad might be regarded as a characteristic type on the Jewish Literary Left. He was not an assimilationist by any fair definition because he did not assume the dominant middle-class Christian culture of his society. But he did not identify as Jewish positively by a fair definition, either, because there are no references to anything in Jewish religion or culture that served him well. His Jewish heritage was mainly felt through an awareness that Jews had been and still were victimized by bigots; this led him to take an internationalist identity that required him to champion the cause of what he believed to be the most oppressed group in his own society, African Americans.[32]

Perhaps the most archetypical representative of the Jewish American radical intelligentsia was the writer Howard Fast, in whose books one can find all the non-European peculiarities I have mentioned. A member of the Communist Party from 1943 to 1956, blacklisted, persecuted by the House Un-American Activities Committee, and imprisoned, Fast authored many very popular novels, some of which (such as *Spartacus*) became motion pictures. He wrote three books on the American Revolutionary War period: *Conceived in Liberty* (1939), *The Unvanquished* (1942), and *Citizen Tom Paine* (1943). He also paid homage, however, to the struggle of American Indians in *The Last Frontier* (1941), concerning an attempt by the Cheyennes to return to their native land, as well as to the fight of African Americans against racism in the nineteenth century in *Freedom Road* (1944), prefaced by W. E. B. Du Bois. *Freedom Road* became a worldwide sensation; it has been called one of the most widely printed and read books of the twentieth century.[33] Based on a true story, it describes the life of Gideon Jackson, leader of a group of former slaves during Reconstruction. Abandoned by the federal government, Jackson and his friends take up arms to defend their families against the Ku Klux Klan, but they are defeated and murdered. *Freedom Road* fit perfectly into the specific radical Jewish American empathy with the ordeal of African Americans. News about Auschwitz affected Fast's writing of this antiracist book: "Reports were beginning to filter out of Germany about the destruction of the Jews. All the notes and thinking that I had done for a novel about Reconstruction came together—and every moment I could steal from my work at the OWI [US Office of War Information] was put to writing the new book."[34]

Like novels by Guy Endore and John Sanford, Fast's *Freedom Road* celebrates ex-slaves who take up arms and fight for their freedom against white racism. And these ideas of African American self-defense and armed struggle put the authors at odds with the Communist Party, which did not advocate such radical policies either in 1934 (when *Babouk* was published) or in 1943 (*The People from Heaven*)—and even less so in 1944 (*Freedom Road*), when, under Earl Browder, the Communist Party

USA was officially dissolved for the sake of "national unity" during the war. No party line but rather strong antiracist feelings and a profound identification with the destiny of African Americans nourished these unique Jewish American literary explorations.

Postwar Resurgence (New Left)

A new generation of Jewish radicals appeared in the 1960s around the New Left, the civil rights movement, and the protest against the Vietnam War. Among this generation's best-known representatives were poets and musicians, such as Allen Ginsberg, Bob Dylan (Robert Zimmerman), Phil Ochs, Adrienne Rich, and Philip Levine; feminist writers, such as Marge Piercy, Betty Friedan, Shulamith Firestone, and Susan Brownmiller; and radical intellectuals, such as Abbie Hoffman, Jerry Rubin, Howard Zinn, Nathalie Zemon Davis, Leslie Cagan, Noam Chomsky, Mark Rudd, Susan Sontag, Todd Gitlin, and the attorney William Kunstler.

To this, one could add that in 1962, one-third of the students who attended the Port Huron conference of Students for a Democratic Society (SDS) were Jewish. Jews made up a majority of the Steering Committee of Berkeley's Free Speech movement in 1964. There was a disproportionately large number of Jews among the 1961 Freedom Riders, and of three civil rights martyrs in the Mississippi Freedom Summer of 1964, two—Andrew Goodman and Michael Schwerner—were from left-wing Jewish families.

The Latest Wave

The most recent wave of Jewish radicalism among intellectuals emerged after the large Seattle demonstrations against the World Trade Organization in 1999. Although not as massive as the radical wave of the 1960s, this latest Jewish American radical cohort has developed a rather high profile. One can find several of its representative figures around the Global Justice movement or, more recently, the Occupy Wall Street initiative. Among the best known are several women such as Roseanne Barr, the popular television actress and presidential candidate for the Peace and Freedom Party in 2012; Naomi Klein, social activist and author of *No Logo* (2000), a radical critique of corporate globalization that became an international best seller; and the feminist philosopher Judith Butler.

Far from being constant across time and space, the political cultures of Jewish radical intellectuals vary significantly according to the different generations and the distinct European and American contexts that have spawned them. The comparative approach I have offered, taking into account historical developments, cultural dimensions, and social-political conditions, may help us to understand, at least to some extent, these particularities. As one would expect, many questions remain unanswered. How and why did so many Jewish American intellectuals become radicals (at least until the mid-twentieth century and to some extent even today) when there existed in the United States no mass radical parties and no mass socialist or Communist parties of the sort that flourished in Eastern and Central Europe and to some extent Western Europe, as in France? To that question, as yet I have no answer.

Notes

1. Bernard Lazare, "Le prolétariat juif devant l'antisémitisme," in *Juifs et antisémites*, ed. Philippe Oriol (Paris: Allia, 1992), 155–56.
2. Hannah Arendt, *The Jew as Pariah: Jewish Identity and Politics in the Modern Age* (New York: Grove, 1978).
3. Enzo Traverso, *Les Juifs et l'Allemagne: De la "symbiose judéo-allemande" à la mémoire d'Auschwitz* (Paris: La Découverte, 1993).
4. Walter Laqueur, *Weimar: A Cultural History, 1918–1933* (New York: Putnam, 1974), 73.
5. See Racher Ertel's introduction to Moyshe Kulbak's novel *Lundi* (*Montog*, 1926) (Lausanne: L'Âge d'Homme, 1982). A similar viewpoint can be found many years later, in Isaac Bashevis Singer's novel *Satan in Goray* (New York: Noonday, 1955).
6. See Jutta Scherrer, *Die Petersburger Religiös-Philosophischen Vereiningungen* (Wiesbaden: Otto Hannassowtiz, 1973), 44, 272.
7. Holland is one of the most evident examples of Jewish integration into bourgeois society. There are few Jewish radical intellectuals: Abraham Soep, who was active in the socialist movement in the Netherlands and later became one of the founders of the Belgian Communist Party; Saul "Paul" De Groot, for many decades the indisputable leader of the Dutch Communist Party; among the Trotskyists Sal Santen, who had been active against the war in Algeria; and in the younger generation Joost Kircz, Marxist scientist and philosopher.
8. Lazare, *Antisemitism: Its History and Causes* (New York: International Library, 1903), 285–94, 310–17.
9. One could mention also, in a different cultural sphere, the famous leftist photographers Robert Capa (Endre Friedmann, Budapest), Chim (David Szymin, Warshaw), and Gerda Taro (Gerda Pohorylle, Stuttgart), who became famous for their photos of the Spanish Civil War.
10. We cannot discuss here the other West European countries. For instance, in Belgium during the 1940s we have two eminent Jewish Marxist (Trotskyist) intellectuals: Abraham Leon, born in Warsaw, and Ernest Mandel, born in Frankfurt. Leon, author of a classic essay on the materialist conception of the

Jewish question, died in Auschwitz, while Mandel survived internment in several concentration camps and after the war became one of the best-known Marxist economists and a leader of the Fourth International.

11. My comments on Jewish American radicalism in the second part of this essay are based on the fascinating and insightful writings of Alan Wald on the history of leftist culture in the United States. But I am alone responsible for possible mistakes or misinterpretations.
12. Alan Wald, *Trinity of Passion: The Literary Left and the Antifascist Crusade* (Chapel Hill: University of North Carolina Press, 2007), 180.
13. Alan Wald, *Exiles from a Future Time: The Forging of the Mid-Twentieth-Century Literary Left* (Chapel Hill: University of North Carolina Press, 2002), 191.
14. Ibid.
15. Alan Wald, *The New York Intellectuals: The Rise and Decline of the Anti-Stalinist Left from the 1930s to the 1980s* (Chapel Hill: University of North Carolina Press, 1987), 48.
16. Ibid., 45.
17. Wald, *Exiles from a Future Time,* 39.
18. Isaac Deutscher, *The Non-Jewish Jew and Other Essays* (London, Oxford University Press), 1968.
19. Wald, *Exiles from a Future Time,* 47.
20. Ibid., 62–63.
21. Michael Gold, *Jews without Money* (New York: Carroll and Graf, 1984), 309.
22. Such as, for instance, Nathan Asch (the son of Sholem Asch), Maxwell Bodenheim, Stanley Burnshaw (Bodenheimer), Edward Dahlberg, Daniel Fuchs, Albert Halper, Walter Lowenfels, Carl Rakosi, George Oppen, Edwin Rolfe (Solomon Fishman), Henry Roth, Leane Zugsmisth, and Louis Zukofsky. The Jewish names in parenthesis are those they received from their parents (although in some cases the father had already Americanized his name).
23. Wald, *Trinity of Passion,* 182.
24. Noam Chomsky, *Chronicles of Dissent: Interviews with David Barsamian* (Monroe, ME: Common Courage, 1992), 118.
25. Noam Chomsky, "Notes on Anarchism," introduction to Daniel Guérin, *Anarchism* (College Park, MD: Spunk, 1970), 12.
26. Robert F. Barsky, *Noam Chomsky: A Life of Dissent* (Cambridge, MA: MIT Press, 1997), 137.
27. Wald, *Trinity of Passion,* 185.
28. Nicole Lapierre, *Causes Communes: Des Juifs et des Noirs,* Un ordre d'idées Collection (Paris: Stock, 2011), 300. On the strong links between Jewish and African American radicals in the United States, see Alan Wald, "Jewish American Writers on the Left," in *The Cambridge Companion to Jewish American Literature,* ed. Hana Wirth-Nesher and Michael P. Kramer, 170–89 (Cambridge: Cambridge University Press, 2003).
29. Wald, *Writing from the Left: New Essays on Radical Culture and Politics* (London: Verso, 1994), 178–86, 199–211.
30. Wald, *Trinity of Passion,* 179, 184.
31. Other examples can be found in Wald, "Jewish American Writers on the Left."

32. Ibid. 183–84.
33. Wald, *Trinity of Passion*, 193–94.
34. Howard Fast, *Being Red: A Memoir* (New York: Laurel Trade, 1990), 75. Fast also wrote a novel on Jewish history, *Our Beloved Brothers* (1948), about the Maccabean rebellion. It is far from being his best, but it became very popular among Zionists.

[20]

The Present of Future Things

Alan Wald

Scholars make their own personae, but they do not make them just as they please.[1] Handcuffed to history, I address the field of the Literary Left in ways that cannot be detached from the succession of highly charged, contextualized experiences shaping and reshaping my life. Summing up the composite autobiographical figure emerging from these unceasing engagements is like taking aim at a moving target. A BuzzFeed version would read "Twenty-five Surprising Things You Didn't Know about Alan Wald." I have been tracking my great white whale of Literary Radicalism since high school. Then, during the events of the 1960s, a rendezvous with culture and the Left crystallized into a lifelong pursuit. That decade turned out to be the political Rorschach test of my generation; the passion of its victories and defeats formatted me forever. My scholarly writings will never be understood by reading backwards through my professional career at the University of Michigan; academe was not an end but a vehicle through which other needs and goals might be fulfilled.

As Derek Walcott wrote in *Midsummer,* "To curse your birthplace is the final evil."[2] When history intruded in my existence as an undergraduate at Antioch College, my birthplace was conclusively established. I seized upon Marxism (via Jean-Paul Sartre and Richard Wright) as a compelling if partial and imperfect ethical criticism of the exploitative and imperialistic dynamics that coexisted with Western society's remarkable achievements. In the worldwide eruptions of 1968, I thought I saw a new kind of society in the making through the international alliance of student rebels and working-class militants, the visionary grammar of a historical process suggested by class analysis combined with the imaginative liberties of a metaphor stemming from hope. An observation by Leon Trotsky, Marxism's stern superego, might suggest why such yearnings, their birthplace still uncursed, are with me some forty-five years later: "Ideas that enter the mind under fire remain there securely and forever."[3]

More puzzling is psychology, the life of subterranean passions coiling beneath the surface of the various roles that one serially inhabits. Perceiving the world on dual channels, we grapple with disparate temporal regimes generating the inner, elusive contradictions that define our characters. Mine oscillates between hotheaded emotions, sensing everything at once, and a calibrated intellect relentlessly deciphering how one thing follows another. This leaves me with an inability to resist *any* opportunity to interpret, rushing to hasty judgment too often, and with recurrent aspirations at odds with my temperament and talent. I am convinced that a lack of self-knowledge makes self-deception probable, but how does one differentiate between emotional and factual truth in the realm of hard-wired memories?

Matters that are private, the restless ghosts of my universe, are also the ones that obstinately resist the voicing that precedes comprehension. The traumatizing loss of my father prematurely in 1981 and then the loss of my mother in 2003 brought increased appreciation of their impact on my early life yet not much more. The death of my first wife, Celia, at age forty-five in 1992 after a decade of illness, remains a knotted emotional ache that I will carry to the grave. (Happily this has been offset by the bliss of my romantic partnership with Angela Dillard since 2001.) Curiously, most of my longtime friends, a number of them former students but usually political or scholarly associates, are either a decade or so younger or five to ten years older; almost none are exact contemporaries. As my enemies grow older, I am luckily free of lasting resentments against even those people who aimed to do me harm, yet petty humiliations and embarrassments (including tiny factual errors in my work and some poorly written sentences) are as vivid as ever. I can coolly explain my attraction to literary narratives of exile, unreliable memory, and uneasy citizenship, and all the whys and wherefores for my recoil from those who substitute ideological certainties for the messiness of experience. But I am flummoxed to account for my ironic/sardonic sense of humor that serves largely as an emotional defense as well as my lapses into complete silence in many conventional social situations.

The Making of a Literary Radical

Born in June 1946 in that narrow gap between the closing of World War II and the advent of the Cold War, I was understandably devoid of nostalgia for the preceding era of economic deprivation and the brutalities of the Holocaust. Both were obsessive topics of my tempestuous mother. As soon as I became conscious of the world I never made—one rendered stifling by the hearings of the red-hunters that crowded our tiny television screen, and the air-raid drills (to ward off nuclear bombs) that were a normal part of the school day—I responded with a kind of wary numbness. No matter where I lived—and we moved often, as my father's career on the President's Council of Economic Advisors with Leon Keyserling was interrupted by McCarthyism in 1953—I was keen to move on again.[4] It was my gentle, mild father who regularly read to me, first *Treasure Island* and then *Moby Dick,* which he had studied in an English class at Clark University with a young Charles Olson. After that I was hypnotized by volumes I saw in libraries, on drugstore racks, and in the family study. Emily Dickinson expressed the reason well: "There is no Frigate like a Book / To take us Lands away."[5]

With a sister born three years before and a brother coming nine years after, I knew something of the middle child syndrome: a feeling of being left out and invisible, in contrast to the older child who benefits from all the firsts and the younger who profits from being the baby of the family. But perhaps I just didn't want to put myself out there to be judged by others. I was not at all precocious as a child or young person, compared with my thriving siblings. As a public school student, I had little going for me academically (unlike my sister, gifted in science) or socially (unlike my brother, handsome and athletic). My mother and father, deeply bonded to the New Deal variety of Left liberalism and leading participants in various conservative Jewish synagogues as we moved about, had great expectations of a most conventional nature for all three of us. Nonetheless, I was mired in a fog of mediocrity triggered by a belief that I really had no worthy voice of my own. Still, as they say, you should always keep an eye on the quiet ones.

My parents were both born in 1916, Haskell Wolkowich (he changed his name to Wald in 1938) in Worcester, Massachusetts, and Ruth Jacobs, in Glens Falls, New York, although she soon moved to New Haven, Connecticut. They came from generically poor immigrant families of East European—Polish, Russian, Lithuanian—Jewish backgrounds. My grandfathers spoke with accents and held unskilled jobs, such as working behind a drugstore counter or collecting premiums for a Jewish burial society. Marrying in 1939, Haskell and Ruth were a tall, slim, attractive, and active young couple, returning to graduate school at one point to earn, respectively, a PhD in economics and an MA in educational psychology from Harvard University. In contrast, I felt ungainly, lethargic, ordinary, and alienated, haunted by a feeling that I was embarked on a cryptic quest. This was to be a lonely one, concerning only myself; there was no notion that I might acquire knowledge to guide or sustain others. I would always remain both fascinated by and at arm's length from those who could present their opinions as authoritative.

Figure 20.1. Alan's father, Dr. Haskell P. Wald, né Wolkowich, New Deal economist, 1940s. Credit: Personal collection of Alan M. Wald.

At first I consumed the books that came my way through family and friends. This started with my father's musty old set of the science-minded *Tom Swift* series, followed by my own collecting of *Tom Swift, Jr.* (I was already something of a completest). Next there was the *Tom Corbett, Space Cadet* series (1952–56), along with detective mysteries beginning with the *Hardy Boys* and growing into Brett Halliday's *Mike Shayne* novels, with an intermittent Mickey Spillane read furtively under the covers. As I had some temporary fascination with the military, my father gave me a paperback of James Jones's *From Here to Eternity* (1951) when I was twelve, suggesting that I might learn something about sex in its pages. The search for more sex led to Irwin Shaw, Leon Uris, Norman Mailer, and other World War II writers.

As I began to pick out literature for more philosophical reasons, I was pulled toward politically radical fiction. Perhaps I was born with a Kafka-like rebel Jewish disposition, but the affinity grew deeper as a consequence of the time in which I was coming of intellectual age—that of the beats blending into the civil rights movement. At first the allure was to writers I saw as antielitist literary intellectuals, certainly not professors or scholars. My inner Holden Caulfield, my adolescent loathing of respectability, led me toward characters and authors who were outsiders; my prime literary love was the strike organizer Mac in John Steinbeck's *In Dubious Battle,* who looked like "a scholarly prizefighter, pecking slowly at a typewriter."[6]

I soon understood that, in some baffling way, I would be a writer myself. My earliest experiments, with science fiction and then in composing the story line for *Mad* magazine–type comic strips that a talented Hebrew School friend drew, showed me how writing becomes a means of mastering surroundings, enabling one to gain an almost magical power over emotions, uncertainties, and desires. At the least, typed communications differed from less controlled interactions in that they could be edited and rewritten before going out into the world. A toy printing press enabled me to produce miniature newspapers and magazines for a few friends and myself. Some short stories gained praise from teachers and were published in the school magazine.

Yet I understood instantly, and permanently, that my destiny as a writer would be that of a very minor figure—which suited me fine. Moreover, to be a writer did not mean to become a literature student. This seemed unlikely, as I lacked the fantastic ear and verbal recall of my classmates. Rather, writing was about seeing my life as a long struggle against hidden constraints, leaving me no alternative but to write my way out to freedom. Looking back on my meager literary gifts, I realize that I was blessed mainly with an imaginative freedom that approached surrealism yet never quite crossed the border. I was fascinated with metaphoric poetry and prose that translated the world from one realm of perception into nearly its opposite, which I found instantly in Blake, Nietzsche, Rimbaud, and the like. At the same time, I was both drawn to and cautious about theory. To apply an interpretative concept from Freud (an early interest) to a work of art was exciting. But what if one were to impose it to the point of reordering the work's priorities, excising from vision its subtleties? This caution, a paranoia about being guilty of misrepresentation, was of a piece with an understanding that whatever writing I would do would be generated by a minor ambition—or rather, a great ambition for what I knew would be only minor accomplishments.

I felt that I lacked grand ideas and thought that whatever I wrote would be a practitioner's work (short fiction, journalism, reviewing), not a theorist's, because I simply had no ability to create a system of ideas. My grasp of history and sociology were fuzzy, too. Usually at a loss for either a form or subject matter, I felt as if I were on an odyssey, by metro, in the depths of my self-absorbed psyche, with connecting stops in imaginary states gleaned from television and popular culture: I was an ordinary guy with a factory job, a hitchhiker on the road, a struggling literary critic in Greenwich Village (with a beatnik girlfriend who had long black hair), or even an anonymous crew member of a ship. Weirdly, I always assumed that I would spend time in jail, and to this day I still hoard an internal library of intellectual projects to draw on when I am taken prisoner.

Although most of my initial literary efforts from elementary school into my first year or two of college were in fiction and poetry, I should have known early on that imaginative literature was not where my talents lay. I lacked a naturalist's eye for minute observation; visual descriptions were usually, I thought, the parts easiest to skip in any work. T. S. Eliot was a predictable attraction for me, yet this was due mainly to his plangent mood. My own efforts at verse, which to my later embarrassment were published in college literary magazines, were little more than clumsy efforts to turn adolescent angst into order. I never had, nor would have, any talent for parsing the aural character of language. In poetry I missed out entirely on the appreciation of calibrated rhythms and the witty use of rhyme or assonance. I may have felt the clash and cadence of meter, the ebb and flow of quatrains, yet could not describe these. I also had a distrust of eloquence and intoxicating verbal richness that kept many of the classics (especially romantic poetry) on the back burner. I preferred verse as well as fictional and nonfiction prose devoid of lush emotionalism, writing that spoke with bluntness, or bitter irony, anything to help one see clearly. In all genres I favored clean, unadorned diction, Camus-like spare, deceptively simple lines to inspect intricate facets of the riddles of humanity.Throughout high school I spent time in limbo as a rebel with countless unknown causes. I simply dissented whenever I felt commanded—or even just pressured—to do something by external authority. At my parents' insistence I went through the motions of taking Hebrew and music lessons, both of which went nowhere. In school, the actual words of the Lord's Prayer and the Pledge of Allegiance never passed through my lips, precisely because one was "supposed" to recite them daily. Enviously I watched the television wanderers Tod and Buzz on *Route 66* (1960–64), responded with empathy to the nonconformist antics of the beatnik sidekick Maynard G. Krebs on *The Many Loves of Dobie Gillis* (1959–63), thrilled to the naughty pages of Chester Himes's *Pink Toes* (1961), and reeled in shock from the horrors of Dalton Trumbo's *Johnny Got His Gun.* (Originally published in 1939, *Johnny Got His Gun* was reissued in 1959 and fell immediately into my hands.) My father gave me a paperback reprint of David Riesman's *The Lonely Crowd* (1950) and told me I was "inner-directed," or at least definitely not "other-directed," and my mother had a copy of Paul Goodman's *Growing Up Absurd* (1960) that I devoured.

Whatever story I concocted for the essay on my college admissions applications, I did not graduate from high school with any genuine professional ambition. My first impulse was to emulate Jack Kerouac's *On the Road* (1957), and the work-study program of Antioch College afforded something of a safe simulacrum. I was still baffled as to what I wanted, so it was attractive to be able to extricate myself every three or six months for short-term adventures in various cities. I would return from a job to the campus in Yellow Springs, Ohio, to try once again to find a footing in some academic field that suited my still inchoate needs. For three years, 1964 through late 1967, I held a steady procession of relatively unskilled occupations (bookstore clerk, stock boy, child care worker, social worker, copy boy, planetarium guard, community organizer) in Manhattan, Pittsburgh, the District of Columbia, and Cleveland; embarked on hitchhiking trips around the East Coast and from Paris by way of the Balearic islands down to Tangiers and back up to London; and indulged in many frustrated dreams of sexual pleasure without commitment and experimentations with drug-induced altered states of consciousness that only briefly led to a desired sense of oneness. Details of these occasionally louche escapades will have to wait for another kind of essay. Any nihilism on my part was relatively short-lived; I quickly found that a little of "nothing is true, everything is permitted" could go a long way.

Figure 20.2. Alan at Antioch College and editor of the *Antioch Masses* magazine, 1968. Credit: Personal collection of Alan M. Wald.

New Left and Old

By 1968, I embraced the term "Literary Radicalism" as my object of study. I associated it principally with Randolph Bourne, the World War I–era author of *The History of a Literary Radical* (issued posthumously in 1920). Bourne, who suffered facial as well as bodily deformities, opposed the identification of American culture with Anglo-Saxon culture and broke with his teacher John Dewey over Dewey's view that the United States could spread democracy through military action. I had originally turned to writers on the Left, even before I knew what that term meant, because I just didn't like the looks of the life that seemed to be programmed for me. So it made sense that the voice of such a relatively nonideological writer, whose transnational ideals were not tied to a specific socialist tradition, would reach me early. Lacking political sophistication for a long time, I only recognized that we in the United States were an island of plenty in a sea of world privation; eventually I saw that the dream of an American Century, very much in the air under Presidents John F. Kennedy and Lyndon B. Johnson—as it is today in new forms—depends on a teleology of empire. I had no wish to be implicated in this society's crimes.

I don't deny that guilt was one small part of that attitude. Actually, guilt is the gift that keeps on giving. But it is essential that guilt be channeled constructively into responsibility, solidarity, and commitment. The compelling ideas of socialism about class structure, racism, philosophy, and justice emerged for me during junior high school, first through imaginative literature by African Americans and European existentialists. Being white or having a prepared purpose in life didn't express the way I felt. Although I have no memory of religious feelings and was bored silly by all synagogue activities, I emphasized my Jewish identity, with which I felt entirely comfortable. I always told people about the original family name, an opportunity to explain my ethnicity, and boasted that my father was the founding president of the Beth El Synagogue to which we belonged during our two residences in Maryland. This sense of being part of an outsider, minority group in a Christian country (naively, I was unaware that many Jews identified with the political and cultural establishment) was a stepping-stone to identification with the have-nots and outcasts in any situation. Totally entranced by the civil rights movement from the first news of boycotts and sit-ins, and revolted by small episodes of chauvinism toward Arabs that I witnessed during a 1958 visit to Israel, I was becoming an internationalist before I knew what it meant.

Later I began to formulate my literary-intellectual interests more responsibly. This came as I learned about the Dreyfusard tradition of intellectuals serving as moral guardians over the modern state, although the nonconformity of a John Reed was still more my style. I was an enthusiastic member of Students for a Democratic Society (SDS) from 1965 through late 1967, much influenced by the two former SDS presidents with whom I worked. In the winter of 1965–66 I joined the idealistic Paul Potter on the Economic Research and Action Project (ERAP) in Cleveland, and then immediately after became a student and comrade of the eloquent Carl Oglesby, whom I helped to bring to Antioch in 1966–67 as "Activist Scholar in Residence."[7] That fall, however, during my sojourn at Fircroft College in Birmingham, England, a school with a social justice ethos designed for workingmen (there was a sister college nearby), my socialist identity began to form, and with it commenced an uncomfortable drift away from the charismatic Oglesby. Returning to the United States a few months before the May 1968 events, I joined the Young Socialist Alliance (YSA), an organization that seemed to blend a moderate version of Trotskyism with the New Left icons of Malcolm X and Che Guevara. For six months starting in the spring of 1968, I edited a campus literary-political magazine called the *Antioch Masses* and also wrote (occasionally with coauthor Michael Schrieber) a political column in the *Antioch Record* called "Le Enragé" ("The Enraged One"); "Les Enragés" was the term for leftist Jacobins in the French Revolution, resurrected in the spring of 1968 by situationists and Trotskyists at the University of Paris at Nanterre.

Both the SDS and the YSA allowed me to combine classic and contemporary (often heterodox) political readings with sometimes round-the-clock activism and find out the degree to which the Marxist method really worked to explain or sustain history and social analysis. My conception of socialism as a way of life—not just programmatic points with an organization to achieve them—grew out of formative, free-floating years in the New Left and then was overlaid (but far from obliterated) by the disciplined collective work of the YSA. I adored both.

Moreover, such organizational connections combined with the freedom of Antioch and later UC Berkeley, where I was a graduate student, to enable a grand tour of 1960s radical protest. Some of it was pretty ugly. On September 5, 1966, President Johnson came to deliver an address to nearly 75,000 at the Montgomery Fairgrounds in Dayton, Ohio. About 150 protestors, mostly Antioch College students, formed a picket line by the front gate, where we were pushed, spit on, and variously threatened. Then a smaller group, of which I was part, dispersed and individually passed through security. This involved several women, including Celia Stodola, whom I would marry nine years later, hiding sections of a cut-up bed sheet under their skirts. On different portions of it the slogans "Please Stop the Killing" and "Thou Shalt Not Kill" had been painted.

Figure 20.3. Alan at UC Berkeley as a graduate student and young socialist, with Celia Stodola in the Berkeley Hills, 1972. Credit: Personal collection of Alan M. Wald.

Inside the fairgrounds, about thirty-five of us reassembled in the bleachers. The sheets were then extracted and reattached, and two people raised the ends of one aloft as a banner while the rest of us linked arms in nonviolent protest fashion in a circle around them. Within seconds there was a roar of rage from the crowd, which included people waving Confederate flags, and Johnson stopped speaking. Minutes later at least a dozen fully armed police and private security guards rushed our group, swinging clubs and stepping on our backs and shoulders to rip down the sheet. As soon as it was gone a second sheet was raised and the attack was repeated, to a round of applause from the crowd. We then sat on the ground, arms still linked, with backs facing outward toward a growing mob. As it surged forward, Chief of Police Harlan A. Andrew, according to a Dayton newspaper report, ordered his men to "just walk away," while another officer loudly declared with a smile that "If anything happens to them now, I'm too far back to help."[8] My vision was blocked, but I looked over my shoulder and saw members of what appeared to be a motorcycle gang striding toward us. Then we were kicked and pummeled from above. I instinctively tried to get up to defend myself, but the women and men on both sides grasped my arms even tighter, and I couldn't move. That was it for my "pacifist moment"; I just didn't have what it takes to tolerate that kind of abuse.

In London in 1967, through SDS contacts with the Stop-It Committee (formed by US students at the London School of Economics in 1966), I was present at the famous October demonstration of twenty thousand people in Grosvenor Square, called by the Vietnam Solidarity Campaign. Our group was assembled around a tiny mock tank that we pushed forward as part of a larger section of the crowd set on approaching the American embassy. Suddenly we were charged by baton-wielding police on horseback, a new experience for me that was terrifying. I promptly turned to run but was held back by a former girlfriend from Vassar College who defiantly stood her ground. I recollect no details after that, but someone in the crowd from the Committee of 100 (set up in 1960 by Bertrand Russell) got the idea that I was a US draft resister and piloted my friend and me safely through the chaos to an apartment, where we were fed and stayed the night.

Zelig-like, I seemed to be at every noteworthy event. Most were peaceful and legal mass actions in major cities. But only ten months after Grosvenor Square, club-swinging police chased me through the streets of Chicago. This was August 1968 during the Democratic National Convention. Earlier in the day I had been talking to Paul Potter in Grant Park when suddenly the police stormed into the center in search of a young man who had apparently lowered an American flag. Teargas was everywhere, and we quickly fled the park, running straight into national guardsmen with .30-caliber machine guns as we tried to cross the bridge at Balboa and Congress Streets. We then turned toward the Jackson

Boulevard Bridge to head toward the Hilton Hotel by way of Michigan Avenue. There were thousands of us, and as we drew closer I heard the still-lingering sound of protestors (and perhaps bystanders) being beaten by clubs, choked by teargas, and even thrown through plate glass windows. Then a porcine-looking line in blue charged into our section of the crowd, and remembering Dayton and London, I took off into the darkness under an El.

Eight months after, I was off to California for graduate school on a Woodrow Wilson fellowship, songs of the 1967 Summer of Love echoing in my head. On July 4, 1969, I and Antioch roommate Peter Graumann arrived at our new place of residence in Berkeley, only to find it under National Guard occupation in the wake of People's Park. Assemblies of more than four persons were immediately broken up. But in less than a year, following news of the US invasion of Cambodia, a massive uprising closed the entire Berkeley campus and then reopened it as an "anti-war university."[9] A few months later, Ari Bober of Matzpen (the legendary Israeli socialist organization) launched his national tour that preceded the publication of *The Other Israel: The Radical Case against Zionism* (1972). I was delighted to be asked to serve on the Education Committee to prevent disruption of his talk in Berkeley by pro-Israel fanatics. (It was called an education committee because our purpose was to educate people to behave respectfully during the meeting.) I was far from a hero, let alone a bruiser, but I always felt safe when an activity was organized by the Socialist Workers Party (SWP) of those years, with which the youth group YSA was in political solidarity, steeped as the SWP was in the traditions of the trade union movement. Knowing that veteran militants such as Nat Weinstein, Jeff Mackler, Patrick Quinn, Bill Massey, and Mike Tormey were also on an education committee was reassuring as well.

Why was my Marxism a liberation and not a constraint? In response to their experiences in the Great Depression and World War II, my parents passionately adhered to the tenets of Reconstructionist Judaism. This movement held that religious laws (halacha) must be respected but also updated in light of modern advances in philosophy, science, and historical knowledge. While halacha was never the least bit a temptation, the events in France in 1968 induced me to organize the tropes of Reconstruction around a new intellectual engine: Jean-Paul Sartre's claim that classical Marxism was the untranscended philosophy of our time. Perhaps remembering my father's tender if reserved sincerity, I didn't share the rage of others toward the older generation's liberal politics, although I did more than my part in griping about efforts by my parents to mold me into conformist roles for which I was unsuited. While fully appreciating the profound contradictions of liberalism and its susceptibility for abuse by those with a sinister or self-serving agenda, as could also be the case with Marxism, my first and remaining impulse was to work through those contradictions rather than dismiss liberalism with a sneer. Updating Trotskyism was always going to be tough, and I joined the YSA with eyes wide open about the limitations of its dogmatic adherence to "dialectical materialism," which for me was a starting point of any inquiry and not the endgame. Yet if philosophy and cultural theory were addressed on a low level, it was also through the YSA and the SWP that I was educated about gender, race, labor history, anticolonialism, and many more topics that were then sidestepped or misrepresented even in higher education.

My very first, and unpolished, essay in a national publication, written in 1969 and published in January 1970 in a magazine called *Young Socialist,* urged US radicals to turn to the writings of twentieth-century "Western Marxists" Georg Lukács and his student Lucien Goldmann.[10] Throughout the early and mid-1970s, I contributed prolifically to SWP publications, especially the *International Socialist Review,* edited by the highly competent Les Evans, and by the end of the decade I was under the spell of the dazzling Marxist scholarship of Brazilian-born Marxist-surrealist Michael Löwy. The SWP essays were not assignments but an effort on my part to expand the range of the organization's cultural life by drawing attention to matters receiving notice in the broader Left through new studies or revivals. Topics addressed included radical history, political murals, politics and the novel, and recent scholarship on fellow travelers; specific authors were John Berger, George Lichtheim, Frantz Fanon, Edmund Wilson, Chinua Achebe, Mike Gold, John Wheelwright, James T. Farrell, and Harvey Swados. (Some submissions were not accepted, although the reasons may have been justifiable; Walter Benjamin, for example, was only just coming into the picture in the United States, and I was hardly an expert.) My ideas in these essays derived from what I took to be classical Marxism, but the way of looking at the subjects was my own.

In the SWP, which I joined in late in the summer 1969, it was soon evident that my status could be described as "resident alien." I was drawn to the proletarian/bohemian legacy of the SWP's past while being distrustful of the burgeoning group of younger and in some cases two-dimensional zealots on the make from elite colleges. The midwestern-born leader of this bland but hardworking undeclared faction initially struck me as serious and polite but turned out to be a control freak with a mysterious inner core. Still, he and his disciples were mostly in my peripheral vision, and the truth is that their political strategies of the late 1960s and early 1970s were often sound and professionally implemented. They were far superior to sections of the Left that relied on disruption and public display more than careful planning, and were thankfully remote from the sequence of sectarian Trotskyist split-off groups that started in 1956 (most of those going by the bizarre term "anti-Pabloite").

Besides, if one wasn't interested in fighting for "leadership," which I wasn't, there was something of a live-and-let-live attitude. I never voted in favor of the SWP majority's resolutions but certainly had no intention of undermining the organization. I loyally recruited individuals who showed an interest, and I learned a great deal from the political meetings, forums, classes, and planning of demonstrations. (Sales and proselytizing, however, were circumvented by me as much as possible.) In April 1971, I was an SWP candidate for the Berkeley City Council, an office for which I was monumentally unqualified. More suitably, I had served as the organizer of two large YSA locals and as an alternate member of the YSA National Committee, before I was asked at age twenty-five to resign from the YSA in the fall of 1971. This demand was due to my known lack of confidence in the rising star from the Midwest, who consolidated his reign that year. From then on I was a contented rank-and-filer of the SWP who did simple tasks, wrote literary reviews, and sometimes gave some classes on Marxism and culture.

With my newfound freedom from organizational responsibilities, three Trotskyist veteran writers of the 1930s, all named George, all "Cannonites" (associated with SWP founder James P. Cannon), took an unexpected and extraordinarily generous interest in me. Whatever they thought of my personal politics (we didn't discuss this much at first), they had seen enough of my work to feel confident that I would be competent to accurately research Marxist cultural history. The upshot was that over the next fifteen years they shared much "inside" information, opening many doors. The three Georges, apparently a popular first name for Jewish Americans of their generation—George Novack (1905–92), George Weissman (half Jewish, 1916–85), and George Breitman (1916–86)—meticulously reviewed my research without ever forcing any of their opinions on me and urged that I try to publish in places that I felt were beyond my reach. That may have been my real "graduate school." They served as a wonderful complement to the brilliant scholars and teachers who guided my literary work at the University of California at Berkeley, Henry Nash Smith (1906–86), Larzer Ziff (b. 1927), and Frederick Crews (b. 1933). Developing a scholarly life that had high standards but was decidedly driven by concerns other than one's professional career, I was getting the best of both worlds.

What I also gained in the SWP was an irreplaceable political schooling from the older working-class militants and veterans of 1930s–50s social movements: Asher Harer, Sylvia Weinstein, Berta Green Langston, Frank Lovell, and Ann Chester are a few of the names of individuals still vivid in my memory. At the same time, I didn't share or repeat the legacy of factional tirades against "Shachtmanites," "Cochranites," and so forth, and I was emphatically disaffected from various younger apparatchiks with briefcases who were always on the phone to the national office. (One firebrand orator, Peter Camejo [1939–2008], was among the exceptions to this bureaucratic style.) What kept me a member for over a decade was agreement with a number of specific policies that still are guideposts. I was partly won to the organization by the writings of James P. Cannon on "defensive formulations and the organisation of action," and I was an enthusiast of the SWP approach to building a mass antiwar movement formulated in the mid to late 1960s.[11] But I never found the organization's "big picture" of what was going to happen in the 1970s and 1980s, including who was going to do the "leading" of any social transformation, to be very convincing.

I learned best by being bombarded by a variety of strong opinions, listening with an open mind to individuals who were compelling in their arguments even if incapable of swaying me all the way. This had been the case with Carl Oglesby, and now I felt the same pull from articulate dissidents in the SWP such as Ralph Levitt, Larry Trainor, and others whose convictions about the near future of a resurgent working-class and union movement seemed unwavering. There was one person with whom I felt a stronger intellectual kinship who was entirely different. Robert Langston, a former PhD student of Jürgen Habermas who hailed from Oklahoma, held opinions that always seemed more deeply considered and generous in spirit as well as funnier than mine. Bob's death in Paris at age forty-four in 1977 severed an important link to the SWP.

All the internal SWP debates, it should be noted, were carried out within the framework of a "Leninism" about which no one seemed to agree. Vladimir Lenin had to be mobilized on one's behalf, and our unspoken motto seemed to be "The only thing that stops a bad guy with a copy of Lenin is a good guy with a copy of Lenin." I passively acceded to this, although I saw the traditions of Bolshevism as meaningful to the present only if they could clarify what had gone wrong with previous revolutionary movements and how to prevent a repeat. In the Middle Ages, the argument from authority was considered very strong; for me, in the modern era, it was very weak.

In any case, I'm a person who has multiple elective identities and feel falsely constrained if I have to answer to just one of them. I was comfortable with the broad politics of revolutionary socialism, but the SWP's evolving notions of what was a "Leninist" political organization became increasingly more dubious, and nothing in the following decades has suggested that it was advancing to new ground rather than regressing to what had been known to fail. Whether writing for SWP publications or elsewhere, I simply chose not to describe my views as "Trotskyist" or even use the orthodox jargon of "degenerated workers state" when referring to the Soviet Union (or the standard description of Stalinism as simultaneously "reformist" and "counterrevolutionary"). The alternate terminology employed by those cothinkers abroad who were unbound by orthodoxy—"revolutionary Marxist" as one's political self-identification, "transitional" or "postcapitalist" to indicate Soviet-type societies—seemed more apt, even if the latter appear inadequate today. Also, while I thought of myself as in some sense a "cadre" or at least a "militant," the aspiration to lead an organization or hold some office was less attractive than ever. This is not to my credit. I lacked (and still lack) certain kinds of political smarts. I was terrible at hairsplitting policy, and although I was quick at making criticisms, I didn't have well-defined alternatives. My views were mainly defined by my long-standing attraction to writings I saw in the *New Left Review* and by revolutionary socialists of several generations in Western Europe, Latin American, Africa, and the Middle East who were not embraced (or even discussed) by US Trotskyists.[12]

Nonetheless, while I lived up to no one's expectations as a "party man," it seemed some kind of principle with me to be candid about whatever kind of radical political affiliation I held. This was mostly because of my desire to put an end to the McCarthy era's stigmatizing of Left "membership" and my belief that scholars should not be aloof from organizational commitment. As a result, red-baiters have had to do no research to "expose" my past organizational involvements, and the Federal Bureau of Investigation agents who thickened my file with confidential reports were hardly earning their pay. Throughout undergraduate and graduate years, more treasured than earning any academic degrees—BA, MA, and PhD—was my involvement in SDS, ERAP, REP (Radical Education Project), SNCC (Student Nonviolent Coordinating Committee), CORE (Congress on Racial Equality), SMC (Student Mobilization Committee), YSA, and SWP, and my sympathy for IMG (International Marxist Group) in Britain, LCR (Revolutionary Communist League) in France—the acronyms go on and on. When finishing my doctorate, for which I did not bother to attend the graduation ceremony, the only "profession" I had in mind was that of "professional revolutionary." I even had a self-help manual—*The New Revolutionaries: A Handbook of the International Radical Left* (1969), edited by Tariq Ali.

I came to the University of Michigan in 1975 as an assistant professor, at age twenty-eight, not to begin an ascent up the ladder of academia but as an independent-minded scholar willing to go wherever my research might take me. In the classroom I believed in exposure to every point of view and encouraged students to learn as I had learned—testing ideas out for themselves. As a committed member of the faculty community and proud to be at a public institution, I took inspiration from and did my best to emulate the devotion to literary excellence of Larry Goldstein and Lemuel Johnson, the historical reach of Geoff Eley and Ronald Grigor Suny, the extraordinary teaching of Marvin Felheim and Richard Meisler, and the humane administrative qualities of June Howard and Sidonie Smith. But in terms of the burning social issues of the day, I was a self-disciplined Marxist carrying out a US version of the "Red University Strategy." This was developed by radicals in Western Europe and promoted in the United States through speaking tours of the Belgian Marxist economist Ernest Mandel (1923–95). Mandel was a comet of learning who was famous for *Late Capitalism* (1975) but first came to international attention with the two-volume *Marxist Economic Theory* (1962), which I immediately read upon its English translation in 1968, the year we met. (Dare I call an eight hundred–page book a page-turner?)

In contrast to that wing of the New Left that saw universities as mere accomplices of imperialism and demanded that student activists "shut it down," the Red University idea was to open them up—to put resources in the hands of those who sought to end international war, abolish the ghettos, and make political democracy viable through participatory control of the economy. I confess that, if the ghost of J. Edgar Hoover is surveilling me even today, Mandel's writings provided the gateway drug and I became one of the pushers. Younger Michigan faculty of the 1970s and 1980s (John Vandermeer, Ivette Perfecto, Tom Weisskopf, Cecilia Green, Buzz Alexander, Bunyan Bryant) stormed the barricades of a repressive elite Eurocentric culture believing that scholarship and social justice were compatible. In some cases, we (and our student and community allies) didn't just raise the Jolly Roger of defiance but assaulted the curriculum, priorities in hiring and admissions, and concerns about campus climate with the forward energy of a barreling freight train. Sit-ins, picket lines, teach-ins, building takeovers, demands for divestment, marches on the regents' meetings, petitions, fact-finding missions (for me, Nicaragua during the Contra War in 1986 and Haiti under martial law in 1993), debates, arrests for civil disobedience (I was convicted in February 1987 for sitting in at Congressman Carl Pursell's office), and endless meetings were the alternative university we kept alive and is the one I will remember.

Figure 20.4. Alan in Managua, Nicaragua, with John Vandermeer during the Contra War, December 1986. Credit: Personal collection of Alan M. Wald.

Into the New Millennium

Some of the models stemming from the 1960s about how things might unfold had a good run but then by the 1990s were going on life support. Ageing brings wonderful additions—two much-loved daughters, in my case—but then time is less available. It became increasingly difficult to maintain a balance of theory and practice in the absence of the political coordinates outside the university—the protests in the streets—that were supposed to sustain the equilibrium. Even as we aimed our fire at atrocities in Central America, South Africa, and the Middle East, we increasingly found ourselves speaking in the name of an imaginary internationalism that could never find satisfactory embodiment in any organized mass movement. And, of course, we had made mistakes. Contrary to C. Wright Mills's warning to the New Left against a "labor metaphysic," I was among those who allocated to the trade unions a highly privileged position in the social pantheon and promoted the 1930s Left too much as a normative radicalism.[13] I learned the hard way, in writing scholarly books, that it is just not possible to counterpose a set of totally "correct positions" to all the errors and misdirections of one's subjects. History, I knew but sometimes forgot, is the activity of humanity pursuing its aims, and socialism is not an outcome but a process.

Witnessing unexpected situations, a generation's confidence in the theory of historical trajectory was undermined—probably for the better. Categories that once seemed liberating came to be seen as straitjackets. Our dialectical critique began to feel as frustrating to use as a knife with no handle. In worst-case scenarios, onetime radical spokespersons precipitously suffered the onset of neoconservative derangement syndrome. Some of these offered political recantations that resembled a bad trailer for a Sacha Baron Cohen comedy. Fortunately, I had learned from existentialist inspirers that ceaseless inner conflict is the fate of the truly modern radical; sometimes one needs to boldly embrace the enigmatic to be liberated from the prison house of our own debates, to cast off the practico-inert—Sartre's term for encrusted habits that induce people to reproduce the past in the present. Some of my former students—Howard Brick, Robbie Lieberman, Paula Rabinowitz, Zaragosa Vargas—had become my teachers.

I am not suggesting that I have now politically achieved some Olympian objectivity. For me, life continues as abnormally as ever. What remains permanent is the struggle between my emotional feeling that taking certain political positions is of the utmost urgency and my rational understanding that disciplined and informed reflection is required for praxis. Often it seems as if someone needs to put a sign over my desk: "Just don't do something, sit there!" This need to accept contradictions and tensions applies to research on Literary Radicalism as well. Despite all my study and experience, I am hardly immune to simplistic romanticizations of labor, antiracist, and antifascist politics of the 1930s, 1940s, and 1950s. I still hyperventilate at the sight of a veteran of the Abraham Lincoln Brigade and thrill to the defiant stance taken by mathematician H. Chandler Davis when he faced the vile witch-hunters in the 1950s and went to jail. But one has to remember those old debates (the Russian Question, Spain, and so forth) in order to understand the legacy of the Old Left as it was and not as we would like it to be. Even the most heroic Communists were flawed giants; in their unshakable belief that the Soviet Union was the land of antifascism, requiring whatever aid could be obtained, they ultimately managed to seize defeat from the jaws of victory by discrediting communism as a movement that could improve people's lives. The logic of their theoreticians who justified Moscow's lies and deceptions sometimes rivaled the chief contortionist at Cirque du Soleil.

The problem in my field is that we radicals love our antifascist traditions as no other political entity, and this is what makes it so hard to write good history about the Popular Front, the Spanish Civil War, the Grand Alliance, and post–World War II competition among the Great Powers. Too many fine people were then willing—often by simply not asking questions—to sacrifice humanity to their own dubious vision of "progress." This meant the substitution of slogans of solidarity for personal responsibility, and for the untidiness of experience, as can be seen in the response of many to the ambiguities of Popular Front practice. Like Isaac Asimov's Hari Seldon in his *The Foundation Trilogy*, the

Old Leftists—and here I mean not just Communists—thought they had figured out the laws governing history and society even as their lives became part of patterns and currents indiscernible to them. The Left of today has not transcended a basic challenge posed decades ago by George Orwell: the central problem of how to prevent power from being abused. One may hope that future writings in the vein of how to "Change the World without Taking Power" and in favor of a political strategy of "horizontalism" will eventually assist in producing some new thinking.

Yet I say all this from a position of complete sympathy with the Old Left's humanitarian objectives of internationalism and an economy democratically controlled by the producers, and I am not at all certain that I would have behaved under comparable circumstances much differently than they did. In relation to the new movements such as Occupy Wall Street and Boycott, Divestment, Sanctions, I am a student, not an adviser, although I certainly feel an obligation to raise questions to debate. Righteous superiority has no place in passing judgment on the Old Left, the New Left, or this New Millennium Left. Self-important condescension is like peeing on oneself: everyone can see it, but only *you* get the warm feeling that it brings.

Search for a Method

I followed a curious route for a radical literary scholar of the baby boomer generation. Graduating from Antioch College as a literature major in 1969, with a reasonable background in the classical as well as modernist canon due to my extraordinary teacher Milton A. Goldberg (1919–70), my imagination was also shaped by courses with Oglesby on the literature of rebellion. I had acquired an unusual background in Marxist history and theory mainly from New Left and socialist study groups and carried out independent reading in Walter Benjamin, Georg Lukács, Jean-Paul Sartre, Simone de Beauvoir, Frantz Fanon, some of the Frankfurt School (obviously Herbert Marcuse), and British Communists such as Christopher Caudwell, Arnold Kettle, and Raymond Williams. When I started the PhD program that fall at UC Berkeley, where Marxism was simply not taught in the English Department, I simultaneously enrolled in an off-campus seminar with philosopher Richard Lichtman on the young Marx. The two literary specialties that attracted me were African American literature (Richard Wright, Lorraine Hansberry) and European modernism (Franz Kafka, Virginia Woolf), and my nebulous goal was to formulate a Marxist cultural theory that would advance their understanding.

Yet two years into graduate school, "theory" became a precipitous growth industry in English departments, taking off with the craze over structuralism, and I found myself quietly converting to a new agenda emphasizing history and primary research (including biography) about US writers intimately connected to Leftist social movements. I can't fully explain this turnaround, one that kept me at a distance from the proliferating new generation of Marxist theory-heads who soon engaged poststructuralism, deconstruction, and postmodernism. Perhaps I overreacted by concluding that we held incompatible definitions of "literary theory"; I saw mine as empirically grounded in life and society, while their treatment of texts suggested the Platonic allegory of a soul sprouting wings and escaping the body.

This reaction against what I saw as overly academic Marxism may explain why as a graduate student I chose James T. Farrell, author of the *Studs Lonigan* trilogy, to guide me through the labyrinth of the cultural Left. Farrell was still alive but nearly forgotten as the Irish American novelist who blended tough-guy Marxism with a sensibility bouncing between Marcel Proust and Honoré de Balzac. In choosing him as the subject for a doctoral dissertation in a leading English Department still fixated on classics, where a previous proposal by a graduate student to write on Mike Gold had been turned down, I was well aware that Farrell was no paragon of stylistic or personal respectability. He was regarded as a crude naturalist, and the biographical information in circulation depicted an irascible womanizer who consumed enough booze to render the entire population of Studs Lonigan's Chicago South Side neighborhood insensible.

From our first face-to-face meeting in New York, however, I saw things differently. Drinking and drugs ("uppers") aside, the congenitally disputatious Farrell, whose sidekick I then became for the last five years of his life (1974–79), possessed a temperament that was rooted in an impetuosity stemming from a blend of his political and literary idealism. His passions for socialism and art were set at a pitch of heroic resolution early on, in the 1920s bohemias of Chicago, Paris, and Greenwich Village. After that he committed himself to a struggle that called on the utmost determination of his will and spirit. Farrell left a visible mark on US culture in the 1930s and 1940s on his own terms. He was difficult but worth it.

I just loved the forked consciousness of such restless minds in and around the Marxist tradition: the Richard Wright of *The Outsider,* the Simone de Beauvoir of *The Mandarins,* the Lorraine Hansberry of *Les Blancs.* My extensive personal interviewing of Farrell, and of the many other Old Left veterans to whom Jim introduced me, became decisive for my literary-historical method. William Blake wrote that "[t]he road of excess leads to the palace of wisdom," and in the area of the oral history of leftist writers, no one seems to have followed that road more excessively than myself.[14] Since 1974, when I bought my first tape recorder, I have interviewed or otherwise communicated with writers and their friends, political comrades, and family members—some five hundred people in all. I also went personally to talk to the older generation of scholars who founded the academic field of Literary Radicalism—Daniel Aaron, Walter Rideout, and James Gilbert. Their books, collectively, had been the Rosetta Stone that helped me to translate a past rendered nearly indecipherable by McCarthyism.

I had learned much from moving back and forth between Rainer Maria Rilke's view that art dwarfs criticism and Walter Benjamin's conviction that criticism can sometimes surpass art in teasing out what had been sealed within its cultural forms. Now as a hands-on researcher, I learned all too well what the theorists tell us about memory—that it is a construction, not an imprint. In trying to dredge up the past, we grasp at the imperfect recollections fluttering inside our heads and piece together a story about what might have happened—or sometimes what we wish had occurred. Every oral history must be approached with a morsel of legitimate doubt. And in some cases, the well is just too deep for the truth to be recovered. In writing about myself, such acquired wisdom weighs heavily.

In the 1970s, a rising generation of radicals shaped by the 1960s inaugurated the Marxist Literary Group (MLG), of which I was quite aware but not an early member, and produced groundbreaking journals such as *Social Text,* to which I subscribed immediately but never submitted writing. My natural tendency in responding to competing scholarly approaches on the Left is to attempt to prove my case by producing superior work—not by attempting takedowns, excoriating others as anti-Marxist (which usually leads to a counterproductive debate), or by the cagey positioning of myself among the various schools. I self-identify as a classical Marxist but of a capacious variety who is happy to learn what I can from Western Marxism, postcolonialism, gender studies, and more.

Consequently, in the 1970s and 1980s, I just listened and read during the escalating theory boom and concentrated on my own research. When I wasn't engrossed in socialist political activism, I was either sitting by myself in the Special Collections rooms of libraries or else traipsing from coast to coast in search of old reds to interview about their experiences. In 1979 as an assistant professor, I was most comfortable relating to radicals in the profession by writing short reviews for *Radical Teacher,* which presented itself as more activist and antielitist than MLG because it was linked to social movements. I didn't attend an MLG institute until 1986, a few years after I had engaged in my own more cautious use of theory in *The Revolutionary Imagination* (1983). I felt welcomed for what I had to offer as a cultural historian, and I participated regularly for a decade and a half until the premature death of my formidable comrade Michael Sprinker, who had by then become a central figure in the MLG.

Part of this aberrant itinerary was due to a personal "outlaw" temperament of being "never so lonely as in a crowd"; the bandwagon aspect of the sudden rush toward theory-heavy journals such as *Tel Quel* was off-putting especially because it seemed as if many of my newly converted contemporaries were bypassing Marx and Engels (not to mention Lenin and Trotsky) and seeing Plekhanov only as a target. But maybe I just recognized that I would never be in the same league as the inspirers of my graduate school years, Fredric Jameson and Terry Eagleton. I read Jameson's *Marxism and Form* (1971) almost the day it appeared, and I carefully followed Eagleton's new work on ideology in the *New Left Review.* I recognized that both were the "real deal," far above my own capacity in that discipline, and I didn't want to be a camp follower or hanger-on—although I happily borrowed and adapted their ideas, especially in *The Revolutionary Imagination* and in the chapter on ideology and the novel in *The New York Intellectuals* (1987). Thus, I instinctively gravitated in a direction where I might make a complementary but signal contribution to Marxist scholarship on my own terms through original archival research.

Figure 20.5. Publicity photo for *New York Intellectuals*, 1987. Credit: Personal collection of Alan M. Wald.

Never anticipating that I would find, like, or be able to keep a university position, I wanted to be a sophisticated but lucid writer on literature and politics who was primarily part of an insurgent social movement; one nonacademic fantasy was to be a staff member of a socialist publication, crafting book reviews, essays on politics and culture, and occasionally coverage of labor, antiracist, and community struggles. Harvey Swados was a kind of model I had in mind after I wrote a piece on him in 1971. I read everything by Edmund Wilson and the early *Partisan Review* editors, who were originally outside the academy, but I was mainly looking at sentences and paragraphs of Isaac Deutscher (blacklisted from academe), Perry Anderson (who didn't become a professor until his early forties), Hannah Arendt (who was nearly fifty before she began teaching), and Ernest Mandel (who started teaching around the same age). Noam Chomsky, I suppose, was the main exception among my extrauniversity models: a professor who pushed his right of academic freedom to the limit, speaking out courageously on the burning issues of the moment.

Figure 20.6. Alan with his daughters Sarah and Hannah, Los Angeles, 1988. Credit: Personal collection of Alan M. Wald.

Figure 20.7. Alan with Michael Löwy, Paris, November 1992. Credit: Personal collection of Alan M. Wald.

Figure 20.8. Alan at the grave of Ernest Mandel, Pere-Lachaise Cemetery, Paris, July 1997. Credit: Personal collection of Alan M. Wald.

Figure 20.9. Alan with Tariq Ali, London, 2002. Credit: Personal collection of Alan M. Wald.

The Trilogy

American Night was envisioned initially as part of a single-volume project inaugurated in the late 1990s with an expectation that it would appear at the start of the new millennium. But the material was disobedient. The upshot is three volumes totaling about thirteen hundred pages and issued at five-year intervals: *Exiles from a Future Time* (2002), *Trinity of Passion* (2007), and *American Night* (2012). The publisher is the University of North Carolina Press, with which I began an association in the early 1980s through the nurturing of Iris Tillman Hill. Each volume accentuates a chronological stage: the early 1930s, the antifascist era, and the Cold War. Thus, the big narrative of three decades is crosshatched with self-contained mininarratives, allowing them to be read independently or even out of sequence.

My aim was to reopen the dossier and recount with fresh eyes the story of the (pro-Soviet) Communist presence that was hegemonic within the wider US Literary Radicalism of mid-twentieth-century fiction, poetry, and criticism. In the early 1930s, with the domestic breakdown of the economy and the international rise of fascism, Communism had emerged as the chief radical force in most of the arts. Two decades later it was beaten out of American letters during the "culture wars" of the early 1950s. How was its contradictory presence expressed? How did it evolve? What is its legacy?

Such a book project wasn't dictated by any dearth of outstanding monographs about major elements of this subject, especially concerning Great Depression social realism and McCarthy-era political witch hunts. I've accomplished much grueling original research with which I am pleased, but I make no claims to be the "first" and "only." Nor do I sensationalize my research; the disclosures presented about political affiliations and personal lives of writers are modestly made and heavily contextualized. Since there exists a genuine community of activist-scholars in the field of Literary Radicalism, the three volumes are filled with the names of scores of older specialists, contemporaries, and younger individuals to whom I am variously indebted, not to mention nonacademics from whom I have learned. But I felt that no one else, including the astonishing Michael Denning in his excellent and nearly comprehensive *The Cultural Front* (1998), had really addressed many of the subtleties of the subject in a synthetic manner.

One impediment to everyone's work was widespread secrecy among cultural workers about their Communist Party affiliation, manifest through obscured and sometimes byzantine forms of commitment that I treat as a mode of "converso culture" in connection with "memory loss" and "institutionalized forgetting." For those who lived through McCarthyism, onetime Communist convictions and affiliations became the love that dared not speak its name. Such a trauma causes the rearrangement of mental furniture, and the Old Left veterans and their families themselves became unreliable sources of information. In a disconcerting way, US culture of the late 1940s and 1950s became "de-Communized" in literary history in a manner that recalls the Warsaw Ghetto Uprising becoming "de-Judaized" in Soviet political history.

Moreover, it didn't seem as if the elusive definition of a "Communist writer" had been effectively explored by researchers apropos those who refrained from wearing membership on their sleeve. Previous scholarship depicted writers such as Arthur Miller as just "a liberal" and Lorraine Hansberry as a "civil rights" activist rather than as long-term pro-Communists (whatever the murky details of their organizational affiliations). Then there was the puzzle of "Stalinism," too often evaded or simplified. Whereas conservative scholars demonized Communists, a number on the Left found that if one merely labeled a writer a "progressive," one really didn't have to talk that much about the terrible price of illusions in the Soviet Union.

Presentism cannot be entirely avoided, but well-meaning attempts by radical scholars to create an idealized usable past for the Left can distort the effort to understand real strengths and weaknesses. What one sees in literary history as in political history so often depends on one's priorities, which is not necessarily harmful. But some scholars regard the candid disclosure of very serious political errors or human failings as "red-baiting" or personal attacks. For my part, I'm a devotee of Jane Austen, who said of her own heroines that "pictures of perfection . . . make me sick."[15]

To be sure, I was no novice in the political field and carried my own baggage, which made me uncertain of my suitability to serve as a relatively dispassionate appraiser. Between 1978 and 1994, I published three monographs and two volumes of my collected essays, mainly on the noncommunist Far Left. While I criticized "anti-Stalinism" when it became a mask for antiradicalism, and looked distrustfully at orthodox Trotskyism, the politics of these books was squarely in the camp of revolutionary Marxism and socialist internationalism. This meant that I had a profound critical distance from the politics of Soviet Communism, already expressed frequently, and had no desire to devote years of my life to writing a book merely to take literary Communists down another peg.

Still, I was unquestionably sympathetic to the ideals of the Party rank and file. Moreover, I had accrued plenty of experience as a stalker of literary ghosts, following many traces across the pages of forgotten Left publications to eventually disclose the political and personal truths of writers who lived and worked in the shadow of the rise of fascism, World War II, and the early years of what some now call "the short American century." So, in the mid-1990s I possessed a divided mind about this particular undertaking. For a while I tried on some alternative hats, none of which really fit.

Then near the end of the decade, I was impelled toward a new assessment of Communism's literary presence while editing a University of Illinois Press series called "The Radical Novel Reconsidered." This consisted of paperback reprints of lesser-known left-wing fiction from the middle of the twentieth century. I started to read in unknown territory, departing from the standard lists and bibliographies to seek out what might be seen as heterodox novels, especially by women, writers of color, and gays and lesbians. It turned out to be an exhilarating experiment in literary spelunking, exploring unknown caves and virgin territory. The marginality of a work of art has always been a source of interest for me, and my fascination with uncovering neglected fiction induced me to follow suit in poetry, drama, and Marxist literary criticism when the University of Illinois Press series was terminated for financial reasons. Suddenly I had become a left-wing Isaiah Berlin, picking up the crumbling collected works of half-forgotten novelists or ones considered beyond the pale and sometimes finding high philosophical and political drama in them. (And like Berlin, I expected to be accused of exaggerating the importance of a work in the interest of vivifying a knotty political-intellectual problem.) This unorthodox reading list became the literary basis for the trilogy, which is less about the "radical canon" than largely unfamiliar works, and involves an effort to devise critical methods appropriate to their interpretation.

Communism and Modernism

In terms of writers negotiating the tripwires of Stalinist dogmatism and literary modernism, *American Night* tells lots of different stories in some detail. From the 1970s to the 1990s, I was attempting something like intellectual portraiture, but in this volume I created a full-blown "humanscape," a neologism I borrowed from a personal letter about the 1930s from critic Alfred Kazin to novelist Josephine Herbst.[16] This requires an engagement with far messier questions that flow from the uneasy relationship of one's life to aesthetic categories: What did complex left-wing humans, with their unique biographies of trauma and pain as well as Marxist commitment, and memberships in multiple communities of gender and ethnicity, in addition to class, actually produce over a lifetime? To fully explore the impact of radicalism on art as mediated by the artist, the critic must address not only political and aesthetic challenges and trajectories but ethical and emotional ones as well.

As the book's title suggests, the majority of the stories I narrate in *American Night* are typically marked by personal pain and artistic neglect, by the Communist Party as well as the cultural establishment. My work has often concerned the study of failures, no doubt because I identify so strongly with outcasts. But for my scholarly purpose of re-creating an oppositional tradition, studying frustration is as fruitful as studying success. This is because every ordeal of struggle comes with a lesson for Literary Radicalism, and every lesson lives on in the historical memory I have tried to create as a bulwark against oblivion. And in *American Night,* I tell of writers increasingly at odds with Stalinism (even if they did not think in such terms) while remaining anticapitalist. Ann Petry's first two novels were not treated well by the Communist press, but she had friends in the Communist movement. She and Jo Sinclair (Ruth Seid), a slightly younger parallel writer, are examples of anticapitalist radicals who eventually went their individual ways after intense engagements with Communism, even as political nostalgia profoundly informed their art, *The Narrows* (1953) and *Anna Teller* (1960), respectively. Thomas McGrath, in contrast, was loyal to Stalinist-type politics, but as a brilliant modernist poet he was always embroiled in artistic controversy with his comrades. And so on.

Another generalization that animates the book concerns a growing autonomy in radical writing that might seem counterintuitive in the context of Cold War repression from all sides. Even if a writer genuflected to the Communist Party publicly, at least by making no political criticisms of it, he or she might continue truly dissident work in the private world of art—through poetry in little magazines, popular fiction, and even somewhat commercialized genres as detective and science fiction. (Sometimes pseudonyms and fronts were required.) Even if a writer was not producing work that I mischievously call "Communist literary modernism," he or she might be experiencing a new kind of freedom in no longer being held captive by the kind of "positivist rationalism" and "moral certainty" that prevailed before World War II. Furthermore, as a consequence of the new postwar situation, even the most organizationally connected Communist writers could be more on their own. Instead of the big and dynamic League of American Writers, there were only smaller and weaker formations where the Communist Party was present—the National Council of the Arts, Sciences and Professions; the Committee for the Negro in the Arts; Contemporary Writers; the Harlem Writers Guild; and the New Writing Foundation. Attacks on artistic "formalism" in the Soviet Union were reproduced in the United States, and "people's art" was the Communist aesthetic of choice, but the *New Masses* was dying in the late 1940s and was much less authoritative than it had been in the 1930s. The 1946 Albert Maltz controversy, when the Communist novelist was pressured by the Party to recant his objections to the notion of "art as a weapon," put a damper on critical statements and the kind of writing one might submit to Party venues, but most pro-Communist creative writers had merged into the mainstream during the war and did pretty much as they pleased in their professional and personal lives so long as no political deviancy was suspected. The US version of Zhdanovism was ugly but could be circumvented. And when a literary controversy erupted several years after the Khrushchev revelations and the end of McCarthyism, a group of talented writers (led by Charles Humboldt) simply walked out of the Communist Party and merged with the early New Left.

In writing my trilogy, I operated with the belief that in the coming debate among activists of the Left on what will be the physiognomy of twenty-first-century socialism, the heritage of the self-conscious and self-critical strain of the leftist literary sensibility that I have sought to re-create will be one of the moral and political reference points. But nothing is certain, and the downfall of the Marxist movements we built in the 1960s ought to be profoundly humbling. What remains of the tradition of the Literary Left today looks like a disrupted system, fractured yet conveying information nonetheless if taken up by a new generation trained in the streets as well as the classroom. Where it goes next, however, is out of my control. At the moment, a kind of populist anarchism has displaced socialism as the vocabulary with which radicals discuss politics. If that remains the case, then my trilogy may ultimately be judged something of an archaeological treatise.

The Future of Present Things

Looking back over forty years of scholarly writing, I recognize that I have always thought of Literary Radicalism as having a history of its own, distinctive due to a conspicuous degree of historical self-consciousness. Its practitioners as well as the scholars who study it are frequently joined together with political militants and social movements in common projects marked by shared moments of fun, fury, pleasure, and pain. Moreover, Literary Radicalism has always been about changing the world; its most farsighted proponents have been acutely aware that each "present" faced by the sequence of generations in its lineages affords a multiplicity of possible lines of development. To adapt St. Augustine, Literary Radicalism is about "the present of future things."[17]

Very much like the Mississippi River, the course of the era of Literary Radicalism on which I concentrate—from World War I to World War II, from the New Deal to the Cold War, from proletarian literature to the New Left, from the Popular Front to radical feminism and black nationalism—is shifting, muddy, treacherous, and filled with snags. By 2014, research on left-wing writers has expanded decisively beyond its one-time fixation on the Great Depression, and into the 1950s and 1960s. In culture after World War II, one finds traces of the Marxist experience in a variety of locations from high modernism to middlebrow to pulp, which includes of course gay and lesbian, multiethnic, and women's literature. Even the core language of Marxist-inflected Literary Radicalism can be seen as riven with false friends due to the presence of semantic ambiguity, incommensurable words for concepts, and cryptic coinages.

Figure 20.10. Angela and Alan's engagement photo, spring 2006. Credit: Personal collection of Alan M. Wald.

These problems and much more have produced a sequence of "paradigm dramas" in a series of books that promote methodologies for the study of Literary Radicalism. This study started with Daniel Aaron and Walter Rideout but went on to include Paula Rabinowitz, Barbara Foley, Michael Denning, and many more. Again and again we ask: What are the sets of assumptions, concepts, values, and practices that constitute a way of viewing Literary Radicalism for the community that studies it through several intellectual disciplines? The more one researches the subject—from the intricacies of the domestic Left to its transnational connections—the more it seems that that there is no coherent, comprehensive perspective for the critical imagining of Literary Radicalism. Thus, the trilogy I completed in 2012 is not just a literary history but also a record of my own struggle to understand that history, a journey where each point of arrival has turned out to be a stepping-stone rather than a destination. By the time I reached the era of the Cold War, I found myself composing the history of an absent presence and the writers who abjured or obscured association with it. I am close to concluding that the untranslatability of the movement—due to its plurality and contingency—may have to be the fundamental assumption by which to approach Literary Radicalism.

Figure 20.11. Alan with H. Chandler Davis, Ann Arbor, September 2011. Credit: Personal collection of Alan M. Wald.

At present I am at work on a book-length balance sheet of what was learned from this effort, "Literary Radicalism: A Counter-History." Residues and slippages of memory surround Literary Radicalism to a greater extent than any other politico-artistic trend in modern times. The place of 1920s expatriatism is indelible, and postmodernism is the subject of endless dissection. Curiously, the cultural Left is closer to a "forgotten" moment, even though there is a considerable amount of scholarship about it. Perhaps we should call it largely an "unknown" moment or a "never-known" or supposedly too well-known moment insofar as the extant overall literary histories and public discourse are concerned. But practitioners understand that historically based scholarship about the class struggle is significantly a struggle against a closed past and also means a struggle for the reactivation of the unexpected, the untapped potential of an eclipsed and buried past.

The essays at the core of *Lineages of the Literary Left* were presented in March 2013 against a background of events shaping a new generation of activists: massive convulsions in the world economy from the financial crash of 2008; the great uprisings in the Arab world, with their remarkable mass-based struggles for democracy; and the emergence in the West of spontaneous forms of resistance to austerity politics and its fierce attacks on the lives of millions of people both in and out of employment. As this book appears, I end my profession as a classroom teacher, enabling a new vocation of wielding the "weapons of criticism" as a full-time writer on behalf of many literary and political loves. I see the organizers of and participants in the 2013 conference and this 2015 volume as setting a new intellectual agenda for myself as well as others. I hope I will be worthy of it.

Notes

1. This essay is based on material reworked from several public lectures at the University of Michigan in April 2013 and also from Grant Mandarino, "Outlaws, Rebels and the Revolutionary Imagination: A Two-Part Interview with Alan Wald," *Red Wedge*, June 2013, Part 1 (even though it says "Part 2"), http://redwedgemagazine.com/articles/outlaws-rebels-and-the-revolutionary-imagination-pt-2, and Part 2, http://redwedgemagazine.com/articles/outlaws-two.
2. Derek Walcott, *Midsummer* (New York: Farrar, Strauss and Giroux, 1984), xxix.
3. Leon Trotsky, *My Life* (1930; reprint, New York: Dover, 2007), 432.
4. I was born in Washington, D.C., in 1946, eight years after my father began government service with the Federal Reserve System, the Treasury and Commerce Departments, and the National Security Resources Board. We moved to Chevy Chase, Maryland, in 1951, when my father began his term on the President's Council of Economic Advisors under President Harry S. Truman. But with the switch to the Dwight D. Eisenhower administration, a behind-the-scenes red-baiting attack was launched against Council Chairman Keyserling, resulting in the withdrawal of funding that temporarily disbanded the body. My father then spent part of 1953 as an economic adviser in Korea with the United Nations, after which we moved to Arlington and Belmont, Massachusetts, where he taught in a program at the Harvard Law School and wrote the book *Taxation of Agricultural Land in Underdeveloped Economies: A Survey and Guide to Policy* (Cambridge, MA: Harvard University Press, 1959). In 1955 we moved to West Orange, New Jersey, when he began a job on the Board of Governors of the Federal Reserve Bank in New York, teaching classes at the New School for Social Research. In 1958–59 the family moved to Greece while my father worked as economic adviser to the Bank of Greece under sponsorship of the United Nations. After returning for another three years to New Jersey and the Federal Reserve Bank, in 1962 he finally took us to Bethesda, Maryland, where he served in the Treasury Department, as chief economist of the Federal Power Commission, and then as senior economist and director of the Office of Regulatory Analysis of the Federal Energy Regulatory Commission before his death from brain cancer in 1981.
5. "There is no Frigate like a Book," now a famous poem, was initially a passage from a letter written in 1873, first published in volume 1 of Dickinson's *Letters* (1894).
6. John Steinbeck, *In Dubious Battle* (New York: Penguin Classics, 2006), 14.
7. I have written about some of these experiences in "A Theater for the Poor: Cleveland and SDS/ERAP in the Mid-1960s," *Against the Current*, no. 155 (November–December 2011): 13–18.
8. "Peaceniks Silenced," *Dayton Journal Herald*, September 6, 1966, 2.
9. I coauthored an essay on the events with Jean Savage. See Alan Wald and Jean Savage, "Berkeley Struggle," in *May 1970: Birth of the Anti-War University*, ed. Frank Boehm, 20–22 (New York: Pathfinder, November 1971).

10. Alan Wald, "Marxism and Art," *Young Socialist* 13, no. 1 (January 1970): 25–26.
11. "Socialism on Trial: The Courtroom Testimony of James P. Cannon," Marxists Internet Archive, http://www.marxists.org/archive/cannon/works/1941/socialism/.
12. My disapproval of the new SWP leadership came primarily in the form of protest votes for several oppositional tendencies, "For a Proletarian Orientation" and the "June 19th Tendency," with which I had some partial agreement on issues such as the need to rebuild trade union fractions and turn toward a broader Left vanguard. In 1986, I became a founding member of Solidarity, a multitendency, heterodox organization.
13. This phrase was famously used by Mills in his "Letter to the New Left," *New Left Review* 5 (September–October 1960), http://www.marxists.org/subject/humanism/mills-c-wright/letter-new-left.htm.
14. William Blake, "The Marriage of Heaven and Hell," Academy of American Poets, http://www.poets.org/viewmedia.php/prmMID/19361.
15. From a March 1817 letter to Fanny Knight, quoted in David Nokes, *Jane Austen: A Life* (Berkeley: University California Press, 1998), 520.
16. I'll use this opportunity to offer a correction. The two names were reversed in making the attribution of the quotation in the footnotes to *Exiles from a Future Time* (Chapel Hill: University of North Carolina Press, 2002), 333. However, the mistake was corrected in the paperback edition of *Trinity of Passion* and was not repeated in *American Night.*
17. St. Augustine of Hippo, *The Essential Augustine* (New York: Hackett, 1972), 233.

Studies on the Left: Selected Bibliography of Alan M. Wald

Monographs

1978. *James T. Farrell: The Revolutionary Socialist Years* (New York: New York University Press).

1983. *The Revolutionary Imagination: The Poetry and Politics of John Wheelwright and Sherry Mangan* (Chapel Hill: University of North Carolina Press).

1987. *The New York Intellectuals: The Rise and Decline of the Anti-Stalinist Left from the 1930s to the 1980s* (Chapel Hill: University of North Carolina Press).

1992. *The Responsibility of Intellectuals: Selected Essays on Marxist Traditions in Cultural Commitment* (Atlantic Highlands, NJ: Humanities Press); paperback, 1995.

1994. *Writing from the Left: New Essays on Radical Culture and Politics* (London and New York: Verso).

2002. *Exiles from a Future Time: The Forging of the Mid-Twentieth Century Literary Left* (Chapel Hill: University of North Carolina Press).

2007. *Trinity of Passion: The Literary Left and the Antifascist Crusade* (Chapel Hill: University of North Carolina Press).

2012. *American Night: The Literary Left in the Era of the Cold War* (Chapel Hill: University of North Carolina Press).

Special Issues, Editions, and Coauthored Books

1987. "Introduction," in *Blackness of a White Night: Stories and Poems by Sherry Mangan*, i–viii (Newton, MA: Arts End Books).

1992. "Introduction," in Daniel Aaron, *Writers on the Left,* xiii–xxx, reprint ed. (New York: Columbia University Press).
1993. "Introduction: The Athanasius of Union Square," in James T. Farrell, *A Note on Literary Criticism,* ix–xxxvi, reprint ed. (New York: Columbia University Press).
1994. "The Radical Age of Innocence," introduction to Marion Hawthorne Hedges, *Iron City,* vii–xiv (Beloit, WI: Beloit College Press).
1994. "Lloyd Brown and the African American Literary Left," foreword to Lloyd Brown, *Iron City,* vii–xxxvii, reprint ed., Northeastern Library of Black Literature (Boston: Northeastern University Press).
1995. "Introduction," in John Sanford, *The People from Heaven,* xi–xxxvi (Urbana and Chicago: University of Illinois Press).
1996. With George Breitman and Paul Le Blanc, *Trotskyism in the United States: Historical Essays and Reconsiderations* (Atlantic Highlands, NJ: Humanities Press).
1997. "Soft Focus: The Short Fiction of Sanora Babb," introduction to *Cry of the Tinamou: Stories by Sanora Babb,* ix–xvi (Lincoln: University of Nebraska Press).
1997. "The Wager of Benedict Bulmanis," introduction to Philip Bonosky, *Burning Valley,* vii–xxxv (Urbana and Chicago: University of Illinois Press).
1998. "A Southern Rebel in Cold War America," introduction to Alfred Maund, *The Big Boxcar,* vii–xxx (Urbana and Chicago: University of Illinois Press).
2001. Paul Mishler and Alan Wald, "Introduction," *Color, Culture and Gender in the 1960s,* special issue of *Science & Society* 65, no. 1 (Spring 2001): 5–11.

Book Chapters

1980. "Sherry Mangan," in *American Writers in Paris,* edited by Karen L. Rood, 269–71 (Columbia, SC: Bruccoli Clark).
1981. "James T. Farrell," in *American Novelists, 1910–45,* edited by James J. Martine, 264–76 (Columbia, SC: Bruccoli Clark).
1982. "*Partisan Review* in the 1930s," in *Literature at the Barricades: The American Writer in the 1930s,* edited by Ralph Bogardus and Fred Hobson, 187–203 (Tuscaloosa, Alabama: University of Alabama Press).
1983. "The New York Intellectuals in Retreat," in *Socialist Perspectives,* edited by Phyllis Jacobson and Julius Jacobson, 155–84 (New York: Karz-Cohl).
1986. "John Wheelwright," in *American Poets, 1880–1945,* edited by Peter Quartermain, 434–40 (Detroit: Gale).

1986. Entries on James P. Cannon (62–65), James T. Farrell (131–32), Dwight Macdonald (261–62), Felix Morrow (279), George Novack (292–93), William Phillips (316), and Philip Rahv (325–26), in *Biographical Dictionary of the American Left,* edited by Bernard Johnpoll and Harvey Klehr (Westport, CT: Greenwood).

1989. "Hegemony and Literary Tradition in the United States," in *Language, Authority and Criticism,* edited by Suzanne De Castell, Allan Luke, and Carmen Luke, 3–16 (London: Falmer, 1989). (This is a revised version of "Literary Tradition," *Humanities in Society* 4 [Fall 1982]: 419–30.)

1990. Entries on John Dos Passos (196), James T. Farrell (215–16), Howard Fast (216–17), and Harvey Swados (809–10), in *Encyclopedia of the American Left,* edited by Mary Jo Buhle et al. (New York: Garland).

1991. "Trotskyism in the 1960s," afterword to Michael S. Smith, *Notebook of a Sixties Lawyer,* 180–98 (New York: Smyrna).

1992. "Jewish-American Literary Critics," in *Jewish-American History and Culture: An Encyclopedia,* edited by Jack Fischel and Sanford Pinkster, 127–34 (New York: Garland).

1993. "Culture and Commitment: U.S. Communist Writers Reconsidered," in *New Studies in the Politics and Culture of U.S. Communism,* edited by Michael Brown et al., 281–306 (New York: Monthly Review).

1994. "Communist Writers Fight Back in Cold War Amerika," in *Styles of Cultural Activism: From Theory and Pedagogy to Women, Indians and Communism,* edited by Philip Goldstein, 216–32 (Newark: University of Delaware Press).

1994. "Leon Trotsky's Contributions to Marxist Cultural Theory and Literary Criticism," in *Rebels against the Old Order: Essays in Honor of Morris Slavin,* edited by Boris Blick and Louis Patsouras, 128–48 (Youngstown, OH: Youngstown State University Press), and in Hillel Ticktin and Michael Cox, *The Ideas of Leon Trotsky,* 219–32 (London: Porcupine, 1995). Originally in *Journal of Trotsky Studies* 2 (Summer 1994): 17–41.

1994. "Irving Howe, Socialist Literary Critic," in *Leaders from the 1960s,* edited by David DeLeon, 384–88 (Westport, CT: Greenwood).

1995. "American Writers on the Left," in *The Gay and Lesbian Literary Heritage,* edited by Claude J. Summers, 53–56 (New York: Henry Holt).

1996. "Introduction to H. T. Tsaing's *The Hanging on Union Square,*" in *Into the Fire: Asian American Prose,* edited by Sylvia Watanbe and Carol Bruchac, 341–58 (Greenfield Center, NY: Greenfield Review Press, 1996).

1996. "The 1930s Left in U.S. Literature Reconsidered," in *Radical Revisions: Rereading 1930s Culture,* edited by Bill Mullen and Sherry Linkon, 12–28 (Urbana and Chicago: University of Illinois Press).

1996. "Mary McCarthy and the Left Reconsidered," in *Twenty-Four Ways of Looking at Mary McCarthy,* edited by Eve Stwertka and Margo Viscusi, 69–76 (Westport, CT: Greenwood).

1997. "A Pedagogy of Unlearning: Teaching the Specificities of U.S. Marxism," in *Class Issues: Pedagogy, Cultural Studies, and the Public Sphere,* edited by Amitava Kumar, 125–47 (New York: New York University Press).

1997. "Victor Serge and the New York Anti-Stalinist Left," in *The Ideas of Victor Serge,* edited by Susan Weissman, 99–117 (Glasgow: Critique Books).

1998. Entries on Popular Fiction (620–27), Science Fiction (724–26), and Radical Poetry (671–79), in *Encyclopedia of the American Left,* 2nd ed., edited by Mary Jo Buhle et al. (New York: Oxford University Press).

1999. Entries on Philip Rahv (73–74), Ruth McKenney (109–10), Harvey Swados (179–80), V. F. Calverton (252–53), James T. Farrell (744–46), and Hans Otto Storm (887–88), in *American National Biography* (New York: Oxford University Press).

2001. "Chester Himes (1909–1984)," in *African American Writers,* Vol. 1, 2nd ed., edited by Valerie Smith, 333–47 (New York: Scribner).

2002. "Revising the Barricades: Scholarship about the U.S. Cultural Left in the Post–Cold War Era," in *Socialist Cultures East and West: A Post–Cold War Reassessment,* edited by Dubravka Juraga and M. Keith Booker, 101–22 (Westport, CT: Praeger). Originally published in *Working Papers Series in Cultural Studies, Ethnicity and Race Relations* (Pullman: Washington State University, 2000), 1–20.

2002. "The Costs of McCarthyism," in *Reflections at the End of a Century,* edited by Morris Slavin and Louis Patsouras, 41–57 (Youngstown, OH: Youngstown State University Press). Originally published in *Against the Current* 15 (March–April 2000): 31–38.

2003. "Jewish American Writers on the Left," in *The Cambridge Companion to Jewish American Literature,* edited by Hana Wirth-Nesher and Michael P. Kramer, 170–89 (New York: Cambridge University Press).

2003. "Narrating Nationalisms: Black Marxists and Jewish Communists through the Eyes of Harold Cruse," in *Left of the Color Line: Race, Radicalism, and Twentieth Century Literature of the United States,* edited by Bill Mullen and James Smethurst, 141–61 (Chapel Hill: University of North Carolina Press). Originally published in *Science & Society* 64 (Winter 2000–2001): 400–23, and reprinted in *Harold Cruse's The Crisis of the Negro Intellectual Reconsidered,* edited by Jerry Watts, 139–56 (New York: Routledge, 2004).

2003. "The U.S. Left and Anti-Racism," in *Black Liberation and the American Dream,* edited by Paul Le Blanc, 194–221 (New York: Humanity

Books). Originally published in *Against the Current* 80 (January–February 2000): 23–29, and 84 (May–June 2000): 27–34.

2004. "From the Left: An Interview with Alan Wald," in *Critics at Work: Interviews, 1993–2003,* edited by Jeffrey Williams, 181–201 (New York: New York University Press). Reprint of "The Formation of an Activist Scholar: An Interview with Alan Wald," *Minnesota Review* 50–51 (Fall 1999): 125–42.

2005. "Black Nationalist Identity and Internationalist Class Unity: The Political and Cultural Legacy of Marxism," in *Radical Relevance: Toward a Scholarship of the Whole Left,* edited by Laura Gray-Rosendale and Steven Rosendale, 3–30 (Albany: State University Press of New York), 3–30. Revised version of "The U.S. Left and Anti-Racism," in *Black Liberation and the American Dream,* edited by Paul Le Blanc, 194–221 (New York: Humanity Books, 2003).

2005. "Stevenson, Philip Edward (1896–1965)," in *Encyclopedia of Literature and Politics,* edited by M. Keith Booker, 697–99 (Westport, CT: Greenwood).

2006. "Marxist Literary Resistance to the Cold War," in *Cold War Literature: Writing the Global Conflict,* edited by Andrew Hammond, 100–113 (New York: Routledge). Originally published in *Prospects: An Annual of American Cultural Studies* 20 (1996): 479–92.

2007. "New York Novelists and Poets Respond to the Spanish Civil War," in *Facing Fascism: New York and the Spanish Civil War,* edited by Peter N. Carroll and James D. Fernandez, 130–39 (New York: Museum of the City of New York and New York University Press).

2008. Entries on Michael Gold (568–71), William Phillips (625–28), and Philip Rahv (628–30), in *Encyclopedia of American Jewish History,* edited by in Stephen Norwood and Eunice Pollack (Santa Barbara, CA: ABC-CLIO).

2008. "Cleveland ERAP Project," in *Students for a Democratic Society: A Graphic History,* edited by Paul Buhle, 96–98 (New York: Hill and Wang).

2008. "The Radical 1930s," in *A Concise Companion to American Fiction, 1900–1950,* edited by Peter Stoneley and Cindy Weinstein, 186–204 (Oxford, UK: Wiley-Blackwell).

2010. "Writers on the Left," in *Companion to American Literature and Culture,* edited by Paul Lauter, 427–40 (Oxford, UK: Wiley-Blackwell).

2011. "Steinbeck and the Proletarian Novel," in *The Cambridge History of the American Novel,* edited by Leonard Cassuto, 671–85 (New York: Cambridge University Press).

2011. Essays on Willard Motley (250–73) and Theodore Ward (320–40), in *Writers of the Black Chicago Renaissance,* edited by Steven C. Tracey (Urbana and Chicago: University of Illinois Press).

2013. "Radicalism," in *The Oxford Encyclopedia of American Cultural and Intellectual History,* edited by Joan Shelley Rubin, Scott Caspar, and Paul Boyer, 257–61 (New York: Oxford University Press).

2015. "American Poetry and the Popular Front," in *The Cambridge Companion to Modern American Poetry,* edited by Walter Kalaidjian, 102–15 (New York: Cambridge University Press).

Journal Essays, Interviews, and Longer Reviews

1976. "James T. Farrell and Trotskyism," *Twentieth Century Literature* 22 (February): 90–104.

1976. "The *Menorah* Group Moves Left," *Jewish Social Studies* 38 (Summer–Fall): 90–104.

1977. "The Pilgrimage of Sherry Mangan: From Aesthete to Revolutionary Socialist," *Pembroke Magazine* 8: 85–98.

1977. "Memories of the John Dewey Commission Forty Years Later," *Antioch Review* 35 (Fall): 438–51. (French translation: *Cahiers Leon Trotsky* 3 [July 1979]: 43–61).

1977. "Herbert Solow: Portrait of a New York Intellectual," *Prospects: An Annual Journal of American Cultural Studies* 3: 260–88. (French translation: *Cahiers Leon Trotsky* 19 [September 1984]: 4–16).

1978. "Introduction to 'Snow' by Sherry Mangan," *Michigan Quarterly Review* 17 (Summer): 272–77.

1980. "From Antinomianism to Revolutionary Marxism," *Marxist Perspectives* 10 (Summer): 44–68.

1980. "From Cultural Pluralism to Revolutionary Internationalism: Jewish Identity and the New York Intellectuals in the Early 1930s," *Jewish Socialist Critique* 1 (Spring–Summer): 29–43.

1981. "Erasing the Thirties: Boston's Forgotten Marxist Poets," *New Boston Review* 6 (February): 20–22.

1981. "The Culture of 'Internal Colonialism': A Marxist Perspective," *MELUS* 8 (Fall): 18–27.

1981. "Remembering the Answers," *Nation* (December 26): 708–11.

1981. "Radical Evil" (essay about Stephen Whitfield, *Into the Dark: Hannah Arendt and Totalitarianism*), *Reviews in American History* 9 (June): 260–65.

1982. "Literary Tradition," *Humanities in Society* 4 (Fall): 419–30.

1983. "The Legacy of Howard Fast," *Radical America* 17 (January–February): 43–51.

1985. "Marxism and Intellectuals," *Changes* 6, nos. 11–12: 14–21. (French translation: *Quatrieme Internationale* [Paris], 3rd series, no. 16 [March 1985]: 59–70.)

1985. "The Politics of Culture: The New York Intellectuals in Fiction," *Centennial Review* 29 (Summer): 353–69.

1986. "Tribute to *Burger's Daughter*," *Against the Current* 3 (May–June): 11–17.

1987. "Sculptor on the Left: Duncan Ferguson's Search for Wholeness," *Pembroke Magazine* 19 (Spring): 32–56.

1987. "Theorizing Cultural Difference: A Critique of the 'Ethnicity School,'" *MELUS* 14 (Summer): 21–3.

1988. "Trotskyism, Anti-Stalinism, and U. S. Intellectuals: An Ambiguous Legacy," *International Marxist Review* 3, no. 2 (Autumn): 47–55.

1988. "Victor Serge et la Gauche anti-stalinienne de New York 1937–47," *Cahiers Leon Trotsky* [National Center of Letters and Social Sciences, Genoble] 5 (September): 5–20.

1989. "The New York Literary Left," *Michigan Quarterly Review* 28 (Winter): 130–42.

1990. "From Margin to Center: C. L. R. James," *Monthly Review* 42 (June): 51–56.

1991. "Racist Speech: A Problem of Power," *Against the Current* 32 (May–June): 18–24.

1991. "Remaking Marxism in the 1990s," *Monthly Review* 43, no. 5 (October): 58–63.

1992. "The Subaltern Speaks," *Monthly Review* 43 (April): 17–29.

1992. "In Retrospect: Alfred Kazin's *On Native Grounds*," *Reviews in American History* 20: 276–88.

1993. "Literary Leftism Reconsidered," *Science & Society* 57 (Summer): 214–22.

1994. "Cuba and the U.S. New Left," *Michigan Quarterly Review* 33: 883–91.

1995. "Search for a Method: Recent Histories of American Communism," *Radical History Review* 61: 166–74.

1995. "Contradictions of the Canon," *Minnesota Review* 41–42 (March): 292–97.

1996. "Learning from Labor," *Monthly Review* 46 (February): 53–62.

1996. "A Conversation with Howard Fast, Conducted by Alan Wald and Alan Filreis," *Prospects: An Annual of American Cultural Studies* 20: 511–24.

1996. "Marxism and Intellectuals in the U.S. at Century's End," *Access: Critical Perspectives on Cultural and Policy Studies in Education* 15, no. 1: 99–114.

1997. "The Many Lives of Meridel Le Sueur," *Monthly Review* (September): 23–31.

1997. "The Commitment Conundrum," *Intellectual History Newsletter* 19: 41–44.

1998. "Between Marxism and Pragmatism," *Monthly Review* 50 (October 1998): 47–52.

1999. "The Formation of an Activist Scholar: An Interview with Alan Wald," *Minnesota Review* 50–51 (Fall): 125–42.

2000. "African Americans, Culture and Communism," *Against the Current* 84 (January–February): 23–29.

2000. "The Black Cultural Front," *Against the Current* 86 (May–June): 27–34.

2002. "Strange Communists from the Literary Left," *Chronicle Review: Chronicle of Higher Education* (April 26): B12–B13.

2002. "The Urban Landscape of Marxist *Noir:* An Interview with Alan Wald," *Crime Time: The Journal of Crime Fiction* 27: 81–89.

2003. "Re-Imagining U.S. Literature and the Left," *Historical Materialism* 11, no. 4: 395–404.

2004. "Between Insularity and Internationalism: The Lost World of Jewish Communist 'Cultural Workers' in America," *Studies in Contemporary Jewry: An Annual* 20: 133–47.

2006. "The Legacy of the Cultural Front: An Interview with Alan Wald," *Political Affairs* (August): 6–10.

2008. "Reconstructing the 'Humanscape' of Left Culture and Commitment: An Interview with Alan Wald," *Reconstruction: Studies in Contemporary Culture* 8, no. 1: 1–27.

2009. "The Great Outsider: On the Centennial of Richard Wright, 1908–1960," *Against the Current* 138 (January–February): 15–19. Reprinted in *Red Wedge* (January 14, 2013), http://redwedgemagazine.com/uncategorized/great-outsider.

2009. "Inconvenient Truths: The Communist Conundrum in Life and Art," *American Literary History* (March): 1–36.

2009. "Hero—International Brigade" (essay about James Neugass, *War Is Beautiful: An American Ambulance Driver in the Spanish Civil War*), *Against the Current* 143 (November–December): 17–20.

2011. "A Winter's Tale Told in Memoirs," *Against the Current* 153 (July–August): 19–29.

2011. "A Theater for the Poor: Cleveland and SDS/ERAP in the Mid-1960s," *Against the Current* 155 (November–December): 13–18.

2012. "Three Books about Irving Howe" (review essay), *American Communist History* 11: 127–31.

2012. "Bohemian Bolsheviks after World War II: A Minority within a Minority," *Labour/Le Travail* 70 (Fall): 159–86. An earlier and shorter version of this essay appeared as "Cannonite Bohemians after World War II," *Against the Current* 159 (July–August 2012): 25–35.

2012. "From 'Triple Oppression' to 'Freedom Dreams'" (review essay of books by Dayo Gore, Cheryl Higashida, and Erik McDuffie), *Against the Current* 162 (January–February): 24–27.

2013. "Outlaws, Rebels and the Revolutionary Imagination: A Two-Part Interview with Alan Wald," Grant Mandarino, *Red Wedge*, June 13, Part 1 (even though it says "Part 2"), http://redwedgemagazine.com/articles/outlaws-rebels-and-the-revolutionary-imagination-pt-2, and Part 2, http://redwedgemagazine.com/articles/outlaws-two.

2013. "The Audacity of American Trotskyism: The Indiana 'Subversion' Case Fifty Years Later," *Against the Current* 165 (July–August): 27–31.

2013. "The Passion of Richard Seymour," *Against the Current* 167 (November–December): 25–30.

2013–14. "Heartbeats of Somatic Memory: Jonathan Lethem's *Dissident Gardens*," *Iowa Review* 43 (Winter): 175–79.

2014. "A Political Witch-hunt in the Name of 'Academic Freedom,'" *Against the Current* 169 (March–April): 7–14.

2014. "Astonished by the Present" (essay about Daniel Bensaïd), *International Socialist Review* 93 (Summer 2014): 111–21.

2014. "The Pressure of the Contemporaneous" (review essay of Milton A. Cohgen, *Beleaguered Poets and Leftist Critics*, and Stephen Voyce, *Poetic Community*), *Modernism/Modernity* 21, no. 2 (April): 557–60.

2014. "'A Seemingly Incongruous Alliance'" (review essay about Bryan Palmer, *Revolutionary Teamsters*), *Labour/Le Travail* 73 (Spring 2014): 301–10.

Book Reviews, Notes, and Columns

Reviews for *Michigan Quarterly Review*

James T. Farrell, *The Dunne Family*, 17 (Spring 1978): 263–69.

James T. Farrell, *Literary Essays*, 17 (Spring 1978): 263–69.

Igor Shaferevich, *The Socialist Phenomenon*, 20 (Summer 1981): 315–16.

David Shi, *Matthew Josephson: Bourgeois Bohemian*, 21 (Summer 1982): 525–27.

Maurice Sugar, *The Ford Hunger March*, 21 (Summer 1982): 526–27.

James D. Wilkinson, *The Intellectual Resistance in Europe*, 22 (Winter 1983): 157–58.

Eric J. Hobsbawm, ed., *The History of Marxism*, 22 (Winter 1983): 158–59.

Nelson Lichtenstein, *Labor's War at Home: The CIO in World War II*, 23 (Winter 1984): 147–48.

James D. Cockcroft, *Mexico: Class Formation, Capital Accumulation, and the State,* 23 (Spring 1984): 308–9.
Stephen Whitfield, *A Critical American: The Politics of Dwight Macdonald,* 24 (Summer 1985): 511–14.
Delmore Schwartz, *Letters,* 24 (Summer 1985): 511–14.

Reviews for *Antioch Review*

James T. Farrell, *The Death of Nora Ryan,* 36 (Fall 1978): 506–7.
James T. Farrell, *Olive and Mary Ann,* 36 (Fall 1978): 506–7.
Francis Mulhern, *The Moment of "Scrutiny,"* 39 (Winter 1981): 130–31.
Chris Bullock and David Peck, eds., *Guide to Marxist Literary Criticism,* 40 (Spring 1982): 241.

Teaching Notes for *Radical Teacher*

James T. Farrell, *Studs Lonigan,* 13, p. 44.
Richard Wright, *Native Son,* 15, p. 60.
Amiri Baraka, *Selected Plays and Prose,* 20, p. 36.
Tess Slesinger, *The Unpossessed,* 30, p. 39.
Jane Slaughter, *Concessions,* 36, pp. 33–34.
Paul Buhle, *The Labor Joke Book,* 36, pp. 33–34.
Gary Soto, *The Elements of San Joaquin,* 37, pp. 45–46.
K. B. Gilden, *Between the Hills and the Sea,* 44, p. 40.
Paul Le Blanc, *From Marx to Gramsci,* 53, pp. 41–42.

Reviews for *In These Times*

James Baldwin, *Just above My Head,* December 5–11, 1979, 20.
Freedomways: Lorraine Hansberry Issue, March 12–25, 1980, 12.
W. E. B. Du Bois, *On Sociology and the Black Community,* June 4–17, 1980, 21.
Tariq Ali and Phil Evans, *Trotsky for Beginners,* April 15–21, 1981, 12.
Gayl Jones, *Song for Anninho,* October 7–13, 1981, 18.
James T. Farrell, *Eight Short Stories and Sketches,* October 28–November 3, 1981, 19.
Sez: A Multi-Racial Journal of Poetry and People's Culture, May 5–11, 1982, 18.
Jeannie Wylie, *Poletown: Community Betrayed,* October 10–16, 1990, 19.
Paula Rabinowitz, *Labor and Desire: Women's Revolutionary Fiction in Depression America,* March 25–31, 1992, 19.

Miscellaneous Selected Reviews

James T. Farrell, *Judith and Other Stories,* in *Praxis* 1 (Spring 1975): 142–46.

Norman McLeod, *The Distance: New and Selected Poems,* in *Minnesota Review* 11 (Fall 1978): 107–11.

"The Morality of Book Banning—Shirley Jackson's 'The Lottery,'" in *Detroit News Magazine,* October 22, 1978, 40.

Morris Dickstein, *The Gates of Eden: American Culture in the 1960s,* in *Science & Society* 44 (Spring 1980): 94–97.

Stephen Ingle, *Socialist Thought in Imaginative Literature,* in *Clio* 8 (1981): 104–5.

"American Radicals" (review of Nell Irvin Painter, *The Narrative of Hosea Hudson: Life as a Negro Communist in the South;* Bertram D. Wolfe, *A Life in Two Centuries;* and William Alexander, *Film on the Left*), in *Alternative Review* 3 (November 1981): 24–25.

Maurice Isserman, *Which Side Were You On? The American Communist Party during the Second World War,* in *Nation* 234 (June 12, 1982): 728–31.

Alexander Bloom, *Prodigal Sons: The New York Intellectuals and Their World,* in *American Jewish History* 76 (September 1986): 86–90.

Sacvan Bercovitch, ed., *Reconstructing American Literary History,* in *New York Times Book Review,* September 28, 1986, 35.

Ellen Schrecker, *No Ivory Tower: McCarthyism and the Universities,* in *Boston Review* 11 (October 1986): 22–23.

Edward Shoben, *Lionel Trilling: Mind and Character,* in *Jewish Currents* 41 (March 1987): 22–27.

Michael Parker, *Inside the Circle: A Union Guide to QWL,* in *Science & Society* 51 (Summer 1987): 241–44.

James T. Farrell, *Hearing Out James T. Farrell* and *Sam Holman,* in *Resources for American Literary Study* 15 (Spring 1985): 103–7.

Russell Jacoby, *The Last Intellectuals,* in *Radical Historians Newsletter 55* (May 1988): 1–2.

"Radical Education" (review of Ira Shor, *Culture Wars;* Paulo Freire, *The Politics of Education;* and Bertell Ollman, *The Left Academy*), in *Minnesota Review* 30 (Spring–Fall 1988): 201–4.

Dorothy Doyle, *Journey through Jess,* in *Guardian,* August 16, 1989, 24.

Paul Buhle, *Marxism in the U.S.,* in *Labour/Le Travail* 24 (Fall 1989): 294–95.

Albert Glotzer, *Trotsky: Memoir and Critique,* in *Washington Post Book World,* January 14, 1990, 4; exchange of letters, *Washington Post Book World,* March 4, 1990, 15.

Jonathan Reider, *Canarsie: The Jews and Italians of Brooklyn against Liberalism,* in *Studies in Contemporary Jewry* 6 (1990): 352–55.

A. Belden Fields, *Trotskyism and Maoism: Theory and Practice in France and the United States,* in *American Historical Review* 96, no. 2 (April 1991): 473–74.

Cary Nelson, *Repression and Recovery: Modern American Poetry and the Politics of Cultural Memory, 1910–45,* in *Minnesota Review* 36 (Spring 1991): 110–13.

Carlos Munoz, *Youth, Identity, Power: The Chicano Movement,* in *Against the Current* 33 (July–August 1991): 41–43.

John Sanford, *A Walk in the Fire,* in *Forward Motion* (December 1992): 37, 41.

Cary Nelson and Jefferson Hendricks, *Edwin Rolfe: A Biographical Essay and Guide,* in *Journal of English and Germanic Philology* 91 (July 1992): 464–66.

"Alexander Saxton and the Antiracist Imagination," in *Monthly Review* 45 (July–August 1993): 122–27.

Greg Mitchell, *The Campaign of the Century,* in *Cineaste* 20, no. 1 (Summer 1993): 58–59.

Leonard Wilcox, *V. F. Calverton: Radical in the American Grain,* in *Journal of American History* 80 (September 1993): 733–34.

"The Roots of African American Communism" (review of Robin Kelley, *Hammer and Hoe*), in *Against the Current* 8 (September–October 1993): 33–36.

"The Utopian Imagination" (review essay of new books by Michael Löwy), in *Against the Current* 9 (September–October 1994): 23–26.

Barbara Foley, *Radical Representations,* in *American Literature* 66 (December 1994): 856–57.

Franklin Folsom, *Days of Anger, Days of Hope,* in *Z Magazine* 16 (June 1995): 56–58.

Paul N. Siegel, *The Great Reversal: Politics and Art in Solzhenitsyn,* in *Against the Current* 10 (May–June 1995): 43.

"Learning from Adversaries" (review of Harvey Teres, *Renewing the Left: Politics, Imagination, and the New York Intellectuals*), in *Boston Book Review* 3 (June 1996): 7–8.

Robert Gorman, *Michael Harrington: Speaking American,* in *Labor History* 37 (Summer 1996): 426–28.

Michael Denning, *The Cultural Front,* in *Labour/Le Travail* 41, no. 4 (Fall 1998): 284–86.

Harry Fisher, *Comrades: Tales of a Brigadista in the Spanish Civil War,* in *The Volunteer: Journal of the Abraham Lincoln Brigade Archives* 20 (Winter 1998–99): 5–7.

Michael Löwy, *The War of the Gods,* in *Historical Materialism* 4 (1999): 295–99.

William Maxwell, *New Negro, Old Left: African American Writing and Communism between the Wars,* in *American Literature* (September 2000): 644–45.

Mark Solomon, *The Cry Was Unity: Communists and African-Americans, 1917–1936,* in *African American Review* 34 (2000): 716–18.

Edgar Branch, *A Paris Year: Dorothy and James T. Farrell, 1931–32,* in *Resources for American Literary Study* 26 (2000): 136–38.

Edward Alexander, *Irving Howe: Socialist, Critic, Jew,* in *Studies in Contemporary Jewry* 16 (2000): 362–64.

Sean McCann, *Gumshoe America,* in *Paradoxica* 16 (2001): 285–88.

David Hollinger, *Science, Jews, and Secular Culture,* in *Studies in Contemporary Jewry* 17 (2001): 277–79.

Keith Gilyard, *Liberation Memories: The Rhetoric and Poetics of John Oliver Killens,* in *Socialism and Democracy* 17 (Summer–Fall 2003): 245–51.

"New Black Radical Scholarship," in *Against the Current* 108 (January–February 2004): 32–33.

"Women's Lives on the Left," in *Against the Current* 109 (March–April 2004): 41–43.

Max Elbaum, *Revolution in the Air: Sixties Radicals Turn to Lenin, Mao, and Che,* in *Science & Society* 68 (Summer 2004): 231–33.

Kathryn Olmsted, *Red Spy Queen,* in *New England Quarterly* 77 (September 2004): 505–6.

"In Memoriam: Paul Siegel, 1916–2004," in *Against the Current* 111 (July–August 2004): 43–44.

"Understanding Genocide," review of Enzo Traverso, *The Origins of Nazi Violence,* in *Against the Current* 112 (September–October 2004): 40–41.

David C. Engerman, *Modernization from the Other Shore: American Intellectuals and the Romance of Intellectual Development,* in *Journal of American History* 91 (March 2005): 132.

Andrew Hemingway, *Artists on the Left,* in *Against the Current* 117 (July–August 2005): 28–30.

Jani Scandura and Michael Thurston, eds., *Modernism, Inc.,* in *Cultural Critique* 61 (Fall 2005): 221–23.

Paul Levitt, *Dark Matters,* in *American Communist History* 5 (December 2006): 237–40.

Bryan Palmer, *James P. Cannon and the Origins of the American Revolutionary Left,* in *Against the Current* 129 (July–August 2007): 39–41.

Richard M. Cook, *Alfred Kazin: A Biography,* in *New England Quarterly* 81 (Fall 2008): 525–27.

"Love and Revolution" (review of Lillian Pollak's *The Sweetest Dream* and Lois Young-Tulin's *The Ghost of Leon Trotsky*), in *Against the Current* 140 (May–June 2009): 39–41.

"A Mandel for All Seasons" (review of Jan Willem Stutje, *Ernest Mandel: A Rebel's Dream Deferred*), in *Against the Current* 138 (September–October 2009): 34–37.

Frank Rosengarten, *Urban Revolutionary: C. L. R. James and the Struggle for a New Society,* in *Science & Society* 73 (2009): 128–30.

Ethan Hoffman and Daniel Morris, eds., *The New York Public Intellectuals and Beyond: Exploring Liberal Humanism, Jewish Identity and the American Protest Tradition,* in *Journal of American Studies* 43 (December 2009): 572–74.

John V. Flemming, *The Anti-Communist Manifestos: Four Books That Shaped the Cold War,* in *Journal of American History* 97 (March 2011): 1171–72.

"A Bend in the Labyrinth" (review of Clive Bush, *The Century's Midnight*), in *Against the Current* 160 (September 2012): 31–32.

Review of William Scott's *Troublemakers* and Mark W. Van Wienen's *American Socialist Triptych,* in *American Literature* 84 (December 2012): 887–89.

"Ornery Professors and Academic Freedom" (review of Majorie Heins, *Priests of Our Democracy*), Society for U.S. Intellectual History Blog, August 2013, http://s-usih.org/2013/08/ornery-professors-and-academic-freedom.html.

Walter Howard, *We Shall Be Free! Black Communist Protests in Seven Voices,* in *American Communist History* 13, no. 1 (2014): 65–68.

Phillip Deery, *Red Apple: Communism and McCarthyism in Cold War New York,* in *Science & Society* 79, no. 1 (January 2015): 132–35.

"Fifty Shades of Pulp" (review of Paula Rabinowitz, *American Pulp*), *Against the Current* 175 (March–April 2015): 39–40, 38.

Over sixty other reviews, notes, obituaries, politico-cultural articles, etc., have appeared in various publications in the United States and Western Europe.

Contributors

Tariq Ali, activist, political commentator, filmmaker, playwright, and novelist, is a longtime editor of the London journal *New Left Review* and the author of numerous works of historical and political analysis, including *Street Fighting Years: An Autobiography of the Sixties* (Verso, 2005), *The Clash of Fundamentalisms: Crusades, Jihads, and Modernity* (Verso, 2002), and *Pirates of the Caribbean: Axis of Hope* (Verso, 2006). He is also the author of *The Islam Quintet,* a critically acclaimed series of historical novels from Verso, beginning with *Shadows of the Pomegranate Tree* (1992) and concluding with *Night of the Golden Butterfly* (2010).

Heather Bowen-Struyk, visiting assistant professor of Japanese at the University of Notre Dame, received her bachelor's degree from the University of Michigan as well as her PhD in comparative literature (2001) and has taught at the University of Chicago, the University of Michigan, and Loyola University Chicago. She is the editor of "Proletarian Arts in East Asia" (Fall 2006), a special issue of *positions: east asia cultures critique.* She is the coeditor of a forthcoming anthology of Japanese proletarian literature in English translation titled *For Dignity, Justice, and Revolution* (University of Chicago Press). Her book in progress, "Beyond Red Love: Intimacy, Love and Camaraderie in Japanese Proletarian Literature," deals with sexual politics, class and gender, male comradely intimacy, and the implications of revolutionary politics for couples and the family.

Howard Brick, Louis Evans Professor of History at the University of Michigan, studies the history of social theory in the United States throughout the twentieth century. He is the author of *Daniel Bell and the Decline of Intellectual Radicalism: Social Theory and Political Reconcilia-*

tion in the 1940s (University of Wisconsin Press, 1986), *Age of Contradiction: American Thought and Culture in the 1960s* (Cornell University Press, 1998), *Transcending Capitalism: Visions of a New Society in Modern American Thought* (Cornell University Press, 2006), and, with Christopher Phelps, the forthcoming *Radicals in America: The U.S. Left since the Second World War* (Cambridge University Press). Brick received his PhD in American culture from the University of Michigan, under Alan Wald's direction, in 1983.

Sarah Ehlers, assistant professor of English at the University of Houston, received her PhD in English from the University of Michigan under the direction of Alan Wald in 2012. Her articles and essays have appeared in journals such as *Modern Language Quarterly, Contemporary Literature, Paideuma, Comparative Literature,* and *Against the Current.* She is currently completing a book manuscript on Depression-era radical poetics titled "Left of Poetry: Depression America and the Formation of Modern Poetics."

Dayo F. Gore, associate professor in ethnic studies and critical gender studies at the University of California, San Diego, is the author of *Radicalism at the Crossroads: African-American Women Activists in the Cold War* (New York University Press, 2011) and coeditor of *Want to Start a Revolution? Radical Women in the Black Freedom Struggle* (New York University Press, 2009). Her work has been supported by the Schomburg Center for Research in Black Culture, the Charles Warren Center for Studies in American History at Harvard University, and the Tamiment Library's Center for the United States and the Cold War. Her current research projects include a study of African American women's transnational travels and activism in the long twentieth century.

Konstantina M. Karageorgos specializes in twentieth-century African American literature. She received her PhD in English at the University of Michigan in the spring of 2015. Her dissertation, "Beyond the Blueprint: African-American Literary Marxism in the Period of the Cold War," directed by Alan Wald, investigates the aesthetics of Marxist commitment in African American literature of the post–World War II period. Her work has appeared in *Against the Current,* the *South Atlantic Review,* and *Mediations.*

Robbie Lieberman, professor of American studies and chair of the Interdisciplinary Studies Department at Kennesaw State University, received her PhD in American culture from the University of Michigan in 1984 under Alan Wald's direction. She is the author of *My Song Is My Weapon: People's Songs, American Communism, and the Politics of Culture, 1930–1950* (University of Illinois Press, 1989), *The Strangest Dream: Communism, Anti-Communism, and the U.S. Peace Movement, 1945–1963* (Syracuse University Press, 2000), and *Prairie Power: Voices of 1960s Midwestern Student Protest* (University of Missouri Press, 2004). Recent publications include a book coedited with Clarence Lang, *Anticommunism and the African American Freedom Movement* (Palgrave, 2009), and an article, "'Measure Them Right': Lorraine Hansberry and the Struggle for Peace," published in *Science and Society* (2011). From 2006 to 2011, Lieberman served as editor of *Peace & Change: A Journal of Peace Research.* Her current research focuses on African American proponents of peace in the early Cold War years.

Michael Löwy, research director in the social sciences, emeritus, at Le Centre National de la Recherche Scientifique in Paris, and a French Brazilian Marxist scholar, studied in the fields of literature, sociology, and political theory with illustrious academics such as Lucien Goldmann, Nicos Poulantzas, and Peter Worsley. Löwy has held university positions in Brazil, France, Britain, and Israel and has lectured widely in the United States. Engaged in political activism internationally since his teens, he has developed scholarly interests in a wide range of subjects, publishing on all of them: Marxist philosophy, surrealism, Latin American politics and religion, theories of worker-peasant revolution, ecosocialism, European Jewish messianism, Franz Kafka, romanticism and modernism, and more. Löwy's books include *Georg Lukács: From Romanticism to Bolshevism* (Verso, 1981), *The Politics of Combined and Uneven Development: The Theory of Permanent Revolution* (Verso, 1981), *Morning Star: Surrealism, Marxism, Anarchism, Situationism, Utopia* (University of Texas Press, 2000), and *Fire Alarm: Reading Walter Benjamin's "On the Concept of History"* (Verso, 2005). Löwy's books and articles have appeared in twenty-eight languages.

Julia L. Mickenberg, associate professor of American studies at the University of Texas–Austin, is the author of *Learning from the Left: Children's Literature, the Cold War, and Radical Politics in the United States* (Oxford University Press, 2006), which won prizes from the Children's Literature

Association, the Society for the History of Children and Youth, the University of Texas Cooperative Society, and the Pacific Coast Branch of the American Historical Society. She is coeditor (with Philip Nel) of *Tales for Little Rebels: A Collection of Radical Children's Literature* (New York University Press, 2008), and (with Lynne Vallone) of *The Oxford Handbook of Children's Literature* (Oxford University Press, 2011). She held a fellowship from the National Endowment for the Humanities in support of her book in progress, "The New Woman Tries on Red: Russia in the American Feminist Imagination, 1905–1945."

Nathaniel Mills, assistant professor of English at California State University, Northridge, completed his PhD at the University of Michigan, under Alan Wald's supervision, in 2011. Mills's articles on US and African American literary radicalism have appeared in the *Journal of Modern Literature, Studies in American Naturalism, MELUS,* the *African American Review, Twentieth-Century Literature,* and *Against the Current.* His current book project is a study of the Marxist concept of the lumpen proletariat and its place in the Depression-era writings of Richard Wright, Ralph Ellison, and Margaret Walker.

Bill V. Mullen, professor of English and American studies at Purdue University, is the author of *Popular Fronts: Chicago and African-American Cultural Politics, 1935–1946* (University of Illinois Press, 1999), *Afro-Orientalism* (University of Minnesota Press, 2004), and *UnAmerican: W. E. B. Du Bois and the Century of World Revolution* (Temple University Press, 2015). He is the editor of several books, including, with Fred Ho, *Afro-Asia: Revolutionary Political and Cultural Connections between African Americans and Asian Americans* (Duke University Press, 2008), and is also coeditor of the Class/Culture Series at the University of Michigan Press.

Cary Nelson, Jubilee Professor of Liberal Arts and Sciences at the University of Illinois at Urbana-Champaign, is the author or editor of thirty books, including *Repression and Recovery: Modern American Poetry and The Politics of Cultural Memory, 1910–1945* (University of Wisconsin Press, 1989), *Manifesto of a Tenured Radical* (New York University Press, 1997), *Revolutionary Memory: Recovering the Poetry of the American Left* (Routledge, 2001), and *No University Is an Island: Saving Academic Freedom* (New York University Press, 2010). He is the editor or coeditor of numerous volumes, including *Marxism and the Interpretation of Culture* (University of Illinois Press, 1988), *Higher Education Under Fire: Politics, Economics, and* *the Crisis of the Humanities* (Routledge, 1994), *Madrid 1937: Letters of the Abraham Lincoln Brigade from the Spanish Civil War* (Routledge, 1996), and *The Case against Academic Boycotts of Israel* (Wayne State University Press, 2015). In 2012, he completed six years as national president of the American Association of University Professors. *Cary Nelson and the Struggle for the University: Poetry, Politics and the Profession* (SUNY Press, 2009) is a collection of essays about his life and career.

Paula Rabinowitz, professor of English at the University of Minnesota, is also affiliated with the Department of American Studies; the Department of Cultural Studies and Comparative Literature; the Department of Gender, Women's and Sexuality Studies; and the Program in Moving Image Studies. She earned her PhD in American culture at the University of Michigan in 1986 under the supervision of Alan Wald. Rabinowitz's books include *Labor and Desire: Women's Revolutionary Fiction in Depression America* (University of North Carolina Press, 1991), *They Must Be Represented: The Politics of Documentary* (Verso, 1994), and *Black & White and Noir: America's Pulp Modernism* (Columbia University Press, 2002). With Cristina Giorcelli, Rabinowitz edits the four-volume series *Habits of Being* (University of Minnesota Press). *American Pulp: How Paperbacks Brought Modernism to Main Street* appeared in 2014 from Princeton University Press. She has held Fulbright Distinguished Lectureships in American literature and culture at the University of Rome III and the East China Normal University in Shanghai. Rabinowitz is editor in chief of the *Oxford Research Encyclopedia of Literature.*

Joseph G. Ramsey, lecturer in English and American studies at the University of Massachusetts–Boston, is coeditor of *Cultural Logic: An Electronic Journal of Marxist Theory and Practice* and a frequent contributor and editorial board member of the journal *Socialism and Democracy.* His current editorial projects include a forthcoming joint issue of *Cultural Logic* and *Works and Days* titled *Scholactivism: Transforming Praxis Inside and Outside the Classroom.* His most recent essays include reflections on teaching Assata Shakur's autobiography to undergraduates and analyses of the politics of communist interracial solidarity in the fiction of Richard Wright, Ralph Ellison, and Guy Endore.

T. V. Reed, Lewis E. and Stella G. Buchanan Distinguished Professor of English and American Studies at Washington State University, is the author of *Fifteen Jugglers, Five Believers: Literary Politics and the Poetics* *of American Social Movements* (University of California Press, 1992) and *The Art of Protest: Culture and Activism from the Civil Rights Movement to the Streets of Seattle* (University of Minnesota Press, 2005), and more recently, *Digitized Lives: Culture, Power and Social Change in the Internet Era* (Routledge, 2014) and *Robert Cantwell and the Literary Left* (University of Washington Press, 2014). Active in digital humanities, Reed also is the author/manager of the website Cultural Politics: Resources for Critical Analysis (culturalpolitics.net) that includes sites on digital cultures, environmental justice, cultural studies, popular culture, social movement cultures, and interdisciplinary cultural theory.

Rachel Rubin, director of the Center for the Study of Humanities, Culture, and Society at the University of Massachusetts–Boston, teaches popular culture, immigration, labor studies, and American literature. From her first book, *Jewish Gangsters of Modern Literature*, a study of the figure of the Jewish gangster in the leftist literature of the 1920s through 1940s in Russia and the United States (University of Illinois Press, 2000), to her most recent book, *Well Met: Renaissance Faires and the American Counterculture*, an exploration of the Renaissance Faire as a formation of the New Left counterculture (New York University Press, 2014), she has been interested in the complex ways that politics, literature, and popular culture mutually constitute each other. Rubin has also published an edition of the autobiography of Polly Adler, the infamous New York City madam; a cowritten book on immigration and American culture; and a coedited book on radicalism in the New South. Currently she is finishing a book of interviews with a wide array of artist-activists, ranging from artist Betty Saar to novelist Maxine Hong Kingston to rapper Boots Riley of The Coup. Her next project explores the culture significance of the education of radical Africans in the Soviet Union in the post–World War II era.

E. San Juan, Jr., emeritus professor of English, comparative literature, and ethnic studies at Washington State University and the University of Connecticut, was recently a fellow of the Harry Ransom Center, University of Texas, and of the W. E. B. Du Bois Institute, Harvard University. San Juan has taught at Brooklyn College, CUNY; Wesleyan University, Connecticut; Leuven University, Belgium; Trento University, Italy; Tamkang University, Taiwan; the University of the Philippines; and Ateneo de Manila University. His recent books are *Racism and Cultural Studies* (Duke University Press, 2002), *In the Wake of Terror* (Lexington Books, 2007), *Critique and Social Transformation* (Mellen, 2009), *US Imperialism and Revolution in the Philippines* (Palgrave, 2007), *Toward Filipino Self-Determination* (SUNY, 2009), and *Between Empire and Insurgency: The Philippines in the New Millennium* (University of the Philippines Press, 2015).

James Smethurst, professor of Afro-American studies at the University of Massachusetts, Amherst, is the author of *The New Red Negro: The Literary Left and African American Poetry, 1930–1946* (Oxford University Press, 1999); *The Black Arts Movement: Literary Nationalism in the 1960s and 1970s* (University of North Carolina Press, 2005), which won the James A. Rawley Prize from the Organization of American Historians; and *The African American Roots of Modernism: From Reconstruction to the Harlem Renaissance* (University of North Carolina Press, 2011).

Harvey Teres, professor of English at Syracuse University, is the author of *The Word on the Street: Linking the Academy and the Common Reader* (University of Michigan Press, 2011) and *Renewing the Left: Politics, Imagination, and the New York Intellectuals* (Oxford University Press, 1996). Teres, a former labor organizer in the factories of Chicago, has titled his forthcoming book *Somebody Loves Us All: Dialogues on Aesthetics with Ordinary People.* It is an oral history in which local citizens speak about their encounters with beauty. His dozens of essays, articles, and reviews have appeared in many scholarly journals.

Chris Vials, associate professor of English at the University of Connecticut–Storrs is the author of *Realism for the Masses: Aesthetics, Popular Front Pluralism, and U.S. Culture, 1935–1947* (University Press of Mississippi, 2009). His second monograph, *Haunted by Hitler: Liberals, the Left, and the Fight against Fascism in the United States* (University of Massachusetts Press, 2014), is the first comprehensive cultural history of US antifascism, spanning the 1930s through the 1990s. His work has also appeared in *Criticism, Against the Current,* and *Science & Society,* among other venues. His new project examines the fraying appeal of neoliberal temporality in US culture and what this bodes for the country's class composition, racial formation, and projects of empire abroad. He has also been actively tackling the issues of public higher education funding and of academic labor through the American Association of University Professors and the United Auto Workers.

Alan M. Wald retired in June 2014 as the H. Chandler Davis Collegiate Professor of English Literature and American Culture at the University of Michigan. He currently serves on the editorial boards of *Against the Current* and *Science & Society,* writes and reviews for scholarly and socialist publications, and is working on a book about methods in the study of Literary Radicalism.

Mary Helen Washington, professor of English at the University of Maryland, College Park, specializes in twentieth- and twenty-first-century African American literature and the black Literary Left of the 1950s. Her books include *The Other Blacklist: The African American Literary and Cultural Left of the 1950s* (Columbia University Press, 2014) and three edited collections of African American literature: *Memory of Kin: Stories about Family by Black Writers* (Random House, 1991); *Black-Eyed Susans and Midnight Birds: Stories by and about Black Women* (reprint, Doubleday/Anchor, 1990); and *Invented Lives: Narratives of Black Women, 1860–1960* (Doubleday/Anchor, 1987). From 1996 to 1997, she was president of the American Studies Association. Her current project examines the black Left and racial postmodernism(s).

List of Illustrations

www.ingramcontent.com/pod-product-compliance
Lightning Source LLC
Chambersburg PA
CBHW060304100726
47907CB00002B/283

* 9 7 8 1 6 0 7 8 5 3 4 5 9 *